THE COLLECTED WORKS OF
WALTER BAGEHOT

VOLUME TWELVE

THE COLLECTED WORKS OF
WALTER BAGEHOT

EDITED BY

Norman St John-Stevas

The Letters
(in two volumes)
with an introduction by
the Editor

VOLUME TWELVE

THE ECONOMIST · LONDON

The Collected Works of Walter Bagehot
This volume first published 1986
© *The Economist* 1986
Reprinted 1986

PRINTED AND BOUND BY STEPHEN AUSTIN AND SONS LTD
HERTFORD ENGLAND
set in Monotype Fournier 11/12 *point*

THE COLLECTED WORKS OF
WALTER BAGEHOT

VOLUMES I & II · LITERARY ESSAYS
VOLUMES III & IV · HISTORICAL
VOLUMES V, VI, VII & VIII · POLITICAL
VOLUMES IX, X & XI · ECONOMIC
VOLUMES XII & XIII · LETTERS
VOLUMES XIV & XV · MISCELLANY

Dilectissimae
NINAE BURGIS
Amicitiae causa
Collaborator collaboratrici
Hunc libellum dedicavit
N.St.J.S.

CONTENTS

Volume Twelve

Illustrations	x
Acknowledgments	xi
Editor's Introduction to the Letters	1
Note on the Text	69
Abbreviations	73
The Letters 1831–1853	75

Volume Thirteen

The Letters 1855–1877	353
Index of Correspondents	681
Index to Volumes XII and XIII	683

ILLUSTRATIONS

Letter to his Aunt Reynolds, *c.* 1832   facing page 76

Letter to his father, December 5, 1851   facing page 322

ACKNOWLEDGMENTS

I wish to express my warmest thanks to those at *The Economist* who have given help and encouragement throughout the processes of editing and publication: Mr Hugo Meynell, Miss Lyn Chawner and, especially, Mr Leslie Gardner, who has been associated with the edition from the very beginning until his retirement in 1984. Their contribution has been vital, and so has that of the designer of these volumes, Mr Grant Gibson, and of our printers, Stephen Austin and Sons, whose heroic labours I salute. Mr Leslie Watkins deserves a special word of appreciation.

I am deeply grateful to the late Mr Robert Bagehot-Porch, who presented me with most of the original Bagehot letters in my collection and, as holder of the copyright, gave permission for publication. I am also indebted to Miss Mary Bagehot for the publication of two early letters (including the first known to have been written by Walter Bagehot). Other descendants of the Bagehot and Stuckey families and of Eliza Bagehot's sisters have been generous in answering questions and allowing me to examine pictures and other material in their possession. I am especially indebted to Mr Michael Churchman (whose wife is a descendant of Vincent Stuckey) for drawing up the Family Tree of the Stuckey and Bagehot families which is reproduced, with his notes, in Volume XV.

The letters exchanged between Walter Bagehot and Eliza Wilson during their engagement are second in importance only to the family letters; and I am most grateful to Messrs Faber and Faber, to whom most of the originals were presented by Mrs Barrington after publication of *The Love-Letters of Walter Bagehot and Eliza Wilson*, for permission to publish. Thanks are also due to Professor Philip Larkin, Librarian of the Brynmor Jones Library, University of Hull, where the collection is deposited, and to the Library's archivist, Mr Norman Higson, for his kind assistance.

Four interesting letters are owned by Mr Richard W. Lyman, President of the Rockefeller Foundation, who kindly supplied

ACKNOWLEDGMENTS

photocopies and gave permission for publication. The existence of these letters was made known to me by Sister Martha Westwater, and I am happy to record my thanks for this and other assistance given by her while she was working on the MS diaries of Eliza Bagehot in my collection. In 1984 she published *The Wilson Sisters*, based largely on the diaries, and she has contributed an essay on the sisters to the final volume of this edition.

A copy of Bagehot's evidence before the French Commission of Inquiry into the Monetary Circulation was kindly obtained for me by M. Emmanuel de Margerie, French Ambassador in London from March 1981 until November 1984, and my thanks are due to him and to the Librarian of the Bibliothèque Nationale.

The Earl of Stockton and Lord Wilson of Rievaulx, admirers of Walter Bagehot, are thanked for permission to reprint their tributes to him in Volume XV.

To the authorities of the following institutions I am indebted for permission to publish MSS in their collections and for the helpfulness of their librarians: the Bodleian Library; the British Library; the British Library of Political and Economic Science; Dr Williams's Library; the John Rylands University Library of Manchester; Hertfordshire County Record Office and the owner of the Bulwer-Lytton collection, the Hon. David Lytton Cobbold; King's College Library, Cambridge; the Department of Palaeography and Diplomatic, University of Durham; the National Library of Ireland; the Public Record Office; the Library of University College, London.

Requests for information have met with prompt and helpful response from Mr Jacques Barzun; Mr G. S. Chisholm, Secretary of the Travellers' Club; Mr Piers Dixon of Brooks's; Mrs Elinor Foster, Records Officer of University College, London; Mrs Margaret Gaskell, Librarian of Girton College; Miss Joan Gibbs, University of London Library; Mr Anthony Lejeune; Mr Robert H. Moon, Chief Executive and Clerk, Woodspring District Council; Mr Nigel Nicolson; Mrs Kathleen Tillotson.

This edition owes much to the resources of libraries and the expertise of their staff, and I wish to express special thanks to the British Library, the London Library, the University of London Library, and the House of Commons Library.

I should like to thank the Lord Chancellor, Lord Hailsham, for advice on Latin.

ACKNOWLEDGMENTS

Finally, I must express my warmest thanks to Nina Burgis, researcher in name but collaborator in fact who has been assiduous, patient, tolerant of all my demands, and an enthusiastic helper over this final phase.

Norman St John-Stevas

34 Montepelier Square,
London SW7.

EDITOR'S INTRODUCTION TO THE LETTERS

The letters and their classification

Bagehot's letters covered virtually his whole lifetime, and although inevitably many have disappeared, sufficient remain to provide fascinating and interesting insights into the different periods of his life. The letters have been reproduced here as a *continuum* but broadly speaking they fall into five sections.

The first section may be described as 'early letters'. It opens with a letter written when Walter was about five years of age in 1831 and ends with the last letter he wrote on 26 May 1842 from Bristol College before going up to University College, London. Some of the letters were written while Walter was a pupil at Langport Grammar School but the vast majority were composed at Bristol College where he continued his studies. They were written to his father and mother resident at Herd's Hill. Bristol College had been founded in 1831 by a group of Unitarians and laid particular emphasis on science. It could boast some talented teachers including John Addington Symonds who lectured on medicine, Dr Prichard, Edith Bagehot's brother-in-law, who gave a course in the history of civilization, and Dr William Carpenter, the eminent physiologist. Walter entered the College in 1839 at the age of 13 and remained there until 1842.

The second section of the letters is again made up principally of letters to his parents, although there are also a number to his friend of University College days, Richard Holt Hutton. They were written from London where Walter was in lodgings while an undergraduate at University College. He had been sent there in 1842 at the age of 16, Oxford and Cambridge being ruled out because his father objected to their doctrinal tests. Missing out on the ancient universities was not at this period a great loss. University College, the 'Godless institution' of Gower Street was at this time a far more lively and intellectually stimulating place than the still unreformed ancient universities with their torpid colleges, 'hotels without bells' as Walter was later to call them. Furthermore, the education provided by University College with its emphasis on mathematics, science and political economy, as well as the classics, was the natural sequel to Walter's early training at Bristol. These letters come to an end in November 1846.

The third period opens with Bagehot's graduation with first class honours in 1846 and covers his period of postgraduate study at London University, his reading for the Bar, the publication of his first essays and his visit to Paris in 1851 where he witnessed Louis Napoleon's *coup d'état*. This made a profound impression on him and influenced his thinking for the remainder of his life. It was from Paris that he wrote seven brilliant letters published in the *Inquirer*, the Unitarian paper flourishing at the time. Bagehot's sympathy with Louis Napoleon outraged the readers of the *Inquirer* but they constituted the first public sign of his genius.

Bagehot then retired from London, and partly to share the family burden of his mother's intermittent periods of insanity, took employment in the family bank of Stuckeys at Langport in 1852. In 1855 he helped to found and became joint editor of the *National Review* with R. H. Hutton and there is an interesting correspondence with Hutton describing the teething troubles of the new publication and the problems of getting it financed and launched.

The fourth section of the letters covers the period of Bagehot's engagement to Eliza Wilson in the autumn of 1857 down to their marriage in the spring of 1858. Eliza's health even at this stage was delicate, although in fact she survived her husband by 44 years. Much to Walter's chagrin, she was no sooner engaged than she departed to Edinburgh to be treated for eye trouble and headaches by a Dr Beveridge who had a considerable following at the time. The ardent suitor naturally enough, did not appreciate this period of separation, but posterity has been the residuary beneficiary since it afforded an opportunity for an exchange of letters which covered not only the personal feelings of the lovers but a wide range of contemporary political, social and literary matters.

The fifth and final section of the letters covers Bagehot's life from his marriage in 1858 to his death in 1877. Throughout this period Bagehot was immersed in the world of affairs and like many busy men even in an age of letter writing preferred to communicate verbally

EDITOR'S INTRODUCTION

when circumstances allowed rather than by letter. Bagehot's sister-in-law, Mrs Russell Barrington records that Bagehot never kept any letters he received save those from his parents, James Wilson, and Richard Hutton.

Mrs Guy Barrington, wife of Bagehot's nephew by marriage, seems to have destroyed many letters on the death of Mrs Russell Barrington in 1934. Any letters which *The Economist* may have had in its possession did not survive the destruction of the office premises at 6 Bouverie Street in May 1941 after an air-raid. Despite these gaps and depredations they cover many of the political and intellectual issues of the period. They include correspondence with his father-in-law, James Wilson, who was appointed Financial Member of the Council in India in 1859, where he died in 1860, and letters written during his period as editor of *The Economist* which lasted from 1861 until his death in 1877. This period also saw a number of unsuccessful attempts by Bagehot to enter Parliament.

Correspondence with Gladstone is included. Bagehot much admired Gladstone and his feelings were reciprocated. Gladstone, especially when he was Chancellor of the Exchequer, consulted him on a number of the financial and economic issues of the day. As a result, Woodrow Wilson described Bagehot as 'a sort of supplementary Chancellor of the Exchequer'.[1] These were the years of the publication of his three great works: *The English Constitution* (1867), *Physics and Politics* (1872) and *Lombard Street* (1873), and the letters give glimpses of the background to their writing and publication. He was labouring on his final work *Economic Studies*, published posthumously in 1879, when he died.

Early letters 1833-1842

The earliest letters of Walter's to have survived were written in 1831-2, when he was between five and six years of age. The first is a short note in pencil to his Uncle Watson; the second is written in huge letters half an inch high and the signature is bold and strikingly similar to that of his maturity. It was written to his Aunt Reynolds, his father's sister, who lived at Hampstead, an Evangelical of strongly anti-Papist

---

[1] 'A Literary Politician', *Atlantic Monthly*, November 1895, (Vol. lxxvi, p. 672).

views. Her low-church attitudes evidently did not commend themselves to the high Anglican Mrs Bagehot. The letter already shows that capacity for observation which was to be such a dominant feature of Bagehot's thinking. The pious little boy repeats to his aunt what he has heard his mother saying.

'My very dear Aunt,' he writes, 'I thank you for the book you sent me, and Brother thanks Uncle. I want to ask you for another Daily Food for Christians, because keeping this sometimes in my pocket and reading the text and poetry in it every morning, it is nearly worn out, and I am afraid I shall lose the leaves; Mamma is afraid you will think me a bold and troublesome little boy, but she says I am yet so ignorant, that I do not know, but I am doing you a favor,[1] I do not agree with her: I hope you do not either.' The letter indicates that the young Walter had already acquired the capacity to please which is an intrinsic part of charm, a judgement confirmed by another extract from the letter: 'Baby cannot walk yet he always says R goes for Uncle Reynolds'.

The letters exchanged at this period are between Walter and both his parents but mainly between father and son. The majority were written while Walter was at Bristol College and are interesting for the insight they give into the affectionate and trustful relation between parents and child and for the clues they give to the development of Walter's future character. The warmth of his parents' affection is clear throughout the letters. To his mother he was their 'treasure' or, 'the blessing'—while his father not only showed his affection for him but took the keenest interest in his son's education. Walter responded in letters which could be mistaken for lecturing but were in reality making up to his father for the formal education which the latter had never received. A little vignette of the relation between the two comes in a letter of 21 May 1838 when Walter writes to his mother: 'I am just come from bathing, and Papa went to see me swim ("was not that an honour") and said if I took pains this year I should do wonders next year.' Writing to his son, whom he had left at a seaside resort, Mr Bagehot writes: 'The mail with its four horses soon took me away from you on Friday and carried me through a very pretty country to Taunton where Bob was waiting for me and brought me home just about the time of your fifth dip as I calculated.' (17 June 1833.)

When Walter left home for Bristol College, his father missed him

[1] The original spelling has been reproduced in all the letters.

profoundly: 'I travelled on to Cheddar with my thoughts wholly fixed on you, and with a parent's prayer for your happiness, and I believe I have thought of little else since my return; and both Mamma and I are longing to hear from you.' On 22 August 1839 his father writes: '. . . you may picture us to yourself, wandering about at Herd's Hill, still admiring its bright mornings and serene and beautiful moonlight nights, although having lost in you one of its greatest charms, we cannot feel the same lightheartedness we sometimes did when you were at home, and I hope to do again, when you return.'

Walter's character is clearly evidenced by the letters. He was a religious boy by nature, going to church twice on Sundays as was the custom and apparently quite happy to do so. His religious turn of mind is illustrated by a letter to his father of 7 November 1841: 'I have finished Moore's Life of Byron; it is useful to contemplate a great mind, struggling in the darkness of scepticism; and divested of the assurance of a future life which the Gospel conveys to our hearts. It shows us how little worldly fame, even when it is of the most exalted description can compensate for the cheerless gloom which unbelief throws on the future.' A sermon by Mr Russell Carpenter on, 'the evils of a visionary disposition, as rendering us unfit for the duties of active life, and as having a tendancy to make us selfish and careless of those around us', evidently made a deep impression. (Letter to his father of 13 March 1842.)

From an early age, Walter was earnest about his studies. While at Langport Grammar School he sends his father accounts of the lives of Alfred the Great and Julius Caesar as well as of the battle of Marathon and his mother is treated to a very long account of the life of St Augustine of Hippo, the 'bulwark of orthodoxy'. (25 November 1838.) At Bristol College his application intensified. A twentieth century schoolmaster might well be astonished at the range of a 13 year-old's studies; Walter was reading Virgil, Euclid, Xenophon and Livy and studying algebra, Latin, Greek, German, science and astronomy to which he eventually added shorthand! He brooded over the integral calculus and Newton's *Principia*. He describes himself as revolving 'at the sound of a bell as much as any Londoner at the sound of Bow Bell'. (Letter to his mother 19 August 1839.)

'I think I look horrid learned', he writes on 25 September 1841, 'with four books open before me at once'. He was clearly working too hard. 'My heart smites me to talk of sleeping, since I fell asleep in the most curious way last night over my books, and slept ever so long, and I had not done anything particular in the daytime either.' (Letter of February 1841.) He was reluctant to accept hospitality from his parents' learned friends in Bristol because of the inroads this would make on his study time. What he describes as his 'amusing book', namely Addison's works 'containing all his papers in the Spectator etc in one volume' would not strike present day contemporaries as being particularly relaxing. (Letter of 8 May 1842.) He kept Boswell's 'Life of Johnson' as a treat when he was tired. A treat of another kind was peering at the 'couple of skulls' which a boy had lent him when he was studying Dr Prichard's Craniology. (Letter to his father 26 April 1842.) The other boys evidently did not share his studiousness and he complains about being interrupted at his work to go and play cricket. Although it improved his circulation and kept him warm he was relieved to get back to his Virgil. 'Excuse this stupid letter,' he writes to his mother on 19 August 1839, 'but I have written it in the midst of an incessant noise.'

His anxiety is shown by his absentmindedness. On one occasion he went in to bathe wearing his flannel waistcoat—'for which I got soundly laughed at as was of course to be expected'. (Letter to father 16 May 1841.) He was also concerned about his father's health and anxious that he should not go down to the counting house after dinner in the winter. At times he appears disorganised, getting the time wrong and allowing letters to fall out of his blotter onto the ground.

Yet it was by no means all gloom and his wonderful sense of fun flashes out from time to time. His sense of humour becomes apparent early; in a letter of 18 May 1839, written to his mother before going to Bristol College, he writes, 'I have read the review of Doctor Cumming's work in the *Monthly*, and like him much better since I find he thinks Egypt a delightful country and advises some persons to go out with the intention of building a boarding-house for the sick, travellers, etc. I hope someone will take his advice. I have some thoughts of spending a month or two there!' The 'little apple-eating animal' breaks through at times: 'Only five weeks to the holidays. Hip, hip, hujia, hujia.' On 2 December 1841 he is found writing to his father: 'I have jumped over half a dozen and skipped all about the room, thinking how soon I shall come home; and see you all again.'

Walter far preferred life at home but he was not unhappy at school as his first letter to his mother from Bristol shows: 'I like it quite as

EDITOR'S INTRODUCTION

much as I expected and rather more!' (19 August 1839.) But like all schoolboys he was at times homesick and in a letter to his mother of February 1841 he writes: 'I do long to be with you all again; and I picture you all to myself, as I am sitting in the long evening all alone: Watty doing his sums, and Papa endeavouring in vain to instil into him some small glimmering of what he is about, and "somebody" (query who!) asleep sound as possible in the armchair.'

He treated his schoolfellows with what Alastair Buchan has called 'fastidious contempt'.[2] At the same time he had two close friends, Edward Fry and Killigrew Wait whose friendship lasted throughout his life. He also made the acquaintance of Constantine Prichard, the son of the famous doctor. 'Constantine Prichard is at home', he writes to his father on 7 April 1842, 'I was much struck by his beautiful forehead and brow, so very intellectual and expressive; certes he is by far the best looking of the Prichards; only time can show whether he is the cleverest.'

These friends apart, Walter tended to be a lonely child, his quizzical attitude to his school fellows had come out during his period at Langport Grammar School. 'The water has got up into the Moor,' he writes to his mother on 1 November 1838, 'which occasions great commotions in the school for fear it will be too wet to have a bonfire and let off fireworks. T. Paul surmises that they have let the water in because the boys shall not have a bonfire; but the fact wants confirmation, he having, as I can learn, no authority for it but in his own thoughts.'

He was not always popular with the other boys partly because he declined to take part in their games. 'Last night I was before the conversation with Mr Bromby concerning the places, rather low spirited for I had been *made* to play a game at prisoner's base. So I went up to comfort myself, looked into Shelley which is my restorative.' (Letter of 11 April 1840.) On another occasion he was given a licking by his companions for *not* breaking the rules. (Letter to his father 6 May 1840.) This extract from a letter to his father gives a clear idea of his attitude of somewhat supercilious superiority to his school fellows which they cannot totally have appreciated: 'You no doubt remember that Master Thatcher, who was locked up, for stealing, and telling mistakes &c. &c.; and that I said I feared no ammendment would arise if he once came out; I am very sorry to say that it is even

The Spare Chancellor, p. 31.

so, as I said; on Sunday he was let out and he behaved prettily well for the first two or three days; but he went on gradually getting worse and worse every day until yesterday evening when only 2 others were up, he took some turpentine (of all the things in the world) and put it into the fire: and when he was accused of it by the servant he denied [he had] taken any, and said he knew nothing at [all about] it: but there was some gone, and a strong smell in the room, so in goes the servant to complain to Mr. Bromby that someone had taken the turpentine; when she got half way, Thatcher ran after her, and told her that he had taken it and nevertheless she told, and Thatcher got a stout licking and returned to his old habitation.'

Equally revealing is his description of his declining to go with the other boys to Ryan's Circus. He described it as 'a kind of low theatre where I believe they act by dumb show; it is also the resort of juglers, mountebanks etc. etc. A most unintellectual place. I am therefore very glad I went to Mr. Osler's as the other boys would most likely have made me go, as they all went—I should have looked most foolish; and acquired the sincere hatred of all the boys for my mugging if I had stayed and passed thereby a faint censure on their amuzement. It would have interfered also with my studies as I should not have had time to do anything after 12 oclock at night (at which time they came home) and as it was I came home before ten and had all the time till they came for doing my work, reading etc etc.'

Like other clever schoolboys he was highly competitive and anxious about his place in class. On 7 December 1839 he is found writing to his father: 'I have not yet accomplished the desirable task of getting up to Wait, I got up to him once and by some very unlucky turns of fortune I fell again and am now about the same as when I last wrote, rather worse for another boy is above me of the name of Bowman, I hope I shall not fall below him also; may God give me strength to say His will be done. I however shall certainly try with all might, to surmount all obstacles and to keep my place if possible.'[3] In another letter he recounts how he received an invitation from Mr Osler to accompany a large party to the railroad, 'which I declined as I did not wish to lose marks in any way; and this afternoon there were no marks given so I might as well have gone'.

During this period one is able to see Walter's aesthetic sense

---

[3] cf. Letter to his father 22 August 1841.

developing. His life long devotion to the poetry of Shelley begins at Bristol and he is moved by the lyrics of Euripides: 'The lyric odes which form the Chorus of the piece [*Medea*] are very beautiful and moreover understandible which is not a very usual thing in the ancient tragic writers some parts of whom the most learned are obliged to give up in despair.' (Letter to father 22 August 1841.) He was always moved by mountains and tells his father about a geographical lecture on Switzerland illustrated by slides: he found the Alps most impressive. Throughout his life he retained his aesthetic sensibility for scenery.

Walter's world was not bounded by the school walls. He could escape to Red Lodge, the home of Dr Prichard, on Sundays and enjoy stimulating intellectual company. 'I dined at the Prichards a day or two ago. The Doctor had two friends there talking about the Arrow-headed character and the monuments of Pentapolis, and the way of manufacturing cloth in the South Seas.' Bristol itself was a thriving town with much going on and he tells his father in March 1841 how he is going to run down and take a look at the outside of the *Great Western*. He describes it as 'one of the most noble productions of art in the present day'. In May 1842 he attended a lecture on animal magnetism or, 'as it is more properly termed, Mesmerism. It does seem most wonderful.'

From his parents and relations at Langport he gained glimpses of the great world. While he was still at Langport Grammar School in 1839 the bedchamber controversy was at its height. Walter wrote to his mother: 'We are all going on very well without you, and Papa and I have such nice chats about Sir R. Peel and the little Queen. Papa has quite made up his mind since he had read our friend the Duke's speech that the Queen did quite right and blames "the Right Hon. Baronet" for making the ladies of so much consequence since they could only use the ladies' privilege of railing against everybody and everything.' (Letter of 18 May 1839.)

The controversy about the Corn Laws was beginning and Walter was sceptical about their value. In the *Stockdale v. Hansard* dispute he was firmly on the side of the Commons. On 20 May 1841 his mother writes to him about a concert which she attended in London: 'We were close to the Directors' box and the only disappointment I had was (for the Queen, we knew, was not to be there) that we were behind the Duke of Wellington, and that he never turned round, and alas! looks quite, quite old and tottery—and decrepit. I still hope the mind beams on, but the body is certainly going the way of all flesh ... Lord Ellenborough and various other stars glittering about—and latish in the evening there was a little bustle, and in came the star of stars with his suite, Prince Albert, who is very, very handsome, and talked and chatted with all around in a very affable manner.'

The behaviour of the British representatives, Lord Macartney and Lord Amherst in China, when they refused to perform the kowtow before the Emperor aroused Walters's strong approval. His analysis of the incident shows acute political awareness. 'Lord Macartney was better in this respect than Lord Amherst; when I first read it, I thought that performing the kotow was only as commading themselves to the customs of the country, in which they were travelling; but if we had performed the kotow, it would have been published by the Chinese all over Asia, that the King of Britain had done homage and was the vassal of the emperor of China.' (Letter to father 17 March 1840.)

Walter left Bristol College in the summer of 1842. His cousin, G. H. Sawtell, noted that he had gained greatly in self-confidence and had become an excellent conversationalist. He was vivacious and high spirited, and it was in this frame of mind that he set off on the next stage of his education at University College in London.

University College, London 1842–1846

Walter arrived in London in the autumn of 1842. He did not care for it as a place. Whatever his later sophistication he always remained firmly a countryman and a Somerset one at that. Furthermore, Victorian London before the days of clean air acts remained semi-permanently, particularly in the winter months, wreathed in smog and smoke. The drains which dated from the 18th century befouled the atmosphere. To make matters worse, Walter's lodgings were at 39 Camden Street, then as now an especially dreary and depressing part of London. 'I must confess,' wrote Walter to his mother in October 1842, just after his arrival, 'to having felt rather dismal, when Papa left me at the University in the midst of a thick London fog; and I cannot say but I felt rather dismal occasionally since, when I think of Herd's Hill and you all sitting quietly and happily down amid all its beauties, while I am toiling here in the midst of dust and smoke.' He confesses to his father that, 'although I keep up my spirits as well as I can, my thoughts ever and anon wander back again, to the calm beauties of Herd's Hill, in the midst of which I have of late spent so many Sundays'. (Letter of 23 October 1842.)

The passing of the years did not reconcile him to the capital. Four years later he is writing to his father: 'It is no compliment to say that I want to come home exceedingly; for I am so tired of London that I should be glad to be out of it on any terms. My dislike of London came on quite suddenly, as it always does, two or three days ago. I know from experience that it will not go off till I have had a run in the country for a short time. I shall, as you know, soon have to come back to bricks and smoke, but this must be endured. I think the people who come up to London "for the season" must be insane; or they must have different tastes from mine.' (25 June 1846.)

In such a setting it is not surprising that his health which, unlike his spirits, was never robust, suffered. Apart from colds and coughs he was also subject to headaches made worse by attacks of torturing self-doubt. In the summer of 1848 when he took his M.A. and was also awarded the gold medal for moral and intellectual philosophy, he was in so weak a state that he had to lean on a friend's arm when he went up to receive the medal. He writes of suffering from 'a cold and a croak', which cannot have been improved in the atmosphere of a city which seemed to him 'mere diluted smoke'. (24 March 1848.) Yet he was carried through everything by his own bubbling inner vitality. 'I have in general pretty good health,' he writes to his friend Edward Fry on 1 May 1846, 'though at the present time I am a good deal troubled by rather severe headaches. But I verily believe I am the happiest person living. I have such a flow of good spirits as no calamities I think could long interrupt, much less exhaust. As for melancholy without apparent cause natural to some minds, I do not know what it means. I am not over-sanguine as to the future in general, but I have a sort of reckless cheerfulness that gets on very well without the aid of hope. Perhaps it may be unfeeling and unsympathising to be so completely happy, but I do not know how to help it.'

Apart from the prospects of returning to Herd's Hill he was kept cheerful by escapes to his uncle and aunt Reynolds who dwelt in the clearer air of Hampstead.[4] Both were Evangelicals: Mr Reynolds had experienced an early conversion and had been instrumental in founding the low-church paper, the *Record* and Mrs Reynolds was befuddled with her notions about the Romanising Newman and the Pope. Bagehot suffered her diatribes with detached good humour: 'She believes that Newman is most likely bribed to become a Roman Catholic—at all events that he will be no loser in money matters by the change. As the Pope is a bankrupt it seems unlikely he should have much spare cash to send over to bribe English heretics. I never could understand what you told me in your letter about Mrs. J— thinking it required great grace to be a nun or a monk. If it means simply retiring from the world and living a life of contemplation in one place, I do not think that there are many things easier and pleasanter ... A monk's life *is* very captivating to my imagination as you know, but I do not think that I could persuade myself into its being right. I do not think Mr. Newman will fill England with monasteries. A monastery beside a railroad would be a curious mixture of the customs of different ages. The extreme of physical inaction and the extreme of bodily exertion would be side by side.'

One advantage of being in London was that Walter was able to hear many of the great orators of the day. Together with his friend Richard Holt Hutton he tracked them down in different parts of London. They could not listen to Parliament since Barry and Pugin's Palace was in course of being built and the legislators were confined to cramped quarters. But they could and did attend the stirring meetings of the Anti-Corn Law League whose campaign for free trade was at its height. They heard Cobden, of whom Bagehot was already a 'worshipper', and Bright, W. J. Fox, Henry Vincent the Chartist, and Daniel O'Connell. In his memoir of Bagehot, Hutton writes: 'Bagehot and I seldom missed an opportunity of hearing together the matchless practical disquisitions of Mr. Cobden—lucid and homely, yet glowing with intense conviction,—the profound passion and careless, though artistic, scorn of Mr. Bright, and the artifical and elaborately ornate periods, and witty, though somewhat *ad captandum*, epigrams of Mr. W. J. Fox (afterwards M.P. for Oldham). Indeed, we scoured London together to hear any kind of oratory that had gained a reputation of its own, and compared all we

[4] They lived at Cannon Place, Hampstead.

heard with the declamation of Burke and the rhetoric of Macaulay, many of whose later essays came out and were eagerly discussed by us while we were together at college.'[5]

Walter gives his father an amusing account of the meeting of the Friends of Ireland at Covent Garden in a letter of 18 March 1844: 'Certainly if good coats and clean linen were taken as the best tokens of the strength or weakness of a political party, the Repealers would be weak indeed, for as Dickens somewhere says the greater part of them seemed to have quarrelled with their washerwomen in earlier youth and to have taken a fixed resolution never to make it up. Two striking peculiarities in the assembly were the unaccountable disposition of the people in the dress circle to go down into the pit, and their striking familiarity with the Irish accent and the Irish howl.' In September 1843, it is evident from internal and external evidence that he made a brief visit to Dublin and at a Repeal meeting heard O'Connell speak. This is the only indication we have that Walter Bagehot ever visited Ireland.

In July 1844 Walter made his first trip abroad with the Reynolds', his aunt apparently being prepared to brave the contact with Popery. They travelled through Belgium and Germany to Switzerland. Walter responded to both art and nature. In the journal he kept for his parents he writes: 'The Cathedral at Antwerp is the most delicate Gothic building in the world according to the guidebook, which also states that Napoleon compared it to Mechlin lace, and Charles 5th said it ought to be kept in a case. At Ghent we saw a beautiful likeness in wood of Charles 5th of the most spirited kind on a celebrated chimney piece in the Palais de Justice. Whoever wants to get an admiration of Rubens let me come to Antwerp. It has thoroughly converted my Aunt Reynolds who is not in most cases, as the family know, a convertible person. The descent from the cross, of which you have the print in the drawing room, is beautiful.' He was less impressed by observing the Sisters of Charity handing out pieces of meat to the deserving poor. It was objects which moved him and he writes of what he considers 'much the most beautiful object I have seen on the continent. I mean, a statue supposed to be by Michaelangelo in the Cathedral of Notre Dame of the Virgin and Jesus. The delicacy of the

---

[5] Prefatory memoir to *Literary Studies* edited by Richard Holt Hutton, 2 vols, Longmans 1879, 1, xvi.

figures, the infantine simplicity of Jesus and the motherly anxiety of Mary who is looking down at him as he sits on her lap give a grace to the whole group too impressive to be forgotten, but which I can't put into words.' He was, deeply, moved by Rubens *Crucifixion*: 'The tears came too fast to my eyes to let me look any longer. I didn't state this publicly for it might look like affectation, yet why it should, I can't see.'

Although he was impressed by the command which Catholicism exercised over the minds of the people and by the way in which the fine arts 'are pressed into the service of Catholicism', (Letter to father July 1844) he remained unmoved by the Catholic Church's intellectual claims. As Hutton puts it in his memoir: 'What attracted Bagehot in the Church of Rome was the historical prestige and social authority which she had accumulated in believing and uncritical ages for use in the unbelieving and critical age in which we live,—while what he condemned and dreaded in her was her tendency to use her power over the multitude for purposes of a low ambition.'[6]

Walter enjoyed college life, even in its attenuated London form, and made some close friendships. His was not a large circle but the friends he did make were grappled to himself with hoops of steel. Richard Hutton was his closest friend, who after his death wrote a moving and perceptive memoir. Hutton was drawn to the 'lad with large dark eyes and florid complexion' from the moment he heard him plying Professor De Morgan with incisive questions during one of his lectures. Hutton was in fact a pedestrian version of Bagehot. He lacked Bagehot's vitality and originality and intuitive genius but he had the good sense to recognise all these qualities in Walter. Hutton was never in the least jealous of his friend's genius and recognised it simply and gratefully for what it was. Other friends of this period were William Caldwell Roscoe and Timothy Smith Osler, a distant cousin.

In his essay on Oxford Bagehot reflects on the part that a college plays in education in a passage which is clearly autobiographical. 'All that "pastors and masters" can teach young people, is as nothing when compared with what young people can't help teaching one another. Man made the school: God the playground. He did not leave children dependent on the dreams of parents or the pedantry of

---

[6] *ibid.* xxvii.

tutors. Before letters were invented, or books were, or governesses discovered, the neighbours' children, the outdoor life, the fists and the wrestling sinews, the old games—the oldest things in the world—the bare hill and the clear river—these were education. And now though Xenophon and sums be come, these are and remain. Horses and marbles, the knot of boys beside the schoolboy fire, the hard blows given and the harder ones received—these educate mankind. So too in youth—the real plastic energy is not in tutors or lectures or in books "got up", but in Wordsworth and Shelley; in the books that all read and because all like—in what all talk of because all are interested—in the argumentative walk or disputations lounge—in the impact of young thought upon young thought, of fresh thought on fresh thought—of hot thought on hot thought—in mirth and reputation—in ridicule and laughter—for these are the free play of the natural mind, and these cannot be got without a college.'[7]

Outside the charmed circle the other undergraduates viewed him with considerable reserve. His manner was often supercilious. 'We used to attack him,' writes Hutton 'for his intellectual arrogance—his υβρισ we called it, in our college slang—a quality which I believe was not really in him, though he had then much of its external appearance. Nevertheless his genuine contempt for what was intellectually feeble was not accompanied by an even adequate appreciation of his own powers. At college, however, his satirical "Hear, hear", was a formidable sound in the debating society, and one which took the heart out of many a young speaker; and the ironical "How much?" with which in conversation he would meet an over-eloquent expression, was always of a nature to reduce a man, as the mathematical phrase goes, to his "lowest terms".'[8]

As he grew older Walter became mellower and gentler but, as Hutton points out he never had in any high degree, 'that sensitive instinct as to what others would feel, which so often shapes even the thoughts of men, and still oftener their speech, into mild and complacent, but unmeaning and unfruitful, forms'.[9] It was this inability to appreciate the feelings of others which later formed a major obstacle to his entering Parliament.

Walter's stock amongst his fellow students suffered a severe

---

[7] *Collected Works*, VII, 354–5.
[8] Memoir, xvii–xviii.
[9] See 'Memoir', xix.

depression when he embarked on a little moral initiative of his own. His sensitive conscience brought on a domestic crisis in the home of Dr Hoppus, where he was lodging. A fellow student and lodger, instead of attending lectures or going to Sunday evening services was passing his time with some loose women of the town and, Walter gathered, was about to start another young man along the primrose path. Most young men then, and virtually all today would have shrugged their shoulders at something which was not their business but Walter felt impelled to intervene. He reached this decision only after some sleepless nights. Writing to his father he shows both his motivation and his doubts. 'I have for some time suspected, although I have tried to disbelieve it, as long as I could, but one of my companions Jessop has exceedingly improper connections, and that he is in the habit of visiting them at times when Dr. Hoppus thinks, he is engaged at college, and on Sunday evenings, when he is thought to be at church. Now certainly I feel, that it cannot be my duty to allow this state of things to continue; I do not think it would be doing right either to Dr. Hoppus or to Jessop himself; yet the office of talebearer is so invidious, and in general so contemptible that I confess that I am exceedingly loath to undertake it.' (Letter of 30 October 1842.)

Nevertheless, Walter decided to act when he learnt that Jessop was going to introduce another fellow student, Collier, to the women. What made his predicament worse was that Jessop evidently was a good natured character of considerable charm and Walter felt drawn to him. He clearly needed reassurance from his father that he had done the right thing: 'I need not tell how much anxiety this has cost me, or how much I dislike the duty I am going to perform, but my resolution has not been taken without the most careful deliberation, and I may add earnest prayer.' A further complication which he confided to his father was that Mrs Hoppus was expecting confinement and he feared that the shock of the revelation might upset her should she learn about it.

His father supported his son's judgement. Meanwhile, the unfortunate Jessop was sent away and Collier's father was sent for. He removed him from the house leaving Walter uncertain whether he would return. It seems probable that Dr Hoppus did take him back again subject to a strict régime. The other students seem to have sent Walter to Coventry. He writes to his father: 'The step I have taken has of course made my companions exceedingly angry, and for this I was prepared: they do not however break forth into any abuse, nor have any painful scenes of a quarrelsome nature occurred, on the contrary, they do not speak to me "either good or bad".' (Letter of 3 November 1842.) The other boys did not quickly forget the incident and it caused him difficulty in getting elected to the debating society in January 1843. The incident caused Bagehot considerable upset: 'It is my first taste of the troubles of life,' he wrote to his mother; 'henceforth I shall perhaps never be wholly free from them.'

The painful incident was left behind and forgotten but it remains a curious and significant one because it gives an insight into the earnest, religious and scrupulous Walter Bagehot who later became submerged but never entirely vanished in the sardonic, no nonsense, experienced man of the world. It certainly took courage to take the action he did and showed a highly sensitive moral nature but is there not a touch of priggishness about it and also of naïveté? He seems to have experienced in himself no moral weakness and was therefore perhaps intolerant of it in others.

Walter was assiduous in attending his lectures. These were of a high order since the students paid the professors directly for the course they attended. This was a splendid incentive for giving interesting instead of dull lectures. Augustus De Morgan was professor of mathematics. Henry Malden taught classics as did George Long, noted for his dry learning and caustic irony. The idiosyncracies of his teachers caught Bagehot's quizzical eye and his comments foreshadow the botanical like analysis of writers and statesmen of his maturity. Writing to his mother on 23 October 1842, he sets out an intriguing gallery. 'Professor De Morgan has *one* eye, and a large white face, rather like Mr. Paul in his manner. He lectures very well, and seems as interested in mathematics, as if he were lecturing on them for the first time, and had not been going continually over the same ground these ten years. Mr. Malden, they say, was a moderately pleasant looking man before he had the smallpox, but certainly now he is, as pitiful a looking creature, as man ever saw. I like him, I think the best of all; he gives us an immense quantity of information on all manner of subjects; and seems quite delighted if you go and ask him a question which I have done once or twice. He dresses in clothes which look as if moths had been long their familiar inhabitants. Professor Long I don't like so much, he is by no means *so* interesting, *and* is exceedingly minute not to say almost tiresomely so, but he may improve as he gets more accustommed to the class, and we get more accustommed to him.'

From the letters we can also see Walter's emerging and developing views. His liberalism was never in doubt and his belief in progress is remarkably confident. 'You ask,' he writes to Edward Fry, 'is England going down hill? I cannot think so. I see a gradual progress in history, especially in the History of England. I cannot suppose that this is now going to stand still. There never yet was a nation while getting freer and freer, more and more intellectually instructed, and morally better and better, which ever stopped. I think England is in this condition; the progress of the Arts or life, of material civilisation, has been for two centuries of unexampled rapidity, and I think that the mental progress has also been vigorously carried forward, though I do not think it has been *equally* quick. The lower classes of this country are ignorant, but the last generation is better than the preceding ones, *our* generation more instructed than the last; it is for us to see to the next.' (Letter of 1 May 1846.)

His aversion to Disraeli, which lasted all his life and prevented him from giving an objective assessment of the great Prime Minister emerged early. Writing to his mother in February 1826 he says: 'I wonder D'Israeli had not more sense than to come out at this time of day with a protectionist speech. Everybody knew that he was no reasoner, and knew nothing of the question, but he need not have made both facts so painfully evident. His assurance gives him great advantage as a political adventurer—a man with any modesty could hardly have ridiculed Sir R. Peel so long for having no principles, and then opposed him when he proposed to establish a very comprehensive one, as a fundamental constitutional maxim . . . I am no worshipper of Sir R. Peel, nor a very firm believer in his thorough sincerity but I do hope that he will persevere in his present course of not condescending to answer Disraeli. The moral weight of the latter being nothing; his accusations would only gather weight from Sir Robert's condescending to answer them.'

Bagehot never got the true measure of Disraeli. He was alienated from him by what he considered his showiness and his 'false melodramatic tastes'. This prevented him from seeing the substructure of principle that underlay Disraeli's policies and pyrotechnics. The Dizzy affectionately held in reverence by the nation, adored by the

EDITOR'S INTRODUCTION

Queen, and fascinating to posterity, escaped him. Interestingly enough, his hostility to another pet aversion, Carlyle, had not emerged at this period. In a letter to his mother of November 1845 he says: 'At first his style seems uncouth and unpleasant, and his opinions fluctuating and absurd. But after a little time his mind grows insensibly in your estimation and you get to see that small assertions which look hasty and immature do really arise from much careful thought, and are parts of a large and coherent system of opinions.' He evidently did not share his mother's admiration for the Duke of Wellington whom he claimed had 'no rival in the art of making "naïve" speeches. I should not wonder if he has a concealed system of logic, in which the fundamental test of a good argument is its beginning by begging the question.' (Letter to his mother, 28 March 1846.) Cobden on the other hand was a subject of admiration: 'I am enthusiastic about, am a worshipper of, Cobden.' (Letter to Edward Fry, May 1846.)

In another letter to Fry he sets out some of his views on literature. '... diffuseness seems to me the besetting sin of our recent literature. In poetry it is worse than in prose, for when the intellect is addressed, it is no harm to follow out principles and reasonings into their most minute applications. But in poetry, and indeed in eloquence where the feelings of the poet are expressed, and the feelings of the orator's hearers are addressed, to give numerous details and to repeat the same details more than once seems like a botanist who, in delineating the beauty of flowers, should recount the number of stamens they possess. *Some* details are essential in poetry, because no affections cling to general ideas, and to pale unhealthy looking abstractions, but the poet's genius and taste are shown in their combination and selection, not as some poets seem to imagine in their accumulation. I hardly know any recent poetry not chargeable with too great prolixity except perhaps the lyric parts of Campbell, and the very best parts of Shelley and Byron.' Bagehot, admirer of poetry though he was, always thought it should be 'soon over'. 'I am an impatient reader of merely pretty poetry though not, I trust, without enthusiasm for the great masters of the poetic art, nor untouched by the beautiful expressions of feelings and aspirations, which earnestly long for what is infinite and eternal.'[10]

---

[10] Bagehot mentions that he likes Hood's poems. 'Of very recent poetry I think they are perhaps the best. They show quickness and delicacy of feeling, and a very happy fancy

EDITOR'S INTRODUCTION

In later life, Bagehot often mocked at things German, particularly the teutonic penchant for abstraction combined with detail. We find him writing about Kant: 'It is a great pity that he had so little power of explaining his meaning. His vast and barbarous terminology is enough to terrify any Englishman, but one who like myself is a fanatical devotee in the service of metaphysics.'

One characteristic which emerges from the letters and which remained with Bagehot throughout his life was his dislike of dealing with detail and minutiae. Even after years of association with *The Economist* he was unable to correct a proof satisfactorily. The slapdash quotations with which his essays are peppered and the curious mistakes and lapses in the letters are also traceable to this source. Bagehot was well aware of this shortcoming. 'The defect in my mind which is the proximate cause of it,' he writes to his father on 7 May 1846, 'is I think, that I have very great difficulty in that "making a thing complete", which Mr. Long is constantly inculcating on us. I would much rather exert my mind really very hard for a short time, than attend for a long time to a great number of comparatively easy things. My mind is very apt to wander when the subject to which I have to attend is a collection of easy details . . . It is the same defect of mental constitution I believe, which makes me such a wretched observer. Observation requires or rather implies a constant attention to a considerable number of minutiae and this which is to many a rest is to me the most irksome labor.' This characteristic made him unsympathetic to the linguistic and grammatical study of the classics. What interested him in the ancient authors was 'the historical instruction, literary beauty and speculative philosophy which after all are the real sources of the value of the records of antiquity'. He claimed that he did not undervalue precise acquaintance with detail and nicety in classical writings but it was not an occupation for him. 'It is absolutely necessary that *some* persons should become well acquainted with them, and thoroughly investigate and discuss their difficulties. But my taste does not lead me in that direction, nor is my mind fitted especially well for such pursuits. It is very possible that the defect of mind which renders minute investigation in matters of small intrinsic importance very irksome to

capable of very good ornamental work. The great depths of the human heart are only for those of a great creative imagination, and where among living poets shall we find that greatest of God's gifts. However, Hood was a man who took his knowledge of mankind not from tradition but from his eyes."

me, may have influenced my reasonings on this point more than I am aware of.'

Education was another topic discussed, this time with his mother. He was especially perplexed by the problem of what religion to teach in a religiously pluralist society. 'You would do the state a great service if you could point any way in which the state could teach religion to *all* its subjects, when those subjects held different creeds, and believed many of them that the creeds of others would doom them to misery for ever. The religion taught in a national system of education ought in my view to be a national religion. But in England we have no *national* religion. One part of the nation believes one thing, and another believes that the creed of the first is fatal to their salvation. Why the very rulers who are to select the religion have every sort of diversity of opinion, and are we to postpone all education till they agree?' (Letter of 9 September 1846.) Bagehot did not satisfactorily resolve this question and took refuge in the conclusion that literacy was of more fundamental importance than theology. 'Really one does hope with Carlyle that after "a thousand years of ineffectual consideration, England really will find courage and capacity to teach all Englishmen 'the alphabet' ".'

Other subjects touched on include India, morality and belief and the practice of the law. He was never an imperialist and later came to detest Disraeli's ambitious foreign policy, and even at this early stage he was remarkably detached about the Indian possessions. 'We generally acquiesce pretty easily in the doctrine that we have the right on our side, and as most of the Indian nations know nothing of European international law, it would not seem a difficult matter to put them in the wrong.' (Letter to his mother, February 1846.)

There are signs too of his distrust of arid moral and abstract religious speculation. Few minds he thought could tolerate the self scrutiny necessary to profound acquaintance with a religious philosophy 'if unaided by that constant call to *action* so necessary in all subjects that have any near kindred with morals.' (Letter to his father 16 May 1846.) 'Certain it is that the constant promise of Christ that those who *do* his will shall know of the truth of his doctrine is unaccompanied by any promise of success to inactive speculation however earnest and conscientious.' This pragmatic view of the nature of morality is shown again in his travel journal of August 1844 from Switzerland when he is reflecting on Thorvaldsen's monument commemorating the sacrifice of the Swiss guard who gave up their lives in defending Louis XVI. Their apparently pointless action was recognised as heroic and hence the monument. Walter comments: 'The moral feelings of mankind are as usual in the right.' Another subject about which in correspondence with his father he shows an almost obsessive concern is the morality of advocacy. 'Do you think there is any ground for saying that the average morality of barristers is lower than that of the rest of the community?' (Letter of 15 August 1846.) He regarded the practice of advocacy as the most disreputable part of a lawyer's calling but seems to have concluded that it could be justified.

These rather solemn discussions are rendered more diverting by their being placed in the context of matters of ordinary domestic concern which he raises with his parents. Thus we find 'No collar of the sort you mention is to be found in my stores' immediately preceding a discussion of Burns, Carlyle, Shelley and Frederick Schlegel. (Letter to mother November 1845.) The passages of discussion on national religious education conclude with, 'Has Watty *really* got a coat small enough for him? They must have amazing microscopes at Hyam's.' (Letter to mother 9 September 1846.) The strong affection for his parents runs through the letters. Writing to his father on 23 October 1842, he says, 'I thank you, for your most kind letter; your affectionate sollicitude for my welfare, believe me, is a blessing, I would not lose by any fault of mine, and in no other way can I lose it, for any other blessing which the world can bestow. If both our lives are spared and God grant that they may be so, may we have that communion in thought and affection which only real sympathy in each other's feelings can give.' But he can be stern too when the occasion requires it and he does not hesitate to rebuke his mother for sending a letter in the name of his brother young Estlin to the Duke of Wellington. (Letter of May 1846.)

London and Langport August 1846-December 1856

Despite his doubts, his ill health and his headaches, Walter continued to garner academic laurels. His first class in classical honours in 1843 was succeeded by another first when he took his B.A. in

EDITOR'S INTRODUCTION

October 1846 and won a scholarship to continue his studies for the M.A. This had the double advantage of giving him an opportunity for higher work and helping him on towards a career at the bar which at this time it had been accepted he would pursue. In 1848 he took his M.A. and was also awarded the gold medal for moral and intellectual philosophy.

The letters afford enlightening glimpses of his life during this period. He seems a little breathless and occupied with many things: 'As you say the time does go away *so* fast,' he writes to his mother on 9 September 1846, 'that one has no time to do anything. It sometimes seems to me as if by the time I was well and satisfactorily up in a morning, it was time to go to bed.' His absentmindedness remained: 'This letter was written yesterday, and ought to have been put into the post. But when I came in long after post time, I was astounded to see it on the chimney piece still.'

We also get shafts of Bagehot's sunniness and brightness. 'He [Alfred Norman] says that Mr. Rowland Hill is very unpopular in the post office, as his measures show a tendency to the reduction of salaries, which is not the kind of reform most agreeable to the *receivers* of salaries.' (Letter to mother, 6 February 1847.) Later she receives an amusing account of the British Association meeting at Oxford and Prince Albert's visit. 'Dr. Faraday is here, and gave a statement that they can now by recent discoveries turn diamonds into coke, but it does not seem that they can turn them back again; so that jewellers will not suffer . . . Ehrenberg the great animalcule finder is there; he looks rather like a squashed animalcule himself.' The account of Frank Newman's party is equally diverting: 'Mr. Stanley is a little man with grissly black hair, and piercing black eyes that look like a Jew's; very singular and clever looking. I went to a queer party at Newman's a night or two ago. He manages a party worse than anybody I ever saw. A good many ladies and a good many gentlemen, but none of the gentlemen knew any of the ladies except Mr. Newman, and one gentleman who, being married, vigorously fought shy of his own wife. All the ladies worked dismally in a meek way; and the men talked politics and metaphysics in another room, Newman peering through the folding doors at the ladies, being afraid, I suppose, they would make a rush and swamp his proof "that all philosophy began in nonsense".' (Letter of 18 December 1847.)

Walter, however, thought that he himself was sobering up. He writes to his mother: 'I *do* seem to get very old as you say. I am not such a thorough boy as to spirits as I was a couple of years ago: but I am boy enough still: and more so than some of my contemporaries ... I was not in great force having an amazing headache, though I hope nobody found it out: as I am not in favor of the publication of diseases.' (Letter of February 1848.) The letter ends 'love to all. How is my hunter?'

In fact, Walter's gaiety bubbled on. Writing to his friend Roscoe on 6 September 1848 he says: 'I have just seen Osler and Sandford at the British Museum. I'll tell you a way of reading German law that seems to work. Put a Savigny on the table before you; and an unwholesome looking white hat beyond it: then look over the Savigny plaintively at the white hat. If anyone seems watching, turn over a leaf and read with your lips voraciously. It seems to work.'

He developed his gift for arresting description: 'The levee at Somerset House the other day also is considered to have gone off well. The Chancellor was not quite up "to the swing of the humbug" and did not comport himself with much dignity or éclat. His method of proceeding was to lurk beind the door and when any one was announced to rush out and shake hands with him greedily. A good many people took him for a waiter and wondered at the intensity of his affection. Of all people Sir Robert Inglis was there looking very jovial and complaisant. Lord Brougham looked very old and horribly ugly. If he were on his trial I think a jury would not require much evidence beside his face to convict him of a sufficient number of crimes, and the older he gets the worse he looks.' (Letter to father 15 May 1849.)

On 8 May 1851, his mother is treated to a vivid and at times hilarious account of the opening of the Great Exhibition. 'The only accurate idea that I can give you of the Exhibition is that it is a great fair under a cucumber frame: the booths very numerous and the glass case very well painted: only it must be one of the swiss fairs where they sell everything from the best jewellery down to needles and thread. The day was most brilliant and the crowd enormous, both of which were essential to the goodness of the spectacle as the palace would be cold and icy without inhabitants and sun is required for the proper apportionment of light and shade and the due appreciation of the painted roof . . The Queen sat in the centre with the crowd around and behind her, and I was lucky enough to get a place in the front row of one of the galleries immediately overlooking the chair of state, and almost exactly over the head of your aged and infirm friend the Duke of Wellington.' The unamplified voices of the principal participants were lost in that great fane and Bagehot could pick up only fragments: 'I fancied that I caught two or three words of the archbishop's grace or benediction but I am not sure: at any rate I heard a sermonic tone of voice which was a great satisfaction. I suppose the Archbishop was inserted in the programme to please the foreigners who are in the habit of consecrating railways and all sorts of secular places: otherwise I think he might as well have been left out as there was nothing there in keeping with him, —nobody minded him and the Queen looked as if she wished that he would leave off. The court looked brilliant enough as far as the men went: the foreign magnates very well got up, our Cabinet ministers like town criers and the Lord Chancellor like a butler on the stage— There was a strong light upon them, and a tree behind—a real tree growing in the ground and just coming into leaf—which threw them out well and was original and picturesque looking.' Walter was disappointed with the United States pavilion and says that the only impression to be gathered from it was that, 'in that country they are extremely well off for soap. They have an immense compartment all to themselves at the end of the nave and nothing hardly in it except busts in soap of the Queen and other people. It must be amusing to wash yourself with yourself and great relief from the wretchedness of the employment.'

The sprightliness is there again when he is in Paris in 1851–52: 'I observe that dances like wheelbarrows are much the same in all countries, and nowhere propitious to people too muffish to waltz. One has to fall back on elderly creatures and express edifying sentiments in bad grammar.' (Letter of January 1852.) Walter apparently could never dance satisfactorily. In an earlier letter to his mother he writes: 'I have added what *I* call waltzing to my other accomplishments. It differs from what other people call by that name, not only in the step which is of my own invention, but also in its having no relation whatever to the music, and by preserving its rotary motion in a great measure by collisions with the other couples. It's very amusing running small French girls against some fellow's elbow, it's like killing flies years ago. There is, however, the inconvenience that one does not like to ask the same girl twice; she might say she had not insured her life, but if you are careful to select a fresh subject for each experiment, the pastime will succeed. I do not fancy it pleases the girls; he dances *tout seul* ("all by himself") I heard one of them say in great indignation to her female friends, as if a fellow of my age could be expected to keep time with her or with the music either, and it pleases me, it being a new, if not humane excitement, and is better than talking feeble philosophy in out of the way corners.' (Letter of 26 December 1851.)

The later letters of this period contain not only gay accounts of external events but important passages of self-analysis, rare in Bagehot's correspondence until his engagement, since he had a reluctance—probably because of his mother's affliction—to talk about his feelings. He was aware of his friend Hutton's tendency to melancholy and writes to him on 7 January 1853: 'You must employ yourself moderately on *something that you like* and keep up your spirits. I hope you will do the latter, and indeed I think you will, for I have observed that people who are naturally inclined to melancholy and like you would never be made awfully happy by any good fortune are not (after the care) so much depressed when they have *invested* their low spirits in real care. A buoyant person like myself who is rarely dismal, and not inclined to bemoan himself for other peoples calamities, is liable to be much disturbed when he has to be dismal because something has happened to *himself*. But this is not your way.'

The meaning of this passage is somewhat obscure but Bagehot is evidently contrasting his own temperament with that of Hutton, partly for purposes of self-analysis but also to help his friend. What he writes tallies with many of the things he says to Eliza his betrothed, such as the passage in the letter of 1 December 1857: 'I am cheerful but not sanguine—I can make the best of anything but I have difficulty in expecting that the future will be very good.' Bagehot appears to be saying that if one tends to live for the day one is not rendered miserable by friends' calamities however much one may sympathize with them. On the other hand, when one does take this view of life, and has a capability for great enjoyment, a grief or loss of one's own casts one down completely, and the future offers little promise of hope. This was evidently Bagehot's own situation.

In a later letter to Hutton, Bagehot comments on his own limitations of feeling. Discussing Hutton's motivation for wishing to visit his wife's grave in the West Indies, he suggests that such feelings should be resisted: 'They are not "suitable to such a being as man in such a world as the present one". I am a very bad judge,—for tho' susceptible enough to cold irritable pain, I know very little of the higher kinds of affection and suffering. Still I cannot think such a tendency of feeling—at least not such an indulgence of it in action—suitable to the plain, manly, sensible sort of human life. I assure you it is not healthy.' (Letter of December 1856.) Bagehot was evidently aware of the deficiency of his feeling life and concludes another letter to Hutton with these words: 'I hope wherever you go you will feel sure of my affection, cold I may be, but inconstant I certainly am not.' The coldness was to be cured by Bagehot's love affair with Eliza Wilson. His character was not cold but his feelings were inhibited and it required the advent of Eliza to release them and enable him to express them.

Bagehot was studying hard during this period. He was imbibing the principles of political philosophy, political economy and metaphysics. In the economic field he was already familiar with the writings of Adam Smith but added the works of Ricardo and Tooke. He also began to read a journal, founded four years before, *The Economist*. But Bagehot never confined himself to academic work. He read widely in literature and took a keen interest in the events going on in the world. As a result we are able to know something of his religious and political views from the letters which have survived. A typical and splendid letter is that which he wrote to Hutton on 20 September 1848. He starts off by discussing the Newman brothers and quite rightly, in view of John Henry's intense self-awareness, rejects Hutton's opinion that he has 'less than the average of self-consciousness'.[11] Both the Newmans he thinks, 'combine with a great facility of analyzing to a certain extent, a great disinclination (and almost an inability) to analyse further'.

From the Newmans, he moves to St Paul and expresses his approval of Martineau's view that Paul's whole soul was absorbed in a wish for a triumph of the truth: 'This was inextricably connected no doubt with a love of God and Christian persons: beyond these he had only one intense wish, as far as I can see, viz. to do his duty whatever that might be: I do not imagine that he was defective at all in the sense of

---

[11] Thus Newman refers in his *Apologia pro Vita Sua*, 1864 (Chapter I), to his resting at the age of 15 'in the thought of two and two only supreme [in 1865 edition 'absolute'] and luminously self evident beings, myself and my Creator'.

personal sin: but I do not think he cared the least what his own position hereafter might be so long as the truth triumphed: he had an intense wish to perform whatever *work* was given him but no anxiety about what the nature of that work might be.' Bagehot goes on to reject the arguments against celibacy put forward by Charles Kingsley's *The Saint's Tragedy*: he suggests that it may be held that 'the highest life is an imitation of Christ's not only in its spirit, but in its characteristic circumstances'. He concludes that St Paul 'argues satisfactorily that it is essential to an *absorption* in the highest end of human action: this is undoubtedly the teaching religion in such a manner as effect a diminution of sin among mankind'.

Then comes an interesting reflection that no man should begin 'to put down the disinterested part of his original nature, unless he has thoroughly put down the selfish and the unnatural: it wd. be an awful thing and yet it must have happened often after conquering the affections to succumb to the appetites'. One justification for marriage is the necessity in most men 'to keep a strong habitual feeling of disinterested affection . . . towards existing persons whom they habitually see and it is very difficult to do this in the case of friends, because they are dispersed so widely, and have such different spheres of duty. You know Arnold's saying that a family or religious intercourse with the poor was necessary for an Englishman. I think it might with pains be generalized into a complete view of the subject.'

Bagehot recognised that feeling in religion was not only an emotional but an evaluative faculty. Commenting to Hutton on an article on Luther in the *Christian Remembrancer* he expresses his interest but criticises it for failing 'in appreciating Luther justly in connection with faith or the influence of affections in religion: nevertheless what he says is instructive as I had overlooked this view of Lutheranism in great measure. The defect of his writing to me is that it is not the writing of a man who has a personal feeling of great difficulties, that is not a deep feeling. It is the state incident to a mind that has acquiesced in the creed given to it by education: and not felt the need of personal search. Hence he is unintentionally unjust to eager men like Luther and Arnold: who speak earnestly and hastily while their minds are yet running on, and are too impatient to speak to say always what is the truth.' (Letter of January 1848.) Martineau's theology is splendidly dismissed: 'His idea of God is a large pale pressure operating universally wh. is imcomplete.' (Letter to Hutton, 8 October 1855.)

EDITOR'S INTRODUCTION

The references to Newman show, even at this early stage, the influence he was exercising over Bagehot's mind. Writing to his mother on 8 December 1849 he notes: 'Mr. Newman the Catholic has been publishing a volume of sermons lately which are rather remarkable both in themselves and as he has not published anything with his name since he joined the Catholic church. They are very keen and acute like all his writings and much more decisive and conclusive than his writing used to be, and he seems altogether much more in his natural place than in former times.' He was drawn to Newman's poetry and rather unkindly draws a comparison between him and Hutton as verse writers. Hutton had sent him a hymn he had written and Bagehot was not encouraging: 'Nobody but Newman can contract with his imagination for a supply of verses.'

Bagehot's views on secular subjects also flash out. The finest example of this is the letter written to his mother on the London of the Chartist riots in 1848. Bagehot was a student at Lincoln's Inn at the time and in the manner of his successors in the general strike of 1926 had been pressed into service. The letter is brilliant both in its description and analysis. 'The benchers came down to be sworn: *not* looking very dangerous as they are old and rickety and much addicted to port wine. However they hobbled down. The students are more vigorous certainly but decidedly as likely to make a row as to prevent it.' The chances of this were reduced by their being forbidden to go to Kennington Common; instead they had to patrol Lincoln's Inn. Walter had his reservations: 'I wanted to shirk it but I found it was reckoned disreputable, and men talked patriotism and so I went and was sworn in.' His judgement was that the elements for a serious riot existed in London: 'I suppose there is as much misery and recklessness there as in any equal space in the whole world: but I do not believe that these Chartists have any organized scheme that will prosper, or that they could hold Irish troops in discipline; and a London mob though brutal and fierce is not inventive like the Parisians, and has not spontaneous discipline of the French.' As to the Chartists, there was 'a great parliament or convention of them sitting in John St. about half a mile from here; where very violent language is delivered to the world gratis by men in dirty shirts; one barrister whose business was not overwhelming presides—His name is Earnest Jones with red whiskers and red hair. I do not think there is much *fight* in them; but there is a deal of talk. However, with the mass of wretchedness and recklessness that exists in London, the slightest spark is dangerous and must not be neglected.' A letter written a few months later to Roscoe which discusses Mill, partnership and Keats amongst other things is also bright and sparkling. (Letter of 6 September 1848.)

In 1849 Bagehot discusses Mill on population and marriage with Hutton. 'I suspect that Mill thinks profligacy a less crime than a marriage on insufficient means, and taking only rather extreme cases of the latter, it would not be easy to find a proof that the consequences (which is the only test of morality that he would allow of) were not worse in the former case than in the latter. Of course on higher grounds it is clear that profligacy is far the worst.' (Letter of 1 March 1849.) He will not accept Mill's axiom that children ought not to be begotten unless they can be maintained in comfort. 'The real principle as it seems to me, is that persons ought not to marry unless they are morally sure that the moral dangers to themselves from remaining single are greater than those to wh. their children would be exposed from the poverty and suffering into which they would be born.'

Bagehot supported Lord John Russell on the question of Jews being allowed to take the oath and admitted to the House of Commons. (Letter to father, 7 August 1850.) On slavery, Bagehot did not take a high principled abstract view and his pragmatic approach comes out in a letter to Hutton of January 1853 when Hutton was in the West Indies: 'Have you seen anything of the blacks? It can't be a pretty study, but it may be an instructive one. People are quite wild here again about slavery, as strong as they ever were when there was a *bonâ fide* agitation in this country on the point. I should like to know accurately what comes from emancipation, taking it as a question of sacrifices. I can imagine many cases in wh. slavery is good for a population, but none or not many in which *traders* can be trusted to be slaveowners. It may answer in rural villages where they only supply their own demand, and where the notion of the slaves being "capital" is extremely secondary, but never in a mercantile community where that notion is the main one and the notion of moral and personal dependence extremely faint.'

Bagehot was equally cool and detached about Ireland and never felt any deep sympathy with the Irish. As a Liberal supporter, he agreed with disestablishment of the Irish Church but was strongly opposed to both Irish republicanism and nationalism. He did not feel deeply for the sufferings of the Irish people. In a letter to his mother of 6 February 1847, he takes an untypically Benthamite view of the attempts to alleviate suffering in Ireland: 'The whole system of public works is an evil,' since it makes the Irish look to the English government for charity and encourages them to neglect the land. The Irish were included in that category 'masses of unknown men' for whom, according to Hutton, he felt little.[12] 'I do not think,' writes Hutton, 'he had at any time any keen sympathy with the multitude ... And that he ever felt what has since then been termed "the enthusiasm of humanity", the sympathy with "the toiling millions of men sunk in labour and pain", he himself would strenuously have denied. Such sympathy, even when men really desire to feel it, is, indeed very much oftener coveted than actually felt by men as a living motive; and I am not quite sure that Bagehot would have even wished to feel it.'

The foreign countries on whose affairs he comments in the letters are France, Austria, the United States and Poland. Writing to his mother on 24 March 1848, he is highly critical of Louis Philippe: 'This is the second lesson of what king-craft and diplomacy are worth in the hour of trial.' He thought the King's supporters scoundrels and humbugs. As to the fall of Metternich: 'It shows the weakness of the system, and of every system which counts for nothing the opinions and convictions of the great mass of its most intelligent subjects.' He is supercilious about the United States and while he later recognised American greatness he never visited America and thus was not able to exercise his faculty for seeing things acutely when looking at them closely and for himself. On Clough's visit to America he writes to him in October 1852: 'Do you expect to find America "instructive"? I should think for a visit it wd. be very much so. I rather like that rough active pecuniary life, but I doubt whether it wd. be *perfect* for a very long time. Besides they are so dyspeptic.'

He had as little sympathy for the Poles as for the Irish; when Martineau was counselling an intervention in Poland in an article in the *National Review*, Bagehot adopts an attitude of cold realism: 'It appears to mean that you are to go into Poland and raise a standard of revolt—without in the least knowing whether the Poles have any capacity or desire for freedom—about which he admits there are no

[12] Hutton *op. cit.* xliv–xlv.

data—but on the *chancs* of their having some—wh. either means that you are to desert them, if you do not find them up to the mark, or that you are to maintain them or attempt by endless war to maintain them altho' they are unfit—both which are absurd. Beside, you wd. have the active opposition of Austria and Prussia, the active sympathy of the *rouge* party abroad which last wd. mean the horror and alarm of all conservatives here at home.' (Letter to Hutton, 13 January 1856.)

The two friendships during this period which were of the most significance to Bagehot were those with Hutton and with Clough. Hutton was more dependent upon Bagehot than Bagehot upon him, and at this stage Bagehot was the more reserved of the two, but their closeness was never in doubt. When Hutton received an offer to become editor of *The Economist* from W. R. Greg, acting as an intermediary for James Wilson in 1856, and proposed first to make a sentimental journey to the West Indies to visit his wife's grave, Bagehot sent him some astringent but wise advice. 'I have thought over *very* carefully what you tell me of Greg's offer, but I cannot think you are acting rightly. You have now an opportunity wh. may not occur again of *fixing* yourself in an established post, likely to be useful and permanent, and give you a fulcrum and position in the world wh. is what you have always wanted, and is quite necessary to comfort in England. I do not think you ought to risk it for the sake of *holiday*. You may have been right to ask it as a beginning of the negotiation for it may be a gain to *you* to get it, but it seems to me quite out of the question to make it a *sine quâ non*. Offers of this kind are not to be picked up in the street every day.

'As to holidays, it is one of the lessons of life to learn to be independent of them. They are scarcely to be obtained by people in regular employment except in very fortunate circumstances. I have some right to say this myself for except when I was at Roscoes last autumn I have not been a week without doing *some* business. I do not say very much, but still some—enough to deaden the mind for more than four years. I assure you, if you seriously mean to work hard in England—and you *require* a good deal of work to keep your mind healthy—you must not hope for any such long gaps. At any rate I feel very strongly that you ought not to make the having one an essential condition of obtaining so good a position.' (Letter of December 1856.) Nevertheless, Hutton left for the West Indies on the assurance that the offer would be kept open until his return.

EDITOR'S INTRODUCTION

Clough, according to Hutton, had 'a greater intellectual fascination' for Bagehot than any of his contemporaries. What attracted him to Clough? It was, thought Hutton, that Clough had as a poet 'in some measure rediscovered, at all events realised, as few ever realised before, the enormous difficulty of finding truth—a difficulty which he somewhat paradoxically held to be enhanced rather than diminished by the intensity of the truest modern passion for it. The stronger the desire, he teaches, the greater is the danger of illegitimately satisfying that desire by persuading ourselves that what we *wish* to believe, is true, and the greater the danger of ignoring the actual confusions of human things.'[13] This law of intellectual suspense had a dangerous lure for Bagehot. It could have paralysed him and he might himself have ended with what he described as Clough's 'fatigued way of looking at great subjects'. Clough, having been pulverised by Dr Arnold and winnowed by Dr Newman was in fact a burnt out case and Bagehot might have become one. As it was, he was saved from scepticism by the inherent bouyncy and thrust of his own nature and in part by Clough's unhappy example.

Both Bagehot and Clough were concerned with University Hall, a hall of residence for London University of which Clough became head. Hutton tells us that he did what he could to mediate 'between that enigma to Presbyterian parents—a college-head who held himself serenely neutral on almost all moral and educational subjects interesting to parents and pupils, except the observance of disciplinary rules—and the managing body who bewildered him and were by him bewildered'.[14] In a letter to Hutton of 1 March 1849, Bagehot gives a graphic account of Clough: 'He is a man of strong, and clear though not very quick intellect: so that I feel like a gnat buzzing about him. He has a great deal of imagination, and has written a good deal of poetry; a proportion of which is good, though he unfortunately has been in the Highlands and talks of barmaids and potato-girls and other operative females there in a very humiliating manner as it seems to me though Roscoe defends it. You would, I think, agree with me in thinking with me that his mind is defective in severity of moral feeling and in the conception of law generally as applied to morals. But he is evidently a man of great honesty and moral courage with an immense deal of

---

[13] Hutton *op. cit.* xxxvi.
[14] Hutton *op. cit.* xxxiv.

feeling. C. Prichard says his mind was injured he thinks by an overstrained asceticism when he first knew him at Oxford, and has never recovered from the evil. Roscoe and myself put him into the Principalship.'

Another friend of these years was Henry Crabb Robinson, an eccentric old bachelor, who had been the friend of Goethe and Schiller as well as Wordsworth and Coleridge and who entertained young men at breakfast parties, gatherings more remarkable for their intellectual than their bodily sustenance and the guests frequently suffered from the agony of famine. 'The more astute of his guests,' wrote Bagehot, 'used to breakfast before they came, and then there was much interest in seeing a steady literary man, who did not understand the region, in agonies at having to hear three stories before he got his tea, one again between his milk and his sugar, another between his butter and his toast, and additional zest in making a stealthy inquiry that was sure to intercept the coming delicacies by bringing on Schiller and Goethe.'[15] According to Hutton there was only one guest canny enough to eat first and that was Bagehot. He sometimes seems to have treated Crabb Robinson rather haughtily and didactically and when they were discussing the *National Review* and Crabb Robinson expressed some doubts Bagehot wrote to him '*I* consider myself a man of business and shd. not engage in such a scheme unless I thought the business aspect fair and reasonable . . . you are to remember, as far as social connections go, reviews—especially new reviews—are not written by the high literary *noblesse*—but by accomplished paupers—barristers, ministers and outcasts—who are not so well known to people of high standing, as they may be to people of low. I think we may hope for a few good pens of name—but we must beat Grub St. for clever padding.' (Letter of 5 April 1855.) Alistair Buchan points out that such a letter was good going for a man of 28 writing to one who was 50 years his senior.[16] However, one may forgive him for that, since it is in this letter that he invents the new word 'padding', still in use today.

In his essay on Hartley Coleridge (1852) which in part is a self-portrait, Bagehot quotes a passage from Keats's preface to *Endymion* which well represents his own state of mind as he concluded his period of study in chambers in 1857: 'The imagination of a boy is

---

[15] *Collected Works*, IV, 481.
[16] *The Spare Chancellor*, p. 78.

healthy, and the mature imagination of a man is healthy, but there is a space of life between, in which the soul is in a ferment, the character undecided, the way of life uncertain, the ambition thick-sighted.'[17]

After completing his studies at University College he moved in the winter of 1848, into the chambers of Mr Charles Hall to read for the Bar. He was being torn in different directions. His father wanted a legal career for him but his mother would have preferred him to come home and work in the family bank. As is clear from the letters, Bagehot's attitude to the law was ambivalent. In some way he found its complexity intellectually fascinating but in others the dread 'minutiae' were both pedestrian and restricting. In December 1848 he tells his father that he does not care for the work in chambers and that it provides 'a capital way of picking up a headache'. He told his father that the difficulties of the law were mainly 'of quantity'. 'No one thing is to a mind that has been properly disciplined, very difficult to grasp and master in and by itself: but unless great care is taken, while new matter is being laid hold of, the old matter slips away. So that the great requisite for success in law is roominess of mind, to take in and hold at once a large number of considerations. I find the work rather fatiguing at present. My eye is not practised enough to see easily the contents of a law paper. I do not know what are the material and what the immaterial parts; and groping all through masses of papers is a tiring operation...' (Letter of December 1848.)

Hutton, on the other hand, maintained that he thoroughly enjoyed his legal studies.[18] Walter's attitude was more nuancé. Writing to his friend Killigrew Wait after he had decided to give up the Bar he writes: 'I was sorry though to have to do this since in some respects legal studies suited me very much better than any other pecuniary pursuit is ever likely to do . . . As to your notion of doing anything *well*, it is so many years since I abandoned the idea that I cant now quite enter into the feeling. My difficulty is in doing any thing *at all*.' As for special pleading, he describes it as the 'champagne of life'. His intellectual reservations about the law aside, there is no doubt that Walter felt that he should play his part in shouldering the family burden of Mrs Bagehot's insanity. He gradually became more relaxed about it. A letter to Killigrew Wait in which he speaks about the

---

[17] See *Collected Works*, I, 151.
[18] See 'Memoir,' xlvi.

matter is a distinct advance, at earlier times he could not mention it, even to Hutton. 'I am not destitute of domestic anxiety myself, as my mother who many years ago was subject to attacks of delirium, has of late fallen into a good deal of habitual delusion and aberration, which, I fear, will end in ultimately disqualifying her for society. Indeed except with her oldest friends who are quite used to her, it has done so already. I suffered a good deal when I first put this steadily before me, but this is some time since and one can "grieve down" a good deal. But it is an odd world after all.' (Letter of 5 January 1853.)

His decision to abandon the law was communicated to his father in a letter of August 1852: 'I have decided to do so at this juncture—utterly and for ever.' Hutton is right when he concludes that the decision was a wise one: 'He was sure that his head would not stand the hot courts and heavy wigs which make the hot courts hotter, or the night work of a thriving barrister in case of success.' Had he chosen the Bar as a career those three works of genius would probably never have been written and his life might have been rendered even shorter.

By the summer of 1851, Walter's period in chambers was over but he was still anguished and undecided about his future. In August, encouraged by Roscoe, he wisely decided on a temporary change of scene and left London for Paris. He could not have timed his visit better since he was able in December to witness at first hand Louis Napoleon's *coup d'état*. He had the advantage of speaking French fluently though, as he said himself, with a '*horrid* accent'. (Letter to Crabb Robinson, 25 December 1851.) From Paris Bagehot wrote seven brilliant letters published in the *Inquirer*, the Unitarian paper.[19] The letters are an extraordinary combination of rollicking cynicism and profound good sense. They outraged the *Inquirer's* readers by eulogising the Catholic Church, defending Louis Napoleon's use of force, attacking the freedom of the French press and maintaining that the country was totally unfit for parliamentary government. Bagehot's 'fast' politics, as Hutton called them were more than racy, they contained in embryo some of the fundamental ideas of his maturity, his Burkeian concern for the preservation of the social fabric, his belief in the importance of national character, and his conviction that British parliamentary institutions could not be exported indiscriminately.

---

[19] *Collected Works*, IV, 15–84; the text of the letters are given there together with an introduction and assessment by the editor.

EDITOR'S INTRODUCTION

His private letters to his mother repeat some of the sentiments expressed in the published ones but do not parallel them entirely and contain some interesting further insights and ideas. Such was his zest and so high his spirits that he seemed to have helped build the barricades in the streets of Paris though his sympathy lay with the other side.[20]

Alastair Buchan remarks on the strain of 'high spirited bumptiousness' which characterizes Bagehot at this period.[21] Hutton says that he was full of life and courage at this time and 'was beginning to feel his own genius'.[22] The letters both private and public are splendid and have a dash and verve which Bagehot never surpassed.

Bagehot's support for Louis Napoleon comes out clearly in his letters to his mother 'I wish for the President decidedly myself as against M. Thiers and his set in the Parliamentary World; even *I* can't believe in a Government of barristers and newspaper editors.' Bagehot was lodging with a middle class couple, the Beins, and Mr Bein declared to him: 'I do not approve of this violence and *coup d'état*, but I am for the President because he's for "the tranquillity" '. 'People want to be let alone; it is clear that the Republic has been *burgled* and if the President were turned out no one knows who would come in.' (Letter of 7 December 1851.) He reassures Mrs Bagehot that despite the excitements life goes on: 'Don't suppose society here is at an end. People eat their meals—the shops are open. Rachel is to play tomorrow.' He sends his father vivid eye witness accounts of the scenes in the Paris streets after the *coup d'état* and has an arresting description of the Montagnards—'men whose faces I do not like to *think* of— yellow sour angry fanatical, who would rather shoot you than not'. Bagehot, however, conducted himself with circumspection and escaped danger: 'It is a bad habit to run in a Revolution—somebody may think you are the "other side" and shoot at you—but if you go calmly and look *English*, there is no particular danger.' (Letter of 5 December 1851.)

Walter also regales his mother, who always brought out his gaiety

---

[20] Letter to Hutton of December 1851: In the letter, Bagehot says that he 'superintended the construction of three'. It is not quite clear whether this should be taken literally or not.
[21] *The Spare Chancellor*, p. 66–7.
[22] 'Memoir', xliii.

and sense of humour, with an account of a conversation between two French ladies: 'Your friend Madame Meynieux pitched into his [Louis Napoleon's] private character yesterday at a great pace. She was arguing with a French lady whom I did not know. I have never heard two people talk so fast and so well at the same time. M. Meynieux and myself looked on open mouthed and in perfect silence. I could not talk that pace in English, much less in French, where I require five minutes to express four ideas. I listened patiently for a long time. The French lady was for the President and your friend violently against.... She don't at all approve of the common Red Socialist, indeed the weak point of the system is that no Socialist will ever associate with any other; all I know is that, as they say in the kitchen, somebody is to "keep company" with somebody.'[23]

After his return to London in the summer of 1852, Walter finished eating his dinners and in the autumn was called to the Bar, but he then retired to Langport to live the life of a country banker and an embryonic man of letters. He never regretted his decision. Meanwhile, he settled down to learn the techniques of his trade. On 7 January 1853 he writes to Hutton: 'I have devoted my time for the last 4 months nearly exclusively to the art of book-keeping by double entry, the theory of which is agreeable and pretty but the practice perhaps as horrible as anything ever was. I maintain too in vain that sums are matters of opinion—but the people in command here do not comprehend the nature of contingent matter and try to prove that figures tend to one result more than another which I find myself to be false and they always come different. But there is no influencing the instinctive dogmatism of the uneducated mind. In other respects I approve of mercantile life. There is some excitement in it, if this does not wear off—always a little to do and no [we]aring labor, which is something towards perfection.'

Nevertheless, he missed the intellectual stimulus of London and his friends: 'It is stupefying to live in the country: one gets into a rut of ideas and society, the same since our great grandfathers fell asleep, from which living tomb nothing after a short time will ever save one.' Hutton reveals that he never stayed more than six weeks at a time in the country without finding some excuse for going to London.

---

[23] Bagehot indicated that the French did not criticise his deficiencies in the language—'they only cut you up afterwards like a rotten potato.' (Letter, Paris, December 1851.) Nothing seems to have changed!

Country activities did not attract him save for hunting. 'Hunting,' writes Hutton, 'was the only sport he really cared for. He was a dashing rider, and a fresh wind was felt blowing through his earlier literary efforts as though he had been thinking in the saddle, an effect wanting in his later essays, where you see chiefly the calm analysis of a lucid observer.'[24]

He did not care for balls and all 'the little blue and pink girls, so like each other', a sentiment which Hutton attributed to his 'extreme shortness of sight'. The country at times made him feel restless.[25]

Banking gave Bagehot leisure to both read and write and during his Langport period he produced some of his finest critical essays. Bagehot had published his first literary essay, a review of Bailey's *Festus* in the *Prospective Review* for November 1847. *Festus* was a poem highly thought of at the time of publication but which has commanded less favour since. Robert Birley paid it the back-handed compliment of including it in his book *Sunk Without Trace*, an account and anthology of works which at one time commanded critical acclaim but on which judgment has been revised.[26] Bagehot's essay on Hartley Coleridge came out in 1852 as did that on Oxford. Both appeared in the *Prospective Review*, as did 'Shakespeare—the Individual', which appeared in 1853. 'Bishop Butler' followed in October 1854. The *Prospective* failed and on its ruins Martineau, Bagehot and Hutton founded the *National Review*, and here in the 50's he published essays on Cowper, the first Edinburgh reviewers, Gibbon, Macaulay, and Shelley. Bagehot never lost his verve, as the essay on Lord Althorp showed which was published as late as 1876, the year before his death, but youth and the Somerset air certainly brought out the best in Bagehot as these essays show. They were republished in 1858 under the rather forbidding title *Estimates of Some Englishmen and Scotchmen*, but partly because of this did not attract much attention at the time, save from the *Inquirer* which paid off old scores by printing a savage review. Hutton was surely right when he says: 'I hardly know any book that is such good reading, that has so much lucid vision in it, so much shrewd and curious knowledge of the world, so sober a judgment and so dashing a humour

---

[24] 'Memoir', xlv–xlvi.
[25] See letter to Hutton of July 1853.
[26] London: 1962.

combined.'[27] 'Certainly,' Hutton concludes, 'the literary taste of England never made a greater blunder than when it passed by this remarkable volume of essays with comparatively little notice.[28]

The National Review 1854-1855

One of the principal preoccupations of Bagehot during his period at Langport was the founding of the *National Review* and there are many references to it in the letters of this period. It was to continue from where the *Prospective* had left off but with a new title, new finances and a new approach. A number of patrons were found including S. D. Darbishire, a friend of Martineau's, Lady Byron, Bagehot and Crabb Robinson. Bagehot played a central role in getting the periodical launched. Religion and theology were to remain matters of central concern but it was not to be so 'inhumanly divine' as the *Prospective*. The prospectus was possibly written by Bagehot and made clear its political and religious aims. 'As Englishmen, we place unbounded confidence in the bases of English character,—its moderation and veracity; its firm hold on reality; its reverence for law and right; its historical tenacity; its aversion to *a priori* politics, and to revolutions generated out of speculative data.' The political purpose of the review was to define the conditions under which the various national characters and institutions had developed themselves and to assess their appropriateness for their people. In literature the aim was to be analogous. 'We wish as before to secure a more constant reference to ascertained principle than we think is now common; but, at the same time, we shall not try to apply arbitrary canons to all writers and all ages, but rather to examine and describe the real features of great literary nations and writers, and explain the manner in which the genius and circumstances of each have influenced the works they have bequeathed to us.' In a letter to Martineau of 18 March 1855, Bagehot set out three points for the guidance of the *National*: 'The clear expression of certain characteristic religious ideas, 2ndly. the

[27] 'Memoir', xlviii.
[28] 'Memoir', l.

treatment of the principles of politics, as contrasted with essays on the details of business, 3rdly. a *taking* style in criticism.'

Its approach to the religious and theological discussions of the day was to be liberal but not excessively so: 'We want Liberals who tho' they belong to a sect are more attached to liberal christianity than to their sect—or at any rate are willing to cooperate with persons who mis-pronounce Shibboleth.' (Letter of 14 January 1855.) On the higher criticism Bagehot wanted a sympathetic and open attitude. 'The Bible must be treated in a human manner. It is a terrible superstition—'. (18 August 1855.) A literal approach to the scriptures was, he thought, 'the grossest Protestant superstition'. (Letter to Hutton, 29 July 1856.) A letter of 25 December 1856 contains a full and interesting discussion of Bagehot's views on the Gospels. 'I am more and more disposed to believe that these are not the narratives of eyewitnesses at all—but embodiments of traditions dating from the second generation.' He was struck by what he described as 'the extreme opposition' of the gospel of John. According to Hutton in his Memoir he eventually came to reject the apostolic origin of the fourth gospel.[29] He found it difficult to accept that three first hand narrations would omit a whole system of conceptions and doctrines recorded by a fourth. 'Again the character of Christ is given I think in the way traditions represent character, and not as contemporary narrations give it. Tradition chooses its points. It gives the characteristic features of a character only and omits all others. Somehow it wont believe any others.' He contrasts the old and the new approach to the gospels: 'The old theory was that they were written by the "Spirit of God". I think—or am inclined to think—they were composed by intense, half inspired, most affectionate storytelling impulse—Of course, with this sort of view the question of Christs nature is simple. Any sort of incarnation requires to be proved by the most close positive historical testimony.'

Bagehot wanted the Review to be eirenic in its approach to theological controversy. 'You theologians are too intolerant of one anothers crochets,' he writes to Hutton on 18 August 1855. He wanted Jowett to remain in the Church of England although he found 'his views about as consistent with the worship of the Grand Llama'. Furthermore he did not see why Stanley should not stay in the Church.

[29] p. xxxii.

He gives a clue to his thinking in another letter to Hutton of 1 February 1856: 'I think certainly I shd. not reject an article for assuming the Deity of Christ—but I cannot allow an article to go in assuming—or defending the textual authority of Scripture.'

Bagehot's judgments on potential contributors are astringent and at times funny. One contributor, Donne, is described as 'a fogey'. He goes on, 'you seem to feel it in his style. He bows over a joke so respectfully.' As to Dr Hinck, who was a would-be contributor on farming, he is dismissed with the words 'Agriculture is one of the consequences of the fall'.[30] Of Martineau he writes: 'You see all great divines respect the *World* and he thinks the World is the same thing as Chapman and Hall.' (Letter to Hutton 4 March 1855.)

His concern and affection for Hutton and his clear-sighted judgment concerning him is plain from a letter to Crabb Robinson of 17 August 1853. 'He is the sort of man to get on, I should say, in literature for he has great energy and accuracy and is to be depended on for doing any sort of work right which you will agree with me, is not very common.' He also gives him some good advice. 'Never argue with any one whom you wish to persuade is a rule with *no* exceptions I think,' he writes on 4 March 1855. He advises him not to take on a joint editorship of the *Prospective*. 'As to the reason of one person's not editing the Inquirer and the Review, it seems to me wholly *parsonic* and worth nothing.' (Letter to Hutton: 20 July 1853.) One other periodical which is mentioned is *The Economist* and Bagehot's comment has an ironical connotation in view of his later editorship of the paper. He comments astringently on the articles: 'It is simple type. I think Wilson must hope that they wont be read. He should print a heading to that effect at the beginning of the article, if he means to retain any of his present staff.—It is beyond all limits.' (Letter to Hutton, 25 December 1856.)

Love letters 1857–1858

In December 1856 a chain of events was set in motion which was destined to alter Bagehot's life radically. Through W. R. Greg, a close friend of James Wilson, the founder and proprietor of *The*

---

[30] Letter to Hutton, 18 August 1855.

Economist, Bagehot gained the idea of contributing to the paper. Greg and Martineau provided an introduction for Bagehot to Mr Wilson and he was invited to visit him at Claverton Manor, near Bath. His visit was to gain him both an additional career and a bride.

Wilson's six daughters at Claverton awaited the arrival of the political economist with the unpronounceable name without undue interest. But this visitor was quite different from all the rest of Mr Wilson's callers. He gained the hearts of the girls by turning his big dark eyes upon them and exclaiming, after their governess had left the room: 'Your governess is like an egg!' Emilie Russell Barrington, the youngest daughter records: 'We at once saw she *was* like an egg! From that moment he rose in our eyes from the status of political economist to that of a fellow creature.'[31] The six brotherless daughters were delighted with their high-spirited caller and it was a surrogate brother that he was soon to become. The eldest daughter, Eliza, a striking beauty with Titian-like red hair, made an immediate impression on Walter. Nine months later she consented to become his bride. On 4 November 1857, Walter proposed to Eliza in the Claverton library, and on 7 November at the Hertford Street house in London, she accepted him. James Wilson had found not only his missing son but also an ideal son-in-law. Nevertheless, the thought of losing one of his daughters made him ill and he retired to his bed.

The meeting at Hertford Street had been but a break in Eliza's journey on the way to Edinburgh, to be massaged by a Doctor Beveridge who was then enjoying a certain vogue. At the same time a financial panic spreading from the United States reverberated in London. Eliza was immured in Edinburgh, Walter in the purlieus of the City which created the opportunity for an extended lovers' correspondence for which Eliza was grateful. It enabled her as she put it 'to understand' her fiancé.

The letters primarily set out the emotions of the lovers, as one would expect, but they cover a variety of other topics, including politics, economics and literature. Writers such as Matthew Arnold and Trollope pop in and out of the pages. The letters show Walter as warm, passionate, impulsive and impetuous: they sparkle with his sense of fun and humour. Eliza, on the other hand, is revealed as

[31] *The Life of Walter Bagehot*, pp. 229–30.

rather cold and reserved by nature but she steadily warms under the impact of Walter's ardour. She was 25, six years younger than Bagehot but in some ways was the calmer, more mature and stronger character. She was well read and much admired for her Grecian profile. Like her mother, Elizabeth Preston, she was much preoccupied with her health and frequently spent days and later weeks in her room with migraine and other indispositions. Like so many Victorian women, she spent a great deal of her time prone on her sofa, but again, like many of those ladies, she proved more robust than was expected and survived her husband by 44 years, dying in October 1921 in her 89th year.

Walter's feelings had long been a dormant part of his personality, now they erupted with volcanic force. 'No one can tell the effort it was to me to tell you I loved you,' he wrote to Eliza on 22 November 1857. '—why I do not know, but it made me gasp for breath, and now it is absolutely pleasure to me to tell it to you, and bore you with in every form, and I shd. like to write in in big letters I LOVE YOU all across the page by way of emphasis. I know you will think me very childish and be shaken in your early notion that I am intellectual, but I cannot help it. This is my state of mind.' He goes on: 'I have just read your letter in that light—and I go about murmuring "I have made that *dignified* girl *commit* herself—I have I have" and then I vault over the sofa with exultation. *Those* are the feelings of the person you have connected yourself with.'

The strength of his own feelings surprised him and this is a recurring theme of the letters. Writing on 2 February 1858 he reflects: 'That I could ever have for anyone the passionate, intense love which I now have for you, would have seemed quite incredible to me then. I had passed such a rigid and firm life that I could not have fancied myself capable of being changed at once and so soon.' Walter was excited and uplifted as well as disturbed by his new found feelings: 'You must not suppose because I tell you of the wild burning pain which I have felt—and at times tho' I am and *ought* to be much soothed, still feel—that my love for you has ever been mere suffering. Even at the worst there was a wild delicious excitement which I would not have lost for the world.'[32] Later he tells her: 'I begin to comprehend now that one may have an intense, *absorbing* and yet a *happy* passion. I have been feeling a little *wild* the last day or two, but I know that this

---

[32] Letter of 22 November 1857.

EDITOR'S INTRODUCTION

is wrong, and struggle against it. I hope I may soon see you, and you will *charm* it away.'[33]

Like so many people in love he felt an intense gratitude for the reciprocity: 'The principal feeling I have now towards you is a kind of gratitude for *your* affection. I am afraid my imagination is beginning to take in *really* the idea that you *can* care for me, and the *gratitude* I feel to you for it is one of the most calm gentle and delicious feelings which I have ever experienced. I am sure I never did anything to deserve such a blessing and I wish I could feel more worthy of it.' He goes on: 'You now fill my whole thoughts, and color all one's future, and have done so for many months in various shades of pain and pleasure, anxiety and delight, that I can hardly fancy what my mind was before you took possession of it. I have a vague notion that there used to be a great blank and a dreary sense of feelings for which there was no object and seemed likely to be none. I little fancied last January what I shd. stumble upon in the course of it. May God bless us *both*, my dearest this new year and all years to come. I think my love for you *has* made me more spiritual and better than I was before. I am sure it ought to have, considering what you are. *Do* love me *always* and *always* for I *must* love you. *That* feeling at least, as *I* believe, God has made unchangeable. May *He* bless you now and always.'

Eliza at first seems to have been rather alarmed by these outpourings which she called Walter's 'rudeness'. Walter was aware of this. 'You have a certain *shy dignity*,' he writes to her on 29 November 1857, 'which is *inexpressibly* attractive to me, but my admiration naturally and I think healthily takes the form of sauciness jokes and all manner of rubbish. I cd. not go on with you for a moment without it. I cd. not express myself, and I cd. not be with *you* without trying to express myself, as I am, and we really know each other better and are *closer* to one another's *real* hearts by it. I never felt the slightest notion of being, or having been, rude to you when rightly interpreted but late at night I sometimes scratch down things very roughly—and I fear they might *seem* what they were not intended to be.'

Warmed by Walter's ardours, Eliza responded, but she was not fitted by nature to give him an equal response. Writing to him on 4 December 1857, she says: 'I *believe* my real nature is very womanly, I mean that I love to *lean* on a stronger nature, though I may appear

[33] Letter of 14 February 1858.

to be somewhat independent on the surface. I *can* stand alone if I must, but it makes my heart heavy to have to do it—Zeno has invented a word for me which she means as a term of reproach and weakness—she calls me a "womanite".'

She got used to his quirky chaffing. 'We would have a real Sunday talk to begin with, and then you would cheer me with your jests and nonsense, the more *nonsense* the better as far as I am concerned, and I think you like to talk what you call "rubbish" to me. Do you know, I feel quite joyous at the bare possibility of having you here.' (Letter of 7 December 1857.) She also had fears—which seem to me to be justified—about her being able to give either an adequate intellectual or emotional response. She writes of a feeling of awe 'at even partially understanding such a mind and being what I am to such a heart. Affection like ours *is* awful and gives such new significance to life,—at least to me it does. It seems such a *power* in life, instead of the mere *episode* I fancied it to be. I cannot say that the feeling is different to what I imagined it, except in being infinitely more *intense*, but its effect upon life, even to its furthest horizon, seems *startlingly* strong. I feel our existence through time and even eternity *bound together* in a manner I *could* not have imagined.' (Letter of 1 December 1857.)

These signs of a thaw brought from Walter an ecstatic response. Yet the gap remained. 'I don't *like* to read of women suffering,' she wrote to Walter in a revealing letter on 17 January 1858, 'and always felt angry with lady-novelists who laid bare "wounded hearts"—(men don't know if they are writing what is true or not and may be excused for guessing)—; it seemed to me they were betraying their sex. But joking apart, I don't think the majority of female writers give their female characters as much *control* over their feelings as well-conditioned women exercise. Of course, there are over-sentimental people among women and *perhaps* a good many of them,—but not more surely than there are absurd men. Miss Bronte made me feel quite *savage* and I could not bear the idea of men reading her books.' With this may be contrasted a letter from Walter of the same date.

'I am writing to you on Sunday Evening, which is the time I like to write to you best, because I feel the quietest and descend the most into my *real* self, where my *love* is strongest and deepest. So you know I always have a fancy at such times that our love makes us somehow alone together in the world. We seem to have a deep life together apart from all other people on earth, and which we cannot show, explain or impart to them. At least my affection seems to isolate me in the deepest moments from all others, and it makes me speak with my whole heart and soul of you and to you only. And perhaps this isolation is one reason why deep love makes one feel—at least in some moments so religious—All the distracting world seems to be gone and we seem to be alone together in the sight of God. I have often felt a sensation of solitude in great scenes of nature, or in some deep summer day when the sky seems so lonely and so pure—but I never felt before—even in thought, alone in the presence of God with another human being,—and I cannot help feeling this, *dearest*, with you whenever I have time, and my real heart is not crushed by the details of life and my intense love can take the view that is most natural to it. From this I suppose it comes that there is a kind of consecration in my feelings towards you quite different from anything which I have ever fancied or experienced in the least degree before. You *must* not mind my writing to you in this way, my own dearest, for I must in a letter to you say what is in my heart or say nothing at all. I must speak *out* my heart if I speak at all—It is my nature.' He concludes by saying that he wishes he could tell her how much he loves her: 'But that is impossible—it will take a lifetime to show it to you.'

This passionate missive did provoke a response. 'I like your Sunday-evening letters *best* too, my dearest, *dearest* Walter,' she wrote on 20 January 1858, 'for you do go deepest into your *heart* then and it is *intense* happiness to me to read what it dictates to you. I not only "don't mind", but I *love* to hear what you find there, for nothing proves to me so well how different a relationship we have to *each other* than to any other human being, than the being *able* to express our *deep* feelings to each other. Not only could I never before express my real mind *wholly* to any one but it made me feel shy to listen to other people's feelings and I avoided it whenever I could. *Now* it is genuine pleasure to me to read and hear of *your* deep feelings and no effort to write of mine to you. I understand the feeling of "isolation together" that you have; it was something very like it that made me tell you I could and did feel *eternally* bound to you and that our spirits will never part.'

Walter's cheerfulness also infected her. '*Now* we shall laugh *together* all our lives,' she writes on 27 January 1858, 'and weep too, for we must expect rain as well as sunshine, but I feel as if we shall have a good deal of the latter—and that we can bear the former better *together*. Affection like ours is such a power for buoying one up through life that I feel quite cheerful about the future and *believe* we shall float very peacefully over life's waves.' Spurred on by Walter, Eliza discovered unsuspected depths in her own nature. 'The world always seemed *more* of a shadow than a substance,' she writes to him on 12 February 1858, 'though I knew that some people do find real substance in it and therefore it is folly and affectation or morbidness to call it all *hollow*. But I feel more every day that I have got what my *soul* wanted, a deep, earnest nature to rest upon and I bless God for it, my own *dearest* Walter. It is *real* life, I feel, that is going to take, I may say that has taken, the place of the dreary, aching sense of no satisfaction in the world and the half successful but wearying attempt at self-support.'

Her sense of irony is also sharpened. 'Julia is very pleased at Mr. Hutton's marriage,' she writes to Walter on 10 January 1858, 'and says she hopes he will look less melancholy now, poor man.' And on 1 February 1858, she writes about her Aunt Julia: 'I am going to leave her your essays and have pointed out the one on Shelley to her as being particularly *metaphysical*, so she will be deep in it soon no doubt, for she has a notion she likes metaphysics and reads Emerson &c., and picks out all the books from the philosophical library that seem to treat of the "nature of the soul", whether their authors were ever heard of or not.'

Walter not only expressed his feelings to Eliza but he analysed them as well and the letters contain many passages of self-revelation. In spite of his high spirits he was inclined to take a realistic or pessimistic view of the outcome of actions. 'I think I should warn you that in practical things I have rather an anxious disposition—I am cheerful but not sanguine—I can make the best of anything, but I have a difficulty in expecting that the future will be very good—The most successful men of action rather overestimate their chances of success in action. I cannot do this at all. I have always to work on the bare, cold probability. My energy is fair, and my spirits very good, but this difficulty of intellect I have always had. If you *will* soothe me in this it will be almost too great happiness—though *you* are a little anxious naturally too. Still we will have headaches in life together and that will be to me *immense*.' (Letter to Eliza, 1 December 1857.)

EDITOR'S INTRODUCTION

His views on reputation and fame were moderate and balanced. 'I am afraid I am callous, possibly proud, and do not care for mere general reputation. Of course it wd. be a pleasure if it shd. come but it is a thing which no man ought to make necessary to his happiness, or think of but as a temporary luxury, even if it shd. come to him. First rate fame—the fame of great productive artists is a matter of ultimate certainty, but no other fame is. Posterity cannot take up little people, there are so many of them—*Reputation* must be acquired at the moment and the circumstances of the moment are matters of accident.' (Letter to Eliza, 4 January 1858.)

Eliza had revealed to him that she had imagined herself earlier in love with an artistic dilettante, Conway Shipley. This prompted Walter to make a comparison between his own character and that of Eliza and to indulge in a little analysis of her needs. 'I fear you overrate my earnestness, but I have a spring and elasticity in my nature which will be very good for you. You would not have been happy with a person of idle habits, however good otherwise. Some of your father's tastes have descended to you, and you could not have borne a *pottering* husband. Besides I maintain that people in practical life have better, at least more *disciplined* tempers. Nobody in real action ever has quite their own way, and therefore they understand how to concede a trifle or two at times and don't know they are doing it, whereas idle people who have only themselves to consult, can hardly give up any point, or if they do make such a merit of it as to be even more provoking than their refusal. If you want arguments for marrying me, I assure you I will write any number, quite an article on the subject. I assure you you require someone with settled tastes and pursuits which you can understand. These *vagabonds* would never do for you after a year or so.' (Letter of 14 Feburary 1858.)

Walter refers to his wildness and certainly he was exasperated with some justification by Eliza's continual changes of plan. 'What drives me wild is the constant hope of seeing you, and then the disappointment. It quite unsettles me, and I can hardly attend to anything at all, and when I do only by a *strong* effort.' (Letter of 16 February 1858.) He says quite erroneously that Eliza has the most culture and also the deeper nature. 'The only thing I maintain is that I have a spring and energy in my mind which enables me to take some hold of good subjects and makes it natural and inevitable that I should write on them. I do not think I write well, but I write, as I speak, in the way (I think) that is natural to me, and the only chance in literature as in life is to be yourself. If you try to be more you will be less.'

Walter writes from Claverton that what he enjoys is balanced conversation. 'What I always like so much here is the mixture of chaff and sense—chaff and currency one might say. I get tired either of sense or nonsense if I am kept very continuously to either, and like my mind to undulate between the two as it likes best. There are some sporting people coming to dinner who will I much fear bring neither sense nor nonsense, but the heavy matter which is compounded of both.' He goes on to tell her of his absence of mind and his life-long habit of talking to himself: 'I am *very* absent here and your sisters caught me talking to myself which I very often do, but it is only the absence of mind for which you are responsible—the selfish conversation is a very old habit.' (Letter of 1 February 1858.) After the death of his mother, Alastair Buchan records that the old habit returned: 'But the father of one of the present residents of Langport used to tell him that about this time Bagehot would roam the lanes on horseback talking aloud to himself, and that the farmers and farmhands would leave their ploughs and flocks and hide under the hedgerows to catch what he was saying.'[34] Bagehot always enjoyed conversation but needed what he calls a 'nudge' to provide him with the stimulus.

Walter's deep and tempestuous feelings for Eliza led him to a highly personalised view of marriage which he expressed at this time to Hutton in a letter of 2 December 1857. He is discussing George Sand's views on marriage and adds his own: 'I am inclined to think that the sacredness of marriage does cease when affection wholly ceases on both sides and am inclined to doubt if the continuance of the union is then even *innocent*. I do not believe this wd. ever happen with such an affection as people ought to marry on—it is perhaps a point of faith that all real unions of souls are eternal—but people might mistake less deep feelings for this real union and these lesser feelings might go off and I doubt if it is then *right* for them to live together—The voluntary element can only come in I fancy, when the affection goes off on one side and continues on the other, and I am inclined to doubt the self-sacrifice theory even there. It wd. end in hollowness, hypocrisy and wd. not after all do any good to the

[34] *The Spare Chancellor*, p. 194.

person not loved.' He did not conclude that this should be a ground for dissolving marriages by law, since he conceded that the state of the affections could not be tried in open court, but it led him to the conclusion that it would be 'most improper' to make adultery a criminal offence.

Some of Walter's likes and dislikes are glimpsed in the letters, including his love of scenery and his dislike of music, the latter probably stemming from his experiences with his imbecile halfbrother, Vincent Estlin, in his youth.[35] Walter did not care for suburbia and liked what he called 'real country', of which he found his ideal in Somerset. 'I like to be either at the focus or the untouched natural exterior.' (Letter to Eliza, 15 January 1858.) He could find lakes and mountains too overwhelming. 'At the English lakes the beauty is at times too great, the air seems loaded—you cannot draw a deep breath and it seems as if you were living on confectionery—a little sickening and not quite natural. And in mountainous scenery, *real* Swiss mountains there is too much agonizing sublimity—too much snow and such *very* sharp peaks.—and you are not quite happy that way. I own I really like best rough *hill* scenery like Scotland and the south part of North Wales, where there is vigour enough to arouse and elate you, and yet not enough sublimity to pain you. I cd. not live in a mountainous country—I mean really snowy sharp mountains—or on a lake of over sensuous beauty like Rydal Water, but if I had my choice I wd. live in a country of wild hills and soft lakes where there was real power in the landscape and loveliness too, and not a frightening inhuman amount of either.' (Letter to Eliza, 14 January 1858.)

As for music he seems always to have found it an annoying and distracting noise.[36] This contrasted sharply with the love of music which was shared by all the Wilson sisters. 'If you knew what it is to have a sister who plays *Beethoven*,' writes Eliza on 1 December 1857, 'you would understand that a piano can be a solace and a stimulant in life, and if you knew the *thoughts* it sets my mind floating in, you

---

[35] For an example see the incident of the clocks recounted by Henry Sawtell, *Collected Works*, I, 35.
[36] According to his sister-in-law, Emile Russell Barrington, Walter towards the end of his life (inspired by Emilie's love of music and the Lewes's admiration for the violinist Joachim) 'conceived the idea that possibly he might get to understand in what consisted the great influence music possessed over many natures'. She opines that had he lived he would himself have come to appreciate music, but death intervened. See *The Life of Walter Bagehot*, p. 414.

would think it "all right".' In another letter of 25 January 1858, when she is discussing the wedding of the Princess Royal she reverts to the theme: 'There is but one thing I feel inclined to envy in her wedding, and that is the one *you* probably would think the most objectionable part, *dear* Walter, viz: the *music*. It seems to me that fine music would really hide all the people (it is the living creatures looking on that are the most *nervous* thing about it!), but then to *me* it is like voices in the air while to *you* it is only *noise*.'

Walter took a dim view of the medical treatment from Doctor Beveridge which occasioned Eliza's absence in Edinburgh, and his letters are punctuated with acidulous and mocking references to the 'rubbing' which he persisted in calling it. She tells him that the treatment is to be continued in London and he replies: 'I am also rejoiced that there is also to be a rubber in London, that if you retain your affectionate sentiment for this alleviation, you may obtain it within rational limits. If you are right and headaches can be cured in this way, friction will become ubiquitous; small boys at every corner (like the shoe cleaners) will call out, "Rub your neck, Sir, rub your neck" and all the world will be rubbed.' (Letter of 17 January 1858.) Again on 14 January 1858, he tells her: 'I think the Beveridge-mania is a form of intoxication—from the name you wd. expect that it would be —and not compatible with temporary sanity.' It is clear that Walter regarded Eliza's 'illness' as what it was, namely psychosomatic: 'All these head diseases are somewhat in the mind.' (Letter of 4 December 1857.) Instead of rubbing he counselled 'cheerful, *easy* excitement' which would be better for her headaches than anything else. (Letter of 1 December 1857.)

Throughout her life Eliza, like so many Victorians, was concerned with her health, an obsession which she caught from her mother. Her diaries are punctuated with accounts of headaches, illnesses, days in bed, etc. Walter's health on the other hand really was delicate and in the end his complaints proved fatal while the lethargic but robust Eliza survived to a great age.

Walter's sense of fun bubbles up throughout the letters, on 18 November 1857 he tells Eliza that 'a small party is always pleasanter. There is not so much competition for the food.' He describes W. R. Greg (later to become his brother-in-law) as he saw him at the custom house: 'He had a mild happiness as if he were confiscating goods.' (Letter of 11 January 1858.) In his next letter he informs her that, 'it may be *elevating* to be engaged to a young lady in a much higher latitude, but it is not at all pleasant'.

They are also rewarding for the peppering of little vignettes of the period. He tells Eliza on 18 November 1857, that he went with her father to see the antiquities of Halicarnassus. 'They are a set of odd legs, arms and bodies of Greek statues just arrived and alleviated our feelings very much. It happened in this way. We drove past the British Museum on our way home, and Mr. Wilson asked if I had seen the new reading room and as I had not, he forthwith took me to see it. We were ushered in to old Panizzi, who was doing nothing in a fine armchair, and he proposed we shd. see the venerable fragments just arrived from Greece. I am not sure, however, that we appreciated them. I have an unfortunate prejudice in favor of statues in *one* piece, at least in not more than *six* pieces, and these are broken up very small indeed, and it is a controversy whose arm belongs to whose body— but I believe real lovers of art admire those perplexities. On the whole however we spent our time cheerfully, and in consequence the Chancellor of the Exchequer and a heap of Scots bankers were kept half an hour waiting.'

The financial panic and its consequences break into his outpourings. 'All banking rests on credit—and credit is rather a superstition. At any rate it is adopted not from distinct evidence but from habit, usage and local custom, and when there is *panic* floating in the air no one *ought* to feel so comfortable as usual. There is *nothing whatever* in our own business specially to make me anxious. On the contrary, I believe few similar concerns wd. look so well if examined; and I am not in any real sense anxious;—still it is not pleasant to live upon opinion just when all business opinion is disturbed. Your father foretells a very rapid revival—and I think he is right, though perhaps some more banks may go first.' (Letter of 1 December 1857.)

We also catch sight of the redoubtable Julia Cameron before she embarked on her photographic career (but she did not commend herself to Walter): 'I had a pleasant evening at Wimbledon last night. The only defect was that Mr. Greg had gone into captivity to an over-fascinating woman, a Mrs. Cameron. She has been a professional beauty and appeared in a nocturnal sort of silk robe surmounted by a red head-dress. She has taken to the *mind* on the waning of her exterior charms and is a friend of Tennysons, and talks of "sweet ideas" and "hard facts". Greg went into utter captivity to her, and she seems a lion in the Putney suburb. I came up with Clough in the train and asked him if he knew her—and he made an excrutiating face and said "I believe there *is* a *woman*". Her husband was an influential member of council at Calcutta, a much better sort of creature with white hair.'

Walter gives Eliza his balanced views on social life: 'I hope you enjoyed Lady Palmerston's. It is all nonsense or morbidness, as you say, to call the world *all* hollow. It is an object of the greatest *intellectual* interest to those who have the mind and opportunity to study it. The mistake is to treat it as giving more than any intellectual interest ever can. The deepest part of the soul after a little revolts at anything merely intellectual. Such things seem trivial and unworthy when forced on us as substitutes for what is deeper.' (Letter of 14 February 1858.) Earlier he had told her: 'You have too much soul to be satisfied with the surface of life, though if your soul is satisfied too, you would like the grand *shine* on the surface of life much more than you fancy.' (Letter of 11 February 1858.)

Walter's psychological acumen was often acute. In a letter to Eliza of 24 February 1858, on her father's leaving office, he comments: 'I breakfasted with Mr. Wilson this morning. He seemed to anticipate glory in opposition and to have a sensation of freedom in having to maintain only what it pleased him to maintain and to have no offical etiquette to restrain him; but he will feel the non-arrival of the Treasury bag in a Long Vacation, if Lord Derby could live so long. I cannot dream that he will, still the political world is so strange that no case is ever desperate.' Greg praised Bagehot for a letter published in *The Economist* on banking and thoughtlessly added 'Better than any of your literary things Bagehot—' which evoked the comment that this was 'paying a compliment and spoiling it rather'. (Letter of 29 November 1857.) He also gives Hutton some advice applicable to contemporary motorways: 'If you live in the country, live near the shores of a railway—*quite* near, it is a great saving of mind and *anxiety*.' (Letter to Hutton, 6 January 1858.)

The lovers' letters tail off inevitably into a discussion of wedding and housing arrangements but even these are rewarding. Walter gives his *imprimatur* to the proceedings in characteristic style: 'I quite approve of your sisters having a dance after our wedding. They will then be anxious to push you out, as they cannot commence till you are gone, and I shall bear you away with greater facility. Don't you think you shd. go away from the Church? You will never get up the hill without the donkey, which might look odd at the head of the bridesmaids; only I rather make a point of the wedding breakfast—with my habits it wd. be painful to miss the *meal*, so I advise being original and having the breakfast *first* and driving off on the lower road from the Church. I suppose this wont be allowed. I have been at a wedding where the bride and bridegroom had a separate breakfast by themselves,—but can you be quite sure of having good food in private at such a moment of confusion. I think it is a risk, and that it is better to *pretend* to be social and appear openly. You dont know how pleasant it is to think that *you* can think of the details of the crisis. You shall "go smash" exactly as you like. Surely that is freedom.' Walter goes on to comment on Eliza's trousseau: 'By the interest and letters that are spent on your trousseau you seem to be likely to have apparel now which will be enough till the end of your life. I approve of this, as I shall *save* by it—Let me advise enduring materials—(canvass, I am assured, wears well) at any rate—if that is not ladylike which I am too ignorant to be quite sure of—something which will stand the wear and tear of life—it would be pitiable to be found in old age with only gossamer gowns. [Footnote:] What is gossamer?' (Letter of 17 January 1858.)

This light-hearted concluding rhetorical question evoked a factual reply from the literal-minded Eliza: 'Still I won't have any *gossamer*! *That* is the fine threads some insect weaves in the night and that you see between the leaves and branches on sunny mornings and is *not* a word in a lady's wardrobe vocabulary. Gentlemen being in general ignorance of the latter, have recourse to figures of speech in talking of ladies' dress and believe I imagine ball dresses to be made of gossamer.' Eliza reciprocates Walter's interest in her trousseau by discussing his mode of dress: 'Our French friend says that men never look like anything but *crows* in their modern costume. Now if you will be *original* on our wedding day, I will ensure your being looked at and I shall be a great gainer thereby. It will be in character since it is considered *original* in you to marry at all.' Walter's sprightliness had evidently struck an answering chord in his staid fiancée. She used her superior knowledge of the fashionable world to give Walter advice on his costume: 'Your tie is not approved by the family congress for the occasion, though admired. It is believed you should have a lighter one and much smaller. They say what Mr. Wood wears is the proper size. I think one like your lilac, but in blue, would look very well.' (Letter of 13 April 1858.)

Partly through her absence in Edinburgh, partly through lethargy, Eliza delegated the task of house hunting happily to Walter. The furniture was to be hired from Westbury which was evidently let. 'I empower you to offer to Mr. Wilson,' wrote Walter with characteristic frugality, 'to pay for the upholstery whatever he may *now* be making of it. I am sure he wd. not wish to *gain* by a family transaction.' Walter considered four houses, two of them at Clevedon. One of them had a large aviary and an apiary with hives. 'What an addition to a domestic circle,' he commented. One house he describes as being furnished 'on the principle of never allowing any place to be vacant on which anything no matter how useless *could* be put. It is not mean—but it is "petty".' (Letter of 22 January 1858.) In the end they decided to take Sir Arthur Elton's house *Bella Vista* at Clevedon but they changed its name to *The Arches*.

On 21 April 1858, the couple were married in the church at Claverton, but neither of Walter's parents were present as it was considered that the excitement would have been too much for his mother, and Mr Bagehot stayed behind at Herd's Hill to keep her company. The day was bright and hot and the guests were able to stroll on the Claverton lawns after the ceremony while a Hanoverian band played. 'Nobody shed a single tear,' wrote Walter to his mother on 23 April 1858, 'Eliza was a most composed bride,—a little anxious at the crisis but very cheerful after it was over. Vincent Wood made a splendid "best man" only that the multitude *would* think he was the bridegroom. Mary was much admired and all the bridesmaids were very animated and nice. There was wonderful oratory at the Breakfast. A Mr. Moffat (MP for Ashburton) proposed *our* health in a copious and *eloquent* manner and spoke of the "hundreds of thousands" who had read my writings—whom I myself shd wish to see particularly. Sir William Topham proposed the health of the bridesmaids in very clever speech in a sort of Lord Palmerston style. He is a man about the Court, captain of the yeoman of the guard and understands the "touch and go" style of oratory rather well. My attention was rather however distracted from what he said by wondering that *"that* man" shd. be speaking at my wedding. Few people seem so far off my beat.'

In the afternoon the couple left for their honeymoon in the west country, six white satin slippers being thrown after the carriage as it

disappeared down the drive. Guests had their dance to solace themselves for the loss of the bridal pair. Walter stopped the carriage at Frome to send his mother the following brief pencilled note:
'My dearest Mother,
We are married. Everything went off well, and my wife sends her love. Yours with greatest affection, Walter Bagehot.'

The years of marriage 1858-1877

After marriage, and thanks both to his own talents and the influence of his father-in-law, James Wilson, Bagehot was able to play an important part in London's social, political and intellectual life. He formed friendships with the Lowes, the Cornewall Lewis's, Matthew Arnold, and George Eliot, amongst others. Society as such had little or no attraction for him but he liked to go to political parties, hear the gossip and learn what was going on. As Bagehot himself jotted down: 'Living really in the political world is the greatest possible gain in a political country: knowing at first hand what others know at second hand only. The characters and the play of political life are not otherwise accessible.'[37] The Lubbocks became friends and he established a close intimacy with the Carnarvons. Writing to Eliza in September 1863, he describes a visit to their house: 'I have been at Highclere, Lord Carnarvon's, who is one of my sort, and has run to mind, and wanted me to help keep his house more decently reasonable while the fast people were there. We had Lord and Lady Ashley, Lord Stanhope (Lady Carnarvon's brother), Lady Dorothy Neville—a pretty woman with an old husband, and several young men. The women wore wonderful dresses, and we played cards rather high, always in the evening and sometimes in the morning—at least some people played in the morning—I kept my character for wisdom and did not. Lord Carnarvon will be Secretary of State for the Colonies when the Tories come in. Lady Carnarvon is very clever and literary—at least with *snaps* of Literature. They will be *people* for some years to come, for they are both clever, very ambitious and have a beautiful place near London to entertain in.'

In 1859 his article *Parliamentary Reform* was published and pro-

---

[37] Quoted by Emilie Russell Barrington in *The Servant of All*, II, 137.

vided those who opposed democratic theories with some telling arguments. Much praise was lavished on the article which appeared in January, and the following March Bagehot brought it out as a pamphlet when it aroused even greater interest. On 1 April, James Wilson gave a special dinner for the author and his admirers, attended amongst others by Lord Grey, Lord Granville, Gladstone, Cardwell, Robert Lowe, Thackeray and Sir George Cornewall Lewis. 'It will really be a very fine collection of public animals,' wrote Walter to his wife. (Letter of 31 March 1859.) He went on: 'I take it as a new idea to have a dinner party of both sides on a division night—particularly a division on a fundamental question "affecting the constitution of our country" as one says in articles, and I hope the novelty will prosper.'

In August of the same year, James Wilson took a fateful and indeed fatal step when he accepted appointment as Financial Member for India and Chancellor of the Indian Exchequer, with the duty of visiting India and reforming its chaotic finances. He set off in October, accompanied by his wife and three of his daughters, Matilda, Zenobia and Sophia. During this period many letters passed between James Wilson and his son-in-law on both Indian and British affairs. Of the many letters from Bagehot only one has survived in which the difficulties created by Trevelyan, the Governing Minister, who opposed Wilson's policy and published without authority a confidential memorandum, were fully discussed.

An amusing letter from Bagehot to Zenobia Wilson is also still extant. 'We shall be very curious to hear your first impressions of the Calcutta people as soon as you have seen them,' he writes on 8 January 1860. 'Pips is afraid the society is dreadfully *middle* class, and hopes you will not get provincial. Please say when you find it coming on and what [it] is like and where you are conscious of it first—We do not do anything particular in this country, that I know of. I believe an accumulation of detail was sent out to you via Southampton but I cannot write that kind of thing not having the preliminary gift of knowing whether it happens or not.'

'The great change of late to me is that having the Economist to look after I come to London and call on public characters and sit (like Jet) with my mouth open hearing what they say. I do not say much myself, but I think if I was 50 and a cabinet minister, *would* not I talk platitudes? It must be such a pleasure to say that two and two make four and see people take it in or seem to as a new truth, and *then* to say they make five and find people swallow that too. I am sure if they treated me in that way, I shd. not say anything. I shd. assent—for I consider old people and great people have a right to it—and besides it is *easy*.

'Vincent Reynolds (small man with regular features) is married to a huge girl—something like a Jack in the box—with a great laugh, but he has not as yet complained. I suppose all the people you see are either high up in the service and dreary, or low down in the service and nobodies. The middle people are seldom much anywhere.'

In August 1860, Wilson contracted dysentery and died. His death occurred on 11 August but it took four weeks for the news to reach England. Oblivious to their loss, Julia and Eliza, the Wilson daughters, were staying at Clevedon, when on 12 September Julia opened *The Times* and read that they were bereaved. Bagehot recorded that the scene was a terrible one for a time. Wilson's last days were filled with thoughts of his daughters but his last words were 'take care of my income tax'.

Up to this point, Bagehot had led a triangular life, passing between Bristol, where he was manager of Stuckey's Bank, Clevedon and Langport, and London. Now a major change took place. He resigned from the management of the Bristol bank and supervised its work in London, sharing a house with the Wilsons in Upper Belgrave Street. In 1861, Hutton resigned the editorship of *The Economist* and Bagehot became editor of the paper as well as its director, a post he held until his death. He took charge of the whole family and became a substitute father to them all. He counselled Matilda against marrying Captain Hill, a rake and spendthrift; and when Julia eventually married W. R. Greg, helped with the arrangements. With Walter there was usually a hitch. The night before the marriage was to take place at St Stephen's, Gloucester Road, the solicitor's clerk bought the marriage settlements round in a hansom cab, but while he was seeking to gain entrance the cab drove off with the settlements. Walter insisted on postponing the marriage for two hours so the settlements could be copied out again, but in the event the cabman returned with the original so that there were two sets available at the wedding. There had been a similar hiatus at Emily's wedding to Russell Barrington in 1868 when the wills which Walter was in charge of disappeared. But all was well in the end. 'The wills are found,' Walter noted, 'They went down to be brushed with my evening clothes.'[38]

---

[38] *The Life of Walter Bagehot*, p. 406.

Bagehot was a member of both the Metaphysical Society, a group of eminent Victorians who met to discuss philosophical and religious questions, and also of the Political Economy Club. Although he delivered two papers before the Metaphysical Society, Hutton notes that he seldom spoke in it. He adds that Bagehot told him shortly before his death 'that he shrank from such discussions on religious points, feeling that, in debates of this kind, they were not and could not be treated with anything like thoroughness'.[39]

During the London years Bagehot wrote more on economic and political than literary subjects. From 1859 to 1877 he contributed two articles (sometimes more) nearly every week to *The Economist* on current affairs. He did however continue some literary work. On 6 June 1859 he is found writing to Eliza: 'I am grinding on at Milton, and have done ever so much; but it is very bad and will be very long.' Certainly the reader today seems to hear the noise. These years were also made memorable by the publication of his three great works *The English Constitution* (1867), *Physics and Politics* (1872) and *Lombard Street* (1873). In addition he gave evidence on banking matters to the Select Committee of the House of Commons and a similar committee in France.

Despite the many calls of London life, Bagehot never lost touch with his roots in Somerset. Visits to Herd's Hill were regular to see his mother; there were also the fortnightly meetings of the directors of Stuckey's Bank to attend and the meetings of Wells and Taunton Quarter Sessions, Bagehot having been made a local J.P. in 1861. He also liked to escape for a day or two to the country when he had something special to write so that he could do so undisturbed.

In middle life, he made a number of attempts to enter Parliament, but was not successful, a major disappointment. He had great difficulty in gaining a candidature. He was a brilliant conversationalist but not an orator. Hutton records: 'As a speaker he did not often succeed, his voice had no great compass, and his manner was somewhat odd to ordinary hearers.'[40] He was not always tactful and had a manner of direct speech which did not commend itself to selection committees. He infuriated the public meeting at Manchester by telling them that in London they were considered extreme supporters of

---

[39] 'Memoir', xxxii.
[40] 'Memoir', lxii.

EDITOR'S INTRODUCTION

democracy. In the contest for the London University nomination he alienated the Conservatives by foolishly accusing Disraeli of personal corruption. The truth is that he had nothing of that grain of opportunism which is part of the make-up of the successful politician. He would not stoop to conquer.

In 1867 at the age of 41 Bagehot had his first serious illness and two years later had a bad relapse. In 1870 the mother to whom he was so deeply attached and for whom he had cared all his life died suddenly. He felt her loss deeply. 'The *worst* of it is,' he remarked, 'that by many it was looked on as a relief.'

Visits abroad were made and the Bagehots frequently changed houses, moving from Upper Belgrave Street to Wimbledon and then to various addresses in Kensington, finally settling at 8 Queen's Gate Place which was decorated with William Morris papers and De Morgan tiles. 'William Morris,' said Bagehot, 'is composing the drawing-room as he would an ode.' Morris had selected blue damask for the curtains and upholstery in the drawing-room. 'They bring me sample threads every two or three months, but the curtains don't come.' It was probably lying on his sofa under these curtainless windows that he caught the chill which was to lead to his death in March 1877.

One of the letters allegedly written during this period was to Emily Davies. I have been unable to trace the original of this letter although there is some documentary evidence for it. The sentiments although they fit in with Bagehot's conservative views on women's rights, strike me as being rather too violent and I am not wholly convinced of its authenticity. 'I assure you I am not an enemy of women,' he declares. 'I am very favourable to their employment as *labourers* or in other *menial* capacity. I have, however, doubts as to the likelihood of their succeeding in business as capitalists. I am sure the nerves of most women would break down under the anxiety and that most of them are utterly destitute of the disciplined reticence necessary to every sort of co-operation.' This sounds more like Queen Victoria than Bagehot.

W. R. Greg's letter to Matilda Wilson on 6 April 1860 telling her about his visit to Paris with the Bagehots, on the other hand, has the ring of authenticity. 'You never saw such people as Walter and Eliza for appetite and unpunctuality. They grubbed at 9, at 11, at 2, sometimes at 5, always at 6, and usually again at 11 or 12, with a snack in the interstices. The sofas and floor presented a most distracting chaos of Newspapers, old and new, chocolate, gloves—(—generally odd ones)—tea cups, lemonade, pats of butter, statistical returns and Blue books, physic bottles, fragments of bread, half-eaten pears, and the like, all accumulating from the day of our arrival to the day of our departure, and never cleared away. We generally spent half an hour a day in getting together a quorum to consider when and where we shd. dine,—and another half an hour in settling what to have for dinner. You may suppose what it was to a man of my habits. I got so demoralised with it all that I lost my two purses within a week—mainly from laying them down or dropping them on the floor à la Mrs. Bagehot.'

Correspondence takes place between Bagehot and C. H. Pearson about the *National Review* and with John Morley concerning Bagehot's contribution to the *Fortnightly*. Most interesting is the letter to Pearson in which Bagehot discusses whether Hutton should edit or write for the *National Review*. 'I quite understand,' writes Bagehot, 'that there is to be no exclusion of the Mauricians, as such, from the National Review—As far as they are Liberal churchmen I think it is very important to include them, and to make it known that we include them. Hutton's case is a very peculiar one. For the last few years his mind has been travelling from heterodoxy to orthodoxy and he has become inevitably and most naturally inclined to think most of and be most anxious to write concerning the new truth which was breaking upon him. The old truth—the old negations if you like—in which he was bred up were comparatively tame to him even when he still adhered to them. Now this state of mind is, I think, seriously incapacitating in the Editor of a *reforming* review. I do not so much care *what* a man holds as *how* he holds it. If a man is inclined to look with lurking partiality on whatever *is* believed and to look with suspicion and to treat with deprecation all common doubts (and this is pretty much Hutton's case) he ought not to be the governing spirit of an innovating periodical . . . I only wish that as a recent convert to old doctrines he shd. not give the principal tone and predominating aspect to the review. I shd. describe the review as open to all liberal churchmen, and to all religious heretics. Of course these words are vague but practical alliances of this sort are always vague.' (Letter of 1 September 1862.) Bagehot did not want Hutton to be an editor but was content to have him as a contributor.

Bagehot first met Gladstone in 1859 at the dinner party given by James Wilson to celebrate the publication of Bagehot's *Parliamentary Reform* and in November of that year, after his return to the Government as Chancellor of the Exchequer under Palmerston, he began a confidential correspondence with Bagehot at *The Economist* about his financial policy. Bagehot's first reply on taxation was written on 2 November 1859. Further exchanges took place but Bagehot and Gladstone were not in full agreement. Bagehot did not share Gladstone's views on the desirability of abolishing direct taxation. In 1861, Bagehot played a leading role in discrediting Robert Lowe's scheme to replace the income tax with a match tax.

Yet Bagehot had a profound admiration for Gladstone, whom he hailed as 'by far the greatest Chancellor of the Exchequer of this generation', and in 1860 he wrote a long appraisal of him in the *National Review*. It was by no means merely adulatory of the future grand old man and it must have been a mixed experience for him to be so lectured. After Bagehot's death, Gladstone wrote to his widow: 'I remember feeling, and I still feel, how true the article on myself is in the parts least favourable to my vanity.' Bagehot became a regular visitor at Gladstone's breakfast parties at Carlton House Terrace and it was at one of these functions that he told Gladstone's daughter, Helen, that 'he knew what a nut felt like when it was going to be cracked as he once got his head caught between a cart and a lamppost'. Bagehot followed Gladstone's career with the closest attention. On the whole he was sympathetic but he had reservations about Gladstone's new style of democratic leadership which emerged in the '70s. He was implacably opposed to Gladstone's plans for home rule for Ireland.

Gladstone's letters must be read as a whole to appreciate their full flavour. A good example of his style occurs early on in the correspondence. One of Bagehot's first acts on taking over *The Economist* had been to write privately to Gladstone to make some inquiries about the basis of his financial policy. Gladstone replied in terms which are described by Alastair Buchan as 'a model of the master's double talk'. 'All matters in these departments for the coming session are as yet in embryo, and I know nothing to guide a journalist at this time except general principles. If I had a journal, I would, with the amount of reserve I might find necessary, and no more, aim at showing again and again the profitableness of remissions which reproduce revenue by enriching the people; and this in quiet comparison with vast outlay on military establishments, which especially when suddenly and violently enlarged, tend in many ways to produce the very evil they aim at averting.' (Letter of 29 November 1859). Bagehot picked up a little of the style himself as can be seen in his letter to Gladstone of 30 April 1861, when he sends him his article on the American constitution declaring: 'I should not, however, send you my article if what I have heard called the "Plenary power of *not* reading" did not place the remedy in your own hands.'

Another typically nuancé letter from Gladstone is evoked on 15 October 1863 by Bagehot's essay on Sir George Cornewall Lewis and on 12 June 1865, a letter to Gladstone from Bagehot asking for his support for the Liberal candidature at Manchester secures a splendid piece of circumlocution in response. 'Dear Mr. Bagehot,' writes Gladstone, 'It would be very great presumption on my part, in expressing an opinion as to your qualifications for Parliament, were I to connect that opinion with any particular constituency. But of the qualifications themselves neither I, nor, as I believe, anyone who knows you can have any doubt whatever; and undoubtedly they point, of themselves, to the class of our great commercial and manufacturing constituencies in an especial degree. If thorough acquaintance with economic science, extensive and accurate knowledge, ready and practical habits of business and a conciliatory disposition, go to fit a man for the representation of these great national interests, it certainly appears to me that your fitness must stand without dispute in the first rank.' The burghers of Manchester dealt summarily with this splendid epistle. Bagehot wrote: 'I had a letter from Mr. Gladstone recommending me, but it was of no use. They said, "If he is so celebrated, why does not Finsbury elect him?"' During 1865, Gladstone was in close touch with Bagehot and among his papers is a note of that year to send his private memorandum on financial policy to a number of distinguished persons including Bagehot. They were in close touch again in 1866 over the failure of Overend Gurney. When he was Chancellor of the Exchequer again in 1873, Gladstone wrote an enthusiastic letter of thanks to Bagehot for sending him a copy of *Lombard Street*.

Bagehot and Newman never met, but throughout his life, Bagehot had the greatest admiration for him and followed with the closest attention that extraordinary pilgrimage which took Newman from the Church of England to the Church of Rome, a journey which epitomised in some ways the theological and ecclesiastical history of nineteenth-century England. In Bagehot's ever present awareness of the unseen world he was closely akin to Newman, for whom he felt a profound sympathy. He knew Newman's *Parochial Sermons* almost by heart: 'The Invisible World' and 'The Greatness and Littleness of Human Life' were constantly in his mind. He took *Lyra Apostolica* on his honeymoon and read the poems to his wife, supplementing them with readings from the Anglican theologian Frederick Denison Maurice.

Bagehot's thought was akin to Newman's in many ways. Both resisted the facile optimism of the period: both felt a profound affinity for the past: both, influenced probably by Moehler and Schlegel, stress the paramount importance of national character as the basis of political order. Newman in his book *Development of Christian Doctrine* applied evolutionary ideas to theology as Bagehot did to society in *Physics and Politics*. Both distrusted Disraeli, but while Newman approved of his imperialism, Bagehot was always cool and often hostile to such attitudes. Only one letter exists from Bagehot to Newman, written on 1 April 1868; Newman never seems to have corresponded directly with Bagehot. However, he had noticed a favourable mention of his works by Bagehot in the *National Review* and accordingly sent a copy of his poems to Hutton to be forwarded to Bagehot. The poems evoked a heart-felt letter of thanks: 'I have known those in the Lyra by heart for many years,' wrote Bagehot, 'and am deeply gratified at being brought into personal communication with one whose writings—amid much difference of opinion—have fallen so deep into my mind. I should hold that some of the poems would have an intrinsic claim to a permanent place in English literature, but independently of this they are quite sure of it as yours—The mental history of the last thirty years in England will always—or at least very long—be matter of great interest and the *Apologia* is a piece of such *easy reading* that it is sure to colour the historians whole mind—and it will pass among quiet people who care more for biography than history. Taken with this commentary, the poems *must* have permanent place, and according to the *coldest* criticism I can make many of them *ought* to have that place of themselves.' Bagehot ends his letter with the words, 'with the greatest respect of *very* many years standing'.

One other Oxford figure who emerges in the letters is his friend and distant cousin Constantine Prichard, Fellow of Balliol. In a letter to Hutton of October 1869, Bagehot writes: 'Constantine Prichard is dead, leaving a large family not well off, I fear. The old world of our youth breaks up, and the *best* people get the *worst* of it.'

A number of points of interest should be noted from the letters of this period. The extent of the influence which *The Economist* exercised in the '70s is shown by the letter Lord Granville wrote to Bagehot on 11 October 1870 during the Franco-Prussian crisis. He requested that *The Economist* would not publish any articles 'which will give thoughtful Germans reason to believe that they have just cause of complaint against us'. Sir Henry Maine's praise of *Physics and Politics* in a letter of January 1873 must have given Bagehot a special pleasure. So must that which came from W. S. Jevons, the economist, for *Lombard Street* in a letter of 23 June 1873. He hailed the book as 'by far the best account we have of the working of our banking system, and your wonderful power of delicate analysis and description has never been more strikingly applied even in your *English Constitution*'.

A letter of 6 July 1873 to J. E. Cairnes, the leading academic economist of the time, contains an interesting discussion of the main argument of *Lombard Street* and the relationship between the Bank of England and other banks, and the note issue. Cairnes paid Bagehot the compliment of incorporating his argument in his *Leading Principles*. The letter ends on a typically Bagehotian note: 'I am very sorry to hear that you have a difficulty in reading for I suppose it is to you as to me almost the gratest pleasure in life, and I am still more sorry to have written you so much as it is *not* a pleasure to read my handwriting.' On 21 June 1874, he wrote to Cairnes praising this book as 'the greatest contribution to *abstract* political Economy that has been made for very many years'. Again it was to Cairnes that he outlined his views on the colonies. 'I have just read your essay on "Colonization": *I* agree but neither the Colonies nor England will. If you stood for a popular constituency you would have that essay thrown in your teeth; it would be said that you wanted to dismember the Empire, and this is very unpopular. The smaller people are the more they wish to belong to some large aggregate.' On 10 December 1875, Bagehot is found writing to Lord Grey discussing the purchase of the Suez Canal shares of which he disapproved. Again it is in a letter to Lord Grey of 2 September 1874 written from the Auvergne that he regrets the revival of imperialism in France: 'There is great distress since the War and the people look back to the Empire—literally as to a *golden* age.'

Bagehot's spirit of fun was not extinguished in his later years, although it did not bubble up so freely, and there are signs of it in his letters. Writing to Inglis Palgrave on 28 May 1873, about the publication of *Lombard Street* he remarks: 'The covers of my book were put on by the publisher when I was ill, and I nearly had a relapse when it came in them.' In another letter to the same recipient of 3 November 1873, he says of the editor of the *Edinburgh Review*: 'I knew Reeve was of no use. He only likes "hashed meat"—ideas which [have been] used before. Anything new is horrid to him.'

Bagehot was a member of both Windham's and Brooks's and in April 1875 he achieved the coveted distinction of election to the Athenaeum under rule 2. 'The committee elected me yesterday at the Athenaeum quite cheerfully,' he wrote to Eliza on 14 April 1875. 'By the rules they can only elect nine persons a year and those "who have attained eminence in Science, Literature, the Arts or for public services". I wonder in which *my* eminence is.'

All his life, though childless himself, Bagehot loved children. On a visit in 1874 to the prospective new house at 8 Queen's Gate Place he commented on the rocking horse in the hall: '*That's* the best thing in the house.'

Walter Bagehot's death

March 1877 was cold and blustery and consequently Bagehot had contracted a chill. Hutton recalls their last meeting: 'The last time we met, only five days before his death I remarked on the vigour and youthfulness of his look, and told him he looked less like a contemporary of my own than one of a younger generation. In a pencil-note, the last I received from him, written from bed on the next day but one, he said, "I think you must have had the evil eye when you complimented me on my appearance. Ever since, I have been sickening, and am now in bed with a severe attack on the lungs." Indeed, well as he appeared to me, he had long had delicate health and heart disease was the immediate cause of death.' On Tuesday, 20 March, Bagehot set off from Queen's Gate Place to make his annual Easter visit to his father at Herd's Hill, stopping at the Athenaeum on the way to the station to cast his vote for the election of George Trevelyan, son of James Wilson's old rival in India. The long journey and the delay in the cold night air at Yeovil station had made him worse and he became even more gravely ill. Eliza Bagehot recorded the events of his last days in her diary in a detail unusual for her. On arrival at Langport on the Tuesday he saw his father for the last time. On Friday he played cribbage with his Aunt Emma, a game which he enjoyed although bezique was his favourite. On the Saturday he was supposed to be better and Eliza lay by his side all the morning cutting open the leaves of a new copy of 'Rob Roy' which she read. Walter had always maintained that the extrovert Scott was ideal reading for a sick room. He complained of his weakness and in the afternoon tried to exert himself moving his pillows about. Eliza attempted to help him and his last words were characteristic: 'Let me have my own fidgets,' then he called her to him and fell asleep across the bed breathing loud and hard. 'Gradually the sound quieted, till, as the sun was setting the end came peacefully—painlessly.' Eliza wrote in her diary that Mr Bagehot was informed 'who cried much'. The sound of those sobs echo down the years as do the reverberations of the grief contained in Eliza's laconic three words. Thomas Bagehot had lost the joy of his life, the treasure on whom was centred all his hopes. The world too had lost by the premature extinction of a man of genius. 'I should never have known how great a man Walter was,' remarked his father, 'had I not survived him.'

NOTE ON THE TEXT

This edition collects for the first time all known letters of Walter Bagehot—almost half hitherto unpublished or published only in part—and a selection of those written to him. There are 407 letters, 250 transcribed from manuscript or photocopies of manuscript, the remainder (many surviving only as extracts) from printed sources. Of these sources the most important is the *Life of Walter Bagehot* by his sister-in-law, Mrs Russell Barrington (first published in 1914; reprinted 1915 as Vol. X of her edition of the *Works and Life*). It is to Mrs Barrington that we owe our knowledge of many letters no longer extant, which she quoted whole or in part, and she was responsible for the preservation of many of his original letters, especially those from three important correspondences: the letters to his parents, 1832-52; letters to and from Richard Holt Hutton, 1843-58; and those exchanged between Bagehot and Eliza Wilson during their engagement, 1857-8. She drew extensively on them in the *Life* of Bagehot and in *Servant of All*, her biography of her father (and Bagehot's father-in-law), James Wilson, and she published almost all the letters of the engagement period in *The Love-Letters of Walter Bagehot and Eliza Wilson* (1933).

Many of Bagehot's letters and papers which had been in Mrs Barrington's possession were destroyed after her death, but some 180 to his parents and to and from R. H. Hutton escaped destruction and are now in the editor's Bagehot collection.[1] Two early letters, one to his Uncle Watson and one to his mother, are owned by Miss Mary Bagehot. Two letters to his mother (8 April 1848 and 8 May 1851) and two to Hutton (8 October 1855 and 25 December 1856) were presented by Mr Robert Bagehot-Porch to Professor William Irvine as a tribute to his *Walter Bagehot* (1939), for which he had made available his

[1] See the editor's Preface to the *Collected Works* (I, 21-2). The nine letters from Hutton are not given as texts in this edition, but have been used for annotation when they throw light on a letter of Bagehot's. They are: 13 September 1843 from Nottingham; 18 September 1844 from Bath; 7 October 1844, dated from 'H.P.K.C.'; 29 December 1844 from Bath; 30 August 1846, 13 September 1846, 5 October 1846, undated of ? late October 1846, and 16 November 1846, all from Baden.

collection of Bagehot letters. After Irvine's death these four letters came on the market and were bought as a gift to Mr Richard W. Lyman, President of the Rockefeller Foundation. They were not among those quoted by Irvine, although his book does include quotations from five letters of which the originals have not been traced.[2]

Most of the correspondence between Bagehot and Eliza Wilson, 1857–8, has also been preserved, since Mrs Barrington presented the manuscripts (apart from seven of Bagehot's letters) to the publishers of the *Love-Letters*, Faber and Faber, who deposited them in the Brynmor Jones Library, University of Hull. They include one letter of Bagehot's and two of Eliza Wilson's not printed in *Love-Letters*; these are published for the first time in this edition, and texts of those already printed for which originals are in the Hull collection have been corrected from the manuscripts.

Bagehot's side of one major correspondence, that with his father-in-law during Wilson's time in India, 1859–60, was almost certainly destroyed by Bagehot himself when they were returned to him following Wilson's death; one letter alone survives in a typed copy (10 June 1860). Most of Wilson's letters were printed by Mrs Barrington in *Servant of All* and the *Life* of Bagehot; their texts have not been reprinted in this edition, but they have been drawn on for annotation. However, the Wilson Papers in the Bodleian Library contain letters from Bagehot to Zenobia and Matilda Wilson and to Mrs Wilson, first published in this edition, as well as a letter from W. R. Greg to Matilda Wilson, describing Walter and Eliza in Paris in 1860, included as a text,[3] and letters about the breaking of Matilda's first engagement, quoted in annotation. The editor's Bagehot collection includes the manuscript diaries of Eliza Bagehot for 1859, 1861, 1864, 1866, 1867, 1869, 1871, 1872, 1874–7, and these have been used in the annotation and dating of letters in the edition.

Bagehot's letters to Crabb Robinson and one to James Martineau are in Dr Williams's Library; all but the earliest (written from Paris in 1851) are concerned with the founding of the *National Review* in 1855. Other material in the Library, especially Crabb Robinson's manuscript diaries, has been used for annotation and dating of letters from Bagehot, including those about the appointment of Clough to the

---

[2] 8 October 1839, 7 March 1840, 26 May 1842, 15 October 1842, 2 September 1846.
[3] 8 January 1860, 6 April 1860, 1 October 1860, 7 February 1861, 16 January 1870.

NOTE ON THE TEXT

Principalship of University Hall. Bagehot's letters to Clough were first published in *The Correspondence of Arthur Hugh Clough*, ed. Frederic L. Mulhauser (1957); for this edition the texts have been corrected from the originals in the Clough Papers, Bodleian Library. The Clough Papers also contain a note from Bagehot to Francis Turner Palgrave, printed for the first time in this edition.

Of other collections of Bagehot letters preserved in English libraries the most important correspondence is that with Gladstone, 1859-73, in the Gladstone Papers, British Library, and the Giffen Collection, British Library of Political and Economic Science. Twelve letters from Bagehot survive (all included in this edition) and twelve from Gladstone (three printed here as texts, the remainder drawn on in footnotes). Those letters already printed in Mrs Barrington's *Life* (all of Bagehot's and a selection from those of Gladstone, some in the form of extracts) have been corrected from the manuscripts. Seven of the letters from Gladstone have been traced only in Letter-Book copies in the Gladstone Papers, British Library (they do not appear in the index to the Papers, but may be found in the indexes to the Letter-Books for 1859, 1860, 1863 and 1864). Another correspondent to whom Bagehot wrote at length on political and economic subjects was the third Earl Grey; the Grey of Howick Collection, University of Durham, contains eleven letters from Bagehot to Grey, not previously published. The edition also includes letters to three economists: W. S. Jevons (manuscripts in the John Rylands University Library of Manchester), J. E. Cairnes (manuscripts in the National Library of Ireland), and R. H. Inglis Palgrave (manuscripts in the editor's Bagehot collection and in the Library of King's College, Cambridge, to which they were given by Geoffrey Palgrave Barker). None has been previously published, apart from two of the three letters to Jevons, which appeared in his *Papers and Correspondence*, ed. R. D. Collison Black and Rosamond Könekamp (1972-84).

Other unpublished letters are from manuscripts in the Library of University College, London, where Bagehot's student notebooks are also preserved, the Avebury Papers and the Carnarvon Papers in the British Library, the Bulwer-Lytton Papers, owned by the Hon. David Cobbold, and deposited in Hertfordshire County Record Office, and the Pearson Papers, Bodleian Library.

The letters are printed in chronological sequence (apart from the last letter Bagehot is known to have received, placed immediately before the last he wrote), since it has been possible to date almost all undated or partially dated letters to a month, and often within days, and the few exceptions can be conjecturally placed in a particular year.

Headings give the name of Bagehot's addressee or that of writer and addressee (in letters to Bagehot and those of which he is the subject) and the date; dates supplied editorially are placed in square brackets, and preceded by a query when conjectural. Head-notes give the source of the text, manuscript or printed, and evidence of dating, where a date is omitted, incomplete or has been found to be incorrect. Bagehot, especially during his boyhood, occasionally writes the date of the previous year; most can be corrected from integral postmarks (e.g. 22 June 1841, 2 March 1842), others from content (e.g. 13 April 1842, 14 January 1855). He also dates incompletely throughout his life and sometimes omits the date in his letters from London of 1842–52; content or their place in a sequence has been used to date these letters in most instances (e.g. 23 May 1846, 20 September 1848, 12 July 1858). Content has also permitted the supply or correction of dates for letters quoted in the *Life* (e.g. 27 September 1843, 28 June 1847); two of Mrs Barrington's misdatings may be due to Bagehot's making an error in the year (18 May 1839, wrongly given as 1838, and a letter of 1845 placed in 1844 and here conjecturally dated 26 May 1845), and one is clearly owing to her misreading of his hand (26 December 1851, wrongly printed as 26 October 1851).

Texts transcribed from manuscript follow the original almost exactly, reproducing Bagehot's spelling, punctuation and capitalization. Mis-spellings, frequent in Bagehot's schoolboy letters, are indicated in a footnote only when likely to mislead or puzzle the reader; omission or misplacing of the apostrophe has been reproduced without a footnote; the omission of opening or closing brackets and quotation marks has been supplied without square brackets, and Bagehot's occasional use of double quotation marks has been standardized to single. Words inadvertently omitted have been supplied in square brackets without a footnote. When words are missing through damage to the original (in early letters often by a tear at the seal or the cutting out of a stamp) a footnote describes the damage and conjectural readings have been supplied, where possible, in square brackets. Two normalizations have been made: ampersand has been printed as 'and' (except in the invariable form '&c.'), and in contractions raised letters have been lowered and followed by a stop (e.g. 'Mr.', 'wd.') and

NOTE ON THE TEXT

omitted letters have occasionally been supplied for the sake of clarity (e.g. 'Ec[onomis]t'). The lay-out of the letters has been followed, except that the few dates written at the end of a letter have been printed at the head, and all postscripts have been printed following the letter, even when written at the head, in a crossing or in the margin.

Texts of letters from printed sources follow the original exactly, except that obvious misreadings have been replaced by a correction in square brackets with a footnote. Addresses, dates, salutations, endings and subscriptions have been normalized by the removal of italics and capitalization.

Abbreviations

Collected Works   *The Collected Works of Walter Bagehot*, edited by Norman St John-Stevas

RB, X   *The Works and Life of Walter Bagehot*, edited by Mrs Russell Barrington. Vol. X. The Life, 1915

Servant of All   Mrs Russell Barrington, *The Servant of All. Pages from the Family, Social and Political Life of My Father James Wilson*, 2 vols, 1927

WB   Walter Bagehot

THE LETTERS

1831

To JACOB WATSON,¹ [?1831]

MS: Miss Mary Bagehot
DATE: probably several months before next letter from reference to 'Baby' and handwriting

My dear Uncle,

Is the mast of the Britannia up?² The other day I saw a dancing dog. Papa³ bought me a french polish Gun in Bristol. Baby⁴ begins to talk and papa thinks he will walk by the spring.

WALTER BAGEHOT.⁵

---

¹ Letter addressed 'Mr Watson/Bridgwater'. This was WB's great-uncle, Jacob Watson (1769?–1839); second son of the Revd Thomas Watson (born Kettering, Northants; Unitarian minister at Bridgwater from 1755 until his death in 1793) and his wife Mary, née Codrington (d. 1774); Jacob's sister Mary married Robert Bagehot of Langport, WB's grandfather.
² Not a famous ship (H.M.S. *Britannia* was launched in 1820, and the Cunard liner *Britannia* in 1840); presumably a ship in Bridgwater harbour, perhaps owned by the trading company in which WB's father was a partner.
³ Thomas Watson Bagehot (1796–1881), merchant and banker, of Langport, Somerset, son of Robert Codrington Bagehot, of Herd's Hill, Langport, and his wife Mary, née Watson. In 1823 he married Edith Estlin, née Stuckey. The Bagehots and the Stuckeys dominated Langport from the mid eighteenth century: they were partners in the carrying trade on the Parret, and in the banking business established by Samuel Stuckey in 1770. T. W. Bagehot was one of the principals in the mercantile and shipping business of Stuckey and Bagehot (later the Somerset Trading Co.), and from 1825 a director of Stuckey's Bank, as well as Vice-Chairman and Managing Director of the Langport branch after the death of his brother-in-law in 1845. The Bagehots were a cultivated Unitarian family; WB's correspondence with his father demonstrates the latter's love of books, political commitment (he was a Whig and a free-trader), and his concern about the boy's education. See 'A Short Biography', *Collected Works*, I, 30–34.
⁴ Watson Bagehot (1830–81), son of T. W. Bagehot's cousin Charles, a naval officer in poor circumstances. After his mother's early death Watson, a sickly baby, was adopted by WB's parents. In a letter of 4 June 1832 (MS Miss Mary Bagehot), Mrs Mary Bagehot described him as so deformed that he might never walk. At the time of his death he was in the family business, living at Heale House, Curry Rivell, and left a widow and two daughters.
⁵ The letter is written in pencil, and the writing is not as well-formed as that of the next letter though the signature is almost identical.

1832

To MRS J. S. REYNOLDS,[1] [?1832]

MS: Mr Norman St John-Stevas
DATE: probably 1832, since said to have been written when WB was 'about six years old' (RB, X, 77)

My very dear Aunt

I thank you for the book you sent me, and Brother[2] thanks Uncle.[3] I want to ask you for another Daily food for Christians, because keeping this sometimes in my pocket and reading the text and poetry in it every morning, it is nearly worn out, and I am afraid I shall lose the leaves; Mamma[4] is afraid you will think me a bold and troublesome little boy, but she says I am yet so ignorant, that I do not know but I am doing *you* a favor, I do not agree with her: I hope you do not

---

[1] Mary Anne (*d.* 1863), second daughter of Robert Codrington Bagehot and a sister of WB's father; she married John Stuckey Reynolds in 1819.

[2] His half-brother Vincent Estlin (1806?–69), only surviving child of Edith Bagehot's first marriage, who had been feeble-minded from birth. He died at the family home, Herd's Hill, Langport, of diabetes and asthma (entry in the diary of WB's wife, Eliza, 14 July 1869; MS Mr Norman St John-Stevas).

[3] John Stuckey Reynolds (1791–1874), prominent member of the evangelical community in London, best remembered for his foundation of the Home and Colonial Training Schools and as one of those who established the *Record* newspaper in 1828 as the organ of ultra-evangelicalism. Son of John Reynolds of Manchester and his wife Ann, sister of Vincent Stuckey, the banker, and of WB's mother. According to the *Memoir* of Reynolds by 'A Friend' (quoted in Mrs RB, X, 78–9n), his devotion to religious and philanthropical causes—the result of a sermon on the dangers of worldly advancement—began in 1823, when he was at the height of his Treasury career and had been offered a seat in Parliament. After giving up his political prospects he remained in the Treasury until 1835, when he became manager of Stuckey & Reynolds, the London branch of Stuckey's Bank. Mrs Barrington records WB's lifelong attachment to his Aunt and Uncle Reynolds, and his respect for his uncle as a first-rate judge of a horse (RB, X, 78–9).

[4] Edith Bagehot (1786?–1870), youngest daughter of George Stuckey and his wife Edith, *née* Beedal, and sister of Vincent Stuckey. In 1806 she married Joseph Prior Estlin (*d.* 1814), son of the Unitarian minister John Prior Estlin of Bristol, who was a friend of Southey and Coleridge. There were three sons of the marriage: the eldest was mentally defective (see n. 2 above), the youngest died in 1821 at the age of eleven, and the second in 1829 following a carriage accident (see letter of 10 May 1842, n. 1). She had been a widow for nine years when she married Thomas Watson Bagehot, her junior by ten years, a connection by marriage of the Estlins (see letter of 21 May 1838, n. 1). Their first child, Watson, died in 1827 at the age of three; WB, their only other child, was born 3 February 1826. Edith Bagehot had great liveliness, humour and charm; she was also a devout Churchwoman, who helped to build a church at Westport (see letter of February 1841, n. 2). But her life was shadowed by bouts of insanity, which began after the tragic loss of three of her children; she had sometimes to be sent away for treatment, but often WB was able to bring her back to herself. See 'A Short Biography', *Collected Works*, I, 30–35.

Papa and I have been playing a good game of Top.

William Wood and I have some fun together sometimes Baby cannot walk yet, he always says R goes for Uncle Reynolds. All send their love and to dear Kate too

Your affectionate Nephew
Walter Bagehot

Letter to Mary Anne Reynolds, [?1832].

either. The new man servant James 2nd is come to-day, our James is going upon the Hill[5] Papa and I have been playing a good game of Top.

William Wood[6] and I have some fun together sometimes Baby cannot walk yet he always says R goes for Uncle Reynolds. All send their love and to dear Kate[7] too

Your affectionate Nephew
WALTER BAGEHOT[8]

T. W. BAGEHOT to WB, 17 JUNE 1833
Test from RB, X, 80–1.

Langport,
17th June, 1833.

My dear Boy,

I cannot let Miss Jones[1] go without thanking you for your letter. I assure you I wish myself back again with you[2] very much indeed and should be glad to hear the sound of the dashing waves and to climb the rocks and brave the deep and journey about with Mamma and you

---

[5] To join the household of WB's uncle, Vincent Stuckey, at Hill House, Langport.
[6] William Stuckey Wood (1826–70), elder son of the Revd William Wood and his wife Julia, eldest daughter of Vincent Stuckey.
[7] Orphaned daughter of William and Amelia Norman; a relation of the Bagehots, who often stayed with the Reynoldses and at Langport (letters from Mrs Mary Bagehot to Mrs Reynolds; MSS Miss Mary Bagehot).
[8] The letter is written in huge letters half an inch high. The signature is strikingly similar to that of WB's maturity.

* * *

---

[1] The governess engaged for WB when he was five; she remained with the family for forty years (RB, X, 77).
[2] The letter was addressed to 'Master Walter Bagehot, Blue Anchor'—a seaside resort near Minehead.

picking spicata—but I must not think of it yet, for little or great boys must not be idle either, and I must do my work before I play. The mail with its four horses soon took me away from you on Friday and carried me through a very pretty country to Taunton where Bob was waiting for me and brought me home just about the time of your fifth dip as I calculated.

Mamma tells me you are becoming a poet and I shall look forward some day or other to our having a 'Sir Walter' in our own family.

Your sword[3] is sent, and as tomorrow is the anniversary of the battle of Waterloo, I suppose you will be very grand on the occasion. How would you have liked living at Brussels when the cannons began to roar and the soldiers were summoned to the field?

I must close directly as Miss Jones is just going off in the phaeton.

To EDITH BAGEHOT, [?1836–1837]

MS: Miss Mary Bagehot
DATE: reference to Watson's lessons suggests 1836 or 1837

My dear Mamma I write this to thank you for my marbles by which I was very much surprised, expecting nothing of the kind but which as you may well believe were very acceptable; being very nice large ones but enough of marbles. You will no doubt be glad to hear that I do sense verses now but not that papa and myself were three hours about it but the one if you remember I did one day seemed to me nonsense. Watson is now learning Musa[1] and says he can say it but I can not help thinking that it is in a fashion but it is fair to say that he has said a lesson or two better than I ever heard him say anything. Being no scribe I must have done. I hope you will be at home soon[2] and both Watson and I will be delighted to see you for we have missed you very much. I remain your affectionate child Walter Bagehot. Watson and myself send many kisses and love.[3]

---

[3] See WB's 'Hartley Coleridge': *Collected Works*, I, 145.

* * *

[1] Latin noun given as the example of the first declension in the *Eton Latin Grammar*,

MAY 1838

To EDITH BAGEHOT, 21 MAY 1838

MS: Mr Norman St John-Stevas

Langport
May 21st. 1838

I was very much disappointed, my dearest Mamma, at not receiving a letter from you, however I suppose, that I must do as they do in France i.e. the best they can.

I am just come from bathing, and Papa went to see me swim (was not that an honour) and said if I took pains this year I should do wonders next year. But enough of myself.

Uncle Estlin[1] came yesterday and said after he had seen poor Uncle Mitchell,[2] that he had never known an instance of one who had for so long a time been totally unconscious, perfectly recovering the use of his faculties, and if they were not restored, it would certainly be a mercy if it should be the will of the all wise God to remove him from his sorrowing friends on earth to the mansions of everlasting bliss.

I had not time to do my lessons for you, either today or yesterday, I have been so busy but I think it would rather puzzle me to say what I

---

primer used by most schoolboys at this date; Watson was probably having his first lessons at home with the governess before following WB to Langport Grammar School (see next, n.3).
[2] The letter is addressed 'Mrs Watson Bagehot/at Mrs Stothard's/St James's Place/Kingsdown/Bristol'. This may have been one of the periods when she was sent away to recover from a bout of mental illness (for another, see WB's allusion in his letter of 1 November 1838 to her absence during September–October 1838).
[3] At the foot of the page his father wrote: 'I do not know what you will think of our darling's letter but as it is his own I preferred sending it to anything else'.

* * *

[1] John Bishop Estlin (1785–1855), surgeon, of Park Street, Bristol, son of John Prior Estlin and brother of Mrs Bagehot's first husband; in 1817 he married Margaret (d. 1821), sister of Thomas Watson Bagehot. Estlin, elected a Fellow of the College of Surgeons in 1845, was one of the first ophthalmic surgeons in England; a Unitarian and member of the Lewin's Mead, Bristol, congregation, of which his father had been a minister, he devoted much of his time to such causes as religious toleration, the education of the poor and the abolition of slavery.
[2] George Michell, surgeon, of Langport, husband of T. W. Bagehot's sister Emma; died 25 May, 1839, aged 54.

was about all day yesterday but today I had a very difficult proposition of Euclid, which with the writing out and all kept me nearly two hours.³

Papa says he thinks he shall be obliged to go to London the beginning of next week and if he does how do you think, I shall manage without you both; but if I cannot bear to be away from you both a week now I wonder how I shall be able to bear it for a whole six months when I go [to] the *heretical* college⁴ as you call it.

I have just looked at my watch and find that I shall scarcely have time to fly down with this to Papa for him to add a few lines. And believe me that I remain yours in great haste.

WALTER BAGEHOT

Give my love to uncle and Aunt Stuckey.⁵ On a second look at my watch I find that I have falsely alarmed myself since it is only half past four instead of five: is not that like me.

---

³ At eight or nine WB had been sent as a day-scholar to Langport Grammar School, where he was a pupil of the remarkable William Quekett (1767–1842), master of the school from 1780 until his death; three of Quekett's sons achieved eminence in their own fields (see their entries in the *DNB*), and the fourth was Secretary of Stuckey's Bank.

⁴ By this date it had been decided that WB should continue his education not at a public school (as his mother would have preferred) but at a Bristol school which had recently come into existence to meet the needs of parents in Bristol and its neighbourhood debarred, by lack of means or dissenting religious beliefs, from giving their sons a public school education. This was the Bristol College, projected in 1829 by a Council of prominent Bristol citizens, many of them doctors and men of science and including as prime movers John Bishop Estlin and Dr James Cowles Prichard (also a brother-in-law of Mrs Bagehot); it was financed by subscribers to its £50 shares, who formed the proprietary body. The College (consisting of separate junior and senior departments) opened in 1831, and offered in addition to the classics, mathematics and Hebrew, teaching in science and modern languages. Its most controversial feature was that although the principal officers were all churchmen (most of them Cambridge graduates and several in Holy Orders), entry was open to all denominations and the Church of England teaching provided was optional. Fees were kept low (never rising much above £20 a year), and it was not a boarding school but arranged for boys to be accommodated in the homes of professors and tutors. That it survived only until 1842 in spite of the excellence and range of the teaching was due in part to local hostility to dissent (a rival Church of England college was founded in competition), and in part to lack of capital: the numbers never rose above 100 boys, and it proved impossible to move the school from its temporary quarters in a house in Park Row to a building of its own. (Information from *Outline of the Plsn of Education to be pursued at the Bristol College*, 1830, advertisements, and reports of Annual General Meetings and other items about the College in the *Bristol Mercury*, 1838–41.)

⁵ Vincent Stuckey (1771–1845), banker and merchant, of Langport; son of George Stuckey and brother of Edith Bagehot. His wife Julia (1781–1861) was the daughter of

MAY 1838

T. W. BAGEHOT to EDITH BAGEHOT, [21 MAY 1838]

MS: Mr Norman St John-Stevas
DATE: written on same sheet as last; postmarked 22 May 1838, and clearly written same day as last

My dearest Edith,

Walter has just brought down his scrawl and altho' I have rather lectured him both for its manner and matter I have consented to send it on his promising to be more particular as to both the next time he writes.

We were both much disappointed at not hearing from you this morning and I can scarcely help thinking that a letter from you has been mis-sent—we wish to know how you are and what you are doing and when you have settled to leave town for we have had enough of your absence and shall be glad to welcome you home again—Your leave of absence however will not expire for a week or more and I must not recall you before it has—By that time I suppose I shall be in town, but we will not be ungallant enough to pass each other on the road and you must therefore decide on leaving London Monday or staying till I return which I trust I shall be able to do on Saturday week, but I cannot yet fix when I am to go from hence as the Committee on our bill[1]

Vincent's uncle, Samuel Stuckey. They were marreid in 1801, when Vincent gave up his career in public service to join the family business; and after inheriting a large sum in 1810 he greatly expanded Stuckey's Bank, by opening new branches and by absorbing smaller local banks. In 1826 his was the first bank to take advantage of new legislation to form itself into a joint stock company, Stuckey's Banking Co.; he was the leading country banker of his day, and a spokesman at Parliamentary inquiries for the joint stock and private banks which had the right to issue their own notes. Hill House, where the Stuckeys lived, was Langport's social centre and a meeting place for Stuckeys and Bagehots. The company of her cheerful gregarious brother helped to preserve Edith Bagehot's mental equilibrium. See 'A Short Biography', *Collected Works*, I, 29–31.

* * *

[1] Presumably the Select Committee on Joint Stock Banks, which was nominated 30 April and began hearing evidence 29 May, although no representative of Stuckey's or other West of England banks gave evidence; the bill, which became law in August, dealt with the conditions for legal action by a Joint Stock Banking Company against its members or by its members against the company.

will not be settled until Monday—As well as we can now judge the business is likely to come on tomorrow or Thursday week—Poor George is in much the same state as when I wrote yesterday—If any thing rather more conscious, but looking more ill and like the dying man—For the first few days he was not like that, but more like a breathing corpse—Mr Estlin has no idea that he can rally and thinks it most probable that he will linger on and sink from debility ere many days are past or that some other stroke or paralysis will lay him low at once—Poor fellow—He found out yesterday that he was paralysed and was much distressed for the moment and his look and manner were to those around quite heart rending. What a thing to awake and find half your body dead!

Adieu, my dearest dear. I have not a minute more—

Ever affy yours

T W Bagehot

To T. W. BAGEHOT, [OCTOBER 1838]

Extract in RB, X, 82; undated, but clearly before 13 October 1838 (see next)

Since you have told me to give an account of the battle of Marathon in my own words, I will do it to the best of my ability.[1]

To T. W. BAGEHOT, [13 OCTOBER 1838]

Extract in RB, X, 83, dated 13 October 1838

Since you were pleased with my account of the battle of Marathon, I will try to succeed better in that of Mantinea.

---

[1] According to Mrs Barrington, there followed 'a short but excellent account of the battle'

NOVEMBER 1838

To EDITH BAGEHOT, 1 NOVEMBER 1838
Extract in RB, X, 82

Langport
Thursday Evening, 1838.

This day is the first of November. Oh, how different from the last two! The comparison makes me feel so happy that you are not gone away ill.[1] I am in a great deal better spirits since Papa came home. I know it ought not to be so, but I can't help it.

The water has got up into the Moor which occasions great commotions in the school for fear it will be too wet to have a bonfire and let off fireworks. T. Paul surmises that they have let the water in because the boys shall not have a bonfire; but the fact wants confirmation, he having, as I can learn, no authority for it but in his own thoughts. I have to write the Life of Alfred the Great for Papa. I find it rather difficult, more so I think than the Battle of Mantinea. I have read his reign in Hume[2] who doesn't of course breath a syllable about religion but praises him most extremely on account of his improvements in the English Law and Literature.

To T. W. BAGEHOT, [?8 NOVEMBER 1838]
Extract in RB, X, 83, dated 8 October 1838, but almost certainly after letter of 1 November which refers to writing the Life of Alfred

My dear Papa,

I will now, as you requested, attempt, and I hope to your satisfaction, the Life of Alfred (justly surnamed the Great). I shall consider Alfred in his double character of a prince and scholar, and to render his reign intelligible I shall give a short account of the Anglo-Saxons down to that time.[1]

[1] She was visiting her sister-in-law, Mrs Reynolds, at Hampstead (RB, X, 82).
[2] David Hume's *History of England*, first published 1754–61, and from 1793 with *Continuation* by Smollett, long remained the standard (and most readable) history.

* * *

[1] Followed, according to Mrs Barrington, by 'a very long essay full of instruction'.

NOVEMBER 1838

To EDITH BAGEHOT, [25 NOVEMBER 1838]

Extract in RB, X, 83, dated 25 November 1838

My dear Mamma,

I will now attempt the life of St. Augustine of Hippo. This bulwark of orthodoxy was born at Tagaste, a town in Africa.[2]

To T. W. BAGEHOT, [18 DECEMBER 1838]

Extract in RB, X, 83, dated 18 December 1838

My letter to Mamma contained, as you know, an account of St. Augustine; this one will contain a brief[1] life of Julius Caesar.

To EDITH BAGEHOT, [?DECEMBER 1838]

Extract in RB, X, 83
DATE: sending the last of six essays written October–December 1838

This letter will contain an account of Socrates.[1]

To EDITH BAGEHOT, 18 MAY [1839]

Text from RB, X, 81–2, dated 18 May 1838—an error for 1839, since about the Bedchamber crisis

18th May, 1838.

We are all going on very well without you, and Papa and I have such nice chats about Sir R. Peel[1] and the little Queen. Papa has quite made up his mind since he had read our friend the Duke's speech that

---

[2] 'A very long account of the Saint follows' (RB, X, 83).

* * *

[1] Mrs Barrington comments 'not very brief'.

* * *

[1] Said to be 'a very lengthy one'. Mrs Barrington describes the six essays (not reprinted in her edition of WB's *Works*) as 'remarkable as the work of a boy of twelve', since they showed that WB 'had already learned how to read' and 'to grip the main points of his subject, and could manage his detail with creditable skill' (RB, X, 83).

* * *

[1] Sir Robert Peel (1783–1850), leader of the Tory party, had been sent for by the Queen, following Melbourne's resignation, but had refused to take office (see n. 2).

the Queen did quite right and blames 'the Right Hon. Baronet'[2] for making the ladies of so much consequence since they could only use the ladies' privilege of railing against everybody and everything. I have done my lessons most days and of course find I cannot do them nearly as well without you, particularly the French. Remember my French dictionary. Do you think I ever can survive two days' holidays without you? I think I may say *possibly*; but I suppose, or rather am certain, that I shall miss you very much. I have read the review of Doctor Cumming's work in the *Monthly*,[3] and like him much better since I find he thinks Egypt a delightful country and advises some persons to go out with the intention of building a boarding-house for the sick, travellers, etc. I hope some one will take his advice. I have some thoughts of spending a month or two there!

And now, my dear Mamma, I must conclude with entreating you to remember that everywhere you carry the thought of your affectionate son,

WALTER BAGEHOT

Excuse bad writing for, as Jenny Deans says, I have 'but one and ill pen'.[4]

T. W. BAGEHOT to WB, [AUGUST 1839]

Extract in RB, X, 86.
DATE: soon after T. W. Bagehot parted from WB at Bristol College on Friday, 9 August (see next)

I travelled on to Cheddar, with my thoughts wholly fixed on you, and with a parent's prayer for your happiness, and I believe I have thought of little else since my return; and both Mamma and I are longing to

---

[2] The Whig sympathies of WB's father, rather than the Duke of Wellington's statement of 14 May to the House of Lords concerning the 'Bedchamber' crisis, must have been responsible for his assigning the blame to Sir Robert Peel. The Duke spoke of the Queen's position with respect and sympathy; nevertheless he insisted that Peel had no alternative to resignation once the Queen had refused his request to remove certain Whig ladies of her household, appointed by the previous government; he said that he would not himself have taken part in any government without that mark of the Queen's confidence, since such ladies must be supposed to exercise political influence.
[3] William Fullarton Cumming, *Notes of a Wanderer, in search of health, through Italy, Egypt, Greece, Turkey, up the Danube, and down the Rhine*, 1839, had been favourably noticed in the *Monthly Review* for May 1839 (4th Series, II, 1–11).
[4] In the postscript to Jeanie Deans's letter to Reuben Butler: 'Excuse bad spelling and writing, as I have ane ill pen' (*Heart of Midlothian*, Ch. VII).

hear from you. I drank tea at Cheddar in the room in which we had so happy a breakfast the day before; and afterwards, when the rain ceased, strolled up the hill among the rocks, which, in the shade of the evening, looked very beautiful and grand. I moralised a little there, and then set off; but before I came home, both Felix and I were heartily tired, and I had a sad headache.

To EDITH BAGEHOT, 19 AUGUST 1839
MS: Mr Norman St John-Stevas

Bristol August 19 1839

My dear Mamma

I shall begin my first letter to you from the Bristol college by telling you that I like it quite as much as I expected and rather more. Mr. Bromby[1] is very kind but I have not very much as yet to do with him: for I do not say any lessons at all to him: nor I shant until I come into the seniors.—I have now to give you a little account of my studies &c &c. I shall begin from the time that I parted from Papa, just before the college bell rang, for I revolve at the sound of a bell as much as any Londoner at the sound of Bow Bell.[2] Well then Papa left me that instant before he was quite out of sight the bell ran[2] and I posted off with all convenient speed to do my Virgil, which was not very very hard work particularly as I had done it all before.—I have been in the midst of writing this interupted[2] by a request to go and play cricket, to which as I was very cold I acceded. I shall now proceed with my narration. After my Virgil I did my Ellis and the next morning my Kenrick.[3] Sunday I went to Lewinsmeed where Mr. Russel Carpenter[4] preached, his text was, 'Whatsoever is not of faith is sin.' And in the

---

[1] The Revd John Edward Bromby (1809–89), acting principal of the College, 1838–40, succeeding the first principal, Joseph Henry Jerrard; fellow of St John's College, Cambridge, 1834–6, BD, 1845, DD, 1850. He left Bristol College to become principal of Mortimer House, Clifton, and ended his career in Melbourne, where he was Master of the Grammar School and an Honorary Canon. WB boarded with Bromby in Park Row.
[2] Thus in MS.
[3] William Ellis's *A Collection of English Exercises. Translated from the writings of Cicero only, for school-boys to retranslate into Latin* (1782, often reprinted) and John Kenrick's *Introduction to Greek Prose Composition. From the German*, 1828.
[4] The Revd Russell Lant Carpenter (1816–92), Unitarian minister; fifth child and second

afternoon I went to church[5] were[2] the clergyman preached on the text give a reason of the hope which is in you, he gave a long definition of hope saying that it was the belief of Cristianity.[2]—I work two or three hours out of school as I told Papa I should and I read the lessons and one chapter [   ][6] Languages, which I generally w[ish f]in[ish]ed.[7] This morning I took down the [notes] of which Mr. Lang[8] gave out on the Greek Testament which same notes I shall have to say at the examination.

And now my dear Mamma by beging[9] you to excuse this stupid letter but I have written it in the midst of an incessant noise and I hope to write a better next time, and believe me that I remain your affectionate son.

W BAGEHOT

I really was very much surprised at Papa's illness as I did not see that he was at all unwell when he left Bristol. Excuse mistakes.

T. W. BAGEHOT to WB, [?22 AUGUST 1839]

Extract in RB, X, 86, where it is said to be 'ten days later' than his first letter to WB; probably the letter received by WB 23 August (see next)

I wish I could be with you, but as that cannot be, we must gladden each other's hearts by writing as often as we can, and telling each other, not only what is passing without, but within us, and keeping up a constant interchange of thought. Everything good is interesting to

---

son of the Revd Lant Carpenter (see letter of 7 December 1839, n. 9); educated at his father's school and then at Bristol College until 1833, when he became a theological student at Manchester College, York. After his father's health broke down in 1839, Russell returned from London (where he had been reading with Dr Hutton) to undertake the ministerial work of the Lewin's Mead congregation. He espoused the causes of anti-slavery and temperance—leaving his congregation at Bridgwater in 1849 when he discovered that the chapel's endowment came partly from public-houses (see Frances E. Cooke's 'Short Memoir', prefixed to R. L. Carpenter, *Personal and Social Christianity*, ed. J. Estlin Carpenter, 1893).
[5] For WB's attendance at Unitarian and Church of England services, see *Collected Works*, I, 32.
[6] Letter torn; about 6 letters lacking.
[7] Letter torn.
[8] The Revd Thomas Francis Layng (1808–74), head of the junior department, 1838–41; graduate of Sidney Sussex College, Cambridge, DD, 1845; previously headmaster of Chipping Camden Grammar School and later headmaster of Bristol Cathedral School and Hereford Cathedral School.
[9] Thus in MS; WB probably intended 'I end by begging'.

us, and we long for your letters as much as you could wish. . . . It must be Stummy's[1] province to give you a history of the important events that are constantly, as usual, occurring here—the Kite flying, the Gull crying, etc., etc.; but you may picture us to yourself, wandering about at Herd's Hill, still admiring its bright mornings and serene and beautiful moonlight nights, although having lost in you one of its greatest charms, we cannot feel the same lightheartedness we sometimes did when you were at home, and I hope to do again, when you return.

To T. W. BAGEHOT, 23 AUGUST 1839

MS: Mr Norman St John-Stevas

Bristol August 23 1839

My dear Papa

I shall begin this my second letter by thanking you for your most welcome one, which I expected two or three days before, though I had no right to at all, and you may believe I was overjoyed when as I was going out of college I met Mr. Bromby who told me that there was a letter for me at home, and when I came home I found and wept over it. I must too appollogise to you Aunt[1] and Stum for not mentioning you in my letter, but I wrote the latter part of it in the midst of an incessant noise and I am certain you all know me two[2] well to suspect me of any want of affection.

---

[1] The nickname of WB's foster-brother Watson.

* * *

[1] Emma Michell (1799?–1893), Thomas Watson Bagehot's youngest sister, widow of George Michell; after her husband's death she seems to have divided her time between the Bagehots at Herd's Hill, and the widowed J. B. Estlin and his daughter Mary. She died at her residence, 3 Upper Belgrave Road, Clifton, 11 January 1893 (*Bristol Mercury*, 13 January 1893).

AUGUST 1839

Today I have at school said some Xenophon 30 lines and yesterday 50 the reason of todays being less than yesterdays is that we did some in fractons,[2] I don't think here they make much account of Euclid or rather I should say don't do much of it, for we only do two or three Propositions on a Monday morning and most boys use here a certain Elringtons,[3] but I use a Simpson, which has all the signs $= < > \therefore \because$ &c &c.

Yesterday I was kept in an hour for talking, but do not you think it was rather severe, for I only spoke six words, but I suppose it was necessary as with thirty boys ('more or less') in a class order could not be preserved if there was any talking and there were several others in the same predicament, and one of them had two hours.

Tomorrow morning's work is not much, for we have only to write some Ellis, and prepare about 50 lines of Virgil which last is play seeing I have learnt it all before. I will try to get up early and finish the rest tomorrow morning before college. Sat. Mor. I could not my dear Papa finish it this morning as intended for I was too tired to get up. And I have not very much time now as I have college work which will take me the best part of two hours and this afternoon I have to go to Mrs. Prichard's.[4] Give most fond love to Mamma and Aunt and Stum. Part of my work is[2] afternoon is the Last Proposition of the 3rd. book and the 1st. of the 4th.

And now my dear Papa I must conclude by wishing that we may meet again in health and happiness. Meanwhile believe me that I remain

Your affectionate son

W Bagehot

I forgot to give this yesterday to the boy to be put into the post office. I am wondering whether I shall find a letter at Uncle Estlin's.

---

[2] Thus in MS.
[3] Thomas Elrington, Bishop of Leighlin and Ferns, *Euclid:s Elements* (1788, and frequently reprinted).
[4] Anna Maria (1790–1858), daughter of J. P. Estlin and sister of John Bishop Estlin and of Edith Bagehot's first husband; married Dr James Cowles Prichard in 1811. According to Mrs Barrington, WB spent most of his spare time at the houses of Dr Prichard and John Bishop Estlin (RB, X, 84).

SEPTEMBER 1839

To T. W. BAGEHOT, 9–14 SEPTEMBER 1839
MS: Mr Norman St John-Stevas

Bristol September 9 1839 Monday Evening

My dear Papa

I shall now begin my journal of my daily work; we are not allowed ever to learn any lessons in college and we cannot learn them perfectly if we would.

This (ie Monday) Morning as soon as came into the school, I said my Euclid 3 propositions, which took till half past ten, this done, we did some Geography and read our account or abridgement of the reign of Edward 3rd. Then at ½ past 11 we went out for our half hour during which on Monday we drill. Then we came in again for an hour during which we were with the writing master. We after that went out for our hour and ½ came in again at ½ past two, and did our Kenrick which is something the same sort of thing as my Greek exercise at Mr Quekett's used to be: only easier; and said some Greek Grammar, and construed some Greek Testament. This is all the work for today but toomorrows[1] work is to be prepared this evening.

Tuesday Evening. Today we in the morning till ½ past 11 did some Algebra; then we went out for our ½ hour and came in and did our Latin Exercise out of a book called Ellis, which is not difficult only long and we also did some Virgil for which we received Marks. I had as many as anyone. After the hour and ½ we came into College and did some German. Dr. Munck[2] says my pronunciation is *very* bad, asked me who had taught [me] and I was obliged to say I had learnt it at home of my mother; then Dr Munck said I had not been taught the pronunciation at all right; but you have as well as I can judge got a very foundation.[1]

Wednesday Evening. This days work has been entirely classical. For in the morning till ½ past 11 we did 2 pages of Xenophon; and after the usual interval of the half hour we did our Kenrick; and in the

---

[1] Thus in MS.
[2] Dr Frederick Muncke, of the University of Leipzig ('Prospectus', *Bristol Mercury*, 12 December 1840). Described by Edward Fry—who had lessons with him before entering the College—as 'a really clever man, but with a vile temper and inveterate proclivity towards lying' (Agnes Fry, *A Memoir of... Sir Edward Fry*, 1921, p. 22).

afternoon Virgil. I am at present the highest in marks by about 30.

Thursday Evening. Today my emploiments have been Xenophon 2 pages in the morning till ½ 11 and in the Half hour drilling; and between 12 and one, a very interesting lecture on chemistry, commonly called from the name of the Lecturer, Falder's Lecture.[3] This afternoon it has been German, Dr Münch has not scolded me any more about pronunciation, so I hope I was better.

Friday Evening. Today in the morning we did Xenophon till ½ past 11 and between 12 and 1 Kenrick's exercises and Grammar; In the afternoon Virgil, rather an easy day. Saturday afternoon. This morning we did our Ellis and Grammar and Scriptores Romani[4] which last are selections from all the best Latin authors, we are now doing some from Livy which I have done before so it is not at all difficult; and after that a Theological lecture; it consits[5] in the boys taking it by turns to read a portion of one of Secker's lecture on the catechism,[6] and after it has been concluded we are asked questions on it. The part of the lecture was the Lord's prayer.

Sunday Evening. I had intended putting this in the post when I went down to Dr. Prichard's[7] to dinner but a note came from Mr. Lean's[8] to say that they were going to Langport and would take a letter for me. Give my love to Mamma, Brother and Stum and believe me your affectionate son,

WALTER BAGEHOT

I am very much disappointed not to have a letter from home on Sunday and the volumes of Hume and Hooke.[9] Uncle Estlin surmises that they were sent by the coach which goes to Bath.

---

[3] Not identified.
[4] An Eton College textbook.
[5] Thus in MS.
[6] Archbishop Secker's *Lectures on the Church Catechism*, 1769.
[7] Dr James Cowles Prichard (1786–1848), physician and ethnologist; his best known work, *Researches into the Physical History of Mankind* (1836–47), was an expanded and revised version of his *Researches as to the Physical History of Man*, 1813; deeply interested in the treatment of insanity, on which he wrote the standard text-book, and appointed a Commissioner in Lunacy, 1845. On the Council of the College, where he lectured on the history of civilization.
[8] James Lean (1774–1849), banker, of Clifton Hill, Bristol; one of the partners in the Bristol branch of Stuckey's Bank from its opening in 1806, and one of the two managers until 1825. His wife Lucy (1777–1845) was the fourth daughter of Samuel Stuckey, and the sister of Julia, Vincent Stuckey's wife.
[9] Hume's *History* and Nathaniel Hooke's *The Roman History from the Building of Rome to the Ruin of the Commonwealth* (4 vols, 1738–71).

SEPTEMBER 1839

To T. W. BAGEHOT, 24 SEPTEMBER 1839

MS: Mr Norman St John-Stevas

Clifton Sep 24 1839

My dear Papa

As I have finished my work for this evening, I will sit down to have a little sweet communion with you. Mamma mentioned in her two last letters a strike for wages among the boatmen;[1] how did it arise; from your having wished to lower, or their having wished to heighten their wages. I should fancy it was rather a serious thing, since those boatmen are not very greatly gifted with the spirit of meekness, and they will be rather apt to vent their rage on those who are willing to work for the reduced wages. I hope in your promised letter you will give me a full account of the '*rebellion*' and its causes and effects.

We have again begun our months work; I was not quite well this morning with a headache and a listless feeling, but however I went to college (as I hate making a fuss about little complaints,) but I was (I fear) rather stupid and the whole morning, at the half hour I tried what a good game of play would do for me, and it made [me] much better, but I don't think I am yet quite the thing. Tonight Mr Bromby has gone out to dinner and Mrs. Bromby, and so the boys '*generally*' as Mr. Dickens would say[2] have not done much work, but I have done all I had to do, and I am writing to you beside notwithstanding the interruption of the rest, who have lately become very quiet. The work for tomorrow is Xenophon, Ellis' Grammar in the morning and German in the afternoon. The Xenophon is by far the most pleasant of the classics to me, since I always said I liked Greek better than Latin, but I demur about its being pleasanter than the German I should like the latter, much better if Dr Munch was not so cross, but I think at bottom he is a good hearted man; he has a great deal of the foreigner about him; and is not a perfect master of the English lan-

---

[1] The Bagehot family business, later the Somerset Trading Co., transported its goods up the Parrett by barge.
[2] Perhaps a reminiscence of 'Boys have generally excellent appetites', in *Oliver Twist* Ch. II. G. H. Sawtell recalled that at Christmas 1838, when floods kept the family indoors at Herd's Hill, Edith Bagehot administered 'alternate layers of the Greek Testament (with her own annotations) and *Oliver Twist*' (RB, X, 65); the novel had been published in November 1838.

guage, which however he speaks very well for a foreigner, I think he is a clever man and knows I believe a quantity of languages.

I had nearly for[gotten][3] to tell you about the Mathematics in which I am seventh, I cannot make out how I am to be so low, but I should think it was in Arithmetic, Vulgar Fractions etc, etc. I shall work harder at Mathematics this Month. At the college there is a boy of the name of Lawrence at the college who has a farm at Wick, did you not say the owner of those fine trees at Wick was of the name Lawrence.

Believe me my dearest Papa that I remain your affectionate son,

I am longing for a letter from you.

WALTER BAGEHOT

To T. W. BAGEHOT, 4 OCTOBER 1839

MS: Mr Norman St John-Stevas

Clifton Oct 4 1839

My dearest Papa

I am half ashamed of not writing to you before, particularly as yesterday was a holiday, but I have been very busy and yesterday I was at Mr. Estlin, and went to the institution,[1] where I spent several hours very pleasantly among the animals, minerals [she]lls[2] &c &c. In the evening of yesterday, I went to Ham Green where Mr. Bright[3] (the invalid of whom you have heard Uncle Estlin speak) lives, it is a very pretty place, woods sloping down to the Avon, which is in itself a pretty moving scene with vessels going up and down every ten minutes and the pretty splash of an oar, as a boat passed by, the calm effect of which is heightened by the stillness of the wood above; I thought of you and Mamma and wished you were with me to enjoy the scene.

The Great Western arrived last night I narrowly missed seeing her as King Road, the mouth of the river Avon, to which she goes, is to

[3] A tear in the paper has removed 6 letters.

* * *

[1] The Bristol Institution for the Advancement of Science, Literature, and the Arts, Park Street, established in 1823, to which was annexed a Philosophical and Literary Society; the institution had reading, lecture, and exhibition rooms, as well as a laboratory and museum. J. B. Estlin was a member of its Council, Dr J. C. Prichard a pro-Director, and W. B. Carpenter one of the Secretaries.
[2] Letters obliterated by sealing-wax.
[3] Richard Bright, merchant. Father of Robert (1795–1869), partner in the great mercantile house of Gibbs and Bright of Bristol, Liverpool and London.

be seen from Ham Green,[4] she has almost brought the news of her own arrival in America being here just at the same time as the ship that brought the intelligence. Two boys of the name of Phillips whom I mentioned in my letter as not having arrived, are now come and are very rum fellows, but good natured and rather Welchy withall. I heard a few days ago of dear Uncle Watson's death,[5] it will be a great trial [to] his daughters as well as to Aunty; as there will be a blank created in the object of their life which it will take some time, to fill up. Have Mary and Sarah fixed any future plan of life, I cannot at all imagine them without Uncle, as all their existence seemed wound up in his; I suppose Aunty will not yet come to Bristol, at least until Mary and Sarah's plans are settled.

As Michaelmas is approaching, don't you think it will be better for Stum to begin Greek, there will be two advantages, one that he will do some Greek which he would not do otherwise and he will do more arithmetic with you than with Mr Quekett and then he will be more under your own eye and if in the evenings you were to read aloud some history as you used to do, I think it [would][6] give him a taste for reading, which [is now][6] a *minus* sign, and will employ the winter evenings as he is getting too old now to go to bed at eight o'clock; don't you remember how fond he used to be of the history of Alexander. I hope you will not go down to the counting house after dinner this winter.

And now my dearest Papa I must wish you good as the bell is going to ring for us to begin work.

Believe me that I remain your affectionate son

W. BAGEHOT

To EDITH BAGEHOT, [8 OCTOBER 1839]

Extract in W. Irvine, *Walter Bagehot*, 1939, p. 34; dated 8 October 1839

I know not why you should want me to answer to the question

---

[4] Isambard Kingdon Brunel's steamship, *The Great Western*, launched from Bristol in 1838; on this her fourth voyage to New York and back, she arrived in Kingroad at 1 p.m. on 4 October, having left New York on 21 September.
[5] Jacob Watson died on 30 September; his estate was left in trust to his son, Thomas Nowel, and two daughters, Mary and Sarah Codrington Watson, with his son, T.W. Bagehot and Edward Bagehot as trustees. Since Jacob Watson was a widower the 'Aunty' referred to by WB must have been Emma Michell, who is said to be going from Bristol to Bridgwater in WB's letter of 7 December 1839.
[6] Letter torn, removing a few letters.

whether I wished to see you. I forbore answering it because I thought the thing spoke for itself. I do wish to see you or rather I long to see once more you and dearest, dearest Papa.

To T. W. BAGEHOT, 10 NOVEMBER 1839

MS: Mr Norman St John-Stevas

November 10 1839

My dear Papa,

I begun a letter in the beginning of the week, but I made it so dirty, that really I am ashamed to send it, therefore I will dash off one to go to night to the post office. Our examination finished yesterday afternoon, in the beginning of the week, I was very doubtful about keeping my place but towards the end of the examination I began to rise, and some papers which were given us on Friday and Thursday, and Saturday, have put me 130 ahead, it is [?in][1] a great measure to my monthly marks, in which I was the most by 69. In mathematics I hope I shall rise I got more marks than any one for Euclid, only two for full. We had a viva voce examination; it is managed in this way; First the master calls up the top of the class, and asks him if can do such a proposition, with the figure and enunciation given. If can do it he gets his marks, if not he returns to his place. Then the next boy is called up, and the same process is gone through; and so on to the bottom of the class; this examination the master asked every boy two propositions. Those who could say neither were requested to stay an hour daily, till they can say the part they were examined on; i.e. with good many all the while they are in the College at least in the junior Department. On Tuesday I shall know my mathematical place, and on Wednesday I will write and tell you the event.

I should have written to you last night, but as soon as ever I was about to begin, Mr. Bromby came in and asked us if we were ready with our Hebrew, we were all thunderstruck, for we had forgotten even that it was the proper day for it. We had a good lesson for about an hour; and learnt most of the proper pronunciation of the vowel points; I had pronounced it all wrong. And we have ever so much grammar to prepare for next lesson.

[1] 2 letters obliterated by sealing-wax.

Mamma will be very glad that we have gone on with it, as she was bemoaning herself that our lessons had been interrupted. I am very glad of it also as it gives some additional work on that evening. You know[2] doubt remember that Master Thatcher, who was locked up, for stealing, and telling mistakes &c &c; and that I said I feared no ammendment[2] would arise if he once came out; I am very sorry to say that it is even so, as I said; on Sunday he was let out and he behaved prettily well for the first two or three days; but he went on gradually getting worse and worse every day until yesterday evening when only 2 others were up, he took some turpentine (of all the things in the world) and put it into the fire: and when he was accused of it by the servant, he denied [he had][3] taken any, and said he knew nothing at [all about][3] it: but there was some gone, and a strong smell in the room, so in goes the servant to complain to Mr. Bromby that some one had taken the turpentine; when she got half way, Thatcher ran after her, and told her that he taken it, and nevertheless she told, and Thatcher got a stout licking, and returned to his old habitation. And now my dear Papa

I remain yours affectionately son[2]
W. Bagehot

Give my love to Stummy and Brother.

To T. W. BAGEHOT, 13 NOVEMBER 1839

ms: Mr Norman St John-Stevas

Clifton Nov 13 1839. Wednesday Evening

My dear Papa

I promised Mamma I would write to day, to tell you the event of the examination, which is that in Classics I am first again, and in Mathematics I am third and the boy above me, only beat me by one mark. I have risen in Mathematics chiefly by the Euclid, I certainly have risen much more than I expected; I am not quite so well satisfied with my Classics, I owe my place entirely to my monthly marks, I did very

---

[2] Thus in MS.
[3] A tear has removed words at the end of 2 lines.

badly at the examination, I only got the highest marks in one thing in the Kenrick or Greek exercises which are not usually my forte; there have been some changes in the class. Wait[1] has gained the second place and that Grace of whom I spoke has risen, and in the bottom of the class there have also been many changes. On the whole I think I must work harder this month, and a great deal harder at the examination.

If you see Aunt Emma will you tell her to make haste and write Cousin Mary about her coming here; we are angry with her for not writing; and as you have not written either, almost think that we are forgotten, but I suppose that you are so much engaged in your business, that you have no time to write even to me. I am afraid this will be but a short letter, as I have very much today though not so much as some times. The family at the Red Lodge[2] have been at Hereford, but were to have returned today.

Give my love to Stummy, Mamma and Brother, and believe me that I remain yours affly

W. Bagehot

Please to excuse this bad writing for it is written in a hurry.

Will you please to send the Edingburgh[3] review and the Arithmetics and the Monthly Reviews. Mr. Bromby takes a Review called Chambers Edingburgh Journal,[4] and he sends it in for the amusement of the boys. It is interesting and gives quantities of extracts from different works, and several stories which are entertaining, and it gives a great deal of instruction.

Only five weeks to the holidays, Hip Hip, Hussa, Hussa.

---

[1] William Killigrew Wait (1826–1902), son of William Killigrew Wait, Bristol merchant; one of the two lifelong friends WB made at Bristol College. Became a prominent citizen of Bristol and its Mayor in 1869; but in 1876 his gift of a new north door for the Cathedral involved him in controversy: the figures commissioned for the door were discovered to represent the four great Doctors of the Western Church, and after a public anti-Ritualist outcry were removed on the orders of the Dean and Chapter. Wait was Conservative MP for Gloucester 1873–1880, and contested the seat unsuccessfully in 1885 (*Western Daily Press*, 15 December 1902).
[2] Elizabethan house in Park Row, Bristol, the home of Dr James Cowles Prichard and his family 1827–45, and for some years thereafter of his son, Dr Augustin Prichard.
[3] Thus in MS.
[4] *Chambers's Edinburgh Journal* was the first of the cheap, popular weeklies to be founded in 1832, the year which also saw the beginning of the *Penny Magazine* and *Saturday Magazine*. Published by Robert and William Chambers at $1\frac{1}{2}d.$, it was a more literary miscellany than the *Penny Magazine*, and although it had not the same stupendous sales to start with, proved to have more staying power.

To T. W. BAGEHOT, 7 DECEMBER 1839

MS: Mr Norman St John-Stevas

Bristol December 7 1839

My dear Papa

I am most heartily ashamed of myself for not writing before but I have been very much engaged in working hard to get up Wait and other things, that I have been unable to do so. I begun a letter at the beginning of the week, but I had not time to finish it and it got so dirty I was obliged to write another with the same matter and lots more beside. First then one cause of my press of business was that there have been some very instructive geographical lectures here[1] which Uncle Estlin Mary[2] and the Prichards have attended and they wanted me to go so I went to one of them, and was very much pleased. He, i.e. the lecturer 'Mr. Smith' has several pictures of the most picturesque and sublime spots in the country which he is lecturing upon, which are painted most beautifully on glass slides and are put into a magic lantern of the greatest power and are reflected on the wall as any other pictures would be. But to increase their beauty he used the oxyhydrogen light as it is called. This composed as the name implies of oxygen and hydrogen mixed together and although each of the elements separately throws out a very insignificant light the two when combined throw out a most brilliant light. He places a white sheet which collected the shadow a moderate distance from the apparatus.

Another thing has been that a man was coming to teach some of Mr. Bromby's boys, short hand and pen making, and I thought you

---

[1] John Smith gave four lectures on 'The Beauties of Geographical Science, and the Wonders of Creation', at the Royal Gloucester Hotel, on 5, 6, 9 and 10 December 1839 (*Bristol Mercury*, 30 November 1839).

[2] Mary Anne Estlin (1820–1902), only child of John Bishop Estlin and his wife Margaret *née* Bagehot (see letter of 21 May 1838, n.1), and WB's cousin; in 1874 WB's wife recorded a visit from Mary Estlin, when she and WB 'told stories of their childhood' (Eliza Bagehot's Diary, 21 April 1874; MS Norman St John-Stevas). Her mother died while she was a baby, and Mary was brought up and educated by her father, whose constant companion she became, assisting him in his work for the anti-slavery cause. She did not marry, and after her father's death worked actively for the benefit of Bristol, where she watched over the Eye Dispensary founded by her father and helped to establish the Hospital for Women. In politics she was an advanced Liberal, and an advocate of the movement for women's suffrage. (Obituary in *Bristol Times and Mirror*, 15 November 1902.)

would have no objection to my learning. He teaches pen making in an hour and shorthand or common writing in six. I have not yet accomplished the desirable task of getting up to Wait, I got up to him once and by some very unlucky turns of fortune I fell again and am now about the same as when I last wrote rather worse for another boy is above me of the name of Bowman, I hope I shall not fall below him also; may God give me strength to say his will be done. I however shall certainly try with all might, to surmount all obstacles and to keep my place if possible. It is not a fortnight to the holidays and I think it is time to settle how I shall come home, a delightful thought. Aunty[3] and myself have been thinking that as she intends going to Bridgewater about the same time I may as well escort her down. My day will most likely be Thursday the 19, and if you my dearest Papa will make that your Bridgewater day, you could take me to our own sweet home. Dulce domum, &c. Do you think this would be a good plan. I do not as yet know what time I shall be able to get away on Thursday I hope in the morning; certainly I should think in the evening. This learning short hand has prevented me from going out, for two Saturdays I went therefore to the Red Lodge last night instead. I have also been at Mr Osler's[4] also this week, a good deal too gay I think, and as I am affraid you will think also. But when I tried to get off Mr Osler's for Thursday I was snapped for Wednesday, and if I had again refused I should have been engaged for another day. So I made a merit of necessity and went; the other boys the same evening the other boys went to a place called Ryan's Circus,[5] which is a kind of low theatre where I believe they act by dumb show; it is also the resort of juglers, mountebanks, &c. &c. A most unintellectual place. I am therefore very glad I went to Mr. Oslers, as the other boys

---

[3] Emma Michell; she often stayed with J. B. Estlin and Mary in Park Street, where she was recorded as a visitor on the day of the 1841 Census (PRO, London).
[4] Thomas Osler (1783–1861), of a family remotely connected with the Bagehots: Vivian H. King, *Some Notes Concerning the Osler Family*, 1914, records the marriage of Priscilla, daughter of William Osler (1676–1741), to the Revd Thomas Bagehot of Langport. In 1822 Thomas Osler married, as his second wife, Maria (1794–1866), daughter of Timothy Smith of Birmingham. He was a secretary of the Great Western Railway Co. in Bristol.
[5] Ryan's Amphitheatre, like Astley's in London, put on the hippodramas (performed on horseback) so popular in the 1830s. The December 1839 programme included an Italian juggler, but the great attraction was 'The Admiration of Europe and America, The Giant of the Wood—The Wondrous Billy—The Elephant!!!', during whose engagement there were no free admissions (advt in *Bristol Mercury*, 30 November 1839).

would most likely have made me go, as they all went. I should have looked most foolish; and acquired the sincere hatred of all the boys for my mugging if I had stayed and passed thereby a faint censure on their amuzement. It would have interfered also with my studies as I should not have had time to do any thing after 12 oclock at night (at which time they came home) and as it was I came home before ten and had all the time till they came for doing my work, reading, &c. &c. Some of the boys were rather glad of so good an excuse to escape their lessons the next day. I am writing in Parks Street where I went to give Aunty and cousin Mary their lesson in short hand for I teach to them all I am taught in that line. The short hand is rather difficult, but will when I have learnt it, will be a great save of time. I forgot to tell you about the geographical lecture that the subject[6] was Switzerland it was most beautiful as you may imagine the lofty Alps towering aloft. We [saw][7] the mer de Glace, which cousin Mary said was like; And we saw Mount St Blanc and saw the travellers ascending to the top, climbing along a place of nine inches in diameter and as slippery as possible with a precipice of unfathomable depth beneath. We saw too the magnificent works which Napoleon and his French army made in passing the rocks, tunnels through the solid rock—They are very busy at Park's street making dresses for a French play, Athalia[8] I believe, which the Carpenters[9] are going to act, and in which Mary is going to bear a part; nothing less than queen I believe. I should not think it much in her way, but I do not know. Aunt is very busy making the crown and things. There are to be some sham diamonds and lots of other finery. And now Papa I must conclude this long letter, which I am sure you deserve for your many letters.

I remain your affectionate son,

W. BAGEHOT

[6] MS reads 'the subject the subject'.
[7] MS reads 'say'.
[8] Presumably Racine's *Athalie*.
[9] The family of Dr Lant Carpenter (1780–1840), Unitarian minister of the Lewin's Mead congregation from 1817 until 1839, when he went abroad for his health and was drowned off Leghorn. He had a school in Bristol (where James Martineau was one of his pupils) until 1829, and advised on the setting up of the Bristol College, though his name did not appear, lest it alarm the High Church party (R. L. Carpenter, *Memoirs of the Life of the Rev. Lant Carpenter*, 1842, p. 357). Until 1836 he took a leading part in the political and scientific life of the city. Among the members of his family united under one roof at this date were his eldest child, Mary (1807–77), the famous philanthropist, and Dr William Benjamin Carpenter (1813–85), the eminent naturalist, later Registrar of the University of London.

Give my love to Mamma, Watson and brother, and tell the middle one that I will write to him soon. Please to excuse this scrawl. Aunty's kind love.

To T. W. BAGEHOT, 26 JANUARY 1840
MS: Mr Norman St John-Stevas

Bristol January 26 1840

My dear Papa

I had written another letter and intended to put into the post office yesterday in the way to college. But as I was going I remembered that I had something to add; so I carried it to college with me, and somehow it fell from my blotting book and was so dirty that I could not send it and so I am just scribling of[1] this as I thought you would be angry if you did not hear. I certainly shall be angry with you and Mamma for not writing to me.

The house of Commons I see by the paper has come to no conclusion in the case of Stockdale and Hansard;[2] I am decidedly in favor of the House of Commons. In the Bristol Mercury there is an very excellent article, it just turns the case, and suppose that Stockdale had brought an action against the court of Queen's bench, its clerk and even Lord Denman himself for something libellous contained in the extract's from its proceedings published by the authority of that court. Would

[1] Thus in MS.
[2] Between 1836 and 1839 John Joseph Stockdale had brought three actions for libel against Thomas Curson Hansard, as printer of a Parliamentary report in the course of which a book printed by Stockdale was referred to as obscene. The actions were heard by Lord Denman in the Court of the Queen's Bench, where in the second action Hansard defended himself on grounds of privilege, while in the third he was instructed by the Commons not to put in an appearance, and judgment was given against him in default. In his judgments Denman refused to accept the House's resolution of 1837 that the power to publish papers printed by order of the House was an essential incident to the constitutional functions of Parliament—i.e. a privilege—and that the House had the exclusive right to define its own privileges; he regarded the privileges of Parliament as part of the law of the land, of which he was bound to take judicial notice: the legal profession and a majority of the House of Lords took the same view. Stockdale v. Hansard was brought up at the beginning of the 1840 session, and Stockdale was committed to the custody of the sergeant-at-arms on 17 January, and the Sheriffs of Middlesex (who had collected the damages awarded by the Queen's Bench against Hansard) on 21 January. In April a Parliamentary Papers Act was passed, by which it was enacted that proceedings, criminal or civil, could not be taken against the publishers of papers printed by either House.

Lord Denman turn round and plead that the privelege[1] of publishing was esential[1] to the usefullness of the court of Queen's Bench. And if the privilege is essential to the usefullness of the court of Queen's Bench, a fortiori to the House of Commons.

In my other letter I gave you some of the sums, I had to do in my head on Friday, they were not very difficult but some of them were *immensely rum*. More rain, the water I should think would be soon in the meadows again; inside our gates at Mr. Bromby's it was 'over shoe' a long way, and it is running down the Park St. in a stream.

I must now conclude as it is time to go to chapel,

I remain yours affectionately

WALTER BAGEHOT

Excuse this horrid *uninteresting scroll*. Will you send my Mary Stuart by the first opportunity, and ask Mamma if my buttoned boots and my tooth powder were sent.

Love to Mamma, Watson and Brother.

To T. W. BAGEHOT, 3 FEBRUARY 1840

MS: Mr Norman St John-Stevas

February 3 1840

My dear Papa

As it is my birthday, I will dash off a letter, though I scarcely know how to spare the time. We are with Mr. Potter, the new master, he is horridly strict, his class say. I shall know more tomorrow I dare say. Mr. Bromby has given some Algebra sums to work out the book he uses is Hind's Introduction. There are sum[1] wacking hard sums in it such rum ones, there was one with some of the terms marked both with a plus and minus sign, the difference then consisted whether the minus was over the plus $\mp$ or the plus out of the minus $\pm$ it was a very hard one and amased[1] me when I first saw it. The was also one with $m+n$, $m-n$ &c &c for there[1] indices; most of them were very easy. There has just this very instant been an arrival, Thomas the Welch boy. You will *jaw* him I suppose for not being more regular in his coming back. We are all come back now the Phillips's arived on Saturday by the packet.

[1] Thus in MS.

I think I told you that Mr. Bromby told me publicly that you told him about my going to bed. The rule is certainly kept much more strictly this term than ever it was before. But whether this is to be attributed to the Usher or to your expostulation I cannot say; a little of both perhaps. I am forty two above Wait in Classics and am 23 the higher than any boy. I shall be very glad, when we have out the marks for our holiday work. I am rather disapointed that I have not heard today as it is my birthday. I must now go to work, I have lots of German to do to night.

I remain yours affectionately
WALTER BAGEHOT

Give my love to Mamma, Watson and brother
    Mrs. Prichard is gone to Ross
    Mary Estlin was ill on Saturday so she did not come home till to morrow.
    Frost is not to be hung Ministers could not very well with so many judges in their favor[2]

To T. W. BAGEHOT, 26 FEBRUARY 1840

MS: Mr Norman St John-Stevas

Clifton Bristol February 26, 1840

My dear Papa

I should have answered your letter before, but I have been very busy. By the by you were wrong in supposing that last week was our examination; It is this week; as it was thought to be a more exact division of the time before *darling* Easter. Mr. Potter is your favourite

---

[2] Added on outside of sheet, which is postmarked 4 February. John Frost of Newport and other leaders of an unsuccessful attempt at armed rebellion in Monmouthshire by local Chartists in November 1839 had been tried on a charge of high treason at a Special Commission in Monmouth, found guilty with a recommendation to mercy by the jury, and had sentence of death passed on them on 16 January 1840. Sentence was postponed pending the hearing in the Exchequer Chamber of a technical objection by defending counsel; the majority of the judges found that the witness list had been improperly delivered, although not to the extent of invalidating the trial, and their finding enabled Melbourne's government to commute the sentences to transportation for life, a decision announced on 4 February. There had been a great volume of petitioning against the sentences, and had they not been commuted, the Queen's wedding on 10 February might have taken place against a background of outbreaks of violence in great towns.

FEBRUARY 1840

I perceive, he gets you on much faster than Mr. Martin; we were amused in mathematics yesterday morning, I intended to have sent you the paper of our sums, but I lent it one of the fellows and he burnt it: However I will try to copy it from one of the fellows and send it you in my next. Will you tell me my mistake in the sum I sent you; I can easily correct it as I have the original paper safe.

I am second in mathematics; a boy of the name of Acraman is top. Wait is 5th and Grace 7th or 8th; Is not it immensely rum. The order in classics is not yet decided I am at present top in marks; Wait Grace and myself are going on very equally, 2 papers only have been given out in which Wait has lost 11 in relation to me and Grace and I are as we were. The usher has been discovered in a *horrid unnatural cram*. I think I told you that some of the boys are learning to fence: so the usher showed of and said he could fence splendidly; However the fellows who were learning to fence brought up the foils and mask and had a good game with him; and everybody declares they fenced as the *experienced* usher. Feb. 28, I am ashamed of myself for not having sent off this letter before, but I think now it is as well to keep it till to morrow when I shall know my marks and order. Grace is at present 10 above, and I am 30 above Wait. If I could but be top in classics, I should be at the head of the Junior Department in 3 things, viz German Classics and Theology and second in Mathematics; but I am afraid I am building castles in the air: to morrow will decide. I scold myself for being so anxious. Feb. 29. The order of our classical standing is out and I am once more at the head of the class, Grace is 2nd, by 10, Wait 3rd.

And now my dearest Papa I will send off this shameful scroll, I remain

Yours most affly.

W BAGEHOT

P.S. Love to Mamma Brother Watson and the rest. By the bye I received a penny and Saturday Magazine[1] from Mr. Phelp the bookseller, did you order them or is it a mistake. I do not like cut them open, till I know.

---

[1] The *Penny Magazine* was a weekly 8-page miscellany, with a strong emphasis on science, and illustrated by woodcuts, then a novelty in magazine publishing; it was launched in 1832 by Brougham's Society for the Diffusion of Useful Knowledge (founded 1826), and like the Society's *Library of Useful Knowledge* (begun in 1827) and *Penny*

MARCH 1840

To EDITH BAGEHOT, [7 MARCH 1840]

Extract in W. Irvine, *Walter Bagehot*, p. 16
DATE: Ash Wednesday fell on 6 March

We had a holiday yesterday to enable us to go to church on Ash Wednesday. I think Papa will storm at our having so many holidays.

To T. W. BAGEHOT, 17 MARCH 1840

MS: Mr Norman St John-Stevas

Clifton Bristol March 17th. 1840

My dear Papa

I would have written to you yesterday only had too much to do what with the German examination, which was this afternoon; I still retain my place at the top. The classics are at present a dead letter in the mark way for as colds are keeping away a great many of the class, Mr. Layng does not give marks, as those who are away would be under a disadvantage. In mathematics I have some sums to send you; 'A had first 18 shillings; and B, when he had paid to A $2\frac{3\frac{1}{7}}{1\frac{2}{9}}$ of £1-11-6, found that he had remaining $\frac{1}{43}$ of what A *then* had, what had B at first'. This is not a difficult one but it is a bother to find the value of $2\frac{3\frac{1}{7}}{1\frac{2}{9}}$ and it takes some time. I do not know yet how to do the sum about the livery, Mr. Potter was too busy to explain it to me today I was not there, when it was done. 'A man possesses $\frac{2}{5}$ of a coal mine and sells $\frac{3}{4}$ of his share for £2000: what is the whole mine worth.' Some thing of the same kind as the one about the widow. I have finished the first volume of the work on China, and I was much pleased with observing

---

Cyclopaedia (1832–44) was intended as an ally to the mechanics' institutions and other organizations for the education of the working classes. These publications, however, proved too difficult for their intended readership and circulated mainly among skilled craftsmen, clerks, and shopkeepers, who also made up the greater part of the membership of the mechanics' institutes by this date (see Thomas Kelly, *A History of Adult Education in Great Britain*, 2nd edn, 1970, pp. 165–67). Looking back on them in 1857, WB summed them up as inspired by the 'half unconscious' idea that 'all will be well when we have a cosmical ploughboy, and a mob that knows hydrostatics'. (*Works*, III, 192.) The *Saturday Magazine* was started by the S.P.C.K. in 1832 as a rival to the *Penny Magazine*, but handed over in 1837 to its publisher, who brought it to an end in 1844.

the conduct of our embassies Lord Macartney and Lord Amherst;[1] they would not perform the kotow or striking the head against the ground 7 times before the emperor of China; and would not take any nonsense from the under mandarins. Lord Macartney was better in this respect than Lord Amherst; when I first read it, I thought that performing the kotow was only as commading[2] themselves to the customs of the country, in which they were travelling; but if we had performed the kotow, it would have been published by the Chinese all over Asia, that the king of Britain had done homage and was the vassal of the emperor of China.

Friday Evening. I beg your pardon my dearest Papa, for not finishing this letter before, but I have been very busy, and I am not at all energetic; on Wednesday I was obliged to get leave to sit up; and I did not stay up till more than 1/2 past ten; and it made me so tired all the next day; and on Thursday I was so tired I went to bed before ten. About the embassies to China [I was] going to say; that the Dutch which was the [? second made] by any European power, hesitated not [? to perform] the kotow not only to the emperor of China him[self][3] but to the letters of his name inscribed in gold; and even to some half picked bones which the emperor of China sent them from his own table. And this embassy instead of being treated as our's was with great observance were hurried about from place to place in rough carts, and sometimes were unable to procure enough to eat. Do [you] not think this shows that we should not allow the Chinese to do just as they like and violate the law of nations by imprisoning our representative; though they were under great provocation from the opium trade,[4] the promoters of which were, certainly, I think very much to

[1] These two embassies represented unsuccessful attempts to open up the vast Chinese market to British trade, in place of the one-sided arrangement by which Britain paid in silver for Chinese goods. In 1793 Lord Macartney's embassy was received by Emperor Ch'ien Lung, but his successor expelled the 1816 mission under Lord Amherst. Such histories of China as Charles Gutzlaff's *A Sketch of Chinese History, Ancient and Modern* (2 vols, 1834), made a great deal of the English refusal to perform the nine prostrations of the kow-tow; the unidentified history read by WB was not Gutzlaff's, however, as he describes the embassies in his second volume (pp. 337, 358).

[2] Thus in MS.

[3] A triangular tear has removed words at the end of 3 lines.

[4] A reference to the arrest by the new Chinese Commissioner of Canton, on 22 March 1839, of Lancelot Dent, head of a large trading firm and president of the British Chamber of Commerce. This was the beginning of an unsuccessful attempt by the Chinese to put down the huge and growing imports of opium by British merchants, which was draining the Chinese economy and leading to widespread addiction; in June 1840 the British demand for compensation for opium destroyed in 1839 brought about the first Opium War and the Chinese loss of Hong Kong.

blame; but our resident was not answerable for for other European nations; nor for every ship of our own and as our government had never authorised it it could not be considered as our act. I must now leave off. Believe me that I remain

Yours affly
WALTER BAGEHOT

Love to brother and Watson

To T. W. BAGEHOT, [11 APRIL 1840]

MS: Mr Norman St John-Stevas
DATE: postmarked 11 April 1840, and with that date added to letter in another hand

Clifton

My dearest Papa

I intended to have sent my last letter to Mamma, a day before I did send it, but I carried it to college in my portfolio, and left it there; so as all the other boys who were going home at Easter had taken their places; I consulted Mr. Bromby and as he thought I had as well go on the Wednesday in the direct coach, and as I had inter nos no objection to an additional day with you; it was agreed that Mr. Bromby should take my place; which is done. I have several sums for you which I copied out of an arithmetic of Wait's, such rum ones. Last night I was before the conversation with Mr. Bromby concerning the places, rather low spirited for I had been *made* to play a game at prisoner's base. So I went up to comfort myself looked into Shelley which is my restorative; and met with some lines on political greatness with this beautiful conclusion 'What are numbers rent by force or custom, man who man would be, must rule the empire of himself, establishing his throne vanquished will, and quelling the anarchy of hopes and fears being himself alone.'[1] In five days I shall be home I hope. I am obliged

---

[1] Shelley's sonnet 'Political Greatness' (*Posthumous Poems*, 1824); WB gives a somewhat garbled version of the closing lines: 'What are numbers knit/By force or custom? Man who would be,/Must rule the empire of himself; in it/Must be supreme, establishing his throne/On vanquished will, quelling the anarchy/Of hopes and fears, being himself alone.'

APRIL 1840

to work hard as Grace is muging[2] immensely being put on his metal[2] by his late fall, Wait is taking it easy. I am very tired so you must please to excuse this short letter.

Believe me yours affly
W BAGEHOT

Kindest love to Mamma Watson and Brother

TO T. W. BAGEHOT, 6 MAY 1840

MS: Mr Norman St John-Stevas

Clifton May 6th. 1840

My dearest Papa

It is a little more than a week since we parted, I have been working moderately hard since I have not been draged out to play, but Thomas gave some corks for staying in which though hard I did not mind. But to day I got a good licking from the same gentleman for nothing at all but amusement, the pretext was that I did not choose to go down Lodge St. (a forbidden place) after Moline[1] to smite him on the ear; I say nothing about blows with foils, kicks &c &c since we came home. There is a new boy come who is a private pupil of Mr. Bromby's and does not go to the college; he is 15 and has only just begun Greek; his name is Honeywill and his father resides half the year in Bristol and half at Portshead. He is rather a boar as Oakes has in consequence of his arrival vacated his bed in George Bromby's room and is come to sleep in mine which is *not* an improvement certainly. And I am not quite so quiet at luncheon now as formerly. He is not a bit of a mug, and excites great commotions in the house by the rapidity of his motions. There was a sum Mr. Potter gave to do at home in Profit and Loss an old enemy of mine you will say. 'A grocer selling tea at 6s. 6d. per lb clears $\frac{1}{8}$ of the money, what will he gain per *cent* by selling at 7s. per lb.' No body could do it, I shall not tell you the answer, that you may have only the same chance as we had to do it. I shall now leave off for tonight as it is nearly prayertime.

[2] Thus in MS.

* * *

[1] Probably Frank Moline: see letter of 27 September 1840, n. 1.

Thursday Morning. Last night when I was going Thomas went in and blew out my candle and made me go down stairs to light; and I said he was a bully and gave a licking but I would not cry though. Do not you [think] this is rather stupid in Hind's common measures, he gives a rule but the two first sums are not done by the rule, but by splitting them into parentheses and, in consequence, I had to puzzle to do by the rule when they were not to be done—I have finished the 2nd volume of China; there is an interesting account of British intercourse with China, and there are many examples of boldness and firmness gaining important points with them. On one occasion when the Amherst went up to open a trade with Amoy and the eastern coast, when they met with the admiral of those seas his first question was, Where do you come from, When they answered from the powerful Kingdom of England, from the petty kingdom you mean. The English made a demonstration of turning him out of the cabin, he began to apologise and his companions said he was so stupid with eating opium that he was not answerable for what he said ! ! !

I must now conclude

Yours affly
W. BAGEHOT

Love to Mamma Brother and Watson. The jaw about brother and stones was before I went away

To T. W. BAGEHOT, [31 MAY 1840]

MS: Mr Norman St John-Stevas
DATE: postmarked 31 May 1840, a Sunday

Bristol Sunday Afternoon

My dearest Papa

Although it is Sunday when, I know, you think there many better things to be done, than writing letters, I must dissent from your opinion in the present case, as I can do nothing else, better as I think reading Paley's Horae Paulinae,[1] which I should otherwise do, inferior to the pleasure of writing to you. My last letter to Mamma was a very

---

[1] William Paley, *Horae Paulinae* (1790; of which new editions continued to appear up to 1887). In a prospectus of the College, Paley's *Evidences* and *Horae Paulinae* are named,

hasty one, as this must also have been, if I had not seized on this little bit of time which is likely to be almost the only one in the whole of this week, which I shall be able to call my own. I shall enclose in this a paper of the sums which we did at last examination, and which put me rather high, in mathematics. They were to be done without arithmetic, or book or paper of any sort. In the 18th. sum there was a mistake, which I have now corrected what must it be sold for *per ton*, every body omitted the per ton, but Mr. Potter vows he gave it out, so authorities differ; I am not a Potterite. There has been another sum given out since, it was this I think but the Paper is at Mr. Bromby's, 'If three men A, B, C, can do a piece of work in 12 days, A and B in 16 days, A and C in 18; what time will each do it in separately.' It is not do it by position.[2] I am obliged to work very hard in Classics. I must be up before six, if it be possible to finish my work; I find getting up early answer better than going to bed, and I think you like it better do not you. I as well as you have not been able to do very much in the Algebra way and I *too* feel the want of companionship; it is very hard in the common measures in Hind. Are you using the first volume of the work on China, for in third time[2] is a geographical survey of the empire; and the map is in the first volume. If you are not using it, and not likely to do so before the holidays would you send; but if you are would you send instead Smollet's[2] 1st. volume. Paley's Horae Paulinae is very interesting it consists, as you know, of instances of such coincidences between the acts of the apostle, and Paul's epistles as are manifestly undesigned, and therefore very unlikely to occur, if either the history was compiled from the history or the letters forged so as to agree with the history. For in both cases the coincidences would be exposed with the most careful accuracy, and not left to be scattered about in different parts of the epistles. [There is][3] a Dr Bevan [?][4] staying here, with a niec[e bot]h[3] 'rum coves' (Red Lodge dialect); they try my risible nerves immensely and even Mary find's hard work to keep countenance sometimes. I must now leave off.

Your affectionate son
W Bagehot

among books prescribed for 'those pupils who are not members of the Established Church', attending theological lectures (*Bristol Mercury*, 12 December 1840).
[2] Thus in MS.
[3] Stamp cut out, removing words in 2 lines.
[4] Unidentified.

JUNE 1840

Give my kindest love to Papa;[5] Watson and brother. I met Mr. Robert Bagehot[6] in Park's Street this morning

EDITH BAGEHOT to WB, 1 JUNE 1840
Extract in RB, X, 88.

Herd's Hill
1st June, 1840.

My dearest Walter,

... It is now fixed that I am to go to London on Thursday next. When I walked round the garden with dearest papa and Watson last evening which was a very beautiful one, and the birds were singing, I thought how often I should wish to be there! but still, with dearest Uncle Stuckey[1] and all the glories of the Parks, I trust I shall do very well.

EDITH BAGEHOT to WB, 5 JUNE 1840
Text from RB, X, 88–9

Sloane Street,
5th June, 1840.

Having just informed your dearest Papa of my safe arrival here, my dearest Walter, I thought I should like to tell you, and to beg you to write.

Uncle Stuckey looking well and cheerful, but calling himself 'very ill' and saying he must go out of town, so hopes I am not going to stay long.

---

[5] Thus in MS.
[6] This must have been Robert Bagehot (?1783–1861), merchant of Bridgwater; Thomas Watson Bagehot and Watson Bagehot were the executors of his will and trustees for his wife and two married daughters, Emma Bowden Trenchard and Louisa Norman.

* * *

[1] Edith Bagehot usually spent part of the London season at her brother Vincent's town house, 126 Sloane Street, which later housed the Catholic journal *The Tablet*: a modern block now occupies the site.

JUNE 1840

Eliza[1] was close to the Duke of Wellington the other evening at the concert of Ancient Music,[2] and alack! thought he was looking very old and shaky. He seemed very attentive to his daughter-in-law, the Marchioness of Douro, who is beautiful. I left husband in the midst of paint and bustle. He talks now of coming up next week (which all hope he will do) and choosing furniture, and then leaving me here to purchase it—and then perhaps I may come home by way of Bristol, and call for you. Just going into Town to buy a new bonnet! I hope you are longing for the holidays, to be with your dear Papa and ever fond mother,

EDITH BAGEHOT

Heaven bless you! I do not like being farther away!

To T. W. BAGEHOT, [18] JUNE 1840

MS: Mr Norman St John-Stevas
DATE: postmarked 18 June 1840

Clifton June 1840

My dearest Papa,

I am sitting to scrible of a letter to you, as I have not much to do tonight. This day last year you went up to see Mr. Bromby, and Mamma and myself were rather frightened, because you did not come home. It does not seem a year does it. I am in much the same state, as when I wrote my last stupid letter to Mamma for which I expect a jaw; the next time I hear from her. I suppose you are returned home again by this time; I shall be coming home I hope, on Saturday week; the public examination being on Friday;[1] O that that day was come and

---

[1] Eliza Stuckey (1808–97), younger daughter of Vincent; in 1844 she married the Revd James Stratton Coles (1810–72).

[2] These concerts were part of the London season from 1776 until 1848; established by a committee of noblemen and gentlemen, and for many years were attended regularly by the Royal family. The chief rules were that no music composed within the past 20 years should be played (at the beginning they were almost exclusively Handelian), and that the Directors in rotation should select the programme. The last of the 12 concerts of the 1840 season took place at the Hanover Square Rooms on 27 May.

* * *

[1] The examinations were held on Thursday and Friday, 25 and 26 June.

that I had got the four prizes I wish for; that is, the first prize in classics; 2nd. in mathematics; 1st. in German; and 1st. in Theology.[2] The most certain prize is the one for Theology but I am not sure of that. There are some subscriptions going round for Messrs. Bromby and Newman.[3] Mr. Newman I do not think has any claim on the Junior department as he has nothing to do with us, but I have subscribed 5s. to Mr. Bromby[4] which is immensely horrible for my pocket; I think I shall need an aditional supply.

I do not know much of my two books and a half of Euclid, but I hope I shall know something about it by Friday. I believe we are to have some German to spout at the public; I would not give much for the people's chance of understanding me, with my horrible pronunciation and lisping. But I suppose most of the company will not care for the understanding as long as it sounds well; and I am determined not to stammer for that would be horrid. You see I am getting up to the swing of the humbug.

In the Paley which yesterday was very interesting, there were some very clear and mathematical arguments to prove that the Epistle commonly called the epistle Ephesians was written to the Laodiceans. One of the leading arguments to prove it was not written to the Ephesians was that it did not resemble any of the epistles written to places which St. Paul had ever visited inasmuch as there are no allusions to any occurrence which happened during St. Paul's residence in that city; and St. Paul had previously resided more than 2 years in that country, it was but natural that he would make mention of some important occurrences which happened at Ephesus. It was fixed to Laodicea by the apostle's commanding the Colossians to read the epistle from Laodicea.

---

[2] WB won second prize in classics; a certificate in mathematics; the first prize in theology (Wait gaining the second); and third prize in German (*Bristol Mercury*, 11 July 1840).
[3] Francis William Newman (1805–97), brother of John Henry Newman; elected a Fellow of Balliol in 1826 after obtaining a double first, but resigned his fellowship in 1830 because his changed religious views would not allow him to sign the 39 Articles. In 1833 he returned from three years as a missionary in Persia, under the influence of Darby, founder of the Plymouth Brethren; excommunicated from the Brethren, he obtained temporary and, in 1837, permanent employment as Classical Tutor at the Bristol College, which he left in 1840 to take up an appointment as Professor of Classical Literature at Manchester. In 1846 he came to London as Professor of Latin at University College, where WB came to know him: see later letters.
[4] Bromby too was leaving the College; at the prizegiving the students presented him with a silver inkstand and Newman with a writing-desk (*Bristol Mercury*, 11 July 1840).

JUNE 1840

I had an invitation from Mr. Osler to accompany a large party to the railroad[5] this afternoon at three o'clock which I declined as I did not wish to lose marks in any way; and this afternoon there were no marks given so I might as well have gone. I must now leave off

Believe me your's affly

W BAGEHOT

Love to Watson and Brother. The former's holidays when.

To T. W. BAGEHOT, 23 AUGUST 1840

MS: Mr Norman St John-Stevas

Bristol August 23 1840

My dearest Papa

I have this instant received your kind and most welcome letter, with Mamma's clear account of the Landslip. I heard from her last night, and a picture of the Landsink as Uncle Stuckey calls it was in the letter. If it is as Mamma describes it, then the picture she sent me is certainly flattering. I do not see, how the Landslip can cease to be visible, though it may lose much of its beauty, without all the land around sinking. If this should happen we shall soon be overrun by the sea, which will be a *cold bath*. I should not of written, I think, to day, as it is Sunday, but that it is more than probable I shall not be able to write to morrow, as I shall begin the Algebra with Mr. Bromby[1] to morrow. He told me to wait till then, as I should see how much time I should be able to devote to Algebra, under the new regulations of the college. I intend to tell him that I think one day with another I shall be able to devote an hour a day to it. Do you think that will be enough,

---

[5] To see the preparations for the opening of the Great Western Railway from Bristol to Bath on 31 August; Thomas Osler was one of the Secretaries.

* * *

[1] Now principal of Mortimer House, Clifton; WB was evidently having private coaching in mathematics from him.

AUGUST 1840

as college work takes me a little more than two hours. I told you if you remember, that Mr. Bromby held forth to the school in our room; but I find that Oakes my informant mistook my question; they say their lessons in the dining room; but the two hours of preparation in the evening are in our room. I do not the least know what I told you about college in the scrap of a note I wrote to Mamma yesterday, which was written at breakfast time, in an incessant noise. I like the new system of judgements better than the old marks, the lowest marks count the best. If you do not make any mistakes in construing your lessons you receive 5 marks; and if you answer quantities of questions beside you will receive one, which is the very best. And if you make such a number of mistakes as to make it evident that you have not prepared the lesson you have [o].[2] I believe I am to do some simple equations out of Bland with Mr Bromby. I am very [glad] Hind and the common measures are done away with.

When I was reading Smollet the other day, I met with a very curious instance of the dislike political men bear to 'the dreary realms of opposition' and how much consistency one party are willing to sacrifice, if they can but embarrass their opponents. When the Whigs were in office, Queen Anne wished them to use their whole influence to pass the bill for the union of Scotland and England through the English parliament. And the Tories unsuccessfully opposed it; And year after year they went on battling, the Tories constantly bringing forward the bill for the repeal of the union. At last Queen Anne quarrelled with her Whig ministers, and the Tories came into power. But Queen Anne made their no longer contending for the repeal of the union an express condition of their taking office. On the meeting of Parliament the Whigs brought forward a motion for the repeal of that union which they had so long supported; and the union was upheld by the influence of the Tories who had so long opposed it. I cannot be sorry that you miss me, and I do not know that I shall try. Write to me again very soon and Believe me your ever affectionate son,

WALTER BAGEHOT

Give my kindest regards to Mamma and Watson and Brother. And uncle and Aunt Stuckey

---

[2] There is a '2' before the 'o'—but it seems to be deleted.

T. W. BAGEHOT to WB, [? AUGUST 1840]

Extract in RB, X, 87–8
DATE: replying to WB's letter of 23 August 1840

I was interested in the account you gave me of what you had read in Smollett. It is sad, indeed, to see to what extent party feeling carries both able, and in the main, honest men; and there is nothing which we have to learn more difficult, and that requires more untiring watchfulness and firmer principle, than the method of preserving the mind from improper influences. A strong love of truth and the seeking it for its own sake, must be the ground on which all our endeavours must rest; but there are too many enemies ready to displace us, so that we must be ever on our guard, and ready to defend ourselves. A love of ease, and an unwillingness to examine into the foundation of things long settled, as far as we are concerned—a fondness for our own opinion, and a dislike of allowing that we were, or are mistaken—are some among the numerous enemies to be resisted, beside the heavy and weighty troops of pounds, shillings and pence, and patronage and power.

To T. W. BAGEHOT, 10 SEPTEMBER 1840

MS: Mr Norman St John-Stevas

Clifton September 10, 1840

My dear Papa,

I have been going to write to you all this week, but I have not been able to find time. We have to mug so hard now four or 5 odes of Horace, and 50 lines of Homer. At Mr. Bromby's school the class who are doing Homer [have] to do at the most 2 or 3 odes at a time. And that all the classical work. And they have not so much mathematical work either as we have, for we do one day four or five propositions of Euclid and another a long paper of Trigonometrical and Algebraical questions. We have not begun Conic Sections yet; I hope we shall not till I get a pretty good foundation in the lower branches of Trigonometry. By the bye you have not sent me Walkinghame's Arithmetic, would you send me the third volume of Smollet's History of England, as I have finished the second.

We have got to do, or rather may do if we please an essay on the probable effects of steam on the future destinies of mankind, and a poem on Circassia, and send them to the principal with a fictitious name. I have not yet settled in my own mind whether I shall do them, I think I shall attempt the essay, but I am not quite clear what to put on Circassia. I should rather like to have some work about it's history, &c &c

The Hebrew is to take an hour out of German and French. Dr. Monke the German master objected strongly, but as there is no other time and I am sure I should learn much in that hour, as Dr. Moncke is occupied with the other class and he would set us to look over what we had to prepare at home. Ever so many of the boys and the usher are talking, about the comparative merits of Yorkshire, and Ireland.

Believe me your affectionate son

W BAGEHOT.

Give my love Mamma and Watson and Brother

To T. W. BAGEHOT, 27 SEPTEMBER 1840

MS: Mr Norman St John-Stevas

September 27, 1840

My dearest Papa

I fully intended you should have heard from me, before this, and indeed I wrote a letter intending to put it into the post office yesterday; but some how or other it has dropped from my blotting case; so I must write a line to day, although it is Sunday. I do not think I have ever been so much occupied, since I have been at the College, as I have during this last week; however I was yesterday fully repaid for all my trouble; for when our judgements for the week were added up I was first by 32, a very large majority for this term. This is the third week I have been first if I can keep my place for one more I shall have the medal.—

We have already this term gone through one book of the odes of Horace: pretty good work for one month I think, and nearly as much as we did in Virgil during the whole of last term. Herodotus is the subject, which causes me the most labor. The part we are doing is not very interesting, being a description of Egypt, and fanciful conjectures concerning the Nile's overflowing in summer; the true theory of which the melting of the snow on the mountains Abysinnia, Herodotus rejects, and adopts a most fanciful one of his own, which gave a deal of trouble, to make out.

With Mr. Bromby I am going to do Trigonometry and Equations alternately. The Equations although Problems and hard enough to make out did not *alone* Mr. Bromby thought give me sufficient practice, in working correctly. Mr. B. gave me the other day a prise for not having any impositions last term, which he had forgotten to give me last term; The Book is Bacon's essays. The mathematics at the college are not in the first class reduced to much order; and for some time it will be rather difficult to adjust the places, but I and F. Moline[1] shall not be far from the bottom. Thomas is the boy who goes from Mr. Bromby's to the college, and is most probably not coming back after Christmas either to Mr. B's or to the college, certainly not to the latter.

I must now conclude.

Believe me your affectionate son
W BAGEHOT

Give my love to Mamma &c &c

To EDITH BAGEHOT, [FEBRUARY 1841]

Extract in RB, X, 89, dated February 1841

I beg leave to remind you that next month I am coming home. And that next month is nearly come. I do long to be with you all again; and I picture you all to myself, as I am sitting in the long evening all alone: Watty doing his sums, and Papa endeavouring in vain to instil into him some small glimmering of what he is about, and 'somebody' (query who!) asleep sound as possible in the armchair, although my

---

[1] This must be Frank, son of Robert Moline and his wife Mary, sister of James Cowles Prichard; the Molines had six sons and six daughters, of whom Frank was the eighth child and fourth son (*Memorials of the Prichards of Almeley and their Descendants* compiled by Isabel Southall, 2nd edn, privately printed, Birmingham, 1901, pp. 36–7).

heart smites me to talk of sleeping, since I fell asleep in the most curious way last night over my books, and slept ever so long, and I had not done anything particular in the day time either. I only succeeded at last in waking myself up by reading some of Rogers' 'Pleasures of Memory';[1] and here is a beautiful simile I have hopped on; something to say poetry, though no disrespect either to your poeticulisings[2] or mine. Speaking of memory he says:

What softened views thy magic glance reveals!
When o'er the landscape Time's meek twilight steals!
As when in ocean sinks the orb of day
Long o'er the wave reflected lustres play;
Thy tempered gleams of happiness resigned,
Glance o'er the darkened mirror of the mind.

To T. W. BAGEHOT, [7] MARCH 1841

MS: Mr Norman St John-Stevas
DATE: postmarked 7 March 1841

Bristol March 1841

My dearest Papa

I am going to answer your two most welcome letters by return of post; business like !!!! This week the college has been rather irregular in consequence of Mr. Booth's[1] having been in bed the whole week, with a bad cold cough &c &c. We have done no mathematics this

---

[1] *The Pleasures of Memory*, 1792, made the banker-poet, Samuel Rogers (1763–1855) famous; the simile WB admired comes from Part I (11. 91–6), and his quotation contains the error 'glance' for 'glass' in the first line.

[2] It was in 1841 that Edith Bagehot published *An Echo*, said on the title-page to be 'for the commencement of a subscription to build a new church, where some of the fold who are now as sheep having no shepherd may thus "Receive the cup of Salvation, and call upon the name of the Lord"'; her introductory note, dated 'Herd's Hill, 1841', explained that the verses, taken from a collection of texts, were in aid of a church to be built 'at Westport, in Somersetshire, whither a poor population have lately gone in consequence of a change in the Parret Navigation'.

* * *

[1] The Revd James Booth (1806–78), of Lava, Co. Leitrim, educated Trinity College Dublin, had replaced Bromby as principal of the College; after its closure he became

MARCH 1841

week at all at the college I am sorry to say, there being no one to take our class, and supply Mr. Booth's place. We have said all our classics to Mr. Swayne,[2] and have done a good deal as we were occupied with them during their usual time and that generally given to Mathematics. His illness has also prevented Mr. Booth, from looking over the examination papers, and I expect as there has been so much delay that the places will never be settled. I do not care much about it.

I have given Mr. Booth my life of Sir Isaac Newton and I do not think he seems enraptured with it, at least he does [not][3] express enthusiastic admiration. I have the life of Galileo to write next; so that I shall have to read the life of Galileo. Which will be an interruption to Potter's Grecian antiquities[4] which is the essence of dryness double distilled. An abridgement of it would be better than the work itself for me at least I should think as there are numerous quotations from the classics and learned disquisitions about minutiae which however interesting they may be to an advanced scholar are comparatively dry and useless to me.

Have you noticed how much the Penny Magazine has improved in this new series. The engravings are excellent; there is an admirable one in the last number from Gainsborough's market cart.[5] There have been some very interesting articles in the last two Saturday Magazines about Canova,[6] the famous Italian sculptor, who was the first to improve the taste of the Italians, and to copy nature and the works of

---

Vice-Principal of Liverpool Collegiate Institution, and was later a lecturer in London for the Society of Arts; FRS, 1846; Vicar of Stone, Bucks, from 1859 until his death. Edward Fry, who entered the College in 1841, describes Booth as 'a most Irish Irishman, a good mathematician, with a considerable knowledge too of classics and philosophy', and an 'inspiring teacher', recalling with delight a history lesson that turned into a discussion of Berkeley's philosophy, when 'the Doctor allowed the whole class to open upon him like a pack of hounds, in support of the existence of matter, and we continued the fight until the school hour was over'; nevertheless Fry attributed the closure in part to Booth's being 'a bad organizer' (Agnes Fry, *A Memoir of... Sir Edward Fry*, pp. 24–5).

[2] George Carless Swayne (1818–92), of a Bristol family, educated at Bristol College and Corpus Christi College, Oxford, of which he was a fellow, 1846–51; returned to the College as Professor of Greek and Roman Literature, 1840; publications included *Prometheus Chained*, in English verse, 1846, and the volume on Herodotus in Blackwood's Ancient Classics for English Readers, 1870.

[3] Supplied in red ink, in another hand.

[4] The 1837 edition (edited by J. Boyd) of John Potter, Archbishop of Canterbury, *Archaeologiae Graecae: or, the Antiquities of Greece*, 1699.

[5] Illustrating the article, 'Gratuitous Exhibitions of Pictures. The National Gallery', in the issue of 20 February 1841 (X, 68).

[6] A series of three articles on 'Canova and His Works', 16 January, 6 February and 20 February 1841 (XVIII, 18–19, 50–1, 60–1).

the Greeks; which were in his time much in vogue. He was also an example of genius surmounting the obstacles poverty and want of education, and rising to the head of his profession. When I go to the post office with this I think I shall run and take a look at the outside of the Great Western. If I had known it yesterday I might have gone over her. I wish I had for I have a great curiosity to see her, as she is one of the most noble productions of art in the present day.

Please to inform Watson that Mamma was looking over his shoulder when he was writing to me *of course he did not know it*!

Love to all Your affectionate son

W BAGEHOT

The musical box is still unfinished I believe.

To T. W. BAGEHOT, 27 APRIL 1841

MS: Mr Norman St John-Stevas

Bristol April 27, 1841

My dearest Papa

I will dash off a line or two to express the feelings of horror which your having gone to the counting house yesterday has excited here. I do not think I shall lose much by staying away that twa' days, as the class had not done much in any branch of their work. Our work consists in Latin of Horace's Satires and Tacitus, and in Greek of Aristophanes and Plato. The Aristophanes is excellent fun, but the Plato is horrid dry.

There have been some alterations in the work some of which are very bad and some good, like all other alterations. One is that the Thursday Evening which used to be allotted to English Composition is now given to Latin Composition as Mr. Booth found we were defficient in that at the last examination before Easter.

I do not think Alfred Estlin's[1] eyes much improved by the last

---

[1] Possibly Alfred Laird Estlin (1826–93), later a solicitor of Somerton, Somerset; he and Joseph Barnes Bagehot were granted probate of Emma Michell's will.

operation, but he is going to have another which is to do wonders. You must consider the last sentence a parenthesis, as I was going to tell you that the last alteration I alluded to was the omission of Locke and the substitution of Greek history and ancient Geography in its place. Please to write as soon as possible and with love to all (horrid formal)

Believe me your affectionate son

W BAGEHOT

T. W. BAGEHOT to WB, 8 MAY 1841
Extract in RB, X, 89–90

8th May, 1841.

Sir Robert Peel's name reminds me of the political (and more especially as connected with politics) the commercial and financial crisis to which we have arrived. Lord John Russell gave notice a week since that the Government had come to a united determination to recommend a revision of our commercial code, with a view of adopting a course free from prohibitary duties in order that our revenue (which now not equal to our expenditure) may be increased, by the increased consumption of taxed articles, to be rendered cheap by the plans proposed, and that commerce and manufactures being freed from monopolies may revive and extend—and the Corn Laws, Sugar Duties, and Timber Duties, the three great hindrances to a liberal course, are to be immediately brought under discussion. Indeed the sugar duties were to be the subject of debate last night.[1] I expect the ministry will

---

[1] On 30 April the Chancellor's budget statement was prefaced by Russell's giving notice that at the end of May he would move for a committee of the whole House to consider the Corn Laws; the Chancellor stated that the Whig government proposed to meet the fourth budget deficit in a row by reducing the duty on foreign sugar and timber and slightly increasing that on colonial sugar and timber, a proposal welcomed by Radicals and Free-traders (like WB's father), although likely to be opposed by some of the government's supporters. On 7 May when the House went into committee on the budget the Conservatives chose to oppose the change in the sugar duties, in which they would have the support of West Indian sugar interests and of the anti-slavery lobby, since the change in duty would let in more foreign slave-grown sugar; at the conclusion of the debate on 18 May there was a majority of 36 against the government.

be defeated by the all-powerful interests who are opposed to them, and they will no doubt dissolve Parliament on the question[2] that the consumers who are to be benefited, may give them support enough if they can. I fear they may, and will be unable to carry, even after an election, their enlightened views, but I rejoice that the time is come for beginning an agitation on this, the most important subject of the time, and as we have the many on our side, and the truth, as I firmly believe also, I will not fear that with time we shall want success.

To T. W. BAGEHOT, [?12] MAY 1841

MS: Mr Norman St John-Stevas
DATE: originally dated 'May 19th. 1841' by WB, but another hand has written '2' over the '9' of '19th'

Bristol May 12th. 1841

My dearest Papa

I have but a moment to spare, but I must dash of a line or two as it is nearly a week since I last wrote. You will be glad I know to hear that English Composition has come into being, and that we are to do that on Thursday Afternoons alternately with Latin and Greek Composition. I have had rather a sell in the history as Mr. Booth has changed Charles the 5th. into the history of England down to the restoration. This isn't near so good. Alfred Estlin's eyes are much improved by the last operation and one scarcely sees anything peculiar in his eyes. I am very sorry to be obliged to leave off, but I recollect I have lots of German to do and it is past six, moreover I have to run to the post-office with this.

Believe me ever your affectionate son.

W BAGEHOT

Love to all

---

[2] The Government neither dissolved nor resigned, hoping to go to the country on the Corn Law issue: Russell had announced on 7 May that they would propose a fixed duty in place of the sliding scale in force since 1828. In the event they were unable to bring forward their corn proposals, but were defeated on a vote of no confidence, 4 June; this was followed by dissolution and their loss of the general election.

To T. W. BAGEHOT, 16 MAY 1841

ms: Mr Norman St John-Stevas

Bristol May 16 1841

My dearest Papa,

I have just received your long and most interesting letter, and hasten to answer it. The interest on the important question now before the house of Commons has even reached us boys, who are certainly no politicans generally. Mr. Booth stoutly defends the existing corn laws, and of course opposes the ministry most virulently. Somerton, Smith, and myself have had some discussions with him, and though of course he had the best of the argument, he having studied the question which we had not, we were by no means convinced.

There is too at the college a boy, or rather youth for he is 19, of the name of Pile the son of West India planter, who feels very strongly against the sugar bill very reasonably I think as it will materially lessen his father's property, which is extensive. It has become quite a joke against Pile to uphold the sugar bill, as he gets very angry or in college phrase '*brittle*'. He has enough of the planter in him too not to give the abolition of slavery unqualified aprobation; though he owns it to be a desirable measure; he says 'Generally it has not worked well; it has increased beggary in a great degree; &c &c, and always winds up with saying that the twenty millions we paid[1] was by no means an equivalent to the planters for slave labor.' I got into the water yesterday for the first time, and like a goose as I was, I bundled in with my flannel waistcoat on for which I got soundly laughed at as was of course to be expected. I must now leave off as I have to write to Mamma.

Believe me your affectionate son

W Bagehot.

Love to all

---

[1] The abolition of slavery in the West Indies was carried by Earl Grey's ministry in 1833, with 20 millions voted as compensation to the planters; the transitional apprenticeship system was ended two years early in 1838.

MAY 1841

EDITH BAGEHOT to WB, 20 MAY 1841
Extract in RB, X, 92

Sloane Street,
20th May, 1841.

Well! my Beloved, I went to the ancient concert[1] and had a most delightful evening in sight and sound. We were close to the Directors' box and the only disappointment I had was (for the Queen, we knew, was not to be there) that we were behind the Duke of Wellington, and that he never turned round, and alas! looks quite, quite old and tottery—and decrepit. I still hope the mind beams on, but the body is certainly going the way of all flesh. I wanted to see his front face and the expression of his eye, but that I could not do. In the box were the Duke of Cambridge, his daughter the Princess Augusta—not handsome even now in her bloom, the beautiful Lady Wilton, Lord and Lady Burghesh, Lord Howe and his sister Lady Susa, Lady Augusta Somerset and some other ladies that we did not know. Lord Ellenborough[2] and various other stars glittering about—and latish in the evening there was a little bustle, and in came the star of stars with his suite, Prince Albert,[3] who is very, very handsome, and talked and chatted with all around in a very affable manner.

---

[1] On 19 May, under the direction of the Duke of Cambridge.
[2] Adolphus Frederick, Duke of Cambridge (1774–1850); his daughter Augusta Caroline (b. 1822), who married the Grand Duke of Mecklenburg Strelitz in 1843; Mary Margaret (d. 1858), wife of Thomas Grosvenor, 2nd Earl of Wilton and daughter of Edward Stanley, 12th Earl of Derby; John Fane (1784–1859), who had the courtesy title of Lord Burghersh until he succeeded his father as 11th Earl of Westmorland in December 1841 and his wife Priscilla Anne (d. 1870), daughter of William Wellesley Pole, 4th Earl of Mornington; Richard William Penn, 1st Earl Howe (1796–1870); Lord Howe's only sister had died in 1820, and 'Lady Susa' cannot be identified; Augusta Rose Blanche Somerset (d. 1913), 6th daughter of the 5th Duke of Beaufort; Edward, 1st Earl of Ellenborough (1799–1890), Governor-General of India, 1841–4.
[3] Prince Albert had married Queen Victoria in February 1840; he was one of the Directors of the Ancient Concerts.

MAY 1841

T. W. BAGEHOT to WB, 22 MAY 1841
Extract in RB, X, 91

22nd May, 1841.

I daresay the excitement of the political world, although it had reached the college, does not interfere with or disturb you much; perhaps to be out of the way of a daily newspaper is no bad thing just now for those who have occupations which require their best attention.

The Ministers, you no doubt know, were beaten on the Sugar Duties by thirty-six, and have given notice that they now mean to take a Debate and Division on the Corn Laws, before they appeal to the Country.

The election will probably be a very exciting one in large towns, especially in the manufacturing districts, and altogether the crisis is a serious one. I am not sorry that it is come, for without this, and perhaps others still more serious, the House of Commons, and above all the House of Lords will not willingly vote a reduction of rents. I do not know what may be the turn which things may take in Bristol, but be careful, my dear, to have nothing to do with it, beyond the quiet expression of your feelings and opinions. Partisanship should be carefully avoided by all who have not had time or experience for forming a sound judgment, for, if otherwise, we are often bound by class to opinions which, if fairly examined, would be acknowledged to be full of prejudice; but which cannot be so tested for fear of disrepute in deserting your party. What makes Mr. Booth a Corn-Law advocate? I hope he has an old rich Uncle with many fine acres, all of which are to be his!

To T. W. BAGEHOT, 22 JUNE [1841]
MS: Mr Norman St John-Stevas
DATE: '1840' is WB's error: letter postmarked 23 June 1841

Bristol. June 22, 1840

My dearest Papa

The hard work of this term is over; the public examination commences tomorrow, and continues to 2 o'clock on Thursday; whereby, in law language, I shall be able to return home by the train, which starts on Thursday, at 10 minutes past four and purports to reach Bridgwater about ½ five. I have got first in Hebrew, but I do not know whether one person will be allowed to carry off more than one prize, or not, however I think they will. I hope I shall be able to prize a good prize for mathematics, as I shall have the third choice—

Tomorrow, I think, I shall get two pounds, from Aunty, as then I shall be able to pay for my boots without bothering with a bill.

All the business part of this letter having been transacted, I think, I may as well shut up shop—

Believe me ever your affectionate son
W Bagehot

Love to all

To T. W. BAGEHOT, 22 AUGUST 1841
ms: Mr Norman St John-Stevas

Bristol August 22nd. 1841

My dearest Papa,

I intended writing to you during the week, but the time has glided on, and I must again steal an hour from Sunday for that purpose.—I am now fully occupied, in all my different college pursuits. I have to contend in classics and mathematics, against those who only learn one of them, which is very difficult. My chief competitor in classics is Perrin whom you will remember to have roundly beaten me in the Junior department; he will again I fear—In mathematics Carrow whom I think I mentioned to you as likely to be my chief competitor has taken only to learn mathematics—French has as yet been a minus sign—Monsieur Dufoure the French professor has not yet made his appearance at college, I suppose from illness—And I have not begun at home, as beginning at the same time will be an advantage—Dufoure is however expected on Monday, and I will let you know the course pursued 'at home and abroad' as soon as I can—Today I have been looking at a very interesting work which Mary¹ has had given her. It is 'The history of Palestine'² the volume of which contains an account of the history of the Jews, with their customs laws &c interspersed with accounts of the nations with whom they came into contact. It is written by the Editor of the Pictorial bible,³ who has been an extensive traveller in the East, and has perfect familiarity with mental customs, habits and modes of thinking—This knowledge is of utmost importance and indeed almost an essential requisite for one, who attempts to illustrate the Sacred narrative.

In Classics at the college, we are reading at the college on[e] of the most beautiful relics of the Greek tragedians, viz the Medea of Euripides—The lyric odes which form the Chorus of the piece are very beautiful and moreover understandible⁴ which is not a very usual thing in the ancient tragic writers some parts of whom the most learned are obliged to give up in despair—The heroine of the play is Medea who has been deserted by her husband Jason, after having saved him in the former part of their lives from many dangers she revenges herself on Jason by poisoning first her children, then him and his second wife—a most horrible story but one admirably calculated for the pathetic.

Edith Prichard⁵ is still very ill; my account last week of her was too favorable, as when I saw Mrs Prichard a day or too ago she gave me a woeful account of her; today I believe she is a little better.

With love to all

Believe me always
Your affectionate son
W BAGEHOT

---

¹ Estlin.
² *The Pictorial History of Palestine*, published by Charles Knight in monthly parts, at 2s. 6d. each, June 1839–August 1840, and in 2 vols, 1840.
³ Dr John Kitto (1804–54); the *Pictorial Bible* was published 1835–8, and the *History of Palestine* was intended as a companion and supplement.
⁴ Thus in MS.
⁵ Edith Prichard (*b.* 1829), youngest daughter of James Cowles Prichard; married in 1852 the Revd Nicholas Pocock (1814–97), historian of the Reformation (*Memorials of the Prichards of Almeley and their Descendants*, p. 37).

SEPTEMBER 1841

To T. W. BAGEHOT, 29 AUGUST 1841
MS: Mr Norman St John-Stevas

Bristol August 29 1841

My dearest Papa

I promised to write to you as soon as I knew anything about the French. There have been changes going on which have given rise to great speculation among us boys. Monsieur Dufour has resigned his situation as French professor, from some causes unknown; it is reported that he was obliged to evaporate on account of debt, which received some countenance from the fact of the utter rascality of the Frenchmen who come over here—Some also say he has something better, but this is very uncertain as neither the place nor value of the new situation seem to be known.

I have begun at home, and am reading Voltaire's Louis the 14th, it seems pretty easy.

This is a very short letter, and I should be ashamed to send it; could I not plead a headache; and also that I have not heard from home since I wrote last.

Believe me ever your affectionate son

W BAGEHOT

Love to all
It is more than *10* days since I heard from Mamma

To T. W. BAGEHOT, [25] SEPTEMBER 1841
MS: Mr Norman St John-Stevas
DATE: postmarked 25 September, a Saturday in 1841

Bristol September 1841
Saturday Afternoon

My dearest Papa

It is more than a week since I wrote to you, or rather to Mamma, and I cannot even plead being more engaged than usual in college work, but some how or other, the time has slipped away, with no more than the firmest resolutions to write every day. My mathematical studies are going on very prosperously, and I think better of my chances of ultimate success; and I find the work I did in the holidays 'no end' of advantage. The differential Calculus is principally learned from constantly working examples; which has always been the point in which I beat the rest of the class; and one feels that after working at the sums for some time, that some though gradual progress has been made—We have finished the Medea of Euripedes and I believe are going to read a play by Sophocles but nothing is yet decided.

French is still at the college as bad off as may be though I go on at home—Monsieur Victor has decamped bag and bagage;[1] but no one else has yet been appointed in his place; and there is a meeting of the council today, which is expected to decide the matter.—The council meet almost every day now, and I believe there is something in the wind about giving up the college[2] although it is said the masters have offered to give up part of their salary, if the council will engage to keep it on two years longer. The meeting of the shareholders is called I should think to decide the question—although I suppose you know better than I do.[3] German is rather in a better condition than usual; owing most probably to Göethe, our new book being much more interesting than any book we ever translated before.—We had to bring a translation of what Dr. Müncke considered one of the finest passages either in proze or verse, I called my poetic powers into play, made somewhat in rhyme, tremendous rum stuff. I had to read it out in the middle of the class; and the mysticism of my reading did not improve the matter; however Dr. Müncke said very good ever so many time; But I do not believe he understood one half of it. It was pretty literal, one good job. The only other poetical attempt was in blank verse; and mine was in consequence I suppose adjudged to be the best by the mob (alias the class) who I should imagine the worst judges of poetical merit in the whole world—Tell dearest mamma her question shall be answered (viz that concerning the Red Lodge) as soon as possible; which means as soon as I know. Horrid unbusiness like this letter will probably pass yours on the road; I hope I shall hear seeing I did not hear last Sunday—Were I not such

---

[1] Thus in MS.
[2] See letter of 21 May 1838, n. 4.
[3] T. W. Bagehot must have been a shareholder.

a truant myself I would kick up a row—My historical studies are going on very pleasantly. I am reading in conjunction with Heeren's Manual[4] which I told you about, parts of the history of Greece; I think I look horrid learned with four books open before me at once. The other two are the atlas and classical dictionary.

Believe me ever your affectionate son

W BAGEHOT

Love to all.

To T. W. BAGEHOT, 10 OCTOBER 1841

MS: Mr Norman St John-Stevas

Bristol October 10th. 1841

My dearest Papa

I intended to have written to you yesterday, but I was prevented by an invitation to dine at Mr. Osler's; I have had one before, which I was obliged to decline to go and see Uncle and Aunt Stuckey at Mr. Leans, so that I have been out twice this week, a circumstance not likely to increase my leizure time—Indeed I have had less time to reading this week than I have ever had within my recollection—For doing mathematics at home with Mr. Booth, has filled up a great deal of time; and we are reading a play of Sophocles at the college, which I find difficult—Smith Osler[1] seems much pleased with University College; the course of instruction there much resembles what it is with us at present, of course with the essential difference of being much more advanced. There seem to [be] no tutors at all analagous to

---

[4] A. H. L. Heeren, *A Manual of Ancient History*, translated from the German, 1828.

* * *

[1] Timothy Smith Osler (1823–1905), son of Thomas Osler (see letter of 7 December 1839, n. 4); a fellow pupil of WB's at Bristol College (but in the senior department) from which he had entered University College, London, where WB came to know him well: see later letters. Fellow of University College 1842, Ll.B. 1848; called to the bar Lincoln's Inn, 29 January 1850; member of the Senate of the University of London from 1859.

those at Oxford and Cambridge; they are indeed rendered quite unnecessary by the longer time which the students are required to spend in the college lectures; as these at Oxford are of very little importance—I was speaking to Mr. Swayne about them and he said the students did not in general among the undergraduates construe near so well as we do at the college, which certainly is not a very exalted standard of comparison—At London (that is at the London University) the examination gets stricter and stricter every year. Somerton is not going up to the Matriculation Examination this year, but is going to spend a year at University College; to perfect himself I believe in Mathematics and the branches of Natural Philosophy which is required for the Pass Examination.

I know nothing new about the prospects of the college. I should imagine the call of three pounds per share would not bring in any very large sum—The history of Palestine which I think I mentioned to you as my Sunday Reading still continues very interesting. I am at present reading the Chapter on the law; which is rather [   ][2] but shows the object of the various and minute [ritual][2] observances which the Law ordained. The Jews had been accustomed to the splendid ritual worship of the Egyptian priests, and a return to simple worship of the Patriarchs would have been almost impossible, at least would have been productive in their minds of a great blank, which was filled previously by the splendid representations of the heathen worship—The recent discoveries in the ruins of Egypt too have thrown great light on the Mosaic institutions, and show that God in pity to the weakness of his people, purified as many as possible of the Egyptian rites and engrafted them on the purer and holier faith he had ordained for his chosen people—

Kindest Love to All—Aunt Reynolds is staying with the Richies[3] at Clevedale—and goes to London on Tuesday I believe; this is rather stale news I suppose. Kindest Love to All—Hint to Mamma. I only had *one* letter last week, Remember also your promise to write again. I shall make a better debtor than creditor I think—I have got the new clothes we settled when you were in Bristol. Believe me ever your affectionate son

W BAGEHOT

[2] Stamp cut out, removing 6 or 7 letters.
[3] Not identified.

NOVEMBER 1841

To T. W. BAGEHOT, 7 NOVEMBER 1841
MS: Mr Norman St John-Stevas

Bristol November 7th. 1841
47. Park St.

My dearest Papa

I begun a letter to you yesterday, but I had a headache and was lazy and so I went on the Downs instead of finishing it; and in consequence I must write to day although I prefer not. The college is not now in the state that could be wished, Mr. Booth has been ill, nearly the whole of the week, and I am afraid is likely to continue so; and without him every thing is of course disordered, and comparatively little is done. Indeed, if the college is to go on with a new building in which all the boys who are not resident in Bristol, should board; Mr. Booth will (I am afraid) neither have health nor capacity for exertion enough to conduct such an institution. This my private opinion; and it is that of the greater of us boys, but if we were to choose masters we should have a rum set, I calculate.

I am doing as much at home now as I can, in preparing for next examination and also in astronomy; although Mr. Booth has not been able to give help in it for some time—I have finished Moore's life of Byron;[1] it is useful to contemplate a great mind, strugling[2] in the darkness of scepticism; and divested of the assurance of a future life which the Gospel conveys to our hearts. It shows us how little worldly fame, even when it is of the most exalted description and[2] compensate for the cheerless gloom which unbelief throws on the future—Unhappiness is very different indeed from melancholy. Byron seems to have had both, the second always even in early life, but the first was the distinguishing characteristic of his after years; when blighted affection and the reprobation of that world, he idolized while affecting to despise it, had rendered him miserable in the extreme. If Moore is correct in the account of his conduct towards his wife; he was certainly not the only one to blame; and he was comparatively speaking the only one punished, he was driven by the outcries of the world

[1] Thomas Moore, *Letters and Journals of Lord Byron, with Notices of his Life*, 1830.
[2] Thus in MS.

from his native land, and the breath of fame on which he had before lived was turned to wormwood. Lady Byron was certainly a 'orrid un' and that 'exactly'; but Moore was too much Byron's friend not as far as ever as possible to throw a veil over his errors. Rather a disjointed letter this, I am rather dull today.

> Believe me ever your affectiona[te son][3]
>
> W BAGEHOT

Mrs. Prichard and Edith are returned but I have not yet seen them. Love to all.[4]

To T. W. BAGEHOT, 2 DECEMBER [1841]

MS: Mr Norman St John-Stevas
DATE: WB's '1842' is an error for '1841', since from Bristol

Bristol December 2nd. 1842

My dearest Papa

This month I am coming home; and 'that's esactly'. I shall probably leave Bristol on the 17th., but I do not know quite for certain. I have just heard from Mr. Booth, that in the meeting of the Council today; they definitively decided to give up the college at *Christmas*;[1] an announcement which surprized me much, although the prospects of the College have been so black for some time past, that I hardly know why it should. Mr. Booth himself seems in a state of great uncertainty

---

[3] Stamp cut out, removing a few letters.
[4] This letter was forwarded by Edith Bagehot to 'My dearest Maria', to whom she wrote a note on the outside; she did the same with WB's letters of 2 December 1841, and 2 March, 13 March, 13 April and 26 April 1842. Her correspondent may have been Maria Mary Stuckey, *née* Michell (1780–1855), widow of Edith Bagehot's cousin, George Stuckey (1775–1823).

* * *

[1] In a note to Maria (see letter of 7 November, n. 4), written on the outside of the sheet Edith Bagehot told her: 'My husband fetches our Blessing next Wednesday and determines then what is to be done with him if the College is given up—I rather think he will return to Mr. Booth's.'

about his future plans; he mentioned something about wishing to take private pupils; but he seemed about as undecided as anything could be —He said he would write to you, and will give you of course a fuller account of his plans than I can do. I am at present engaged in a course of horrid hard work, quite as hard as I ever had I think; that Plato is an invaluable recipe for making anyone's head ache: an effect which it has had on me times without number. I hope, however I have pretty well mastered it; in Mathematics too I am getting pretty well forward, I have nearly finished the part of the Theory of Equations and done a considerable quantity of the Differential Caculus and the eleventh book of Euclid. I was thinking if you have no objection of making the Theory of Equations a part of my holiday work; as I have not been able to so much of it as I could wish: and it is a subject I think, I can work on with by myself. But we can settle all this, when we meet; I have jumped up over half a dozen and skipped all about the room, thinking how soon I shall come home; and see you all again.

> Believe me ever
> Your affectionate son
>
> W BAGEHOT.

Love to all. I am sorry my last letter was unreadable. Of course I must maintain that there is sense, in the German Translation; but on such points my word of course is not worth a tobacco stopper.

To T. W. BAGEHOT, 6 DECEMBER 1841

MS: Mr Norman St John-Stevas

> Bristol
> December 6th. 1841

My dearest Papa,

I cannot and will not let the post go out, without dashing off just a line to tell you, how much I shall be overjoyed to see you—and that I will work like steam, that I may be able to enjoy, as much as possible of your society while you are here. In addition to the work I told you of before I have to write an 'Essay on the comparative advantages of the study of ancient and modern Languages'.¹ Not a very promising subject I am afraid, but I will do my best. It is quite voluntary doing it, and I should not wonder if I were the only one; who does it; however the practice in composition is what I look too—I am still over head and years² in work, and shall I am afraid be wholy² unable to attend the German Examination tomorrow; which I should have wished to do, and to have another try at the poetry, notwithstanding my last 'sell'; by the bye I have two small translations from the classics, which I will copy out and send you; they have been done at little odd times, when I was lazy or tired—

Believe me
Ever your affectionate son

W Bagehot

I shall 'disinherit' Mamma, if she does not write soon—one small note is all I have had for a fortnight.

I hope you can read this as I am in great haste.

To EDWARD FRY,¹ [?JANUARY 1842]

Text from RB, X, 92–3
DATE: according to Mrs Barrington, postmarked 1842 and written during the Christmas holidays; confirmed by WB's reference to Moline's letter of 6 January 1842

Dear Fry,

What could induce you to think I wanted Barker's Latin Dictionary; if you will accept the brute, I can only say you are most welcome to it.

Your doubt about the old question is easily answered; there is nothing to prevent the principle of Young's solution answering: if

---

¹ *Collected Works*, XIV.
² Thus in MS.

* * *

¹ Edward Fry (1827–1918), later Sir Edward, had a distinguished legal career, retiring as a Lord Justice of Appeal in 1892; thereafter he was made a permanent member of the Hague Tribunal, and presided over four commissions. Edward was a member of the famous Bristol Quaker family, son of Joseph, who with his brothers controlled the cocoa and chocolate factory started by their grandfather and at this date still carried on in a

you pare while the weight is suspended, it will break at the point at which you begin; if you take the body away, while you pare, Professor Young's solution remains in statu quo. By the bye, I have written to Young, to thank him for his prompt attention to our question.[2] My governor said it was the respectable thing to do. Could you send me Young's letter, as my governor wishes to see it; it shall be returned promptly. Have you commenced working yet? I am over head and ears in Plato's *Apology of Socrates*, and Bourdon's *Application de L'Algébre a la Géometrie*.[3] The French reminds me to ask how Chalon[4] is (Heaven only knows how to spell the name); if he is convalescent, remember me to him, and if you like, you need not say it was from me, tell him to wash his hands. I have heard from Moline; he had nor received my letter, and when he wrote that (6 January, 1842) had not received a word from England. He writes in good spirits and says he likes his work pretty well, when it is not standing up in water. He could not stand in very deep water, that's certain. Is Booth gone to Dublin? Compliments to your brother,[5] if your Quaker principles do not proscribe that usage of society.

Believe me (I had a mind to put *respected friend* but I shan't),

Yours &c. &c. &c,

WALTER BAGEHOT.

I hope you can decipher this scrawl.

---

small way in Union Street. In Agnes Fry's *Memoir* (pp. 24-5), Edward describes how in January 1841 he and his elder brother (who had previously been educated at home) were sent to Bristol College; this was 'rather a plunge—we were Quaker boys, with Quaker dress and language'—which they retained in face of a 'good dose of teasing'—but he was soon grateful for 'freer air' and superior teaching. At the College WB was two years ahead of him, but they became close friends after its closure, when both joined Booth's small school and shared many classes. In the *Memoir* Fry speaks of 'sparkle and genius' already detectable in WB as a schoolboy, and described him to Mrs Barrington as 'a lanky youth, rather thin and long in the legs, with a countenance of remarkable vivacity and characterised by the large eyes which were always noticeable' (RB, X, 85).

[2] The problem and Young's reply (dated 27 May, perhaps a misreading of '2 Jany') are given in RB, X, 93-4 (with Young's initials given as 'T. R.' in error); their correspondent was John Radford Young (1799-1885), professor of mathematics at Belfast College 1833-49.

[3] By Pierre Louis Marie Bourdon; Augustus de Morgan translated the first three chapters as *The Elements of Algebra*, 1828.

[4] Perhaps the French teacher of the Fry children, 'a M. Chaillu, a funny old Frenchman, who had very little idea of teaching, and used to amuse us with all sorts of stories' (*Memoir*, p. 22).

[5] Joseph Storrs Fry, Edward's elder brother.

To T. W. BAGEHOT, 6 FEBRUARY 1842

MS: Mr Norman St John-Stevas

Bristol. February 6th. 1842.

My dearest Papa,

I had intended answering your last kind letter before this, and was actually on the point of doing so yesterday, when it occurred to me, that I might as well wait till tomorrow; and this resolution concurring with the vis Inertiae of matter was speedily adopted. Things are getting much more comfortable at Mr. Booths,[1] or I am getting more used to them; I was rather dismal at first, particularly when I found I was to be in a class by myself; and that I should not have much companionship or association with other boys. I am beginning too to get steadily to work, which is a comfort, and that has made me much less dismal, and though I shall probably not after all be so comfortable as in the lifetime of the college; still there will certainly I think be no occasion for any immediate change. My classical work, as I think I mentioned to you before, is in Greek Homer, and Demosthenes and in Latin Juvenal and Cicero. Juvenal is much the most difficult of all; he abounds in so many allusions to the niceties of Roman life, and ancient customs, that it is by no means easy to unravel his meaning, and it is not very much after it is found out sometimes. It is however a very excellent book to learn the language and the customs of the ancients; Mr. Booth seems to it[2] better than any of the others. I suppose he mugs more at it. He has a much better knowledge of history and antiquities and Geography, than of the structure of the language and its grammatical distinctions. My mathematical studies are the integral Calculus, and Newton's Principia; which are both very interesting, particularly Newton, who certainly was a *small* brick. His proofs are beautiful simple, and generally pretty easy, but sometimes the very simplicity of his demonstrations, render them difficult. Newton has been much abused by later mathematicians for his decided preference for the ancient Geometry, which has led him in some instances to use long and involved demonstrations when he might have used much shorter

---

[1] After the closure of Bristol College, WB went to the small school opened by Booth in his house on St Michael's Hill: see last, n. 1.

[2] This in MS; perhaps an example of the common nineteenth-century provincial idiom, by which 'know' was omitted following 'ought to', 'seem to'.

ones by employing Algebra. I hope I have expressed myself clearly as I am afraid I am at present rather stupid and thick. I have begun reading Mitford's History [of] Greece[3] as we settled before I went away; it is highly interesting, and generally well written, although some times he hes a fit of using antiquated expressions, and rum words. It is on the whole animated and the author seems to have had a great deal of information, and to have been throughly well read in the whole mass of the Greek writers; since he is constantly quoting them in the notes, and blowing up other people for not 'understanding and rightly explaining the passage'. Mitford is a downright thoroughgoing Tory [? who will][4] not allow one single good or honourable action ungrudgingly to the Athenian democracy; and he seems to think absolute monarchy one of the best forms of government in existence.

I am also reading Boswell's Life of Johnson, which I keep as a kind of treat when I am tired; it is *not* Croker's edition,[5] but an oldish one in one volume; but as the price of Croker's is two guineas and this only five shillings, there is a considerable balance for mine. My English composition for the present is to be, The history of the Successors of Alexander 'from the death of that prince to the birth of Christ'. It will be hardish, and will be very long seeing it is the history of 323 years, and there are a great variety of events and an immense number of wars, which are terribly involved. I have begun it, but have not as yet been able to do much to it. Mr Estlin was telling me today, that he believed there was a class of the old students of the college who attended some lectures of Dr. William Carpenter at his own home, in which case, I suppose you would like me to attend them. Mr. Estlin was not however certain about it; but it is a matter which is easily discoverable.

Believe me ever
Your affectionate son
W BAGEHOT

Love to all

---

[3] William Mitford, *The History of Greece* (5 vols, 1784–1810; continued to the death of Alexander by R. A. Davenport, 1835); its anti-Jacobin tendencies were notorious, and accounted for by its having been written at the time of the French Revolution. Edward Fry recalled that he and WB 'wrote essays on the character of Dionysius of Syracuse, and considered Mitford's defence of his government' (Agnes Fry, *A Memoir of . . . Sir Edward Fry*, 1921, p. 25).
[4] Letter torn at seal, removing 6 or 7 letters.
[5] First published in 5 vols. 1831, and with additions, in 10 vols, 1835.

FEBRUARY 1842

To T. W. BAGEHOT, 15 FEBRUARY [1842]

MS: Mr Norman St John-Stevas
DATE: postmark appears to be '1842', confirmed by references to Carpenter's lectures and to Boswell (see last)

February 15th. 1841
Bristol

My dearest Papa

I have a nice quiet hour after the departure of the rest of the boys, and will use it in writing to thank your for your last welcome letter, which I received on Sunday. Uncle Reynolds as you will probably have heard, had arrived; and is to go on Saturday next. He blowed me up like beans for not eating all sorts of good things, but I did not mind it very mickle.

I hope your back is getting better; and that you are getting well without any of your threatened dosing; which is not a thing to be lightly ventured—I have not been very bright either having had a good deal of headache at night, but to day my nose has been bleeding so that I hope, I shall not have any to night. My work has lately been increased considerably in a way, which I did not expect. You will remember my saying that Mr. Estlin had mentioned Dr. Carpenter's having a class, which attended some lectures of his, which he thought you would like me to attend. I thought that they would be about the same length as they used to be at college, and said I should like much to attend them. But they are four times a week, and one hour and one half each time. Mr. Estlin had kindly spoken to Dr. Carpenter and I have attended the lectures in consequence during the last week, and I suppose I had better continue to do so. The subjects are, I believe, Natural Philosophy, Zoology and Chemistry. I shall never probably have a quieter time for these subjects than I have now; although they have some what put me out in my arrangements, and rather I fancy annoyed Mr. Booth. This last is only a fancy perhaps, but he was not, I believe on the very best terms with Dr. Carpenter.

I have just been reading in Boswell's Life of Johnson, the account of the intercourse between Warren Hastings and Dr. Johnson. There is not much in Dr. Johnson's letters to him I fancy, they are rather seedy, with common place compliments. Boswell praises Warren Hastings to the skies, which is the more disinterested, as it was at the moment of the beginning of his trial.[1]

Believe me ever
Your affectionate son

W BAGEHOT.

Love to all, except Watty, who has grievously offended me—His conscience will tell him how.

T. W. BAGEHOT to WB, 21 FEBRUARY 1842

Extract in RB, X, 94–5

21st February, 1842.

In the evening after I finished my last letter to you, I read Lord Palmerston's speech[1] to your mother. The whole of it was most effective, but one part of it was so eloquent that I cannot help making an extract of it for you. A great deal, you know, has been said by the advocates of the Corn Law about our being independent of a foreign supply of so important an article as our food, which Lord Palmerston contends is a complete fallacy, as we depend on foreign commerce for a market for so great a portion of our manufactures; if we will not buy, we cannot sell, and our artisans and manufacturing population may be starving for want of wages to buy food, however abundant may be our home grown supply. He then adds: 'But, sir, there are larger

---

[1] In Boswell's record of 1781 (see Birkbeck Hill edn, rev. and enlarged L. F. Powell, 1934, IV, 66–70). Hastings's trial had in fact been dragging on for more than three years when the *Life* was published.

* * *

[1] On 17 February, in the debate on Peel's Corn Law bill, the first stage in his 1842 programme of fiscal reform, which was followed by the introduction of income tax and by a general reduction of duties on imported goods and agricultural products. The bill retained the sliding scale, but with as great a reduction in duties as Peel judged would be acceptable to his colleagues and to the House of Lords. Palmerston spoke last in the debate of 14–17 February, in support of Russell's motion for a fixed duty; WB's father quotes the conclusion of what Greville described as 'a good slashing speech' (*Memoirs* [*Second Part*], II, 86). Russell's motion was lost by 123 votes, and in five more nights of debate amendments in favour of total repeal and of higher protection were also defeated.

grounds on which this doctrine ought to be repudiated by this house. Why is the earth on which we live divided into zones and climates? Why, I ask, do different countries yield *different productions* to people experiencing *similar wants*? Why are they intersected with mighty rivers—the natural highways of nations? Why are lands the most distant from each other brought almost into contact by that very ocean which seems to divide them? Why, sir, it is that man may be dependent upon man. It is that the exchange of commodities may be accompanied by the extension and diffusion of knowledge—by the interchange of mutual benefits, engendering mutual kind feelings—multiplying and confirming friendly relations. It is that commerce may freely go forth, leading civilisation with one hand, and peace with the other, to render mankind happier, wiser, better. Sir, this is the dispensation of Providence, this is the decree of that power which created and disposed the universe; but in the face of it, with arrogant presumptuous folly, the dealers in restrictive duties fly, fettering the inborn energies of man, and setting up their miserable legislation instead of the great standing laws of nature.'

To T. W. BAGEHOT, 2 MARCH [1842]

MS: Mr Norman St John-Stevas
DATE: 1842 postmark shows that WB misdated

March 2nd. 1841
Bristol

My dearest Papa,

I most certainly intended answering your last note before this, but I have had a good deal to do, between one thing and another, and I have not done so. I have I think plenty of time for classics and mathematics, although with my additional work, I have considerably less time to myself than before. I have not however found any occasion to shorten materially the time, which I used to give in the evening to either of these subjects, and the principal difference is that I used to learn one of my classical subjects in the morning and that I am now obliged to do so of an evening. Both my mathematical studies, viz. the Integral Calculus and Newton's Principia are extremely difficult, by far more so, than anything which I have met with before, but I hope I am making sure, although slow progress, The Integral Calculus is and must be a work of time, as it can only be learned from long practice in working examples, as there is no general rule whatever; and there [are] a great number of cases, which mathematicians have never yet succeeded in working at all. The Principia is also very beautiful, and like 'the darling Euclid' extremely simple after you have made it out, although before it seems confusion worse confounded. In classics I have read this term, two satires of Juvenal; they are not particularly long, but are extremely difficult, and although some parts are most sublimely beautiful, there is a vast deal of dross, through which as in our own Shakespeare, one is obliged to wade to meet with something to repay the labor. The last one which I read imitated by Dr. Johnson in his 'Vanity of human wishes' which I have been amusing myself with comparing with the original. Johnson has expunged the dross entirely, and is therefore much more pleasant to read on the whole, although I prefer some of the sublime passages of the original to those of the translation—Mentioning Dr. Johnson has reminded me to tell you, that I have finished Boswell's life of him; which is very interesting, what struck me particularly was that amazing love of life which he seems to have had; (I am afraid I should rather have said fear of death). To mention death before him in his last illness, or to dwell on it for any time at any period of his life, was sufficient to call up his most violent anger; and what with him generally accompanied it the most virulent abuse. Like many other great and good men, his practice was not always in accordance with his principles; but the temptations of his career were many and great, while he must demand our gratitude for having been among the very first to consecrate poetry to the reprehension of vice. He certainly had some very curious ideas certainly, such as his preferring Goldsmith's history of Greece to any composition of Robertson, or Hume. No one else would think of advancing such an opinion; since Goldsmith's is a mere compilation confessedly so indeed, without one spark of originality; and the others are long since numbered among the best of our English classics. I am branching off into an essay instead of a letter have written what for me is an amazingly long letter. I am glad Watty does not find the second book so very difficult; may I ask to let him do two propositions instead of one for my sake. Please do not forget your *implied* promise of compensating for your Saturday's note by an additional letter.

Believe me ever
Your affectionate son
W Bagehot.

Love to all.

To T. W. BAGEHOT, 13 MARCH [1842]

MS: Mr Norman St John-Stevas
DATE: 1842 postmark and content (see notes) shows that WB misdated

Bristol 13 March 1841

My dearest Papa,

I hasten to reply to your welcome letter, which I received this morning in due course—I have just been hearing a beautiful, and impressive sermon from Mr. Russel Carpenter; on the text in Genesis 'Behold this dreamer cometh'. He first spoke of the history of Joseph, as affording such evident and beautiful proofs of the beneficent providence of God; and then passing from the literal interpretation of the text; to the evils of a visionary disposition, as rendering us unfit for the duties of active life, and as having a tendency to make us selfish and careless of those around us.

I have just been reading in the Pictorial History of Palestine; the account of the Jewish Captivity and all its attendant circumstances; the writer has shown completely that the disobedience of the Jews and their consequent punishment advanced the designs of Providence in preparing the way for the coming of the Messiah, even more than their perfect obedience would have done, and that thus, while they thought that they were but acting in conformity to their blind and rebellious desires; they were in reality fulfilling the allwise designs of God. Since if they had remained shut up within the borders of their own land, the coming of Christ could not have been made known to the other nations of the world, at least not with nearly the same rapidity, even if it at all.[1] I will certainly bring home the books you mention;

[1] Thus in MS.

and give you all the account of my studies with Dr. Carpenter which you may wish. I conclude that I had better have another suit of clothes, as my present best is not to say good; and my worst is very tight indeed. I have been reading all about the news from India, which must from the accounts be most disastrous. The Examiner states, that it is the greatest reverse, which our arms have ever experienced in India;[2] Sir Robert Peel says that although he thinks the event of the expedition is most disastrous; he believes that the accounts which have at present reached us are much exaggerated.[3] It is to be hoped that he will prove a true prophet.

Believe me ever
your affectionate son
W BAGEHOT.

Love to all.

To T. W. BAGEHOT, [7 APRIL 1842]

Extract in RB, X, 95, dated 7 April 1842

Constantine Prichard[1] is at home. I was much struck by his beautiful forehead and brow, so very intellectual and expressive; certes he is by far the best looking of the Prichards; only time can show whether he is the cleverest.

---

[2] News had only just reached England of the disastrous retreat from Kabul, following the concerted revolt of November 1841 against the British occupation of Afghanistan. On 6 January 16,000 British and native troops marched out of the cantonments, indefensible because cut off from supplies, and on 13 January one survivor reached Jellalabad to tell of their massacre. The *Examiner*, 12 March 1842, described it as 'the greatest disaster that ever befel the arms of our country', condemned the occupation of Afghanistan and restoration of the unpopular Shah Shuja, and criticized the ineptitude of the military commanders.

[3] In answer to a question in the House as to the extent of the disaster; this was also in the *Examiner* report of 12 March. Reports of the massacre were not exaggerated, but the disaster was not complete since Kandahar, Ghazni and Jellalabad remained in British hands; in September 1842 Kabul was retaken and 100 British prisoners released before its evacuation on 12 October.

* * *

[1] Constantine Estlin Prichard (1820–69), fourth son of James Cowles Prichard; scholar of Balliol 1837–42, elected a Fellow 29 November 1842 (the same day as Frederick Temple); ordained 1847, and Vice-Principal of Wells Theological College 1847–50; a prebendary of Wells Cathedral from 1852 until his death. In 1854 he married Mary Alice Seymour (1833–1918), niece of the 9th Duke of Somerset and became Rector of South Luffenham, Rutlandshire. Prichard became an intimate friend of his cousin, WB.

To T. W. BAGEHOT, 13 APRIL [1842]

MS: Mr Norman St John-Stevas
DATE: postmark lacks last figure of year, but reference to India and Cicero show this to be among letters of 1842 misdated 1841 by WB

April 13 1841
Bristol

My dearest Papa,

We have a holiday today; beginning soon you will say seeing we have not been a fortnight yet; and I have only been back an hour or so more than a week. It is as I said denominated a holiday, but I have been passing it, in hard work, which is certainly the best way of getting in[1] rid of what in any other way, is and must be a horrid bore. I have begun some Mechanics with Mr. Booth, and have been a considerable part of this morning puzzling my brains with the *demonstration* of the Parallelogram of Forces, which you will recollect, we learned together experimentally in the work on Mechanics published by the Useful Knowledge Society. It is extremely difficult confusion worse confounded it appears at first sight, but I am nearly master of it now and am beginning to allow that it may *possibly* be beautiful. It is certainly useful, as it is to Mechanics, what the 4th. Proposition of Euclid is to Geometry, the keystone of the whole. I am reading in Classics the second Georgic of Virgil and one of the legal orations of Cicero. It is in defence of a nominal king who was in reality subject to Rome, who had been first of the Party of Pompey, but had afterwards joined that of Caesar; and had even entertained the latter at his house. Afterwards however his enemies at Rome accused him of disafection[1] to the government and added the improbable charge, that it had been his intention to assassinate Caesar, while he was his guest. He happened to be an old friend of Cicero, who defends him with all his eloquence; and succeeded in preventing the condemnation—You have never sent me that Paper, by the bye, about India; do please to send it, as I very much wish to know all about it—Also I have another bill of indictment against[1] that you wrongfully defrauded me of my rightful dues in not sending me a letter on Sunday.

Believe me ever
your affectionate son

W BAGEHOT

[1]Thus in MS.

APRIL 1842

To T. W. BAGEHOT, 26 APRIL 1842

MS: Mr Norman St John-Stevas

Bristol April 26th. 1842

My dearest Papa,

I have a little leizure time, and will appropriate it to writing to you, the rather that my week is nearly expired. I have had less time to myself, since I have been back this time, than I can remember, having had before; by this I mean less time at my own disposal for reading and lighter studies. I have been working hard, at the subjects we arranged, when I was last at home, that is in classics, the orations of Cicero against Catiline, and the first six books of Homer's Iliad. I have in addition to these books, which I am reading with Mr. Booth, begun to read some Sallust to myself, applying to him however when there is any difficulty. The other two books which I am reading are the Georgics of Virgil and the Philippics and Olynthiacs of Demosthenes. Of these last I am writing an analysis; that is expressing as concisely as I can the different subjects and the separate divisions of the speech. This is at the same time a practice in English Composition, and a way of familiarizing my mind with the arrangement and peculiar beauties of these models of eloquence which, if I should become a barrister, will of course be of the highest importance. I am also going on with my historical essay, on Alexander's Successors, on which I spend as much time, as I can, although it is a kind of composition which requires the whole stretch of one's intellect and cannot therefore be done, when I have a headache or when I am not very bright. I have just been reading in Mitford's History of Greece, an account of Alexander's conquests on the country which is now called Affghanistan and Cabool. It is peculiarly interesting just at this time, when the bones of so many of our countrymen are bleaching unburied on their mountains,[1] and when for aught we know the thousands we are now sending out, to avenge their fate, may only be going to become sharers in the same disastrous destiny. The mountaineers tried very much the same stratagems on Alexander, as they seem to have done on

[1] Echoing the *Examiner* of 9 April 1842: 'the bones of 13,000 British soldiers lie bleaching upon the wild mountain passes of Khoord, Cabool and Jugdullat.'

our troops, only they were by no means so united among themselves. They several times made truces, only to break them, which they did, as soon as ever they saw or thought they saw any prospect of advantage. There is every reason to believe that the people were then much the same, as they are now; the historians mention the Brahmins, with a description which exactly applies to them at the present day. The paper is run to *seed*.

Believe me ever
Your affectionate son
W BAGEHOT.

Love to all. Concerning the skulls, I hope I am pretty well master of the leading divisions. One of Mr. Booth's boys has lent me a couple of skulls, and with the aid of a number of Chambers's Information for the people,[2] I am I hope qualified to understand most of Dr. Prichard's Craniology.

To EDITH BAGEHOT, 2 MAY 1842

MS: Mr Norman St John-Stevas

Bristol.
May 2nd. 1842

My dearest Mamma,

I am rather crying shame to myself for not answering your last long letter and *two short* notes, and although I am rather an invalid, will begin to pay off my debt. Being rather an invalid, means that I was rather giddy all day yesterday, and towards the evening became worse; so that Dr. Prichard observed that I ought to have some medicine, and accordingly wrote a mysterious looking prescription; which being translated into drugs became nothing more or less, than a 'calomel pill and black draught'. This was of course taken, and made me very poorly all the morning, but towards the afternoon I felt well

---

[2] Issued in fortnightly numbers at $1\frac{1}{2}d.$ each from 1833; the first of the non-fiction serial publications of W. and R. Chambers, using the production and distribution channels of *Chambers's Edinburgh Journal.*

enough to go to Dr. Carpenter's lecture, which I did not want to miss, and so it may be presumed there is nothing very much to 'speck 'o'—

Aunt Emma, and Mary Estlin depart to Clevedon today; they went down on Thursday for a day, as a sort of trial, and seemed much pleased. They have asked me to come down for a day and I promised I would if I could; and as there is a probability of a holiday on Wednesday, the 'could' will probably come to pass—I went on Friday to a lecture on Animal Magnetism,[1] or as it is more properly termed Mesmerism. It does seem most wonderful. Dr. Canter (that was the name of the lecturer) by moving his hand downwards before a person's face, made him go or appear to go soundly to sleep, and they ran pins into him and a penknife which was a horrid shame I think, seeing that when he *awakes*, he must feel pain. However there certainly was no movement while the sleep continued. He then took out the pins and put his arms and his legs quite stiff, and made him sit in that position for about ten minutes, during which there was certainly no sign of motion or of consciousness any more than if the man had been a log of wood, and Dr. Canter stated that he could remain for any time. Certainly no one in their natural state could remain so long in such an uncomfortable position, without any movement. He then awoke the man by moving his hands laterally in front of his face without touching it however, and the patient woke up immediately. This man was his own assistant. He then magnetized a boy, who used to go to the college, and is now a pupil of Dr. Carpenter's; and set him fast to sleep, in which case certainly there could be no collusion.

With love to all, believe me ever

Your affectionate Son

W Bagehot

— does not deserve to have his Papa come over, saying there was nothing in my letters!!!! he must be corrected—I shall send a Memorial to the authorities—

---

[1] During the 1830s and 1840s there was great public interest in and controversy about animal magnetism or mesmerism. The distinguished physician Dr John Elliotson resigned his posts at University College Hospital, London, following denunciation in the *Lancet* of his public experiments in mesmerism 1837–8. The *Bristol Mercury* of 30 April 1842 gave a brief account of Dr Cantor's first lecture on mesmerism, 26 April, when he put a young man into a 'somnolescent state' and a woman into a 'cataleptic state'.

MAY 1842

To T. W. BAGEHOT, 8 MAY 1842

MS: Mr Norman St John-Stevas

Bristol
May 8th. 1842

My dearest Papa,

I did not go to Clevedon on Friday as I intended; it looked so very rainy in the morning, and likely to be such a wet day, that I thought I had better put it off, and went to Dr. Carpenter's lecture instead. Aunt Emma now wants me to come down next Saturday morning, and stay until Monday; and I do not know but that it would be the best plan, as Saturday is the day when I have least to do. I suppose your coming up with Mamma would be impossible, but it would be so beautiful. Do turn it over in your mind. I have been mugging away very hard lately particularly at Mathematics. I am working principally at my Mechanics, in which in addition to the work by Pratt,[1] which I think I mentioned to you, I am reading a book on the subject by Poinsot[2] the great French Mathematician. It is in French (is not that grand) and it is pretty easy for all that; it is perfectly clear, and one thing follows from another almost as beautifully as in Euclid. It is a great contrast in this respect to Pratt, which seems to me *at present* all in a *jumble*, but perhaps, that is only my ignorance. I have finished reading Mitford's history of Greece, and have commenced reading Fergusson's history of the Roman republic.[3] It is by no means so interesting as Mitford, nor does it so clearly exemplify the causes of the leading events, which occur from time to time. In talent there can I think be no question, but Mitford is decidedly superior—He has in many instances collected a clear and satisfactory narrative of the political struggles of Athens, from widely scattered notices in the various orators, and disjointed references in later historians. I am also reading for my amusing book, Addison's Works; containing all his papers in the Spectator &c in one volume in the People's edition. (Please never to abuse double column books again)—My paper is

---

[1] John Henry Pratt, *The Mathematical Principles of Mechanical Philosophy*, 1836.
[2] Louis Poinsot, *Eléments de Statique*, 1811.
[3] Adam Ferguson, *The History of the Progress and Termination of the Roman Republic* (3 vols, 1783; editions continued to appear up to 1825).

MAY 1842

evaporated, and I cannot write more seeing it is to go in a *Hodge Podge*.

Believe me ever
your affectionate son
W BAGEHOT.

Love to all

EDITH BAGEHOT to WB, 10 MAY 1842
Text from RB, X, 72-3

10th May, 1842.

My dearest Walter,

   . . . I have been reading over many of my beloved Stuckey's[1] letters to dearest Papa this week, and he and I were much struck with the similarity of the style with yours and in affection for his own Mamma—or rather in parental affection I hope you resemble each other. Oh! I have the blessed assurance that that is a feeling which survives the grave and lives purified and anew through all eternity.

   Now that Aunt and Uncle are gone,[2] my popping place is to Mrs. Kent.[3] I scold her much for caring totally (unlike you and Papa and *me* now) about people and their attentions. She has always got some little fad about 'cold manners', default of courtesies and enquiries, and fresh peccadilloes of the kind she punishes by a cross proud look (*entre nous*), and then—there they are—all turned to icicles, and send each other to Coventry! She is just in this way now with ——[4] who has a tendency not to think 'small beer' of himself and to swell out to a barrel or a butt. How one does wish to expand the good in humanity, to repress the bad, and raise all hearts and minds above the petty jealousies of life,

---

[1] George Stuckey Estlin (1809–29), second son of Edith Bagehot's first marriage to Joseph Prior Estlin; he died 10 June 1829, aged 20, as the result of a carriage accident.
[2] Vincent and Julia Stuckey's yearly visit to London.
[3] Not identified.
[4] Thus in printed text.

and fix them upon the sublime views of the immortal soul and its life to come and which is to last for ever!! Instead of which the petty interests, and petty complaints of the body—body, body are filling every mind and occupying every tongue, and yet one must not wish to be '*no*-body' either—by way of a pun for you!

EDITH BAGEHOT to WB, [?MAY 1842]

Extract in RB, X, 75
DATE: probably before or during WB's first visit to Clevedon (see n. 1)

Papa said, 'You can go if you like', but upon my eyes sparkling, and heart leaping, added, 'but I think you had better stay at home'. Now I think both of us are aware, that without him to take care of me and keep me together, as my imagination and feelings are so prone to travel railroad speed, my body must be kept at a more temperate pace, and not be allowed to do too much in a short time.[1]

To T. W. BAGEHOT, 15 MAY 1842

MS: Mr Norman St John-Stevas

Clevedon
May 15 1842
Sunday Morning

My dearest Papa,

I am writing from Clevedon, as indeed appears from the date. It is indeed a pretty place, and there are some spots, which even a Lyn-

---

[1] According to Mrs Barrington this was written when there was some question of Edith Bagehot joining WB at Clevedon without his father; it shows her knowledge of her own mental state and her dependence on her husband's care. In forwarding to Maria WB's letter of 26 April, Edith Bagehot gave her news from his letter to her of 2 May, and said of his proposed visit to Clevedon: 'I have been trying to coax Papa to take Watty and me to Clevedon and meet our dearest, but he says No! he must work hard, and I must stay quietly.'

mouth[1] person might think beautiful, although it is of course more cultivated, and has in consequence not that beautiful and picturesque wildness, which we used to admire in your garden. I went last evening to a pretty little bay in which though not to be for a moment compared to Ringclip, the tide really came in very prettily. It was very calm, scarcely 'a breath the blue waves to curl', only alack there is precious little blueness and mud is not a *necessary* ingredient in sentiment. There is a universal petition that you would come up here. I think you would like the island scenery very much indeed; do not you think you could manage it for a day or two, just a glimpse. Our dear friends are kindly pressing me to come down next Saturday, and if you could come up, &c &c. I shall have rather an easier week next week, as two of Dr. Carpenter's pupils are going into Wales, and he will give no lectures in consequence. I am afraid you will think this too much holiday for me, and if so I will give it up and work on as usual; this you will decide upon. I walked over a most beautiful hill yesterday, and scrambled up another, and saw a most beautiful view, on one side a most beautiful inland scenery, rich and cultivated, and on the other, the sea and rocky hill, between which and the one I was standing there was a most beautifully wooded vale, 'looking serenity' as Shelley has it.[2] I did so wish for you. A letter came this morning, informing us, that a letter had come from Augustine Prichard[3] informing them of his safety. They were of course not a little anxious after that dreadful railroad accident.[4] It was indeed most merciful—[?that he][5] was too late for that train which was the very [one][5] he had fixed to go by. One would almost be [?led][5] to say (as Clive did after twice snapping a loaded pistol at his head and its twice refusing to go off) 'that he was

---

[1] For the seaside holidays WB took with his parents Lynmouth was the place most often chosen, because of its great beauty, 'and together they became intimate with every rock and cranny in the place, appropriating in fancy special spots as their very own' (RB, X, 8–9).
[2] A reminiscence of '... one silent nook ... It overlooked in its serenity/The dark earth, (*Alastor*, 11. 575–6).
[3] Augustin Prichard (1818–98), surgeon; third son of Dr J. C. Prichard; FRCS 1849 MD, Berlin, 1841; surgeon to Bristol Eye Dispensary founded by his uncle, J. B. Estlin and to Bristol Royal Infirmary.
[4] That of 8 May on the line between Versailles and Paris, described by the *Annual Register*, 1842, as the 'most frightful railway accident that ever was'. Three carriages of the train, packed with people who had been attending the King's fête at Versailles caught fire, with the passengers locked in; more than 50 died and 40 were seriously injured.
[5] A tear at the edge of the paper has removed a few letters from three lines.

preserved for something great'.⁶ I suppose you have not written today, not knowing where I should be.

Believe me ever
Your affectionate son
WALTER BAGEHOT

I suppose ——†⁷ is with you again. How does he like his sister now he has *seen* her. Why does not Mamma write to me. It is a *week* since I had even a line from her, and then it was only a line.

†meant for Watty—

To T. W. BAGEHOT, [26 MAY 1842]

Extract in W. Irvine, *Walter Bagehot*, pp, 14-15, dated 26 May 1842

Would you have any objection to my getting Donnegan's Greek Lexicon¹ it is the best work on the subject I believe, and Mr. Booth strongly recommends it and indeed I feel very much the want of some book of the kind. The price is the only objection, as it is about 35 shillings; I am afraid you will think this very expensive, especially as I have lately bought a large Latin dictionary.

To EDITH BAGEHOT, [?1839-1842]

Extract in RB, X, 98; written while WB was at Bristol

I dined at the Prichards a day or two ago. The Doctor had two friends there talking about the Arrow-headed character and the monuments of Pentapolis, and the way of manufacturing cloth in the South Seas.

---

⁶ WB may have met this well-known story in Sir John Malcolm's *Life of Robert Lord Clive*, where Clive says to the friend who has fired the third shot out of the window: 'Well, I am reserved for something!' (I, 44-5). However, 'great' suggests that he was recalling Macaulay's essay in the *Edinburgh Review*, January 1840 (Macaulay, *Essays*, 1843, III, 116).

⁷ The cross and footnote appear to be in WB's hand.

* * *

¹ James Donnegan, *A New Greek and English Lexicon*, 1826, of which the 4th edition, enlarged, came out in 1842. Printed text reads 'Donnejan's' in error.

To EDITH BAGEHOT, [? 19 OCTOBER 1842]

Extract in RB, X, 101.
DATE: 'after a few days residence' in Camden Town; as his father was with him 16 October (see next), probably in the middle of the week

I must confess to having felt rather dismal, when Papa left me at the University[1] in the midst of a thick London fog; and I cannot say but I felt rather dismal occasionally since, when I think of Herd's Hill and you all sitting quietly and happily down amid all its beauties, while I am toiling here in the midst of dust and smoke. More especially I prefer the evenings at home, with Papa reading aloud Sir Samuel Romilly,[2] to those we have here,[3] although I have managed by dint of hard work to get through them pleasantly enough.

To T. W. BAGEHOT, 23 OCTOBER 1842

MS: Mr Norman St John-Stevas

London[1] October 23. 1842.

My dearest Papa,

I am just returned from the chapel, to which last Sunday we went together; the contrast was to me I must confess painful; and although I keep up my spirits, as well as I can, my thoughts ever and anon wander back again, to the calm beauties of Herd's Hill, in the midst of which I have of late spent so many Sundays. This was forced strongly

---

[1] University College, Gower St; known as the University of London from its opening in 1828 until November 1836, when it received its charter and when the University of London was set up as a body empowered to grant degrees to students of University College and King's College. It was designed to provide higher education for those, like the Bagehots, who objected to the religious tests at Oxford and Cambridge, and to offer a wider range of subjects (including sciences and modern languages) than the older universities.
[2] *Memoirs of the Life of Sir Samuel Romilly, Written by Himself, with a Selection from his Correspondence*, 1840.
[3] At 39 Camden Street, Camden Town, where WB lodged with Dr Hoppus (see next).

* * *

[1] WB originally wrote 'Bristol'; another hand has substituted 'London'.

OCTOBER 1842

upon me, when I came back here, where although Dr. Hoppus[2] was very kind, and let me[3] a very excellent work, Dr. Clarke Demonstration of the being of a God,[4] I am glad I am not going to spend every Sunday. We had a very excellent sermon from Mr. Teggart,[5] (have I spelt his name right) on the text of Malachi, 'And the people of God spake often one to another': he enlarged with considerable animation, on the joy we ought to feel in intercourse on the subject of religion, not as he said, to make it the common Table Talk, nor on the other hand a matter of gloomy and dogmatical discipline, but as a link by which we might connect the events ever recurring in this world with that which is to come. The habit must indeed be an important one, to see every event in the relation which it bears to the next; and thus really putting in practice the sublime thought of Burke, 'that the situation of man is the preceptor of his duty.'[6] I know not if I have made myself intelligible, but I hope I have.

I thank you, for your most kind letter; your affectionate sollicitude for my welfare, believe me, is a blessing, I would not lose by any fault of mine, and in no other way can I lose it, for any other blessing which the world can bestow. If both our lives are spared and God grant they may be so, may we have that communion in thought and affection, which only real sympathy in each other's feelings can give.

I am getting now regularly into work; and shall soon I hope be able to give you the account you wish for, of the course of study. We have had a series of most beautiful, although difficult lectures from Mr De Morgan,[7] on the higher development of Algebra, or rather on a

[2] John Hoppus (1789–1875), formerly an independent minister, and professor of philosophy at the College, 1830–66; Ll.D, Glasgow, 1839, FRS, 1841. A follower of Dugald Stewart, with a strong interest in the history of philosophy, but so poor a teacher that 'he almost killed the study of philosophy in the college' (H. Hale Bellot, *University College London: 1826–1926*, 1929, p. 111). Hoppus took in boarders and WB lodged with him at 39 Camden Street.
[3] Thus in MS, for 'lent me' or 'let me have'.
[4] The Wesleyan preacher Adam Clarke's *Discourses on Various Subjects Relative to the Being and Attributes of God*, 1828.
[5] The Revd Edward Tagart (1804–58), minister of the Unitarian Chapel, Little Portland Street from 1833; the sermon WB heard was typical in its simplicity and directness, and his preaching drew a distinguished congregation, including Charles Dickens and his family, who attended the chapel from early 1843 (*Pilgrim Edition of the Letters of Charles Dickens*, III, 1974, pp. 449, 455). One of the proprietors of the College, and later on the Council of University Hall.
[6] In the *Appeal from the New to the Old Whigs* Burke says that God has 'virtually subjected us to act the part which belongs to the place assigned to us the duties are all compulsive'.
[7] Augustus De Morgan (1806–71), mathematician; held the chair of Mathematics at University College, 1828–31 and 1836–66, and its most outstanding thinker and teacher.

new and more extended view which he takes of the symbols of Algebra and on a way which he has of explaining them by Geometry; they were on abstract parts of the subject, and Mr De Morgan goes on rather fast, but he is quite ready to answer any questions, and to solve any difficulties, which may occur to any of us. He seems to take a very great pleasure in imparting knowledge to those who are really attentive, and wish to profit, but those who are not so do not like much. He is not a good driller for an examination, I should think, he does not give his class such specific directions as to what they were to read out of the class, as could be wished—He has however referred us to some articles of his in the Penny Cyclopaedia[8] on positive and negative quantities; they are chiefly the same as his lectures, although he is clearer as lecturer than as a writer. Of my home arrangements I have not much time now to speak. I have arranged as we fixed, about dining every day at half past five, which gives me generally speaking a considerable portion of time every day in the college Library.

Tuesday morning. I have kept this letter on the stocks in hopes of having time to finish it, but I have not, nor have I now as it is quite time to go to college, and I must put into the post office on my way thither.[9]

Believe me ever your affectionate son

WALTER BAGEHOT

Love to all. Many thanks for Mamma's kind letter.

To [EDITH BAGEHOT], [23 OCTOBER 1842]

Extract in W. Irvine, *Walter Bagehot*, p. 23, dated 23 October, without name of addressee

Professor De Morgan has *one* eye, and a large white face, rather like Mr. Paul in his manner. He lectures very well, and seems as interested in mathematics, as if he were lecturing on them for the first time, and

---

For reminiscences of his classes and tributes to his influence, see H. Hale Bellot, *University College*, pp. 81–7. Three of the eleven notebooks containing WB's lecture notes (MSS University College, London) are devoted to De Morgan's lectures, 1843–5, and the earliest notebook, dated 'Christmas 1842', has notes on mathematics.

[8] De Morgan, a member of the Useful Knowledge Society since 1826, wrote 850 of the articles in its *Penny Cyclopaedia*.

[9] The postmark is 25 October. In forwarding the letter to 'Maria', Edith Bagehot told her she had 'a great deal to say' which WB's next letter would explain.

had not been going continually over the same ground these ten years. Mr. Malden,[1] they say, was a moderately pleasant looking man before he had the small pox, but certainly now he is, as pitiful a looking creature, as man ever saw. I like him, I think the best of all; he gives us an immense quantity of information on all manner of subjects; and seems quite delighted, if you go and ask him a question which I have done once or twice. He dresses in clothes which look as if moths had been long their familiar inhabitants. Professor Long[2] I don't like so much, he is by no means *so* interesting, *and* is exceedingly minute, not to say almost tiresomely so, but he may improve as he gets more accustommed[3] to the class, and we get more accustommed to him.

To T. W. BAGEHOT, 30 OCTOBER 1842

MS: Mr Norman St John-Stevas

Camden Town, October 30th. 1842

My dearest Papa,

I sit down in great perplexity of mind to write to you: I do not know, whether the course of conduct I am now taking, will appear to

---

[1] Henry Malden (1800–76), professor of Greek at University College 1831–76, and joint headmaster of University College School with T. H. Key from 1831 to 1842; a member of the Committee of the Society for the Diffusion of Useful Knowledge. At school with Macaulay and at Cambridge, where Malden had a brilliant career. His obituary in the *Spectator* (probably by the editor, R. H. Hutton, WB's fellow-student in Malden's classes) described him as 'Conscientious, delicate, precise, with something in him of the mathematician's as well as the scholar's sense of beauty', and said that his only fault as a teacher was to be so 'careful, painstaking, and elaborate' that he could not cover all the greater Greek authors (*Spectator*, 8 July 1876, quoted in H. Hale Bellot, *University College, London*, pp. 93–4). WB's notes on his lectures in the session 1842–3 are preserved at University College, London.

[2] George Long (1800–79), professor of Greek at University College 1828–31, and of Latin 1842–46; one of the leading authorities on Roman history and law. A contemporary of Macaulay and Malden at Cambridge, where he defeated both in obtaining a Trinity College fellowship; professor of Ancient Languages at the newly established University of Virginia (where he came to know Thomas Jefferson) from 1824 to 1828; he was editor of the *Quarterly Journal of Education* published by the Society for the Diffusion of Useful Knowledge, and of the Society's *Penny Cyclopaedia* and *Biographical Dictionary*. Hutton recalled Long's 'caustic irony, accurate and almost ostentatiously dry learning, and profoundly stoical temperament' ('Memoir' of WB, *Collected Works*, XIV, pp. 00–0, see also H. Hale Bellot, *op. cit.*, pp. 89–92). There are notes on Long's lectures, 1842–4, in WB's University College lecture notes.

[3] Thus in printed text; probably WB's misspelling.

OCTOBER 1842

you right or not, but I can only say, that it has not been taken without the most anxious consideration. I hope I am doing right, certainly I am not doing what is pleasing to me; and I feel it to be my duty to take a step, before the distance between us will allow me to consult you, which would have been the greatest comfort to me. I have for some time suspected, although I have tried to disbelieve it, as long as I could, that one of my companions Jessop has exceedingly improper connections, and that he is in the habit of visiting them at times, when Dr. Hoppus thinks, he is engaged at college, and on Sunday evenings, when he is thought to be at church. Now certainly I feel, that it cannot be my duty to allow this state of things to continue; I do not think it would be doing right either to Dr. Hoppus or to Jessop himself; yet the office of talebearer is so invidious, and in general so contemptible that I confess I am exceedingly loath to undertake it. The immediate necessity of taking some step is, that tonight under pretence of going to a debating society at the college, Jessop is going to introduce another of my companions Collier to these women: this certainly must be stopped and I possess no other means of doing so, but informing Dr. Hoppus *immediately*. I at first thought of threatening them with doing so if they did not consent to stay at home, this evening, but I should have had no means of compelling them to stay, and it would have been impossible for me, to know really whether they went to the college or not. Besides they must have given some reason to Dr. H. for their staying at home as it has been usual for them to go, which reason must have been a false one. I do not think, I should have minded, at least I hope not, the position in which this would have placed me: which indeed will be made worse by the step of telling Dr. H. as I shall most likely be charged with it, and in that case I shall not of course attempt to deny it. What renders it still more painful to me is that Jessop has so much good feeling and is altogether so pleasing, that I like, what I have seen of him, except in this unfortunate affair—

I have expressed my abhorrence of it to him, when I only suspect it, and have I hope as much as was in my power discouraged all conversation on such kind of subjects, but it was not in my power to prevent them altogether. I am now going to seek a conversation with Dr. H. I could not well do so sooner, as the others are only just going to college. I need not tell how much anxiety this has cost me, or how much I dislike the duty I am going to perform, but my resolution has not been taken without the most careful deliberation, and I may add earnest prayer. I will try to snatch a moment before I go to college, to tell you the result, the details I must reserve, but it will give me [very][1] much comfort to hear from you that I shall put this into the post, as I go to college. The conversation is now over. Dr H. was much shocked, and seems inclined to sift the matter to the very bottom; farther indeed than I had supposed, as he intends, if he finds my information correct, to send Jessop away immediately; for this I shall in some respects be sorry, although I cannot but think it essential to Jessop's welfare that he should be immediately removed from London—I cannot say more, as it is more than time for me to go to college, and I have a racking headache, caused I think in great part by my not having slept well for the last night or two, scarcely at all last night, which was spent resolving and doubting on the step I have now taken. Dr H. said that he felt another difficulty, that of not shocking Mrs H.[2] who is expecting confinement—I need not say how much good it will do me, to know that you think I have done right. Dr. H. assured me that he was greatly obliged to me for stating it to him, which makes me hope that I have done so.

Believe me ever your affectionate son
WALTER BAGEHOT.

To EDITH BAGEHOT, [?NOVEMBER 1842]

<small>Extracts in RB, X, 25, 103, undated but clearly soon after last</small>

I hope I have acted right; I have at least the consoling reflection that I tried to do so and that I did not enter upon the performance of a duty to me exceedingly painful in reliance of my own strength, but with the hope of God's allwise direction. It is my first taste of the troubles of life; henceforth I shall perhaps never be wholly free from them, and although overcoming one, may render the others more easy, I felt the other day with some beautiful lines of Wordsworth:—

---

[1] Tear at the seal has removed four letters.
[2] Martha Devenish (*d.* 1853) married Hoppus 1832.

Yet why repine we, created as we are for joy and rest,
To find them only, in the bosom of eternal things.[1]
I must say good-bye as I am scribbling, when I ought to be reading Mr. De Morgan on 'the square roots of unity!'

To T. W. BAGEHOT, 3 NOVEMBER 1842

MS: Mr Norman St John-Stevas

Camden Town. Nov. 3rd. 1842.

My dearest Papa,

Many, many thanks for the kind sympathy of your note, and for the wish it contained, that I might be supported against the temptations, and difficulties I might have to encounter; many have arisen out of this most painful affair; but the consciousness that I have acted right is, I thank God a sufficient support. The step I have taken has of course made my companions exceedingly angry, and for this I was prepared: they do not however break forth into any abuse, nor have any painful scenes of a quarrelsome nature occurred, on the contrary, they do not speak to me 'either good or bad'. This [is] perhaps the very best course for all parties which they could have pursued.—The line of defence they at first adopted, was a total and indiscriminate denial; when this failed, they took the ground of the conversations which I heard being only conversations; and not as they seemed to me recitals of events; and Collier says he saw no harm in the conversations. Mr. Collier his father who lives in London is coming here to day, and Dr. Hoppus informed me that he should probably wish me to repeat in his presence what I stated to him, and told me that he should wish now to make a note of the principal circumstances. The scene of today will probably be an exceedingly painful one, but I hope, God will give me strength to go through it, and to state the truth, as it really occurred.

Friday Morning I had no time to finish this letter last night, and

---

[1] WB's recollections of the concluding lines of 'To the Clouds', from the recently published *Poems, Chiefly of Early and Late Years*: 'Yet why repine, created as we are/For joy and rest, albeit to find them only/Lodged in the bosom of eternal things?'

have only a moment now before I go to college to tell you, that the painful scene of last night is over; it was trying to all of us: Collier's father seemed at first inclined to be very angry, but after talking with Dr. Hoppus for some time, he became much calmer. Collier went away with his father last night, and it is uncertain whether he will return. Dr. H. does not wish to take him back, and told his father so: if however his father should seem to be going to be very strict indeed, Dr. H. will probably take him back. I apprehend from some expressions of his father to him last night, that he has not been very steady before—

I shall not post this letter in the postoffice till I have had your letter, which was promised me this morning—Friday Evening I am only just come home and have only time to thank you for your most affectionate, and comforting letter.

Believe me ever
Your affectionate son
WALTER BAGEHOT—

Love to all—Thank Mamma for her kind letter—

To T. W. BAGEHOT, 16 NOVEMBER 1842

MS: Mr Norman St John-Stevas

Nov. 16th. 1842. Camden St.

My dearest Papa,

I send you with this the answers to your questions. I think there should at all events be, as you think no alteration until Christmas, and indeed until that time I should hardly be able to judge satisfactorily, as to many of the points in question, particularly as to the main one of whether I am to try for honors in both Classics and Mathematics. If I have time, I should much prefer doing so. I do not fancy there would be any advantage in consulting the professors of the College at present, as they will have no opportunity until Christmas of knowing, what I do know, and what I do not, without knowing which they could give no advice. At the Christmas examination I shall have an opportunity of measuring my strength with the rest of the class and of seeing, how I stand with respect to them, which will afford valuable data for determining on the main question. Until that time I will if you think it right, and best, go on preparing for honors both in classics and mathematics. I will as you suggest, take an early opportunity of consulting Smith Osler, the next time I see him which may not however be quite immediately, as he is very little indeed at the college, and our classes are of course different—

In my answer to your first question I said, that there would be a great deal to do beside my work for the classes if I were to matriculate with honors. This will be particularly the case in classics where from want of time a very small portion of the London course will be gone over. But I am persuaded the grand secret is to do perfectly what is done, and that the pass examination for which the Latin and Greek classes prepare tell very much on the examination for honors; indeed it is said in the rules and regulations of the London University, that 'it will be made the basis'; and that the examination for honors is to give the examiners more complete knowledge of the qualifications of each student—There has been a very hard contest for the classical Flaherty[1] this year, a Mr. Bunnell Lewis[2] has gained it: he looks the picture of a worn out student, pale and almost feeble, he seems really to be ruining his health. He has the reputation of being exceedingly diligent although not *very* quick; he must however be very clever as he got the classical scholarship last year.

Believe me ever your
affectionate son
W BAGEHOT.

Love to all. Please to write soon.

---

[1] Scholarship called after the old lady who endowed it in 1836 (H. Hale Bellot, *University College*, pp. 188–9).
[2] Bunnell Lewis (1824–1908), classical archaeologist; fellow of University College 1847, MA 1849, taking the gold medal then first awarded; appointed Professor of Latin, Queen's College, Cork, 1849.

To EDITH BAGEHOT, 24 NOVEMBER 1842

MS: Mr Norman St John-Stevas

Nov. 24, 1842. Camden St.

My dearest Mamma,

I have only a moment to say that I hope, you will send immediately, or that Papa will, such parts of my last letter, as you say, are not intelligible[1]—I think it very possible, that it may be so, as I had a bad head ache, at the time, I was writing it.

If the unsensible parts be too many, please to send the whole letter, and I will rewrite in a better form.

Believe me in great haste
Yours ever affectionately

W BAGEHOT.

I hope Mr. Small gave Richard 1st. a very bad character; Scott gives much too favorable a description of him in Ivanhoe and the Talisman.

To T. W. BAGEHOT, 11 DECEMBER 1842

MS: Mr Norman St John-Stevas

Camden St. Dec 11th. 1842.

My dearest Papa,

Many thanks for your note, which I have just received. I think my Aunt[1] in her kindness has grievously overstated the matter of my illness or rather I suppose liability to illness—although I was not 'feeling

---

[1] The letter of 16 November has several small corrections in pencil in WB's hand.

* * *

[1] Mary Ann Reynolds; WB was a frequent visitor at Cannon Villas, Squire's Mount, Hampstead, where his uncle and aunt Reynolds lived.

very strong' as Aunt Emma would say, at the beginning of last week. I am now however much better, and I hope we shall neither of us be on the sick list when I come home—I think, that will be on Wednesday or Thursday week, but most probably the latter. My examination is to be over at 12 oclock on Wednesday, not knowing the times of the trains I cannot tell whether I could or not come that evening but I should think it possible. Please to send me a train Paper, for I don't know where to get one here, London being *large*. The examinations are to be the Mathematics and the natural Philosophy on Monday three hours apiece. The English language, and Latin also three hours apiece—on Tuesday: Greek on Wednesday for three hours[2]—one thing has surprized me and rather put me out. It is that we are not to be told a single word about how we have done until Midsummer; I cannot conceive the use of this, to the Students certainly none, but the Professors will not be so much pressed for time in looking over the papers as they would be supposing the result was to be made known immediately, and this I suppose is the real reason. I am I hope pretty forward in my preparations, and shall not be much cooped up in a corner at last: I do not however anticipate any very great success, the more so because those who have been at the college longer have from their former experience great advantage in knowing exactly what to prepare for the examination and how to do it. I believe I must stop, as I have some things which I must do before I go to Hampstead. You have the less right to complain of my shortening this letter as it [is] in great part your own doing.

Believe me ever your affectionate son
W BAGEHOT.

Many thanks to Mamma for her parenthetical note.
Love to all.

---

[2] Certificates of attendance, required from candidates for degrees, were granted only to those who had taken the class examinations before Christmas and at the end of session; these 'came to bulk very large in undergraduate life, and they were of portentous length' (H. Hale Bellot, *University College*, p. 298).

DECEMBER 1842

T. W. BAGEHOT to WB, 11 DECEMBER 1842

Extracts in RB, X, 96–7, 85, dated 11 December 1842; 11 December was a Sunday in 1842, RB, X, 96, is therefore in error in assigning the letter to WB's schooldays at Bristol

Herd's Hill, 11th December, 1842.
Sunday Morning.

The education required in the present day must be laid on a wide foundation, and ample time given for raising the structure. A tree and its roots and branches is a better figure. The roots must be deep and firm if the trunk is to grow high and its branches spread widely, and all its parts must grow together. A man's character must be gradually forming religiously, morally, and intellectually, which cannot be done, I think, but through the influence of time and the circumstances which accompany it. If one part of the character be forced too much, it will generally be at the expense of some strength in another, and I often think that we may trace some of the faults of young and old collegians to the too exclusive pursuits of collegiate honours. In saying this, however, I know you will think that I under-rate the exertions that must and ought to be made by them. Temperance is all I wish to inculcate and a wide view of the blessings of education founded in wisdom and virtue. Every day do I feel how much I have lost in not having had such an education as I wish to give you, and you need not therefore fear that anything will be wanting on my part to secure to you its advantages. I do not repine although I feel that there is a world beyond my ken, and that that world of knowledge and usefulness may bring with it more happiness than can be mine. But thankfulness and not mere contentment is the deep sentiment of my heart for the blessings of my lot, and as I have education enough for the immediate duties of my station, and for growing wiser and better for that world where light and truth and peace reign now and for ever, I must be more anxious to make a right use of the talent I have, than disappointed that it is not larger.

During my illness I have had one half day, nay nearly two, of the luxury of the leisure forced on me, and have read some of McIntosh's life[1] with great interest; but Saturday and Sunday, when I was first taken, were days of suffering and annoyance.

JUNE–JULY 1843

Her mind² is in a nervous state, which a trifle seems occasionally to excite and could ill bear any serious burden, so I have not had so much to delight me as in some of my illnesses.

To T. W. BAGEHOT, [?JANUARY 1843]

Extract in RB, X, 103–4, dated at the beginning of WB's second term at University College

I went to breakfast with Smith Osler, this morning, and on his offering to perform his promise of proposing me in the Debating Society, I told him frankly that I thought my being able to get in exceedingly doubtful, and on his inquiring told him the reason.¹ He said that if I would put him in possession of the circumstances of the affair, he would try to get me elected.²

To T. W. BAGEHOT, [?JUNE–JULY 1843]

Extract in RB, X, 108–9
DATE: probably June or July 1843: see n. 1

We have been getting up a new Society¹ to supersede the old one.

---

¹ *Memoirs of the Life of ... Sir James Mackintosh*, ed. R. J. Mackintosh, 1835; Mackintosh, philosopher and politician, was one of the Holland House circle, a contributor to the *Edinburgh Review*, and a coadjutor of Romilly's in his work for legal reform.
² WB's mother.

* * *

¹ The report WB had made to Dr Hoppus of the bad conduct of Jessop and Collier (see letter of 30 October), which had resulted in their removal. Smith Osler, in the tribute he wrote after WB's death, said: 'The first thing I knew about him when he was not long emerged from boyhood was an act of great moral courage' (RB, X, 104).
² Osler must have been successful in securing WB's election to the old debating society: see next.

* * *

¹ Debating Society, which replaced the old Literary and Philosophical Society. H. Hale Bellot records that the old society was still in existence in June 1843, but was probably superseded soon afterwards (*University College*, p. 296). For a debate in February 1844, see WB's letter of 1 March 1844.

JUNE–JULY 1843

Roscoe,[2] Hutton,[3] and myself are the chief prime movers. We have had one meeting to organise the Society, in which *I* was in the chair. Roscoe was unexpectedly prevented from attending the meeting and Hutton fought shy of the honor, which accounts for my elevation.[4] I am to be replied to on Capital Punishments by a Mr. Stowell,[5] whom I don't know personally, but who is reckoned a crack speaker. My motion was very reasonable as there was a lack of subjects at first starting, De Morgan just beginning.

---

[2] William Caldwell Roscoe (1825–59), poet and essayist; eldest son of William Stanley Roscoe and grandson of the historian William Roscoe. The Roscoes were a Unitarian family, and W. C. Roscoe was educated privately in Liverpool and at University College, London, where he was a year ahead of WB and Hutton; after gaining his BA 1843, he was entered at the Middle Temple, and called to the bar 1850. As students WB and Hutton were not yet close to Roscoe; their admiring interest in him appears in two letters Hutton wrote to WB from Heidelberg in the autumn of 1846 (MSS Mr Norman St John-Stevas), when Roscoe came there with his mother, sister (whom Hutton later married) and a younger brother. Hutton was 'decidedly afraid' of Roscoe, but found the whole family delightful, with 'deep religious feeling' and 'our enthusiastic attachment to the personal history of Christ'; William had shown 'how sensitively reserved' he was, though quite without 'haughtiness', and confirmed Hutton's impression that he was 'more formed to appreciate the beautiful than the sublime', while morally 'his conscience must have rather to rouse his will than to direct it'. By 1847 all three were contributors to the *Prospective Review*, as they were to the *Inquirer* a few years later, and many of Roscoe's finest critical essays were written for the *National Review* of which WB and Hutton were joint editors. After Roscoe's early death Hutton published his *Poems and Essays*, with a prefatory memoir, including a letter from WB (see Vol. XIV).

[3] Richard Holt Hutton (1826–97), theological writer, journalist and critic; highly successful editor of the *Spectator* from 1861 until his death: the paper was given its character by his liberal political views, espousal of Christianity against rationalism, and literary judgment. From their first meeting as undergraduates at University College, WB was his closest and most admired friend; his 'Memoir' of WB, in its various forms (see *Collected Works*, XIV) is a valuable biographical source, and he brought out the first collections of WB's writings. Hutton was educated at University College because he was a Unitarian, son of the Revd Joseph Hutton (1790–1860), and himself intended for the Unitarian ministry; but during the 1850s Hutton moved away from Unitarianism, and in later life was in sympathy with high Anglicanism and a devoted admirer of Cardinal Newman. See also 'A Short Biography', *Collected Works*, I, 42–3.

[4] Roscoe was the Society's first chairman. In a letter to WB of 7 October 1844, Hutton wrote: 'Sanford told me the other day that Roscoe is not coming back to town for 2 or 3 months. So we shall have to get a new chairman. We will put you into the chair. Roscoe and Rees both away! Brady is coming to read in town, they say: we must get him. I dare say he will speak well. . . . As Sanford remarks we must get up one or two good debates and increase the society' (MS Norman St John-Stevas).

[5] Not identified.

JULY 1843

To EDITH BAGEHOT, [?OCTOBER 1842–JULY 1843]

Extract in RB, X, 118, undated, possibly written during WB's first year at University College

De Morgan has been taking us through a perfect labyrinth lately; he was quite lost by the whole class for one lecture, but we are, I hope, getting better, and more gleg at the uptake. We have been discussing the properties of infinite series, which are very perplexing—one is harassed by getting a glimpse of theorems and then to find that they are to be taken with so many limitations, that one has still greater difficulty in seeing them at all. My father will understand the difficulty, when he is asked to see how—$1 = 1 + 2 + 4 + 16 + 32 \ldots$ to an infinite number of terms.

To EDITH BAGEHOT, [10 JULY 1843]

Extract in RB, X, 114–15, dated 10 July 1843

My dearest Mamma,

I have just come back from Somerset House, and beg leave to inform you that, in spite of all croaking and forebodings, I am actually past and in the *first class*. Also that I have been further recommended to go in for honours both in Classics and Mathematics. We had no business to hear this till to-morrow, but Hutton and myself with some others, by dint of bothering officials, got admitted to Dr. Jerrard's[1] august presence. He was kind indeed, I think affectionate is the only proper word, and especially congratulated Hutton and myself on our 'distinguished success' hitherto! He said that he strongly recommended us to go in for Classics, and said that though he could not personally give any opinion on Mathematics, he assured us that the Mathematical examiners spoke very highly of us.[2]

---

[1] Joseph Henry Jerrard (?1801–53), fellow and classical examiner of London University. Jerrard, educated at Trinity College, Dublin, and Caius College, Cambridge, had been the first principal of Bristol College, 1831–38.
[2] The extract continues with three sentences from the letter to his father of 11 July ('It is rather an awful... get on it at all').

To T. W. BAGEHOT, 11 JULY 1843

MS: Mr Norman St John-Stevas

Camden St. July 11th. 1843

My dearest Papa,

I snatch a few minutes to tell you, how I am getting on which I flatter myself you will be anxious to hear—I hope on the whole pretty fairly so far—though the worst day tomorrow is yet to come. I hope to get put down which is all I ever expected—the scholarship I never had any hopes of, and so I hope I shall not be disappointed at not getting it, and most assuredly shall not—It is rather an awful circumstance that out of 80 who passed only four had the courage to put their names down, namely Hutton two King's College men and myself. One of the King's College men was faint hearted at the important moment and gave it up so that we are the only *three* candidates. I think I shall probably almost certainly be the last on the list if I get on it at all—

They are I believe very cautious about putting men down, and never have put down more than four on any former year. The King's College man is utterly incomprehensible. Hutton and myself have been working him in all ways to find out what sort he is but wholly without success—He passed in the second class, which is at least a sign of his not being generally well informed on the subjects examined in—If however he does everything that he says he does and as well as he says he does, he has the scholarship out and out—but he has been convicted (or at least there have been exceedingly suspicious circumstances) of what look like bragging or showing off and one does not know what allowance to make for it. About classical honors I have not yet settled—Last night I had thoroughly made up my mind not to go in. I was then very out of sorts indeed very restless and uncomfortable, but tonight I am thankful to say I am much better, and I hope there is no reason to fear breaking down—

Many thanks to my mother for her kind note and to you all for your affectionate interest.

Believe me ever very tired
Your affectionate son
W BAGEHOT.

Love to all—

To EDITH BAGEHOT, 17 JULY 1843

MS: Mr Norman St John-Stevas

Camden St. July 17th. 1843.

My dearest Mamma,

I have just received four letters from home altogether, two from Papa and two from you, for all which I thank you, though I am afraid you have been rather '*dampers*' on my spirits. You will conclude from this exordium that I have chosen not to go in for classical honors, and this is the case. After writing that note to Papa on Saturday I determined on a last trial to see how I should get on. But after an hour's work, I got thoroughly exhausted and went to sleep over my books, and when I awoke, really felt as if I had not two ideas—and this decided me. I had persevered all day against a pain in my shoulder, and a slight difficulty in breathing, which are by no means incentives to hard study. It would have been useless to go in without learnig a whole book of Thucydides, which in the interval there would have been just time for, and but just in my usual state, and not time sufficient in my present state.

I should not have cared so much, if I could have got sleep when I went to bed, but every night for the last ten days I have lain awake for nearly two hours or an hour and ½ after I went to bed, and this makes a good hole in a night of 6 hours at most—Under these circumstances I hope you will think that I have done right; at least in looking forward I cannot but think that if I had gone on and had done my health any serious injury it would have been by no means a soothing reflection that I had lost so good an opportunity of pausing.

Believe me ever
your affectionate son
W BAGEHOT.

Love to all

I had just forgotten to mention, though I did not forget the fact, that I hope to leave London on Wednesday morning. I hope by the ¼ past ten train, and to be at dear Herd's Hill, and with you all at six to dinner—

JULY 1843

To EDITH BAGEHOT, [?17] JULY 1843

Extract in RB, X, 115, dated 17 July from Somerset House; the reference to 'last evening' suggests that WB misdated a letter of 18 July

A change has come o'er the spirit of my dream[1] as will be observed from the date of my letter. I got remarkably better last evening, and have ventured on trying on a forlorn hope. I don't expect to get placed at all, as I have had no preparation or cramming whatever. There are seven of us trying.

To Mrs J. S. REYNOLDS, 26 JULY 1843

MS: Mr Norman St John-Stevas

Herds Hill
July 26th. 1843

My dear Aunt,

Being in a state of very great excitement much in the way of epistolary correspondence is not to be expected. The result for which you will be kind to turn over is most amazing—After all the pros and cons I had no right to expect anything of the kind and did not.
   The result in Classics
   —Barry[1] (Exhibitioner) Kings
   —O'Reilly[2] St. Cuthbert's Ushaw

---

[1] 'A change came o'er the spirit of my dream' (Byron, 'The Dream').

* * *

[1] Alfred Barry (1826–1910), educated at King's College, London, where he took seven prizes in 1843, and at Trinity College, Cambridge, of which he became a fellow in 1848, when he was 4th wrangler and 7th classic. Principal of King's College, London, 1868–83; Bishop of Sydney and Primate of Australia, 1884–89.
[2] Myles O'Reilly (1825–80), of Knock Abbey, Co. Louth, a country gentleman with a great interest in education; one of the Committee for setting up the Catholic University in Ireland in 1851, and acted as Examiner in Classics there at Newman's invitation. A member of the Home Rule party in the House of Commons, 1862–79.

Equal $\begin{cases} \text{W. Bagehot University college} \\ \text{R. H. Hutton University college} \end{cases}$ Equal

Hodgson Pratt[3] University

These were the only five mentioned. I think you have heard me speak of Hutton, and if you have you will know that I consider being equal to him no slight honor. I believe that my English essay was the cause of a good deal of my success. Dr. Jerrard told Hutton that his essay and Mr. Barry's and mine were by far the best and that mine was the best of all. The subject was the Character of Socrates, and the influence of his teaching, and we had to do it without reference to books, and without cramming as the subject was only made known when we entered the examination room.

I do not know whether you will have seen my uncle Edward,[4] who is in town—I believe that all at the Bank is pretty comfortable and Miss Jones is established there and seems at her ease—My Aunt was here last evening and was pleasant.

Believe me
Yours ever affectionately

W BAGEHOT

To T. W. BAGEHOT, 27 SEPTEMBER [1843]

Extract in RB, X, 120–1
DATE: 27 September was a Wednesday in 1843; the letter must have been written from Dublin (see notes)

Wednesday, 27th September.

There are but two events to characterize this day; the first is of a

---

[3] Hodgson Pratt (1824–1907), educated at Haileybury, and entered East India Company's service at Calcutta in 1847; wrote on Indian questions for *The Economist* during 1857; later active in industrial cooperative and peace movements.

[4] Edward Bagehot (?1803–88), younger brother of WB's father. His obituary in the *Langport and Somerton Herald* (11 February 1888) recorded: '[Bagehot] who was one of the principals of the Somerset Trading Company, resided for many years on The Hill, Langport. He was a member of the late Corporation and several times filled the office of Portreeve of the Borough of Langport.'

SEPTEMBER 1843

negative character, that I have not had a letter,[1] but the second is that I have been to a Repeal meeting,[2] and have heard O'Connell—a very remarkable event, to describe which I ought to invoke the aid of every god in the Pantheon, and every saint in the calendar. In sober prose it was a great treat. I never heard any eloquence at all to be compared with O'Connell's. The meeting lasted from two to five, and more than two-thirds of the time was occupied by his speech, or rather speeches, for there were several, as he spoke on every subject which came before the meeting, and these were many. The business commenced by the secretary reading some letters from various branch societies, some of them wordy, which were applauded in proportion to the amount of rant they enclosed. One of these was from the Southern States of America, in which slavery still exists, and which in alluding to some expressions of O'Connell on the subject of Negro slavery, called the god of justice to witness that in opposing 'Emancipation', they were actuated by no motive save a regard to the highest ultimate interests of mankind.[3] All this the meeting heard in perfect silence, until O'Connell rose, and observed that he was perfectly indifferent to the terms of reproach in which the writer of that letter chose to mention him, but he would not allow the cause of Irish Freedom to be sullied by an alliance so unhallowed. He was quite willing to hear; nay! he gloried in the name of fanatic (this was one of the epithets in the letter) if to be a fanatic was to love, and honour the cause of freedom, however it might be opposed by distinctions of man's erecting, whether they were of sect, party, or colour. The invocation to the god of justice seemed to him something like blasphemy. It amounted to imputing to the Ruler of Nations, distinctions between one man and his fellow, founded on the

---

[1] This suggests that WB was in Dublin for several days. Although the present letter is the only evidence of his visit, which is not mentioned in Mrs Barrington's *Life*, there can be no doubt that he was present at the Repeal meeting held in Dublin on 27 September 1843: see n. 2.

[2] 1843 was the most successful year in the short history of the Loyal National Repeal Association founded by Daniel O'Connell in 1840 to bring about the repeal of the 1801 Act of Union; following the return to power of the Conservatives in July 1841, when many Repeal MPs lost their seats, the Association was built up and organized. During 1843 O'Connell held his 'monster meetings', the last at Clontarf on 8 October, and 'repeal rent' was collected from a network of local Associations. WB attended the weekly meeting of the Dublin Association at the Corn Exchange on 27 September; all the details of his account are confirmed by the report in *The Times* of 29 September.

[3] The Repeal Association of St Louis, Missouri, reproached O'Connell for his anti-Slavery speech of 10 May 1843, which caused the dissolution of many American Associations.

bodily difference of colour, which the most enlightened of his creatures had agreed to disregard. I can't pretend to give his words, and even if I could, I could not give you any idea of the voice in which they were uttered. Its higher tones are very dignified and impressive, and the lower ones very sweet, and are heard distinctly in every part of the room. There was much, too, on a proposition made by a Mr. Connor,[4] that no Rent should be paid by the Repealers; O'Connell quite hinted that he was an emissary of the Tory Government and desired to be informed, whether it would not have been but justice to himself, if Mr. Connor had waited until his return before he made a proposition so important, being in truth nothing less than treason. Thence he branched off into a discussion of the present state of the connection between landlord and tenant, and advocated very strongly a plan of which the main feature was to take away from the landlord the right of immediate eviction on the non-payment of rent, and thus to put him on the same footing with other creditors. The second part of his plan was to prohibit by act of parliament leases for any time shorter than twenty-one years, and to give by this means to the tenant a firmer assurance that he would enjoy the fruits of his industry. The audience consisted principally of the Irish not remarkable for the goodness of their garments, and more good-tempered than genteel. At each proposition made by the 'Liberator', there was an impressive *aye*. It was a very tumultuous 'aye' when he proposed that Mr. Connor's name should be effaced from the list of their members. The room was hung round with inscriptions of which these are specimens: 'A people strong enough to be a nation should never consent to be a province'; a better one is: 'Whoever commits a crime, strengthens the hands of our enemies'.

---

[4] William Connor, of Inch, Co. Queen's, had moved such a resolution on 18 September, when O'Connell was not present (*The Times*, 20 September 1843). O'Connell was set on winning concessions from the British government by constitutional means.

To T. W. BAGEHOT, [?JANUARY 1844]

Extract in RB, X, 130–31
DATE: probably January 1844, since the subject is Key's lectures for the session 1843–44 and WB missed the first term, returning to University College in January 1844 (RB, X, 116).

My head is now full enough of queer etymologies,[1] and examples of all manner or changes of all manner of letters. It is not easy to recollect at a moment's notice a number of words in many languages, yet it is necessary to compare the different forms, and thence to rise to more general laws. The subject is yet in its infancy, for the science is not thirty years old, and this adds much to its difficulty. There is no connected system as yet to help the memory. I will write more fully on Monday which I believe is a holiday.

To T. W. BAGEHOT, 27 JANUARY 1844

Text from RB, X, 118–20

39 Camden Street,
27th January, 1844.

My dearest Father,

I took a holiday on Thursday evening to go to the Anti-Corn League in Covent Garden Theatre.[1] It is reckoned to have been a very good meeting though neither of the usual great guns, Cobden and

---

[1] Mrs Barrington explains that WB had begun 'studying etymology with Mr. Key'. Thomas Hewitt Key (1799–1875) held the chair of Latin at University College from 1828 until 1842, when he resigned it to become headmaster of University College School and professor of Comparative Grammar, undertaken at his own request and the first such chair in the country. Hutton recalled that his 'restless and ingenious mind led him many a wild dance after etymological will-of-the-wisps', but he was a stimulating teacher (see H. Hale Bellot, *University College*, pp. 889, 92). WB's notes of Key's lectures on Comparative Grammar survive (MS University College, London).

* * *

[1] The Anti-Corn Law League, founded in 1839, began in 1844 to hold its weekly meetings in Covent Garden and Drury Lane Theatres.

JANUARY 1844

Bright,² were there. Mr. Fox however was a host in himself. Parts of his speech were very fine, and made very impressive by a peculiar but striking manner, and a deep and well modulated voice, and he made the most of the opportunity of going out of the beaten track of Corn Law speeches, afforded him by its being Burns' birthday. He said 'nature made him a poet, and aristocratic protection made him an exciseman'—a very effective parenthesis in his declamation against protection in general. Many passages in his speech were in very bad taste, and though they were those that told best in the pit, they certainly marred its effect on the more cultivated part of his audience. His invective is very stinging, and he has the art to make passages, that are really, I have no question, very elaborately and carefully prepared, seem as if they were struck off the moment without the slightest effort. He had not a single note, and never left a sentence unfinished or went back to begin one again through the whole speech, which lasted a full hour.³

The other speakers were Bouverie⁴ (I am quite sure that everybody who heard him could not blame the Salisbury electors), a Dr. Burnet⁵ and Mr. Milner Gibson.⁶ The last spoke next best to Fox (though there was a great difference between them), and very like a gentleman, in which respect he was unrivalled. The great want in all their harangues was argument, which cannot be mended by any quantity of wit or declamation. One is always tempted to ask, as the landlady did Falstaff, 'What, not a halfpenny-worth of bread to all that sack',⁷ and in treating of a great practical question, and one which as they are themselves

---

² Richard Cobden (1804–65), and John Bright (1811–89). Hutton records that he and Bagehot seldom missed an opportunity of hearing the oratory of Cobden, Bright and W. J. Fox ('Memoir'; see also Hutton's reply to WB's 'remarks on Cobden', letter of 13 September 1843; RB, X, 116–7).
³ The Revd William Johnson Fox (1786–1864), Unitarian minister, journalist and social reformer, was the main speaker; the climax of his appeal for total, immediate and unconditional abolition of the corn laws was a refusal to compromise with the legislature: 'Men of the House of Commons, men of the House of Lords, do as you please, and what you please; our appeal is to your masters' (*Morning Chronicle*, 26 January 1844).
⁴ Edward Pleydell Bouverie (1818–89), elected for Kilmarnock in 1844, after his failure at Salisbury in May and November 1843.
⁵ The Revd John Burnett according to the *Chronicle*; not in the *Clergy List*, and not otherwise identified.
⁶ Thomas Milner Gibson (1806–84), MP for Manchester; one of Cobden's most influential allies and a leading orator for the League.
⁷ Prince Hal on Falstaff's tavern reckoning: 'O monstrous! but one half pennyworth of bread to this intolerable deal of sack!' (I Henry IV, II, iv. 598).

striving to show, requires immediate decision, sound and comprehensive reasoning would seem the most essential requisite, though it is not the one most readily found. Such eloquence as Francis Horner's is what one wants, dealing with the existing question with great precision, but at the same time and by the help of well-grounded and enlarged principles. I have just been galloping over a volume of his life with some of his speeches at the end,[8] which Mr. Reynolds kindly lent me, and which has been an agreeable diversion at times, though I could have wished to have given it more fixed attention as it is well worthy of being studied. He quotes in one place a striking thought from Leibnitz: 'There are secrets in the art of thinking, as in all other arts', and surely seeing accurately how such minds as his were trained to excellence, is not bad education in the art of reflection, and more likely to initiate one into its mysteries, than almost any other. At any rate it is very pleasant to see great minds in their leisure moments, and when they are off the stage; but it certainly does not place genius one whit more within the reach of those who have not it by nature, nor, properly received, does it lessen their greatness, though it lets us into the secret of many faults, which one would not otherwise know of.

To T. W. BAGEHOT, [?23-25 FEBRUARY 1844]

Extract in RB, X, 121-3
DATE: soon after the Anti-Corn Law League meeting of 21 February 1844, but unlikely to be 22 February since WB refers to the meeting as 'on Wednesday' not 'yesterday'.

I was at the Anti-Corn Law League meeting at Covent Garden Theatre on Wednesday evening and witnessed their enthusiastic reception of O'Connell.[1] It was a very imposing sight to see the whole house crammed full as it was in every corner, pit, stage boxes, and

---

[8] Francis Horner (1778–1817); his *Memorials and Correspondence*, ed. Leonard Horner, 1843, which had recently appeared, printed three of his speeches of 1814–15 against the Corn Laws.

* * *

[1] The *Sun* reported that no meeting of the League could be compared with that of 21 February, 'either for the numbers congregated together, or for the enthusiasm ex-

galleries, rise at once at his entrance, and remain standing for more than ten minutes, cheering him the whole time, some waving hats and pocket handkerchiefs, and very many shouting welcome. What made it still more striking was that the crowd outside, which must, from the loudness of their shouts, have been very large, began to cheer several times under the mistaken impression that he was coming, and the audience inside rose each time and cheered, to the very great annoyance of Mr. James Wilson.[2] O'Connell's speech was witty enough, and he continued to express more by the tone of his voice than by anything which he said, the gratitude which he felt for their sympathy when he most wanted it. No man was ever under more disadvantageous circumstances for making a fine speech, as his audience would hardly let him say ten words consecutively without interrupting him by their applause. Certain it is that he was very quiet, nor did he venture on anything half so violent as I have heard Mr. Fox say in the same place, who wound up a long invective against the aristocracy, and the great Pro-Corn Law League, as he calls the House of Lords, with saying that 'he would hurl defiance in their teeth'.[3] The number of people who went away without being admitted was immense, as they posted on the walls of the neighbouring streets in less than half an hour after the doors were opened, that there was no more room. I was on the front of the crowd on the stage, and I could not see a vacant place in the boxes, galleries, or the pit, and we were so crowded that after a great deal of rolling backwards and forwards we carried the platform by storm, very much I have no doubt to the annoyance of those who had tickets for that part of the house and who, relying on the sacredness of the place, came late and found their places occupied. I had to stand the whole evening, but as I heard very well and was very near all the 'dons', I had no reason to complain. It will give you some idea of the enthusiasm that is

---

hibited' (22 February 1844). O'Connell and his principal colleagues had been found guilty of seditious conspiracy on 12 February, after a trial lasting 23 days, and began to serve their sentences in May 1844.

[2] James Wilson (1805–60), politican and political economist, and WB's future father-in-law (see later letters). In his 'Memoir of the Right Honourable James Wilson', WB explains the special value and opportuneness of Wilson's arguments against the Corn Laws in his *Influences of the Corn Laws*, 1839, and in *The Economist*, which he founded in September 1843 (*Collected Works*, III, 332–38). A member of the Council of the Anti-Corn Law League, he often spoke at their meetings, although Mrs Barrington records that 'that sort of agitation was not to his taste, and he would say later that he would be sorry to see other political questions worked in that way' (*Servant of All*, I, 30).

[3] At the meeting of 15 February 1844 (*Morning Chronicle*, 17 February 1844).

felt for him in London, when I tell you that they began to issue tickets at half-past twelve on Monday and that at a quarter before one they had none left in the outer office, and numbers of people were going away without them. Hutton and myself, however, by dint of very great exertions, and contempt of the repeated refusals of all inferior satellites, made our way to the head committee room and by dint of eloquence obtained a ticket apiece there. I don't know whether you have not reason to complain of all this description, but I was very full of it for a day or two, as it was a scene quite new to me, and write now to let off the steam. I must add that I had hardly ever so distinct a notion of the greatness of London, as when I came out, and saw how little inter st all this great assemblage seemed to excite three streets off, and how little effect it had on either the numbers or direction of the throng of passengers.

To EDITH BAGEHOT, [1 MARCH 1844]

Extract in RB, X, 123-4, dated 1 March 1844

I can communicate no intelligence on any matters of fact whatever, except that I went a few evenings ago to hear a chartist lecturer on the present state of the country. His name is Vincent.[1] He is a clever and eloquent man, and by no means wholly in error as to his views of political matters. He is very opposed to the use of physical force, and is half his time talking about Christian principles.

I have been reading some more of Carlyle's French Revolution which I think I told you I had begun. His political opinions are very strange. In fact, I think he utterly disbelieves in the usefulness of any institutions. For Hereditary Monarchy and Hereditary Aristocracy he has a thorough contempt. Representative assemblies he commonly calls National Debating Clubs, the right of suffrage, the power to send the $\frac{1}{5000}$ part of a dumb voice to the central spouting club.[2] Political

---

[1] Henry Vincent (1813-78), Chartist and radical lecturer, known as one of the finest popular orators of his time. From April 1842 his speeches were devoted to the cause of the Complete Suffrage Union, and became more moderate and conciliatory in their tone; many Chartists regarded him as a traitor.

[2] A reminiscence of *Chartism*, ch. ix: 'one's right to vote for a Member of Parliament, to send one's "twenty-thousandth part of a master of tongue-fence to National Palaver".'

science is a hard subject, but this rejection of all the common expedients for governing a community strikes one as strange. He, I think, is for a Natural Aristocracy[3] as he calls it. He thinks that it would be an advantage if the highest minds in every generation were engaged in the actual direction of the state power. But I cannot see why the highest intellects should not be employed rather in communicating new truth to mankind, or labouring to illustrate known truth and to instruct the mass of the population in old and valuable knowledge. This is, I think, a far higher way of influencing the happiness of the world, than the application of physical force to protect men's lives and properties. It is a not unfrequent source of error in such reasonings to confound the influence exercised by the finest minds over their fellow-men by persuasion and conviction with the Government by laws and Acts of Parliament. The two things seem very distinct, but I could quote from writers of very high reputation instances of their being confounded. As far as I understand Dr. Arnold's theory that Government ought to be sovereign over human life,[4] it seems grounded on nothing else but the assumption that the Government by argument and the Government by force must necessarily be the same. We had a debate on a subject very like this a few days ago in our Debating Society. The question was 'whether Government ought to interfere with the dissemination of blasphemous or seditious publications'. I took the negative. The debate was spirited. More like a real description of actual business than I ever knew in a society for the purpose of speaking. Everybody seemed to feel the question to be one of interest and impotance. If you or my father are interested about it, I will send you my speech[5] in a day or two. Mr. De Morgan has lately had an amusing feud with one of his lower classes. Some students would come late, and the professor, to keep them out, locked the door, which has made him rather unpopular.[6] It is not so bad as last year, however, when he told the same class with much bitterness, that they were robbing their parents and insulting him! The rest of the students thought of asking him to take the Chair of Rhetoric in consequence.

---

[3] Cf his demand for 'a *real* Aristocracy' in *Chartism*, ch. vi.
[4] In such writings by Thomas Arnold as *Principles of Church Reform*, 1833, and the preface to his *History of Rome*, 1838–42.
[5] For Bagehot's address in the debate of February 1844, see *Collected Works*, Vol XIV.
[6] See Sophia De Morgan, *Memoir of Augustus De Morgan*, 1882, p. 101.

To T. W. BAGEHOT, 18 MARCH 1844

Extract in RB, X, 130

39 Camden Street,
18th March, 1844.

My dearest Father,

I shall begin with observing that the literary taste of the family is, I fear, at a low ebb. I yesterday received a note from my mother (I have received none from anyone today) in which she enjoined on me not to say anything about the meeting at Covent Garden the other evening[1] on the insulting ground of you being able to see it in the papers. Now it is too bad to have one's powers of description put on a level with a newspaper reporter's! It is degrading to have it thought that one has no better eyes and ears for whatever passes than a man who is the whole time scribbling shorthand! ! ! ! In spite of all injunctions the meeting was so curious, that I shall expend a word or two on it. The 'Friends of Ireland', as the advertisement set forth, would appear to be Irish, or at least Celtic for Repealers, of whom the meeting was for by far the most part composed, and of which the speakers all expressed themselves advocates. Certainly if good coats and clean linen were taken as the best tokens of the strength or weakness of a political party, the Repealers would be weak indeed, for as Dickens somewhere says the greater part of them seemed to have quarrelled with their washerwomen in earlier youth and to have taken a fixed resolution never to make it up.[2] Two striking peculiarities in the assembly were the unaccountable disposition of the people in the dress circle to go down into the pit, and their striking familiarity with the Irish accent and the Irish howl. Nevertheless the chairman,[3] a heavy man in a white waistcoat, called the meeting 'most respectable'. O'Connell's speech will be in the papers for certain, so that I must not lay hands on it, and indeed, excepting its strong Repeal character, there was verylittle

---

[1] The meeting of the Friends of Ireland on 14 March; the *Morning Chronicle* (15 March) described the audience as principally composed of the Irish in London, and said that the 'jokes and merriment reminded us somewhat of a Christmas audience on boxing-night'. O'Connell spoke of the sympathy for Ireland now felt by the people of Britain and emphasized that his aim was repeal of the Union, not separation.
[2] *Martin Chuzzlewit*, ch. XXXIV, in the No. published February 1844.
[3] W. J. O'Connell, grand repeal warden for London.

about it remarkable. He spoke with his hat on, and seemed quite at home, though he was looking, I thought, wan and haggard.

TRAVEL JOURNAL, [JULY 1844]

Extracts in RB, X, 132–5

Bruges.[1] 26th July. A day of sightseeing which begins at six in the morning and ends at nine at night, gives one much to set down, but leaves little time or inclination for doing so. . . . We went to the hospital of the Sisters of Charity, whom we saw in full costume, and it was considered pleasing to see them go round to the sick people in the wards, and give them *gebäckte* meat. I have no notion of that kind of pleasure. It is pleasing no doubt to know that from a sentiment of piety towards Him who is higher than the highest, these women go through a laborious course of trial to be allowed to wait on the meanest of His creatures, but watching them in the lowest part of their functions is not the way to have the most favourable ideas of them. Cutting roast beef, and putting it into plates with the fingers is no doubt a very useful operation, but I should prefer the general notion that a person went about doing good, to knowing that they did this, and seeing them about it. . . . .

I have left myself little room to speak of what I consider much the most beautiful object I have seen on the continent. I mean, a statue supposed to be by Michaelangelo in the Cathedral of Notre Dame of the Virgin and Jesus. The delicacy of the figures, the infantine simplicity of Jesus, and the motherly anxiety of Mary who is looking down at him as he sits on her lap[2] give a grace to the whole group too impressive to be forgotten, but which I can't put into words.

The Cathedral at Antwerp is the most delicate Gothic building in the world according to the guide-book,[3] which also states that

---

[1] WB was making his first journey to the Continent on a tour arranged by Mr and Mrs Reynolds, partly as a consequence of anxiety about his health (RB, X, 118). From 24 July he kept 'a copious journal for the benefit of his parents' (RB, X, 132).
[2] Michelangelo's marble *Madonna and Child* in the Chapel of the Holy Sacrament; the Child is not seated on her lap, but standing between her legs.
[3] From Murray's *Handbook*, which shows that these remarks were made about the

JULY 1844

Napoleon compared it to Mechlin lace, and Charles 5th. said it ought to be kept in a case. At Ghent we saw a beautiful likeness in wood of Charles 5th. of the most spirited kind on a celebrated chimney piece in the Palais de Justice.[4] Whoever wants to get an admiration of Rubens let him come to Antwerp. It has thoroughly converted my Aunt Reynolds who is not in most cases, as the family know, a convertible person. The descent from the cross, of which you have the print in the drawing room, is beautiful as far as colouring is concerned. The body stands out from the canvas which is the more remarkable as being on a white ground. The raising the cross[5] is also fine. None of the paintings by Rubens in the National Gallery, and none that I have ever before seen, give any idea of his full strength. A minute examination will often discover defects in the details of his pictures, and one or two of his faces want expression when one would have imagined he would have put forth all his powers, but for striking and instantaneous effect, I have never seen his equal, and I cannot imagine anything that in this respect would be an improvement on him.

 The last painting which I should wish particularly to recall is a painting of Jesus dead and on the knees of Mary with the Magdalene and the other Mary standing beside her. Mary Magdalene has in a paroxysm of sorrow lifted the hand of Jesus, and is weeping over it. To contrast this with the deep and settled grief of Mary without tears or passion was a noble conception. The tears of the Magdalene and the other Mary are flowing over their countenances, and in the latter it is only a single tear which is beautifully executed. To convey in language a good idea of this picture, and that of the crucifixion by Rubens would require no small share of those powers required for the effort of producing them. The imagination ought to have recourse to every source for the most expressive images of sorrow and suffering, and a yet higher flight in search of illustrations for the suffering and despair of the impenitent thief. The best tribute I can give to them is a statement of the fact that after the rest of the party were gone to look at

---

'delicate Gothic workmanship' of the steeple of Notre Dame.

[4] In the Courtroom, preserved from the original during the rebuilding of 1722–27; the black marble chimneypiece (1528–31) was executed by various artists from designs by Lancelot Blondeel.

[5] The triptychs of *The Raising of the Cross* and *The Descent from the Cross*.

JULY 1844

some Antwerp silk—which, by the way, they lost their way and didn't see—and after throwing all attempts at criticism aside I tried to enter into the conception of the painter, the tears came too fast to my eyes to let me look any longer. I didn't state this publicly for it might look like affectation, yet why it should, I can't see. They are few who would be ashamed of weeping over Lear or Othello, and to come more exactly to the point I am convinced that fewer still would read the narratives in the Gospels, especially St Luke's, if they were not so familiar, without much emotion. In spite of the number of times we have all read them, those who read them in private with attention will find it hard not to pay the same tribute to their deep knowledge of the human heart.

When at Mechlin we afterwards saw another church whose name I have forgotten, in which we saw the picture by Rubens of the Scourging of Jesus,[6] of which we have the print at home. We saw here a priest preaching in Dutch. The meaning was lost on us, though the sound at a distance had an effect remarkably like English. I believe it is less guttural than German to which it is nearly allied, which would make the elementary sounds very much the same as in English, and account for the resemblance I have mentioned, which was felt by all our party. The audience was mostly of the lower class, and the manner of the preacher seemed calculated to attract their attention and did so. All who can read the sermons of Bossuet will not have to learn that eloquence of the highest order is at the command of the Roman hierarchy. Yet it is singular that the art which has for its object the setting forth in attractive and enduring colours and labours of the human mind should be at the service of a system, which sets out with denying the right of private judgment in matters of religion—that is the right of exercising the highest of its powers on the noblest of its subjects.

---

[6] Ruben's *The Flagellation* is not in Mechlin, but in the Dominican church of St Paul in Antwerp, for which it was commissioned as one of a series of paintings by various artists of the Mysteries of the Rosary.

To T. W. BAGEHOT, [?JULY 1844]

Extract in RB, X, 135, written from Brussels

An English gentleman who had resided some months at Mechlin and whom we met in the railroad described the authority of the Roman Catholic priests in that city as so great that a shopkeeper who should offend them would within a week find his shop deserted. If this be not literally true, the clergy must have great power, if a person who had good opportunities of information, and appeared to be an intelligent man, could entertain such an opinion of them.

This uniformity is what many persons in our country are sighing for, but the best description of it is Lord Bacon's,—that all colours are alike in the dark. Ignorance is the surest means of obtaining it. While walking amid the lofty arches of Antwerp Cathedral I could not be otherwise than astonished at the skill with which architecture, and all the fine arts are pressed into the service of Catholicism.

To T. W. BAGEHOT, [?JULY-AUGUST 1844]

Extract in RB, X, 135, written from Aix-la-Chapelle

Mr Reynolds and myself in enquiring about the English service met with a queer character, who seems to act as leading churchwarden. He talked theology at a great pace, but professed never to have heard of the evangelical party, or anything at all contrary to the Church of England being one and indissoluble! He commenced a full detail of the churchwarden's employments in the midst of which we came away. He proved satisfactorily that every subject of conversation could be brought round to a churchwarden's business.

TRAVEL JOURNAL, [?AUGUST 1844]

Extract in RB, X, 135-6, written in Cologne

The streets are gloomy and dirty and narrow, but these are nothing here. Whoever would learn the full strength of the human imagination, the loftiness of human hopes, and the littleness of their fulfilment, let him look on the Cathedral of Cologne. When the original architect drew that plan of the original structure which still exists, and is deemed the finest conception of the Gothic school, he must have felt some swelling pride at leaving behind him a name connected with a structure so magnificent, and some nobler anticipations of the glory his labours would bring to Germany, and of their stimulating effect on the genius of future ages. His name has been lost, and grass has long grown on the unfinished towers that only show what the whole would have been. It is not commonplace declaration to dwell for a moment on so complete a wreck of such aspiring hopes. The Cathedral was begun in A.D. 1248 and received additions till 1509, when the work was stopped, till in 1824 the King of Prussia gave money for continuing the work on its original scale. The choir is now finished, and the rest of the work going on fast, though at the rate of 100,000 dollars a year, the work would last fifty years. The height of the work is well seen from the bridge of boats over the Rhine where the unfinished towers, and also the lower portions are seen far above every other building. The effect of the whole by moonlight, from time to time obscured by heavy masses of dark cloud, with a reflection of the lights on shore in the 'wide and winding river'[1] might, I should think, bear no very distant approach to the celebrated sight of Venice by night from a gondola. I am too much aroused by the beauties of what I have just seen, to be a very fit former of comparisons between it and what I really know—much more than with what I have never seen. They show the skulls of the Magi (or five Kings of Cologne) in the Cathedral and some antiques, but they are too little to be seen or remembered as being there; anywhere else they might have a better chance, but,—I will not break forth again!

---

[1] Byron, *Childe Harold*, III, lv. i.

AUGUST 1844

To EDITH BAGEHOT, 7 [AUGUST] 1844

Text from RB, X, 137–9
DATE: misdated (presumably by WB) 'July' for 'August' as the journal entry for
8 August shows

Nonnenwerth, 7th July, 1844.
6 o'clock in the evening.

My dearest Mother,

I am on an island in the midst of the Rhine, my window opens on it, and the sound of its rushing volume of water is in my ears, and I have been for the last three hours watching the sunset first, and then the shadows deepening over the castle and rock of Drachenfels. If under these circumstances you expect a letter of anything but rapturous enthusiasm you will be disappointed. The very room where I write is strange for it was once a nun's cell. I got so far and only so far last night when I was in a very excited state, and as I am now sitting in the garden beside the Rhine with Rolandseck on my right, and Drachenfels before me I am not now much more endowed with common sense. Rolandseck is famed as the seat of a hermitage built by a lover named Roland, within sight of the nunnery, now turned into a hotel at which I am writing, where his lady love had taken the veil. Schiller has made a very beautiful ballad out of this story,[1] which I have just been reading, and which adds not a little to the interest of the scene.

After I wrote to you from Brussels we went to the field of Waterloo, and returned to Brussels in time to go to Namur by the railroad. The field of Waterloo is not particularly striking as a scene now, though every year of peace adds to the interest of all that is associated with the price the world paid for it. We had a short abstract of the battle by a sergeant engaged in it, found a bullet, examined the holes in the wall at Huguemont, and achieved all the other orthodox and difficult things that have

---

[1] 'The Knight of Toggenberg.' The ruined castle of Rolandseck received its name from the local tradition that the famous nephew of Charlemagne chose this site because it overlooked the convent of Nonnenwerth, where his betrothed was immured, and that he lived there as a hermit for many years; Schiller transferred the scene in his ballad from the Rhine to Switzerland. The convent had been converted into a hotel, with a minimum of alterations, recommended in Murray's *Handbook* for its situation, 'good accommodation and reasonable charges', gardens occupying most of the island, and its excellent fish dinners.

been done by all English tourists since the time of the battle. Mr. Reynolds had so thoroughly forgotten the scene that he could not tell whether any alterations had taken place since you were there. A comparison of dates proved that a large mound of earth with a lion on the top 200 feet high, and very nearly on the spot where the Duke ejaculated, 'Up guards and at em' has been erected since that time.[2] It will be a very enduring memorial and I like it, though my aunt was angry at things being not let stay as they were on the day of the battle. We went from Namur to Liege by the Meuse, which we had heard was beautiful, but which we should not have found out for ourselves. One gentleman said he thought it prettier than the Rhine, but rather neutralised the effect of this, by observing, 'it will be better presently, there won't be so many rocks'. I never understood what the real enjoyment of scenery meant before, and I never expect to experience more of it. Byron has shown most exquisite taste in his selection of Drachenfels as the point of view for his bold description of the Rhine in 'Childe Harold'—the scene is a noble one in itself, the lines in the poem are nervous and impressive when read in England, but it would require a power of illustration as copious and exact as the poet's, to describe the pleasure the poem gives when you can turn from it to the scene it paints. No higher praise can be given to descriptive poetry than that it pleases most when thus read. It is a likeness which looks best side by side with the original. The Rhine does not foam, however, as he says it does, at least not on this spot.[3] It is the calm swift rush of a large body of water, which though perhaps not so imposing in reality when spoken of, because not so easily described, harmonises better with the characteristic attributes of the scene which are repose and grandeur.

---

[2] The Mound of the Belgic Lion covered the bones of the fallen, and had a flight of steps leading to the top, so that it served as memorial and viewpoint. Murray's *Guide* dismisses 'ill-natured censures' of the mound and the lion.
[3] *Childe Harold*, III, lv, 1–4; the passage is quoted in Murray's *Handbook*, including 'the river nobly foams and flows'.

TRAVEL JOURNAL, 8 AUGUST 1844

Extract in RB, X, 136–7

8th August. Still at Nonnenwerth[1] where we mean to linger another day. A place of pure enjoyment of natural scenery is not good for a journal though a happy one to live through. In the morning we ascended Rolandseck—the scene of Schiller's 'Knight of Toggenberg', and in the afternoon we scaled the Drachenfels. The beauty of catching the same landscape in different points of view is very striking at the time, but can only be very generally stated on paper. The obvious points of the scene are on the right bank of the Seven Mountains of which the Drachenfels is the most striking, especially when by twilight it is dimly seen lowering over the river. The hills have generally a peaked appearance which is said to mark their volcanic origin. On the left bank is the hill of Rolandseck with a broken arch of the ruin on the top, which is in exact keeping with the fragments of a tower and wall left standing on Drachenfels. These ruins of feudal strongholds bring to one's imagination the times when these scenes were valued for other qualities than their beauty. Cultivation has covered all their country with green—except these relics. Barbarism has left these stranded wrecks to make us remember that there was a time when her dark waters covered the earth. The windings of the broad river, with island and the old nunnery upon it, complete the meagre outline of the picture.

TRAVEL JOURNAL, 10 AUGUST 1844

Extract in RB, X, 139–40

10th August. We this day left Nonnenwerth with great regret. The lonely stillness of the island in its most sequestered retreats, the 'frowning' grandeur of the Drachenfels and the greener and softer beauty of Rolandseck with the single arch on its summit, took a speedy hold on my admiration, which, in spite of the usual transient

---

[1] WB's University College 'Note Book on Political Economy' contains two pages of notes headed: 'Wages. Notes on Mill—Nonenwerth on the Rhine. July 9th [*WB's error for 9 August*] 1844' (MS University College, London).

nature of such feelings, I hope they will long retain in my memory. We proceeded to Coblenz by the steamer—incomparably the worst way of seeing scenery that could be devised. The river is quite lost. One is hurried from one point to another so fast that one cannot gain an adequate idea of the height of rocks, which everybody that knows scenery at all well very well knows to require time, and what is hastily seen leaves few lasting traces on the mind. I must delay till I have Murray at hand to secure accuracy as to names, the account of the places which most struck me in descending the Rhine to this place. I mean to set down the places that have most struck me in the ascent of the Rhine. Briefly, both because I could not adequately describe them if I would, and I am too tired to do if I could. Nonnenwerth needs no mention in this list; that and the whole scenery of the Seven Mountains are so associated themselves in my mind with the ideas of pleasure and peace, that before I forget them my mind must undergo many organic changes for the worse. Except my home, and some other scenes that I have visited with those I love best, there is no scene that I have ever regarded with so much affection. Stillness and retirement have always a strong hold on me. The flourishing towns now covering the banks of the Rhine, compared with the huts of the serfs which in the middle ages occupied their sites, show the futility of praising more barbarous times at the expense of our own, because their remains with the marks of age on them have the grandeur of antiquity. A scoffer might sum up the remark, that the pleasure these ruins give us, as it arises from its reminding us of other times and modes of living with their pleasing contrast to our own, by saying that we admire them because we haven't to live in them, or to be near their founders. My tendency to prose, or as I call it *speculate* tonight is so great that I shall adjourn, especially as it waxes late.

To [?T. W. BAGEHOT], 12 AUGUST 1844

Extract in RB, X, 139, without name of addressee

Boppart,
12th August.

By staying at Nonnenwerth we have, we think, got a pretty good notion of what Rhine scenery really is, and a much higher opinion of it than do most racing tourists. We mean to go over the rest of the Rhine considerably faster, and get, we believe, to Schaffhausen, and there to enter the north-east of Switzerland, which, always subject to Murray's direction when we have him, we intend to make our object. Seeing Switzerland is not to be done in a fortnight. If I were left to myself I am by no means sure I should leave the Rhine. The beauties of nature are not written so that those who run may read them, and I would not run the risk of losing the full advantage to be derived from a few weeks on the continent by dissipating my attention over a great number of dissimilar objects. More grandeur I shall, I believe, assuredly see there, but I can hardly expect more pleasure than I have already had.

TRAVEL JOURNAL, [AUGUST 1844]

Extracts in RB, X, 140–2

The only day lost since I came out, by a blunder (not of our own, but of the constituted authorities) we lost the steamer from Mayence to Mannheim in the morning. The dullness of the passage in the afternoon with a drizzle, and an ugly country is no pleasing subject of recollection. We stayed at Mannheim instead of Heidelberg, our appointed stage.

Today we richly effaced yesterday's disappointment. We came out to Heidelberg, and saw the castle, a magnificent architecture built at different times, on different plans. Architectural critics lay down their rules against all mixtures of styles, but are hardly sanctioned by the taste of mankind. Those who are fond of seeing how rich in resources the human race have now become, will look with pleasure on a building where many ages have sent their representative: those who are more habituated to look on works of art, as produced from the imagination of a single mind, and those who like to figure to themselves their builders as a single generation, into whose feelings they are to enter, and whose habits they are to realise will not be gratified by finding their usual tastes, illusions, and criticisms wholly disturbed. There is a portion in the rich Italian style, and some parts are very old and rude Gothic. In 1764 it was struck by lightning, and some part was blown up by the French. The large masses of ruin in which the latter lie, especially where shaded with underwood, have a noble effect. I bought a print of the ruin in the state it was in, about 1764, at the period of its most perfect completion.

On Wednesday morning we proceeded to Thun. It was our plan to get on to Lauterbrunnen or Interlacken at the least. But we were so taken with the sight of the lake of Thun, and the Muen, a bold and lofty promontory jutting out into the middle of it, with the glaciers behind it and setting off its sombre colour, that we stayed there, and strolled up to the summer house to see the sunset. I have seen many finer as far as clouds are concerned, but I never before watched the pink tint gradually fading from the 'Alpine snow'. It by degrees crept up the mountains as the sun descended till just before it descended the summits only partook of it. According to an old national custom in Switzerland still, I believe, preserved in retired valleys, this moment was seized to blow the Alpine horn which was re-echoed from hill to hill, and whenever the sound was heard, the shepherds fell on their knees to render thanks to God for the day's light, and their preservation. A similar custom of choosing sunset for a public act of adoration is very prevalent in the East. The fire-worshippers[1] are now well known to every reader of poetry, and Mahomet, whose followers were the exterminators of the fire-worshippers, enjoined on them this same usage.

At Lucerne is to be seen the famous statue by Thorwaldsen erected to the memory of the Swiss guards, who defended the Tuileries on the day of the tenth of August against the populace of Paris. The Swiss lion in the agonies of death has his paw on a shield that bears the 'French fleur de lys'. It is hewn out of the solid rock, and reflected in a pond artificially made in front of it. The dimensions are colossal, but it is only on approaching it very nearly that this is seen. The illusion is so perfect that the most natural feeling is wonder that the lion is in the death grapple should be so perfectly still. Over the monument is written

Helvetiorum, Fidei et Virtuti.

Underneath are the names of those who in the words of the inscription did not shrink from their military oath. Seven hundred and fifty-six were killed and 301 saved—of these last one is now alive and

[1] A reference to the third tale in Moore's *Lalla Rookh*, 1817.

shows the monument. In such a scene the works of art are put to the hard trial as having to be seen immediately after gazing on the most magnificent of the labours of nature. But I felt here nothing like inferiority, the monument is every way worthy to be placed beside the Alps. Of the deed to which it is erected there can be only one opinion— it produced not one single result. The king had taken refuge with the National Assembly, and it was to his weakness that the bloodshed was owing.[2] Yet everyone feels a sentiment of admiration for these men, 'for their faith and valour', and the moral feelings of mankind are as usual in the right, and as usual paying homage to what is in the highest degree beneficial. The habit of mind that leads to courageous execution of what is required by fidelity to engagements, will always be most useful to mankind. I say this to obviate what an objector might induce against the justice of my admiration from my admitting the inutility of the act. He might say how much better for the world and themselves if their lives had been spared by flight. The feelings of mankind are shocked by such reasoning. The intellectual answer is that they themselves had been in the course of their good lives much more benefited by the habits of mind that led to the self-sacrifice, than they suffered by their painful death, and that the world is incalculably more benefited by these habits than by any others.

To EDITH BAGEHOT, [25 OCTOBER 1844]

Extract in RB, X, 142–4, dated 25 October 1844, after his return to University College

Have you seen the article in the last *Edinburgh Review* on Lord Chatham? It is a splendid article, and any person who has read the pages of Macaulay's former essays can be at no loss to discover the author.[1] There is some curious matter about Burton and Sir William

---

[2] In *The French Revolution* ('The Constitution', VI, 7), Carlyle pays tribute to the vain stand of the 'poor column of Swiss' on 10 August 1792, sold for sixpence a day to Louis XVI, who forsook them 'like a king of shreds and patches'; he concludes: 'Let the traveller, as he passes through Lucerne, turn aside to look a little at their monumental lion; not for Thorwaldsen's sake alone. Hewn out of living rock, the Figure rests there, by the still Lake-waters, in lullaby of distant-tinkling *rance-de-vaches*, the granite Mountains doubly keeping watch all round; and, though inanimate, speaks.'

* * *

[1] Macaulay's 'Early Administrations of George the Third: the Earl of Chatham', in the *Edinburgh Review*, October 1844 (Vol. LXXX, pp. 526–95).

Pynsent[2]—of which it is a wonder that there is no tradition in our neighbourhood. There may be to be sure, though I have never heard of it. Pitt's purity and incorruptibility seem to have made a great impression on the English nation, although he certainly connived at many practices which would now be thought, as Lord Ashburton[3] says, 'not over scrupulous'. There are some noble passages in the article, to which I have alluded, especially the concluding page; and this remark of the singular fact, that the last debate in which Chatham spoke was the first in which Burke spoke. 'It was indeed a splendid sunset and a splendid dawn'.[4] The Reviewer would have contributed to the ornamental effect, and the instructive tendency of this article if he had quoted some of the many bursts which tradition ascribes to Lord Chatham, and in which his great strength lay. If I remember right he does not even quote Chatham's celebrated declaration, 'that it mattered not to him on which bank of the Tweed a man's cradle had been rocked'.[5] We find some difficulty now in seeing the real grandeur of this saying. It should be remembered that this was the same year with the publication of the No. 45 of the *North Briton*, and that Chatham was struggling to overthrow Lord Bute's ministry, whose unpopularity in the country was principally grounded on his Scottish origin, and then we can see whether it did not require much nobleness of character to reject the support of this illiberal prejudice. Of the authenticity of this saying there is no doubt, for it occurs in a public letter of Lord Chatham's written at the time. The explanation of Lord Chatham's views on the question of the right of the House of Commons to tax America (which he altogether denied) throws light on the well known peroration of his great speech in the House of Lords: 'My Lords, if America falls she will fall like the strong man, she will lay hold on the pillars of the constitution and pull down the whole fabric along with her'.[5] It is always a pleasing task to quote such sayings of high-minded and highly gifted men.

---

[2] It is surprising that WB did not know the story of how Pynsent left his Somersetshire estate to Chatham, since the column, 150 feet high, erected by Chatham as a memorial to Pynsent, is only three miles from Langport, and there WB 'performed, as a young man, the rash feats which so terrified his mother' (RB, X, 43).
[3] Alexander Baring, 1st Baron Ashburton (1774–1848), financier and statesman, concluded the Ashburton treaty between Britain and America in 1842.
[4] Quoted from Macaulay's article; on the debate on the repeal of the Stamp Act when the House of Commons heard Pitt for the last time.
[5] Both quotations are from the debate on the American Stamp Act of 14 January 1766

DECEMBER 1844

To EDWARD FRY, 26 DECEMBER 1844
Extract in RB, X, 144-45

Herd's Hill,
26th December, 1844.

My dear Fry,

... My health is much mended. My Mother's family has suffered from hereditary consumption, and as my chest was delicate, my friends were alarmed perhaps needlessly. I have never read any of Lord Bacon's Latin works, but his essays ('Advancement of Learning' and the 'New Atlantis') are old favourites of mine. To ask in his day, 'is truth ever barren?'[1] required a nobleness of soul, which I know not how to characterise. His trust in the progress that would be made by unshackled human reason is not to be measured by ours. He may be thought to have lived in the primary formation of civilisation, to have taken his stand on the barren granite, and predicted the rise of luxuriant vegetation and exalted intelligence. I am getting very metaphorical this morning. The breaking up of the frost has set me think[2] again. Macintosh says that diffused knowledge immortalises itself, and I believe he says so truly—are you acquainted with Macaulay's essays?[3] They are very noble works, very eloquent, and I think for the most part wise. His views of English history are very good, and though perhaps a little borrowed from Hallam,[4] are more original than so hackneyed a theme would have seemed to have promised. Perhaps, however, history ought to be continually re-written as each age gets larger views of truth, and more discriminating accuracy in the allotment of praise and blame. No age ought to be content with the views taken by its predecessor of past times, though it ought to be acquainted with them just as much as the boundaries of science are extended by those only who have surveyed the cultivated interior. Write to me as often as you can.[5] I will not insult you by more promises, but I will do my best in future to make my promises more worthy of confidence.

[1] Quotation not traced.
[2] Reading of the original, according to Mrs Barrington.
[3] *Critical and Historical Essays contributed to the Edinburgh Review*, 1843.
[4] Henry Hallam, *The Constitutional History of England from the Accession of Henry VII to the Death of George I*, 1827.
[5] WB was keeping up his correspondence while at Herd's Hill; a letter from Hutton,

EDITH BAGEHOT to WB, [APRIL-MAY 1845]

Extract in RB, X, 145–6, dated in the spring of 1845

I am glad to remember that I always thought and said, the classes you had chosen were the most difficult and also the most abstracted from these general subjects of capacious, just, good, common and elevated sense, which I could better understand and was the most anxious about, since many a mathematician is certainly a learned booby. I used to say too, dearest, that if you could not bear the necessary hard study now, you could not bear the hard study and work of the Bar hereafter, and I think Mr. Estlin seems to think the same, and gives a hint about *business*, whither, as you know, my wishes have always somewhat turned, though I would never for the world say so to slacken or contract what I do hope you will have, a thoroughly good education. But turn your attention a little to business when you are at home, try to understand Papa's cleverness in it, and if very or totally inferior at first, do not be depressed. If he were to die now, which God forbid! I am sure I should at once wish you to understand *what business is*. I have often told dearest Papa, it was a fault more of his habits than his intentions, that he had not, as a matter of course, made you better acquainted with its practical details and mysteries; but all paths are open to good sense, good feelings, good intentions and industry, and, as deep and abstract study is now thought so bad for you, you must seek to apply the stores already acquired in lighter converse and associates, and in more of the practical details, friendships and usages of daily life, and not be so much the studious, mawkish scholar any longer.

EDITH BAGEHOT to WB, [APRIL-MAY 1845]

Extract in RB, X, 146–7, said to be later than last

Your health, my beloved, I trust is not worse. I often hope and pray that it will humble you *where you ought to be humbled*, namely, that

---

postmarked 29 December 1844 (MS Norman St John-Stevas), says: '*Many thanks* for your letter, it was a great help to me. I quite agree; had been thinking about exactly the same subject whenever I had time to think about anything but "my analysis".—I think it is a very fine doctrine of Emerson's and certainly he is its apostle.' He told WB to read Dickens's new Christmas Book, *The Chimes*, which he thought the best thing Dickens had written with one or two passages 'quite sublime'; and he was glad to find WB agreeing with his preference of *Pride and Prejudice* to Maria Edgeworth's *Patronage*.

as you must not *strain* your mind after very high and abstruse *attainments* you will 'exercise yourself' clearly to comprehend and express those which are obvious and easy. Your letter was spelt quite rightly. Mr. Reynolds says your faults at present remind him of his at your age, namely, that you are much fonder of finding out and attacking all authorities where they are wrong than you are of humbling yourself to obedience and deference, and learning of them where they are right. This is true, I think, at least I thought it becoming alarmingly true, but when you were at home last you were all sweetness to me, and I thought there was a manifest improvement (excepting in being so silent when the thoughts of your heart and mind should have expressed themselves), and in your letters of late, excepting this one, which does remind me of some of Mr. Reynolds about you. However, as you say, it is much *better than none*, and clever letters, like clever people, bear being pulled to pieces and found fault with.

EDITH BAGEHOT to WB, [?MAY 1845]

Extract in RB, X, 149–50
DATE: placed among letters of May 1845, and reference to 'your dear uncle' shows that it was before Vincent Stuckey's death on 8 May

Herd's Hill

My dear Blessing,

Your letter of this morning so anxiously expected (on my part I confess fearfully, so I was a little prepared) failed to impart the sunshine some of them bestow, either with regard to your body or mind; but God may chasten and renovate us all through His spirit and send us a happy meeting on Thursday. I cannot argue further on the points[1] as you are your own authority, and are in dear Eliza's opinion and mine, one of the most difficult writers whom we must first *understand* before we know whether we agree or not, and we quite fail to do this first in the letter of today. But, in the meanwhile, till Bagehot's grammar and dictionary supersede the old ones, we must spell and divide not according to *sound*, but the common usage of the schools.

[1] According to Mrs Barrington WB's mother did not understand his arguments in some 'discussion about Disraeli'. This may have referred to his speech of 11 April 1845, opposing the Maynooth Grant (*Debates*, LXXIX, 565–6).

I tremble now for the mathematics, since, as I told Babbage,[2] trying the sense of the obscure and difficult which I did not know, by the sense and reasoning which I did, I was afraid. But this will not improve your headache, darling, for you are never well, nor I either, when you and I have had 'any bit out break'. Let it not disturb the joy of our meeting for there is nothing like 'speaking the truth from the heart' even where people differ, and between parents and children these are the only discussions which really make correspondence interesting and valuable for time and eternity.

Since I came from church I have been telling your dear Uncle that dear Papa, though he thinks you are wrong, scolds me for saying you are so, and said I abused *everybody*, and Uncle said 'so you do, you are the "Senior Wrangler" of the family'. Well! I dare not say 'peace, peace when there is no peace',[3] but sincerely do I pray that all mankind should follow the example of the great humility of our Saviour.

To EDITH BAGEHOT, [? 10 MAY 1845]

Extract in RB, X, 151
DATE: soon after Vincent Stuckey's death on 8 May

Please to remember me very kindly to all on the hill. I have no doubt that now you and my father are left alone, you will feel very much the real greatness of the loss you have sustained.[1] But I think you will soon feel, as those to whom the hourly vacancy is less, already feel, that it is hardly possible long to think of my dear uncle with anything like gloom. All our associations with him were also associations with cheerfulness, happiness, and gratitude, and it is only the natural sadness of recent loss which can render such remembrances melancholy. Gloom cannot long linger round the memory of one whose presence always dispelled it.

---

[2] Charles Babbage (1792–1871), mathematician and inventor; best remembered for his calculating machine, abandoned by the government in 1842 after much public money and a large amount of Babbage's private fortune had been spent on it.
[3] Jeremiah, vi, 14.

* * *

[1] The death of Vincent Stuckey on 8 May 1845.

MAY 1845

To EDITH BAGEHOT, [?26 MAY 1845]

Extract in RB, X, 131, dated 26 May and following letter of 18 March 1844, but 1844 is impossible since Stanley's *Life of Arnold* was not published until 31 May 1844, and WB writes as though familiar with it; probably a misdating of WB's

I had no doubt of your liking Dr. Arnold.[1] I never knew or heard of anyone who did not like him very much, except the editor of the *Record*. A writer in that paper in a Review of Dr. Arnold's life[2] said it was a book to do more harm than good! ! ! If your pleasure in the book makes you sceptical as to this intelligence, I am sorry, and I should hardly have believed it of a 'religious' periodical if I had not *seen* the words myself in its columns. They were so angry as to what he said as to the narrow-mindedness of the Evangelicals, and their neglect of the cultivation of the *intellect*,[3] that they were utterly unable to separate what they thought unjust in his censure from their general impression of his character. There are contemporaries of Arnold superior to him, I think, in quickness of imagination, and subtlety of discrimination and vigour in the reasoning power, but there would be few claimants to a superiority over him in moral energy and *un*fanatic zeal. My father seems in doubt if he would have approved of the Dis-establishment Bill.[4] I have no doubt that he would have done so. He says in his life, that the Irish Church ought to be a Catholic Church in three-fifths of Ireland at least.[5] His system would have come to the French plan of paying the preachers of every scheme of *Christian* doctrine. He would also have compelled those who are not Christians to support some form of Christianity. I do not apprehend that he saw any particular advantage, moreover, in the contributions of individuals passing through the hands of the tax gatherer, and would therefore have been satisfied with making each man pay not less than a given sum to the support of *some* form of Christian worship. But this is too

[1] Dr Thomas Arnold (1795–1842).
[2] A. P. Stanley, *The Life and Correspondence of Thomas Arnold*, 1844; an enormously popular and influential book, which went through three editions between 31 May and September 1844. No review appeared in the *Record* May–September 1844.
[3] In 1831, for instance, he felt that their 'narrow views and technical phraseology' were obstacles to 'the real and practical application of the Old and New Testament, as the remedy of the great wants of the age, social, moral, and intellectual' (*Life*, I, 255).
[4] No Disestablishment bill was introduced in the 1840s, although the subject was frequently canvassed in debates on Ireland, as it was during those on the Maynooth College bill in May 1845.
[5] In a letter to William Empson of 11 June 1834 (*Life*, I, 344).

JUNE 1845

moderate a theory of Church establishments[6] to be much in favour with their usual supporters. Bigots for the voluntary principle (among whom I fancy that I ought to include myself) may doubt whether coercion by legislative enactment is even to this extent a fit way of spreading the influence of religion. I am not, however, going to write an appendix to this letter on Church establishments.

EDITH BAGEHOT to WB, 11 JUNE 1845
Text from RB, X, 73-4

11th June 1845.
Day of St. Barnabas and my
beloved Sluckey's death.

My own Blessing,

A line I must dash off to thank you for yours. I was a *leetle* disappointed to hear that you thought we had better not have the pleasure of your company before next week, and, being thankful you feel well enough to stay, must not, I suppose, say a word against it upon my principle of 'trimming the lamps' vigorously, and 'watching in our various duties and callings with our various talents that we may return those "who have the rule over us" and our Lord His own with usury'; but if Dr. Bright[1] recommends a quicker transition to purer air, which he might, as there is now quite a change in the weather and you suffer from the heat so much, how fervently we shall delight to welcome you.

---

[6] Arnold's idea, expressed in *Principles of Church Reform*, 1833, was an absolute identification of Church and State, in which the Establishment would be made truly national by admitting all except Jews, Roman Catholics and Quakers.

* * *

[1] Presumably Richard Bright (1789–1858), distinguished physician, son of Richard Bright merchant and banker of Bristol (see letter of 4 October 1839); remembered for his identification of 'Bright's disease'. Physician to Guy's Hospital, 1824–43, appointed physician extraordinary to Queen Victoria on her accession; 'as his reputation rose he took the leading position as consulting physician in London' (*DNB*).

JUNE 1845

I need not say I love and value you as much as I loved and valued Stuckey at the same age, more I cannot; but I think my love for you has been happier, more roses and fewer thorns, because you have been since your birth so much more happily situated, and from the least boy ever joined with joy and pleasure in the same mental pursuits I have ever followed the most myself—not that I must ape the literature that you have (though I have always been fond of books, since, as a child, it was often a loud sentence of reproach to me—'Edith Stuckey, do not sit so lost over a book'), for when I was talking over your argument with William Wood, not only Papa had told me I was stupid, by giving me your explanation of the fact about Burke, but Aunt Reynolds gravely said, 'Now Edith, you are not to infer that Walter was wrong because you think him so, for you know you *are* ignorant', which I am quite ready to admit, only I thought to myself—I do like Walter to make that clear to others what is clear I dare say to his own research, so rapidly improving and telling; and when he does, I think I can *sense him*, though profoundity[2] in the subject may still be wanting. I am not sure whether Aunt Reynolds wanted to put you up or me down—both I hope. My elastic mind is daily recovering from the loss of my beloved brother. My mind, like his, *must be cheerful*, from its vivid enjoyment of blessings left; but your dear Aunt is exactly the same. I think of my own brother constantly as if, in the transfer to a purer state, conversation and communion, that I thank God I sought on earth, are still carried on with him—and to indulge and repeat the hope which scripture allows, as one dear friend after another is borne to Heaven,

> That through their Soul as angels bright
> They hover o'er our sphere,
> And shed new beams of grace and light
> On those who loved them here;

and it seems as if your dear Uncle's voice could say to you, in better prose perhaps than my poetry,—'Walter, you must make yourself a clever fellow and be a stay of the family, and a comfort to your mother when I am gone'.

---

[2] Thus in printed text.

1845

To T. W. BAGEHOT [?1845]

MS: Mr Norman St John-Stevas
DATE: No other reference to this Scottish holiday has been found; the watermark is undated. The reference to the end of the season suggests September, which makes 1843 unlikely (a letter from Hutton of 13 September shows WB to have been in England and on the 27th he was in Dublin); in 1844 he had been abroad and in 1846 letters show him in England, while in 1847 he was on the Continent (see letter of ?6 February 1848). Handwriting resembles that of some letters of 1846

Glasgow
Queens Hotel

My dearest Father,

We reached Glasgow on Tuesday morning a little before two A.M. in perfect safety though something tired. I was told that we missed a fine view over the Cheviots by passing them in the dark, but it was I suspect quite worth while missing it to see Glasgow at night. The iron works have large fires on the establishment burning constantly which extend their light for some miles round the city, and are very fine at night. A painter of the Rembrandt school might find them an instructive study.—

We have just bought the ponies well I hope in point of strength and serviceability but not well certainly in point of cheapness. The season here is not yet over and horseflesh is 'up'. We had to give £11 for Watson's pony—a remarkably strong thoroughly Highland pony, irongrey with what ought to be a hog mane if the people here understood aesthetics, and £15 for mine which is a very stout white cob of rather leisurely habits but as strong as a rock and warranted sound. We went on what they call in the differential calculus the exhaustive method—that is we got a list of all the horsedealers in Glasgow out of the Directory and went to them all—The money is more than I calculated on as you will see but it would have been foolish not to have animals well up to their work, which if we can carry out our plan will not be a trifle.

The notion we at present have of our tour is this—we start for Dumbarton as soon as I have finished this note. From thence we go to Loch Lomond along the west shore of which we shall ride, and shall spend a day or two in making excursions through Sir Walter Scott's country. From thence we shall make the best of our way to Fort William. I wanted and perhaps I may still contrive to get in Inverary and Loch Awe upon the way though I do not feel so clear about as I could wish. After that we shall follow pretty much the line of the Caledonian canal which being a hyphen between the northern lakes runs through a fine line of country and if possible get as far north as Cromarty, and sell the ponies at Inverness—at a considerable reduction I fear as the season will then be quite over and Highland ponies can hardly be suitable imports for that market. From thence by steamer to Aberdeen whence there is continuous railway communication to the southward. I do not know that we shall do all this but it is as well to aim high and do what we can. My love and Watson's. I hope my mother's cold is better.

Yours affly

WALTER BAGEHOT

To EDITH BAGEHOT, [?MID-OCTOBER 1845]

Extract in RB, X, 147, dated October 1845 and probably soon after the news of Newman's reception into the Catholic Church had become known on 13 October (*Morning Post*)

My Aunt Reynolds was looking very well, and very brisk. She said, however, that she had been ill, but I never saw her looking better. She believes that Newman is most likely bribed to become a Roman Catholic[1]—at all events that he will be no loser in money matters by the change. As the Pope[2] is a bankrupt it seems unlikely he should have much spare cash to send over to bribe English heretics. I never could understand what you told me in your letter about Mrs. J—thinking it required great grace to be a nun or monk. If it means simply retiring from the world and living a life of contemplation in one place, I do not think there are many things easier and pleasanter. It is completely realising the *laissez faire* system of grappling with the evils of the world. Every one knows on a small scale how easy that is. That bodily penance is considered by most men easier than the everyday work of duty is quite evident from the history of all religions. Then Catholics would say that to live a life of prayer was difficult. But it is surely not so difficult as to live in the world a life of prayer and labour also. A

---

[1] John Henry Newman (1801–90) had resigned his Oriel fellowship on 6 October and on 9 October was received into the Catholic Church by Father Dominic Barberi.
[2] Gregory XVI (1765–1846), Pope from 1831.

monk's life *is* very captivating to my imagination as you know, but I do not think I could persuade myself into its being right. I do not think Mr. Newman will fill England with monasteries. A monastery beside a railroad would be a curious mixture of the customs of different ages. The extreme of physical inaction and the extreme of bodily exertion would be side by side. Nothing passes here of much moment. I have a good deal to do of various kinds, and shall be obliged to take some work with me to Hampstead this evening.

To EDITH BAGEHOT, NOVEMBER 1845

MS: Mr Norman St John-Stevas

Camden St. Nov 1845

My dearest Mother,

No collar of the sort you mention is anywhere to be found in my stores. I have demonstrated to my own satisfaction that it never got here at all; *no doubt* Miss Migs[1] can throw light on this matter as on all others. As to writing home news I have long ago given up that notion as it would be utterly Utopian to expect any sufficient supply to fill a letter once a week. I suppose I ought to condole with you concerning the great Wansworth defeat. I hope Adeline [?Page][2] bears it like a heroine. I advise you to have a small engraving made of her when hearing the news, and a small cup labelled 'Tears' in one corner. It would take exceedingly, and you would be sure of getting her in in April—

As to the question that my father asked me about Carlyle, he wrote in the Edinburgh Review an article on 'Burns' in the 98th no. and an article on the Signs of the Times a number or two before that one entitled 'Characteristics'[3] to which my father refers—Has he read the last article aloud. It is one of the most eloquent of Carlyle's writings in my opinion, although I believe the article on Burns is more generally popular. There is a passage in 'Characteristics' as to the opinions on

---

[1] Perhaps a joking reference to Miss Miggs, Mrs Varden's disagreeable maid in *Barnaby Rudge*.
[2] The name is difficult to read; possibly identical with the 'Adelaide Tagg' referred to in the letter to his mother of ?May 1846.
[3] 'Burns' appeared in the *Edinburgh Review*, December 1828 (Vol. XLVIII, pp. 267–312), 'Signs of the Times', June 1829 (Vol. XLIX, pp. 439–59), and 'Characteristics', December 1831 (Vol. LIV, pp. 351–83); all were included in *Critical and Miscellaneous Essays*, 1839.

religious subjects of the great writers of the last generation especially Shelley and Friedrich Schlegel[4] which I think exceedingly fine, and finer on a second reading. This last peculiarity is one of the most remarkable about Carlyle's writing generally. At first his style seems uncouth and unpleasant, and his opinions fluctuating and absurd. But after a little time his mind grows insensibly in your estimation and you get to see that small assertions which look hasty and immature do really arise from much careful thought, and are parts of a large and coherent system of opinions.[5] Since I came back to London I have read his Hero worship[6] for the first time. It is the best abstract of some of his peculiar opinions that I know of. As it was delivered in the form of lectures it is necessarily more popular and diffuse than some of his other writings. I think there are passages in his essays scattered here and there finer than anything in his Hero worship, but the general style of the latter is far more eloquent. I am quite a disciple of his views on that subject and have been for a considerable time. With regard to his historical applications of them there is some room for doubt but in general I think them pretty accurate. I should strongly advise the book's being ordered to come down to Langport. We *ought* to have it, and if I order it here, I shall have it when I have just read it and don't want it. There is a report here in bookseller's shops that his work on Cromwell which he has been for a considerable time employed on according to floating rumor is now coming out. The reports oscillate between a 'life' of Cromwell and a collection of his 'speeches and letters'.[7] It will be at any rate I should think a defence of him for he is one of Carlyle's idols—heroes as he names them. I hope you observed that he had a statue[8] though you blew me up about it.

[4] 'Hear a Shelley filling the earth with inarticulate wail; like the inarticulate grief and weeping of forsaken infants. A noble Friedrich Schlegel, stupefied in that fearful loneliness, as of a silenced battlefield, flies back to Catholicism; as a child might to its slain mother's bosom, and clings there' (*Critical and Miscellaneous Essays*, III, 312).
[5] For Carlyle's influence during the 1840s, especially on the young, see Kathleen Tillotson, *Novels of the Eighteen-Forties*, 1956, pp. 150–56.
[6] *On Heroes, Hero-Worship, and the Heroic in History*, lectures delivered in May 1840 and issued in book form, 1841.
[7] Chapman & Hall were advertising Carlyle's *Oliver Cromwell's Letters and Speeches, with Elucidations and Connecting Narrative* from the beginning of November 1845 (*Athenaeum*, 1, 15 and 22 November), and the volumes were published 25 November.
[8] Presumably a reference to the controversy about the placing of a statue of Cromwell in the new Palace of Westminster (see the correspondence in *The Times*, September 1845); Carlyle advised against it ('Hudson's Statue', *Latter-Day Pamphlets*, 1850). No statue was placed in the Palace until 1898.

Will you cause it to be conveyed to my father that the *general opinion* as far as I can collect it (which is rather a *limiting* clause) is not considered to be Macaulay's.[9] It is said to be written by the person who wrote an article on Churchill[10] some time back. I thought at one time the last was written by Mr. Macaulay, but do not think so now. It is too confused for his style of narrative and the style is not sufficiently polished.

The article on Defoe[11] is a sound though not a splendid article— It is speaks[12] with very high praise of Defoe though not too high for all enthusiastic admirers of Robinson Crusoe—I think the *cleverest* thing as far as I know that Defoe ever wrote is the appearance of the ghost of Mrs. Veal, which you have heard tell o' in connection with Drelenecourt on death—Scott gives it in his life of Defoe in his collection of Biographies of English Novelists.[13] If an old woman's ghost ever should appear on earth, my conviction is firm and unalterable that she would talk in that sort of rather fussy twaddle. If I had met with it in a grave treatise on Death, I am sure I should have believed it. It looks so circumstantial and undeniable—so like a fact—anybody but Defoe would have made the ghost say something striking which would have spoiled the effect. The post is going out.

Believe me
Yours affectionately
W Bagehot

I have no time I find to read this over. Excuse blunders

---

[9] Either 'it' refers to the article on Defoe in the *Edinburgh* or WB has omitted to name the article after writing the parenthesis.
[10] 'Charles Churchill', in the *Edinburgh*, January 1845 (Vol LXXXI, pp. 46–88), by John Forster, literary editor (and from 1847 editor) of the *Examiner*.
[11] 'Daniel Defoe' by Forster; *Edinburgh Review*, October 1845 (Vol. LXXXII, pp. 480–532).
[12] Thus in MS.
[13] The life of Defoe in *Ballantyne's Novelists Library* was by Ballantyne, not Scott. In his article Forster takes from it the well-known story of the occasion of Defoe's *Mrs. Veal*; a bookseller had published a large and unsaleable edition of *Drelincourt on Death* (a translation of C. Drélincourt's *Les Consolations de l'âme fidèle contre les frayeurs de la mort*), transformed into a best-seller when Defoe furnished him, within a few days, with *The True History of the Apparition of one Mrs. Veal the next day after her Death, to one Mrs. Bargrave at Canterbury, the 8th of September 1705*, in which the ghost recommended Drélincourt as the best book ever written on death.

FEBRUARY 1846

To EDITH BAGEHOT, [26 FEBRUARY 1846]
MS: Mr Norman St John-Stevas
DATE: postmarked 26 February 1846

Camden St. Feb. 1846.

My dearest Mother,

I dare say that you are wondering why I have not written to you according to the compact, but I really have not been able to do so—I have had a good deal to do and have had a sore throat, and influenzaish cold hanging about me which have made me very stupid. I am now however a good deal better, and hope to be quite well again in a day or two. My croak after which you enquire is *quite* gone I believe—I have a tendency to make it sometimes but I can always controul it and generally do. I have got a long essay to write about 'Causation', and the metaphysical theories about it, of which there are not a few. The subject is very mysterious, though most writers say their view of it is complete, and exceedingly simple. I am reading a long discussion of the subject by Dr. Brown[1] who thought that he had explained the whole subject, but I am afraid, he left the matter exactly where he found it, in the most material points. The main difficulty is in analysing the ideas of cause, power, agency, efficiency and efficacy, &c, and in applying them correctly after the analysis to the external world, and to the mind—There is no reason however for turning this letter into a metaphysical essay. Has anybody learnt of anything about the Indian war.[2] Nobody scarcely in England ever knows that we are at war except when there comes a battle, and when heaps of people are killed we wake up to the fact, and wish to know the reason for it. We generally acquiesce pretty easily in the doctrine that we have the right on our side, and as most of the Indian nations know nothing of European international law, it would not seem a difficult matter to put them in the wrong, if its provisions are to be taken as the standard. I have not seen any good account of the merits of the present quarrel

---

[1] Thomas Brown, *Observations on the Nature and Tendency of the Doctrine of Mr. Hume, concerning the relation of cause and effect*, 1805.
[2] The first Sikh war, caused by the annexation of the Sind by Britain. The Sikhs invaded British territory by crossing the Sutlej in December 1845, and were defeated in four battles (18 December 1845, 21-2 December 1845, 28 January and 10 February 1846). The news of the December victories appeared in *The Times* on 23 February 1846.

but the Sikhs have long been troublesome neighbours to us, and are a warlike, though disunited people. The Sutleg (it is spelt all ways) on which the battle was fought, is remarkable as being the extreme limit to the eastward of the conquests of Alexander the Great. It has for some time been the limit of our dominions to the westward. I suppose we shall edge on further in time, as the greater part of our Indian empire has been formed by adding bit to bit from time to time, on the compulsion, it is said, of evident necessity. No doubt we can make out a case of absolute necessity *for* ourselves *to* ourselves, without much difficulty but this has no[t] in general been held by moralists to be a sufficient basis for self-justification. However as I do not profess to have studied the present case, I had better not write a philippic against Indian aggression. Nevertheless as Fox used to say when we were at war with Napoleon to keep the French power within what we deemed its true limits, 'we are only nervous or superstitious about aggrandisement to the West of the Cape of Good Hope'[3]— I cannot see much reason in the geographical distinction between accession of territory in Europe and in India, but I suppose there is some broad line of demarcation as this country has so long acted on its existence.

I have no doubt that my father noticed Sir Robert Peel's remarkable declaration that he thought Lord John Russell could have carried on the government and given a total and immediate repeal to the corn laws. He is a very competent judge no doubt, and I wish I could think so, but it appears to me difficult to see how it could have been done without a new creation of peers. Nor am I quite clear as to the sort of majority for Free Trade that a dissolution at present would have given us. At all events Sir Robert can do it more easily, although one grudges him the distinction of passing so great a measure after so long opposing the principles on which it is founded.[4] I wonder D'Israeli had not more sense than to come out at this time of day with a protectionist speech.[5] Everybody knew that he was no reasoner, and knew

---

[3] This quotation has not been traced.
[4] Peel had resigned in December 1845, after failing to unite the Conservatives on a policy of partial repeal; Russell was unable to form a government because Lord Grey refused to serve with Lord Palmerston, and Peel returned to office with a ministry committed to total repeal of the Corn Laws. The debate on Peel's tariff proposals began 9 February and occupied 12 nights.
[5] On 20 February (*Debates*, LXXXIII, 1318–1347).

nothing of the question, but he need not have made both facts so painfully evident. His assurance gives him great advantage as a political adventurer—a man with any modesty could hardly have ridiculed Sir R. Peel so long for having no principles, and then opposed him when he proposed to establish a very comprehensive one, as a fundamental constitutional maxim. D'Israeli always puts Free Trade into his novels, but he appears to go on the specious theory that the best person to advocate unbending adherence to principle is the person who has adopted first and then rejected all the principles now prominently brought forward on political subjects. I am no worshipper of Sir R. Peel, nor a very firm believer in his thorough sincerity but I do hope that he will persevere in his present course of not condescending to answer Disraeli. The moral weight of the latter being nothing; his accusations[6] would only gather weight from Sir Robert's condescending to answer them. D'Israeli must have [been] wroth, when his friend Smythe[7] took office under the present government. The Young England party made a great fuss six months ago and have already ceased to exist. Ld. John must have been rather vexed at the patronizing way in which Sir Robert talked of his having disappointed him (Sir R.) in not taking the government[8]—his not taking office is a strong illustration of Byron's theory

> Naught's permanent among the human race
> Except the Whigs not getting into place.—[9]

I wonder somebody doesn't tell him so in the house. They must want a laugh with all these heavy speeches. I do not make out from my father's last letter, how much he calculates that the peculiar burdens on agricultural industry exceed its peculiar immunities? I suppose he would remedy the danger to agriculture arising from the greater profits obtainable in mannfactures (on account of the local burdens), by giving some additional immunities to Real Property, and not by putting on a tax on the importation of foreign corn.

---

[6] A reference to his savage attack on Peel of 22 January (*Debates*, LXXXIII, 111–23).
[7] George Smythe, later 7th Viscount Strangford (1818–57), MP for Canterbury 1841–52; in 1844 a member of the 'Young England' movement of Disraeili and Lord John Manners, and supposed to be the original of Disraeli's 'Coningsby'. In January 1845 he had been appointed Undersecretary at the Foreign Office, and he voted with the government in the debates on the Corn Laws in 1846.
[8] 'The noble Lord did disappoint me when he did not at once undertake the formation of a Government on the principle of adjusting this question' (16 February 1846; *Debates*, LXXXIII, 1004).
[9] *Don Juan*, XI, lxxxii.

MARCH 1846

As you say I do not answer your questions, I must tell you that I have read several letters of yours at Hampstead—I understand them pretty well except what you are expecting to get out of the Deaf and Dumb man, who seems 'innocent', and why you still write to the Bishop of Chichester? These I have put down as not to be made out, any more than Kant's investigation into what renders the understanding in general *possible*?

Believe me ever
your affectionate and obedient Son
W BAGEHOT.

Love to all.

To EDITH BAGEHOT, [28 MARCH 1846]

MS: Mr Norman St John-Stevas
DATE: the Saturday after 23 March 1846: see n. 3

Camden St. Saturday afternoon

My dearest Mother,

I have been unexpectedly detained till it is too late to write my usual weekly letter. You shall however certainly hear from me by the next post. I hope my father's cold is better, and 'won't disinherit' him if he does not write to me while he has so good an excuse. Everybody at Hampstead is now pretty well I think except Bella, who has had a very severe attack of influenza, and was still very poorly when I was last at Hampstead. My aunt has not been well, but is now better. Mrs. Norman and Alfred[1] were there on Sunday last, in great spirits as they go to Ireland on the 1st of April. I dined at the Prichard's on Thursday. Mrs. Prichard was very much out of spirits, but the Dr. seemed not so much so and talked pretty much as usual about Niebuhr and the origin

---

[1] Perhaps relations of George Norman, who in July 1851 married Robert Bagehot's daughter, Louisa; on the marriage certificate he is described as 'Gentleman' and the son of George Norman, surgeon, deceased. Alfred Norman was a junior clerk in the Mail Coach Office of the General Post Office in 1847, when he talked to WB about Rowland Hill (see letter of 6 February 1847).

of the Etruscans.² Constantine is in town and going to stay for some time. Many thanks for your note which I received this morning, though it was a note and for your letters during the week, which have been more plentiful than usual lately. I do not understand your admiration for the Duke of Wellington's speech, which seems to me poor though straightforward. How he could talk of 'religious peace' in England and Ireland at this moment appears singular.³ It makes one wonder he didn't make the thing complete and say 'religious unanimity'. A person merely looking at the number of religious sects into which the country is divided would be inclined to hope that we had reached the maximum of religious division, and that any change would rather lessen it, than increase it. However this may be, it is quite undeniable that the Duke of Wellington has no rival in the art of making 'naive' speeches. I should not wonder if he has a concealed system of logic, in which the fundamental test of a good argument is its beginning by begging the question. This letter must go to the post and I must go and write an essay on 'logical definition'.

Yours ever affectionately

W BAGEHOT.

To EDWARD FRY, [?APRIL 1846]

Extract in RB, X, 151–2, dated 'the spring of 1846'

Your brother's poetry¹ is very graceful and pleasing, and what is more

---

² Barthold Niebuhr's *History of Rome*, 1811–32, was the first work to deal with the ancient history of Rome in a scientific spirit.

³ In opposing the Address on the State of Ireland in the House of Lords, 23 March 1846, the Duke voiced his fears for the extinction of the Church of England in Ireland, and said: 'Every system of religion is tolerated in this country; and, above all, we have the advantage of religious peace'; any move towards disestablishment in Ireland would leave untouched political rivalries among contending sects, while ending that religious peace. (*Debates*, 1846, LXXXIV, 1390–91).

* * *

¹ Fry had sent WB poetry written by his brother (presumably Joseph Storrs Fry, known to WB at Bristol College), asking 'his opinion as to its merits' (RB, X, 151). Fry did not publish any of his poetry.

uncommon quite genuine and unaffected. From my former knowledge of him I should have thought quiet, good-natured satire the species of composition for which nature had intended him. I do not know whether either he or you, however, think satire right. To me its best forms seem no unfitting expression of reverential thoughtfulness. I do not think your brother will take it amiss if I venture to recommend condensation to him in any thing which he may write hereafter. I do not mean that there is anything in this piece which I want shortened or omitted, but diffuseness seems to me the besetting sin of our recent literature. In poetry it is worse than in prose, for when the intellect is addressed, it is no harm to follow out principles and reasonings into their most minute applications. But in poetry, and indeed in eloquence where the feelings of the poet are expressed, and the feelings of the orator's hearers are addressed, to give numerous details and to repeat the same details more than once seems like a botanist who, in delineating the beauty of flowers, should recount the number of stamens they possess. *Some* details are essential in poetry, because no affections cling to general ideas, and to pale unhealthy looking abstractions, but the poet's genius and taste are shown in their combination and selection, not as some poets seem to imagine in their accumulation. I hardly know any recent poetry not chargeable with too great prolixity except perhaps the lyric parts of Campbell, and the very best parts of Shelley and Byron. The last (Don Juan excepted) is not *very* chargeable with this fault perhaps. What a command of language and illustration is shown in 'Childe Harold'! What a pity that he had nothing better to say than what an uncomfortable place this world is! After all he might have written a great work if he had lived till now. He was just setting himself to work, and the true cure of despondency and moral scepticism is action—that is right action. Do you know Hood's poems? Of very recent poetry I think they are perhaps the best.[2] They show quickness and delicacy of feeling, and a very happy fancy capable of very good ornamental work. The great depths of the human heart are only for those of a great creative imagination, and where among living poets shall we find that greatest of God's gifts. However, Hood was a man who took his knowledge of mankind not from tradition but from his eyes.

---

[2] Thomas Hood had died in poverty 3 May 1845. On 10 January 1846 Moxon had published *Poems by Thomas Hood*.

I shall have to read some physiology for my degree, but I am as ignorant of natural history as I used to be. If I have any leisure time after taking my degree, I hope to remedy this gross defect in some measure at least. I have been most occupied for the last year in 'science' and metaphysics. I do not know whether the latter science has engaged your attention much. In these days of universal controversy we are constantly required to know the ultimate principles of belief on which the whole superstructure of knowledge rests, and also to be able to detect any false claimants to the title of *self*-evident truths which cannot be proved from others and carry their own certainty with them. These truths having their root in the structure of the mind itself can only be known by a metaphysical enquiry. I have been reading some of Kant,[3] the founder of the modern school of metaphysics in Germany and France. He appears to me to have been a man of preternatural acuteness, no little confidence in himself, to have been very fond of the complexities of an artificial system, and to have been defective in the power of diffusing simplicity over a subject by the constant application of master truths. However he has greatly advanced the study of mental philosophy and to anyone who wishes to cultivate the power to acute discrimination his works may be recommended as constantly requiring the exercise of that faculty. It is a great pity that he had so little power of explaining his meaning. His vast and barbarous terminology is enough to terrify any Englishman, but one who like myself is a fanatical devotee in the service of metaphysics.

To EDWARD FRY, [1 MAY 1846]

Extracts in RB, X, 11, 12, 25, 29; the first dated 1 May 1846, and the others said to be from the same letter

I do not know whether you are much of a free-trader or not. I am

---

[3] Dr Hoppus 'made a minute study of Kant and the Post-Kantian idealists, with whom there was at that time very little acquaintance in England' (H. Hale Bellot, *University College*, p. 110).

enthusiastic about, am a worshipper of, Richard Cobden.[1] I am not very nervous about Lord Stanley and the House of Lords. . . .[2]

You ask, is England going downhill? I cannot think so. I see a gradual progress in history, especially in the History of England. I cannot suppose that this is now going to stand still. There never yet was a nation while getting freer and freer, more and more intellectually instructed, and morally better and better, which ever stopped. I think England is in this condition; the progress of the Arts of life, of material civilisation, has been for two centuries of unexampled rapidity, and I think that the mental progress has been also vigorously carried forward, though I do not think that it has been *equally* quick. The lower classes of this country are ignorant, but the last generation is better than the preceding ones, *our* generation more instructed than the last; it is for us to see to the next. The most hopeful sign of our times is seeing men like Burns and Ebenezer Elliott[3] showing the falsity of that scale of merit, that is graduated according to property, and making the rich to know that there are richer than they.

I am an impatient reader of merely pretty poetry[4] though not, I trust, without enthusiasm for the great masters of the poetic art, nor untouched by the beautiful expressions of feelings and aspirations, which earnestly long for what is infinite and eternal.

I fancy from what you say of my disappointment (having to miss a term), etc,[5] that you have melancholy theories about me. If you

---

[1] This sentence is quoted in the *Memoir* of Edward Fry, with the reading, 'about it, and am a worshipper of Richard Cobden' (p. 34). Fry replied that he was 'decidedly a Free Trader', although he thought repeal of the Corn Laws would not remedy 'social evils', nor was he so great a radical as the leading Free Traders (*ibid.*).
[2] Edward Stanley, later 14th Earl of Derby (1799–1869), had resigned from the cabinet over repeal of the Corn Laws, and was regarded by the Protectionists as their leader. With the support of the Whigs the bill passed its second reading in the Lords by a majority of 47.
[3] Ebenezer Elliott (1781–1849), 'the Corn-Law Rhymer', so called after his best known book, *Corn-Law Rhymes*, 1831. Carlyle had written on Burns (1828) and Elliott (1832).
[4] According to Mrs Barrington, a reference to Longfellow's *Voices of the Night*, 1839.
[5] WB had postponed the taking of his BA from October 1845 to October 1846; surviving letters show that although his health was poor 1844–5, he did not miss a complete term.

wish to keep close to the facts of the case you had better dismiss them. I have in general pretty good health, though at the present time I am a good deal troubled by rather severe headaches. But I verily believe I am the happiest person living. I have such a flow of good spirits as no calamities I think could long interrupt, much less exhaust. As for melancholy without apparent cause natural to some minds, I do not know what it means. I am not over-sanguine as to the future in general, but I have a sort of reckless cheerfulness that gets on very well without the aid of hope. Perhaps it may be unfeeling and unsympathising to be so completely happy, but I do not know how to help it.

To T. W. BAGEHOT, [5] MAY 1846

MS: Mr Norman St John-Stevas
DATE: the day after Disraeli's speech of 4 May: see n. 1; postmark 5 May

39 Camden St. May, 1846

My dearest Father,

I did begin a letter to you on Sunday Evening when I came back from Hampstead, but was too sleepy and stupid to get on with it. Yesterday I had no time to finish it and today it seems better to begin afresh. Have just caught sight of a passage in Mr. Disraeli's speech in the house of Commons last night; where he seemed to be referring to John Mill's Essay on the laws that regulate interchange between nations in favor of reciprocity meaning to apply that principle to *all* duties whatever.[1] I cannot believe however that even Mr. Disraeli would make such a flagrant misquotation. The fact is that John Mill very carefully draws the distinction between duties for revenue and duties for protection, and only applys the principle of reciprocity to the former. But Mr. Disraeli seemed to be arguing from the authority of John Mill that Ld. G. Bentinck[2] and himself should not be treated with such contempt. The essay begins with an allusion in the highest terms of eulogy to Mr. Ricardo's chapter on foreign trade—of the

---

[1] In his speech of 4 May, Disraeli cited J. S. Mill's 'Of the Laws of Interchange between Nations' (Essay I in *Essays on Some Unsettled Questions of Political Economy*, 1844), as stating that 'hostile tariffs must be met by hostile tariffs' (*Debates*, LXXXVI, 88).
[2] Lord George Bentinck (1802–48), leader of the Protectionists in the Commons.

MAY 1846

principles of which the essay by John Mill only proposes to be a development. Ricardo's chapter, John Mill thinks, is the foundation of everything which is 'known' with scientific accuracy on the subject. Of John Mill's opinions there can be no doubt as he has been writing articles against the corn laws for many years in the Westminster Review. I yesterday accidentally met with an article by him written at the time of the passing of the tithe commutation act,[3] which he says 'takes the tithe off the consumer and lays it on the landlord'. Tithe will now no longer operate as any discouragement to cultivation. It will no longer be one of the expenses of production which the price must be sufficient to repay; but a fixed proportion of the rent, that is of the surplus after the expenses are paid. It will be liable indeed to increase, but only as 'the rent increases, and can never under any circumstances be anything but a deduction from the rent'. As this opinion so exactly coincides with that to which you came when you were considering the subject when the corn law bill was first introduced I thought you would be interested in seeing it. Mr John Mill thinks that the reason of so 'unlandlordlike a proceeding was a wish to keep up the corn laws'; and if I understand him rightly maintains that the increased advantage, which the removal of the tithe unaccompanied by an alteration of the corn law would give to the home producer over the foreigner, would cause an increased cultivation of poorer soils, and therefore a rise of rent. So that the landlord would be indirectly counterbalanced for the burden of the tithe which he was taking upon him so long as the corn laws were maintained. Mr. Mill therefore though approving of the provisions of tithe commutation regretted that from not being accompanied with a corresponding reduction of the duties on foreign corn, it operated as an increase of 'protection to domestic industry', and therefore to a comparatively unprofitable employment of English capital.

Apropos of all this Political Economy would you be so kind as to send me the reference to Mr. M'Culloch's article or articles in the Edinburgh Review on 'Absenteeism'.[4] I have engaged to make a speech

---

[3] The article from which WB quotes has not been traced; the same arguments are found in John Pringle Nichol's 'Tithes and the Commutation', commissioned by Mill for the first number of the *London Review*, I (April 1835), 164–73, and signed 'J.P.N.'.

[4] John Ramsay McCulloch (1789–1864), statistician and economist. His view on absenteeism—that it was unimportant whether landlords were resident or non-resident—had first been expressed to a Select Committee in June 1825, and he expanded his argu-

MAY 1846

to prove that the expenditure of the income of absentees in a foreign country does not diminish the wealth of the country from which they emigrate. Brady[5] who is an Irishman is to take the opposite side. From Ricardo's chapter on Foreign Trade, and an essay by John Mill on the 'Influence of consumption on production'[6] I have a clear notion of the general argument, or I should not have undertaken to bring forward the subject. But there are some parts of the questions that seem intricate, and that will require some thought to be able to put clearly in a speech. It will be very good practice however, and I mean to take pains about it.

You will be interested in hearing that the Middle Temple have appointed Professor Long their Reader of Civil Law.[7] It is said that in consequence he will resign the professorship of Latin which he now holds, and attend more than he now does to the chamber practice of his profession. I do not know however whether this is true. The Biographical Dictionary of which Mr. Long was editor seems in a deplorable condition, as the Useful Knowledge Society have recently declared their work terminated, and that their sittings will now cease. They have published a self-laudatory pamphlet[8] stating what they have done, a good deal of which is no doubt valuable. They state that the sale of the Biographical Dictionary was diminishing, that £3000 had been expended on the parts issued and that the existing debts of the society scarcely fall short of their accumulated property. They can however repurchase the property of the parts already issued at a nominal price at any time within three years if sufficient funds should be raised to enable them to complete the work. As you have the parts already issued, I write this to you, though I suppose you have seen it in the Morning Chronicle.

---

ments in the *Edinburgh Review*, XLIII (November 1825), 54–76 (reprinted in *Treatises and Essays*, Edinburgh, 1853). It was criticized—mainly but not entirely from Irish sources—as being inapplicable to Ireland, with its chronic under-employment and labour which did not work for money wages (for an analysis of such criticism, see R. D. Collison Black, *Economic Thought and the Irish Question 1817–1870*, Cambridge, 1960, pp. 77–79).
[5] Francis William Brady, BA London, 1843; called to the Irish bar 1846; later QC.
[6] Essay II in *Some Unsettled Questions of Political Economy*.
[7] George Long gave up his chair on becoming lecturer in Civil Law and Jurisprudence of the Middle Temple, the Benchers having appointed him as an authority on Roman Law. Attendances at the lectures were poor because the course was not compulsory (see letter to T. W. Bagehot, 1 September 1846), and Long soon relinquished the appointment; in 1849 he became classical lecturer at Brighton College.
[8] *Address of the Committee of the Society for Useful Knowledge*, dated 'March 11, 1846'.

Everything at Hampstead in statu quo—Mr. Reynolds is in remarkably good spirits. Many thanks to my mother for her letters.

Believe me ever
Your affectionate Son
W BAGEHOT

To T. W. BAGEHOT, 7 MAY 1846

MS: Mr Norman St John-Stevas

39 Camden St. May 7th. 1846.

My dearest Father,

Many thanks for your two long letters which I will begin to answer before I go out to chapel this morning. I am very sorry that my letters lately have been carelessly written. The defect in my mind which is the proximate cause of it, is I think, that I have very great difficulty in that 'making a thing complete' which Mr. Long is constantly inculcating on us. I would much rather exert my mind really very hard for a short time, than attend for a long time to a great number of comparatively easy things. My mind is very apt to wander when the subject to which I have to attend is a collection of easy details. In mathematics, I do not nearly so much mind the parts which are generally considered as difficult, and which are seldom very long, as the great number of easy applications in which very few others find the slightest difficulty. With most people I suppose it would be fair to conclude that they could do what presents small difficulty, as well as that which would generally be considered more difficult. But I have too often found myself completely deceived in that mode of reasoning with respect to myself ever to venture on it again. It is the same defect of mental constitution I believe, which makes me such a wretched observer. Observation requires or rather implies a constant attention to a considerable number of minutiae, and this which is to many a rest is to me the most irksome labor. I will do what I can to amend my inaccuracy in writing but I hope you and my mother will instantly pull me up if I relapse as I very likely may be tempted to do by indolence and carelessness into my former negligent habits. With respect to the examinations when my headaches were so annoying, I had almost given up the idea of going into the examination of the Latin class, and had resolved to take that of the Roman constitution which would have been much less labor. But as my headaches are now a great deal better, I do not see any reason against my going into both examinations. I shall not do very splendidly, I dare say, in the Latin class.— I think I mentioned to you in answer to a letter in which some months ago you asked for an account of what I was doing, that in classical matters I had found it necessary to make some selection; and that I had determined to attend less to the niceties of grammatical constructions, which differ but very little from one another, to the different readings found in different manuscripts of the same classical author, and the researches of etymology, than to the historical instruction, literary beauty and speculative philosophy which after all are the real sources of the value of the records of antiquity. I do not in the least undervalue that precise acquaintance with every detail and every nicety in the classical writings which forms the pursuit of profound scholars. It is absolutely necessary that *some* persons should become well acquainted with them, and thoroughly investigate and discuss their difficulties. But my taste does not lead me in that direction, nor is my mind fitted especially well for such pursuits. It is very possible that the defect of mind which renders minute investigation in matters of small intrinsic importance very irksome to me, may have influenced my reasonings on this point more than I am aware of. But I cannot on reviewing these considerations see anything in them, that is erroneous, and I think at the time to which I have alluded you concurred in them. Of course as the examination is that of the highest class in Latin in the college, it would be absurd if a great part of it were not taken up with questions on the more evanescent niceties, and elaborate investigations to which I have just alluded. Of course those who have attended more especially to these niceties have a very fair advantage over those who have not. I shall of course attend more accurately to that part of the Latin examination which will also form part of the degree examination, than to the other part of it. With respect to the information about the law I can easily get what is necessary from Roscoe or Osler or any other of the young men whom I know and who are reading for the bar. I can however call on our cousin[1] if you

---

[1] Andrew Kippis Watson: see letter of 3 October 1846, n. 1.

MAY 1846

wish it. Most men from University college go to the middle Temple because that Inn is the only one which recognizes the degrees of the London University as exempting men from two years 'study' or rather two years 'eating dinners'. However as soon as I can get time I will make accurate enquiries on the subject. The political economy of your last letter will require more consideration than I have yet been able to give to it, and I must leave that as well as the other matters connected with my speech to be talked over in some morning's walk. I should have written to you yesterday but that I took a holiday in the afternoon and went with the Prichards and Mary Estlin to Hampton Court. We had a pleasant day, though it was hot, especially as we went in a carriage. Edith Prichard, Mary Estlin and myself came back by water. Mr. Estlin who had been to Twickenham to see Mrs. Mathews turned up on the Thames in a boat and came on board the steamer in which we were. He was very tired and rather querulous. He is not looking very well. He has been taking the chair at some Unitarian meetings, and I have heard people who [were] present talk of the advantage that any public meeting possessed, which was presided over by a *venerable* man. The pictures at Hampton are very splendid, though we had not near time enough for seeing them fully. The Cartoons from being rough sketches, loose[2] much less in engravings, than any other celebrated pictures which I ever saw. I never however saw any engraving which gave adequately the intensity of feeling which Raphael has thrown into many faces and attitudes. In some of the figures there is a grotesqueness at first sight which you lose in the engravings. In many instances this vanished when I got into the right light, but I had not time to find out whether it would do so in all—

The doctor wanted to have dinner in a small room looking out on the road, and seeming very like an oven seven times heated. However we carried eating it on the grass in the park. There are many excellent pictures at Hampton beside the cartoons. The great strength of the collection is in the portraits. The originals of Kneller's portraits of Newton and Locke are there. I never saw any engraving that gave at all adequately the fixed penetrating expression of Newton's eye. I had not to look very long at it, but the eye seemed to me almost poetic and even a little *wild*. Newton was certainly under some sort of mental

[2] Thus in MS.

aberration for a short time in one part of his life, and all his great discoveries were made before that period. I am just come in from Hampstead where all is just as usual, save that Alfred Norman is returned.

Believe me ever
your affectionate son,
WALTER BAGEHOT

I must have seemed very stupid in my remarks on Ld. Bacon in my last letter to my mother, if as she appears to think, I had intended to say that the same book was published to please Queen Elizabeth, and also to say that it was published after her death. Bacon wrote *two* books one an account of the 'treasons' &c. of Lord Essex which I think I called a 'libel', and also a defence of his own conduct in the time of James 1st. who was disposed to favor those who had stood by Essex in his misfortunes.[3] Perhaps what I said was obscure or illegible.

To EDITH BAGEHOT, [?MAY 1846]

MS: Mr Norman St John-Stevas
DATE: perhaps the letter which pained his mother, referred to in the postscript of next; 'Adelaide Tagg' may be identical with the 'Adeline [?Page]' of the letter to his mother of ?November 1845, since WB there speaks of 'getting her in in April'.

My dearest Mother,

I do not wonder at your complaining of my silence. I have been very busy and not especially bright. But the real reason that I have not written to you is that I am very puzzled what to say. You would not like my writing without any allusion to the letters I have lately received from you. Yet as you know what view I cannot help taking of the question of 'authorities' generally, I do not see how you can be doubtful what I should think of your making Brother[1] write to the Duke of Wellington. Nor do I think that you can imagine that what I should say could give you any pleasure in this matter. To your

---

[3] *A Declaration of the Treasons by Robert late Earl of Essex*, 1601, and *Sir Francis Bacon his Apologie in Certain Imputations concerning the late Earl of Essex*, 1604.

* * *

[1] Vincent Estlin.

hoping against hope about Adelaide Tagg² no one has any right to object. We can only state the reasons for thinking that there is no hope whatever, but no one can object to your taking your own view of the matter. Still the question of your writing in Brother's name in such matter is what I should never have expected.

When the letter came in which you told me of it, I felt almost bewildered to think that you should as it seems to me have done anything so unlike your usual maxims of not putting brother forward. But it may be that nothing which I can say, will do anything but make you write again in his name; for I am well aware that you have not much respect for my opinion in such questions. That the letter is *yours* and not Brother's you will of course admit as I have it in your own handwriting that it would be a miracle if Brother wrote the most commonplace letter for himself. Most of those around you have probably heard you say this; at least I have heard it twenty times. Surely you don't imagine that this miracle has been worked—and if the letter is your own why not write it in your own name in a straightforward manner?

I have often heard you say that if you were to die, you should like us to go on managing with Brother according to principles, and that everything should be as far as possible the same to him. But how are we to know what those principles of yours are, if you do not act on them? I perhaps ought not to charge you with not acting on them: but this at least I can say, that I have tried to the best of my ability for ten years to make out your ways of proceeding with Brother, and certainly if there is a thing which I should have said you would never have done, it is that which you have now done. I cannot say that I have read without pain any of the letters which you have sent to me as a 'repository'. But I do not say anything of this. It is not my place to decide what you are to write and what you are not to write, but *do* write them in your own name. Mr. Jacob³ need not have lent you Hermann and Dorothea as the family possess two copies of it: one is upstairs in the cupboard next the Edinburgh Reviews. My father could find it in a moment and you could read it when you liked. I cannot admire it much myself. The merit of Goethe is I think in his lyrical and

---

² See headnote.
³ Probably William Jacob (?1763–1851), widower of Julia Stuckey's sister, Martha; MP for Rye 1808–12; Comptroller of Corn Returns to the Board of Trade 1822–42.

dramatic productions. His aphorisms are very profound too. I will write again in a day or two.

> Yours in haste
> W BAGEHOT

To T. W. BAGEHOT, 16 MAY 1846
MS: Mr Norman St John-Stevas

> 39 Camden St. May 16th. 1846

My dearest Father,

I am just returned from Hampstead, and will not trust to the chance of getting any spare time tomorrow, but will begin a letter now. My Aunt Reynolds called me into counsel concerning carpets; touching which my mother had written to her. I could not however throw much light on the question. If I had been at home I should certainly have moved that the house do resolve itself into a committee to enquire whether or not you and my mother could come to London this summer to buy them. It was the unanimous opinion at Hampstead that a carpet could be got to satisfy my mother, but no one seemed willing to be responsible for getting one which would satisfy you. As however I make out that my mother's letter is merely to ask for information this may seem not to the point now; but it will be, I suppose, before the question is finally settled. It is my opinion that my aunt and uncle would go down to Langport if they were asked sometime soon—I am much obliged for the reference to M'Culloch. I will send you my speech when I have made it, if it is worth sending in my own valuation. I cannot satisfy myself that all which M'Culloch says about the 'profit' accruing to those dealers from whom absentees purchase is exactly correct. It seems to me to 'prove' that it does a dealer no good to purchase his goods. However I will send you my speech. In all other respects the article is very able and convincing. A Mr. Lawson who was Whatelyian professor of Political Economy some years ago, has written a 'confutation' of M'Culloch's theory,[1] but I have not been able to see his work although I have seen an abridgment of his arguments. If the

---

[1] James Anthony Lawson (1817–87), of Trinity College, Dublin; called to the Irish bar 1840, QC 1857, and ended his career as judge of the Queen's Bench, Ireland. Served as Whately professor of Political Economy at Trinity College 1840–45. WB is probably

abridgment be good, I do not think the arguments have much force, except that perhaps one or two of M'Culloch's positions might require a slight modification which would not however at all invalidate his conclusion.

I have been reading lately Blanco White's life[2] which is interesting, that is to people who like myself can read the life of anybody if it consists of personal details in which character can be shown. The accounts of the Spanish clergy in 1800, and previously for some years are such as to make one not astonished at the present state and prospects of that country. What else could arise from the union of a superstitious people without knowledge, a religion of forms and ceremonies, and an atheistic clergy? Whatever may be said, and there is much that may be said for the Catholicism of the middle ages, nothing whatever can be alledged in favor of the gross corruptions of the church of Spain. Blanco White says that Newman and Whately[3] drank tea with him alone one evening at Oxford; which is very curious when one thinks of the different lines which they have since taken—as it was just after Blanco White had become a member of the Church of England and before Newman had in his mind, I suppose, many of the Catholic notions which he has since arrived at. There was little at that time [to] disunite them. Blanco White says that Newman was a 'mystic' by nature, and contrary to what has generally been understood, states that he unlike the rest of the first Tractarians was never inclined to the German Rationalism. Dr. Pusey[4] is well known to have gone a great

---

referring to his *Five Lectures on Political Economy*, 1844, in which Lawson contends that when the landlord in Ireland became an absentee and ceased to demand the services of local tradesmen, the effect was to force labour into less productive types of employment (p. 125).

[2] Joseph Blanco White (1775–1841), a Catholic priest in Spain, who came to England in 1810; he became an Anglican clergyman and eventually turned to Unitarianism. White was a member of the Oriel College common room from 1826 until 1832, when he followed Whately to Ireland; sometimes considered one of the founders of latitudinarianism in the Church of England through his influence on Oxford colleagues. His *Life . . . Written by Himself*, ed. J. H. Thom had appeared in 1845.

[3] Richard Whately (1787–1863), fellow of Oriel, 1813; author of *Elements of Logic*, 1826; in 1829 he became professor of Political Economy at Trinity College, Dublin, and in 1831 Archbishop of Dublin. The occasion referred to by WB was in February 1827 (White, *Life*, I, 438), before Whateley's increasing scepticism and Newman's Catholic views had driven them apart.

[4] Edward Bouverie Pusey (1800–82), fellow of Oriel, 1823; appointed Regius professor of Hebrew and canon of Christ Church, 1828. Pusey joined the Tractarians in 1833, and was their leader after Newman's conversion. He published a book on the causes of rationalism in German theology (in two parts, 1828 and 1830), following a period of study in Germany.

way in that direction in his earlier days and some critics say that his recent changes have been 'a shrinking from logical consequences which it was inexpedient to meet'. The fundamental position of the German rationalism is, I believe, the opinion maintained by Mr. Martineau[5] that supernatural events occurring in connection with a 'supposed' revelation are no proof that the Revelation is true, or that it is indeed a revelation from God. The name Rationalists is however often given to persons who think that no supernatural events occurred in connection with Christianity, that is to the persons who are called anti-Supernaturalists. I am not aware however that there is the slightest ground for imputing to Dr. Pusey any inclination to the theories of the latter; nor that there is evidence for asserting any more than that a general tendency to be dissatisfied with the modern and English views of Protestant Christianity and a tendency to accept the German solutions of the leading theological questions were at one time very prominent in Dr. Pusey's mind.

Blanco White's ability does not much strike readers of his life who are unacquainted with his works. His greatest talent seems to me to have been for giving a clear and rather elegant statement of what was already known. He seems to me to have been incapable of the process usually called 'fixing his opinions';[6] that is making up his mind that after weighing all the arguments within his reach a certain conclusion was proved, and of making up his mind not to depart from it till some *new* arguments were suggested to him. This defect gave his mind a singular want of tenacity and made his views appear incomprehensible to persons whose minds were rigidly fixed to any set of opinions. He has recorded in his journal his resolution to write in English in order to 'anglicize the habits of his *mind*'. The purity and elegance of his English letters are excellent evidence of the extent to which he anglicized his style; but certainly the fluctuating, and nervously scrupulous habits of his mind were utterly different from the tenacity of most

---

[5] James Martineau (1805–1900), Unitarian divine; pastor of Paradise Street Chapel, Liverpool, from 1832, and appointed professor of Mental and Moral Philosophy and Political Economy at Manchester New College, 1840, where R. H. Hutton was later one of his pupils; recognized as an inspiring preacher and writer. His views on Biblical inspiration were influenced by Joseph Blanco White, as appeared in the Preface to the 1845 edition of his *Rationale of Religious Enquiry*, clearly referred to here by WB.

[6] cf. Newman's comment that White's mind was 'helplessly disorganised' (*Letters and Correspondence*, ed. Anne Mozley, 1891, II, 98).

English minds of any grasp and from the easy acquiescence which they exhibit in any habits of mind, and any speculative views that are good enough for practical purposes. It is right however to say that his mind was almost compelled by his singular situation and feeble health, and exclusively religious education to devote himself exclusively to theological studies; and that there are few minds which would bear the internal strife, and anxious aspirations, and stern self-scrutiny necessary to profound acquaintance with a religious philosophy, if unaided by that constant call to *action* so necessary in all subjects that have any near kindred with morals.

Blanco White *did* little or nothing in life; and the history of speculative minds seems to confirm the anticipation of common sense that those only who have a deep *moral experience* themselves can solve questions that derive their difficulty from the complexity of our moral nature, and from the danger of either underestimating or overvaluing the contributions made by conscience to a knowledge of God and duty. Certain it is that the constant promise of Christ that those who *do* his will shall know of the truth of his doctrine is unaccompanied by any promise of success to inactive speculation however earnest and conscientious. Blanco White's life is a very melancholy book. He is always 'chawed up' as Watty said of Lady Willoughby,[7] and one does not always see any sufficient reason for his grievances.

Monday Morning. I doubt if this letter be very intelligible in all parts as I wrote it last night late, but I *hope* that is clear. My headaches are generally a good deal better though I have rather a bad one at this moment.

Believe me ever your affectionate son

WALTER BAGEHOT

Love to all especially to my mother. I am sorry she did not like my last letter any better, and am very sorry if any expressions in it have really given her any pain. But I really cannot see that if what I said, were false, it would have been any such grievous offence to think it true. And as I cannot say that I feel inclined to retract anything which I

---

[7] Possibly Elizabeth, *née* Kennedy, first wife of Sir John Pollard, 4th bart; or perhaps a reference to their reading of *So Much of the Diary of Lady Willoughby as Relates to Her Domestic History and to the Eventful Period of the Reign of Charles the First*, 1844, a fictional diary, published anonymously, written by Hannah Rathbone, containing a good deal of piety.

said in that letter, I must take shelter behind her favorite expression that truth cannot do anybody any harm, in this case at least.

To T. W. BAGEHOT, [23 MAY 1846]

MS: Mr Norman St John-Stevas
DATE: 23 May 1846, from reference to WB's 'Absenteeism' and to Macaulay's speech of 22 May (see n. 2)

My dearest Father,

I have only time for a short note, to go in the same envelope with the speech on absenteeism.[1] The argument of M'Culloch's to which I referred is on page 62 of the review. I quite see the truth of what you say on the subject in the letter which I received this morning. It is clear that if, as you suppose, Robinson Crusoe had all the facilities for laboring, and all the means of production, which are enjoyed by persons in a trading and manufacturing community he would be able to produce as much as they produce. The 'profit' also is and can be nothing else than the excess of what is produced in a given time over what is consumed. But I think your illustration requires one addition. If you suppose Robinson Crusoe to have all the advantages of machinery and the division of labor and at the same time no unemployed capital he would be not only *equally* favorably circumstanced with a person living in a commercial community but *more* favorably circumstanced. When one man is to supply his own wants by previously supplying the wants of others, he cannot exactly know what these latter wants are. He is obliged to accumulate a 'stock in trade' by which he can supply them whenever they are felt. It is a consequence of this a great quantity of capital lies idle for a time. Mr. M'Culloch observes 'Whether they (the manufacturers) directly consume the commodities which they have manufactured, or exchange them for others of an equal value belonging to others has no more to do with profits than it has with poetry or painting'.

---

[1] WB's speech, on the question, 'Does the Expenditure of the Income of Absentees in a Foreign Country diminish the Wealth of the Country from which they emigrate?': *Collected Works*, XIV.

MAY 1846

But if the goods produced be such as were produced only for the purpose of exchanging them for others, it will make a difference to the trader whether they can be exchanged immediately after they [are] ready for sale or some months or years afterwards. The more customers there are, the more circulating and more productive will be the capital of the trader. Mr. M'Culloch's argument appears to me to hold good only for those traders who have the means of selling their goods as soon as they are ready for sale. All traders would be in this position, if they had powers of foresight sufficient to inform them exactly what articles would be required and when they would be required. But these are not the conditions of society under which we live and about which we are reasoning. I think that this will be clear with what I have said in the speech. I have made the reference to M'Culloch more precise in the written speech than it really was in what I *said*. I did not introduce more 'theoretical' matter as it is called than I could help. But as the opponents of absenteeism have advanced a good many singular assertions about 'profits', it was necessary to meet them on their own ground. I shall be glad to know whether you think this part of the argument sound or not. It seems to me quite satisfactory.

I have just seen a little of the debate in the house of commons last night which seems to me the best *debate* that they have had this session. As there is a good deal to be said on both sides, the question is well adapted for discussion. Some passages of Macaulay's speech seemed to be very striking.[2] I do not however see my way quite to his conclusion. I do not see how to avoid the conclusion that there must [be] an immediate reduction of wages; and till I know more than I do at present as to the amount of that reduction, I do not see how to determine the question, would it be desirable for the working classes to submit to that reduction, in order to gain the means of intellectual improvement, and domestic comfort? Whatever may happen in the long run, the immediate effect must be diminished production, and therefore either wages, or profits or both must fall. But I do not see how without

---

[2] The last night of the debate on the second reading of the 'Ten Hours Bill' (a bill for limiting the hours of young persons in factories to ten hours a day). Macaulay spoke for the bill on the score of morality and health; moreover, he denied that 'a great society in which children work fifteen, or even twelve hours a day, will, in the lifetime of a generation, produce as much as if those children had worked less', contending that manufactures would gain from a healthy, well-educated population (*Debates*, LXXXVI, 1028–43). The bill was defeated, and the government saved, by the votes of Whigs and some Protectionists.

knowing the amount of that fall, how we can determine its moral or its physical effects on the working classes. I do not see the objection to giving up an increase of national wealth, if it were accompanied by moral improvement. However I may be able to judge better when I have really read the debate.

I will write to my mother soon, and put no political economy into the letter.

Believe me
every yours affectionately
WALTER BAGEHOT

To T. W. BAGEHOT, 25 JUNE 1846

MS: Mr Norman St John-Stevas

39 Camden St. June 25th. 1846

My dearest Father,

While the examinations were going on, I could not have found time to write more than a very short note. They are now over, and those who have gone through them are left to their own meditations as to their own failure or success. My own meditations are not very promising as in several things I thought I was better prepared than I found I was. There is no use in writing my own opinions and conjectures on the matter however as the event will soon show us certainly how the matter really lies. I never met with any one who was a good judge of how he had done at an examination and of course no one can know how those who are competing with him have done. Mr. Grote[1] is going to

---

[1] George Grote (1794–1871), historian of Greece. A disciple of Bentham and James Mill, and took the lead, with Mill and Brougham, in the foundation of the London University, becoming the youngest member of its Council; he resigned from the Council in 1830 as a protest against the appointment of the dissenting minister Hoppus to a chair of philosophy, but was re-elected in 1849 and succeeded Brougham as President in 1860. One of the small group of Radical MPs, 1832–41, and undertook the advocacy of the ballot, which he brought up six times between 1833 and 1839: his speeches were listened to with respect, but his motions were invariably lost.

preside at the distribution this year in compliment I suppose to the history of Greece which he has recently published.[2] Is it not singular that a Benthamite politician should publish two bulky volumes on the poetical legends of ancient Greece? I have heard that it is rather imaginative in some parts which no one would have guessed from the author's speeches on the 'Ballot'.

I hope to be able to get out of town either tomorrow or Saturday week. I have some work to finish for Mr. De Morgan which will detain me till that time. I believe I shall want £13 to pay Mr. De Morgan. I shall also want 5£ for myself as my wardrobe &c. has been expensive. It is no compliment to say that I want to come home exceedingly; for I am so tired of London that I should be glad to be out of it on any terms. My dislike of London came on quite suddenly, as it always does, two or three days ago. I know from experience that it will not go off till I have had a run in the country for a short time. I shall, as you know, soon have to come back to bricks and smoke, but this must be endured. I think the people who come up to London 'for the season' must be insane; or they must have different tastes from mine. I will now collect all the necessary information about the inns of court. If there is anything to be done immediately I will write to you, but if not we can talk it over in some of our walks in the garden. I suppose if I go to the bar, I am to look forward to two or three years of very dry work at any rate; after that people seem to like it better. It seems a universal rule that noone likes it at first. Roscoe was declaiming to me last night as to the difficulty of real property law. Hutton says he find its less difficult and more disagreeable than he expected. Everybody seems to complain that the recent statutes have not been sufficiently framed on the principles of the old law, and that modern reformers instead of amending the old system have placed beside it a portion of a new one on wholly different principles.[3] Mr. Long said 'that real property law always was a difficult study. But that the

---

[2] The first two volumes of Grote's 12-volume *History of Greece* were published in March 1846; he had been devoted to the subject since his youth, and retired in 1843 from the bank in which he was a partner in order to write the *History*. For WB's tribute to Grote and to the *History*, see *Collected Works*, II, 369–73.
[3] The result of the four reports of the commissioners appointed to inquire into the law of real property, issued 1829–33, was a series of acts removing particular abuses while leaving the substantive rules of the land law untouched; they concentrated on schemes for a general registration of conveyances, a recommendation approved by Bentham, but impossible to carry out without fundamental changes in land law.

old law was comprehensible; and that it was spoilt by statutes which no man could comprehend'. He then began a philippic against Brougham as the ringleader in this sacrilege. Mr. Long is quite I fancy of the old school in legal matters. At least he once told me that Bentham the modern authority for codification was an exceedingly confused man. His recent appointment will enable him to make his views extensively known. I suppose you are watching the slow, but sure progress of the Corn Bill through the house of Lords with considerable interest. I have not read any of Ld. Ashburton's speeches[4] in favor of his 'amendments'. Does he still adhere to the doctrine that wages rise and fall with the price of corn? In 1815 it is remarkable that this was the universal opinion. One man did say something that indicated a doubt about it. But Horner put him down by saying he hoped the house 'would hear no more of such heresies'. Ld. Ashburton who does not seem to get wiser as he gets older may have in this instance kept to the creed of his youth; though he is now doing all in his power to destroy the credit he gained by opposing the passing of the corn law thirty years ago. Do you think that Sir R Peel has made a complete defence of himself?[5] It seems to me that he has answered the charges that have been raked up against him. Mr. Reynolds remarked to me on Sunday; that it was odd Peel did not say 'I could not have said that some thing must be done for the Catholics in 1825, for that was not then my opinion'. He does not any where say that it was not his *opinion* at the time of the speech to which there have been so many allusions, but takes the simply negative argument, 'I did not *say* so'. Straightforwardness certainly is not the most obvious of his good qualities. Did you read Mr. Gladstone's letter to the Canadian legislature

---

[4] Ashburton had been an advocate of free trade in his youth, but in 1846 opposed repeal of the corn laws; during the debates he supported amendments by other peers, and on 22 June moved a resolution against the immediate admission of large quantities of foreign corn now in bond (*Debates*, LXXXVII, 763–66).
[5] On 9 June Lord George Bentinck, in giving notice that he would oppose the government's Irish Arms bill, made a violent personal attack on Peel; he accused him of having hunted Canning to death over Catholic Emancipation in 1827, although—as he admitted to the House in 1829—he had himself changed his mind on the subject as early as 1825. Peel (who had to be restrained from calling Bentinck out) rebutted the change temperately a few nights later, whereupon Disraeli returned to the attack on Bentinck's behalf. On 19 June Peel produced convincing evidence that he had been misreported in 1829, and proceeded to answer Disraeli point by point, enthusiastically cheered by the House (see Norman Gash, *Sir Robert Peel*, 1972, pp. 595–98).

about a fortnight ago?[6] It seemed to me a very excellent state paper, and to be by far the best defence which the ministry have made for their measure. It was very beautifully expressed too, which those who take right views of political economy are not always able to accomplish. It is singular with what completeness and exactness the ministry have adopted Cobden's views. Mr. Gladstone said little which had not been said at the league, but he said it with an elegance which they could scarcely attain and which, it may be, they would despise.

I am much obliged to Watty for his note which though short was more than I deserve for not answering his last. I have not seen William Wood, but I will call on him tomorrow if I can.

Believe me ever
your affectionate Son
W BAGEHOT.

To EDITH BAGEHOT, [?JULY–AUGUST 1846]

Extract in RB, X, 161–2, where it is printed as though part of the same letter as the preceding extract—wrongly, as MS of that letter shows (see letter to Edith Bagehot, 26 February 1846). Since he speaks of the Whigs as 'we', probably after the formation of Lord John Russell's government in July 1846.

It will be a great thing for good thorough Whigs if we get rid of the Irish Church, and if, as you say, Lord Ashley says Sir R. Peel is prepared to destroy it.[1] I wish I could believe that Lord John Russell was ready to pull it down, but he did not used to be; and I think he would

---

[6] William Ewart Gladstone (1809–98) had been appointed Colonial Secretary at the end of 1845. His despatch of 3 June 1846 to the Governor of Canada, Earl Cathcart, argued that Canada would benefit in the long run by free trade in corn and timber, and refused petitions for modifications in the tariffs (*P.P.*, 1846, XXVII, 49–54).

* * *

[1] Anthony Ashley Cooper, Lord Ashley (1801–85), later 7th Earl of Shaftesbury, social reformer and Evangelical churchman, Conservative MP 1826–51. He was a supporter of the Established Church in Ireland, and his diary for February 1844 shows him to have distrusted Peel's defence of that church on grounds of expediency rather than principle. On 31 October 1846 he told Russell of the report 'that the great *desire* of your Government, it may not be actually their *policy*, is to endow the Romish priesthood in Ireland'. (See E. Hodder, *Life and Work of the Seventh Earl of Shaftesbury*, 1886, II, 58, 185.)

prefer endowing the Catholics as well as the Protestants. Lord Grey[2] would go to work in a more complete manner perhaps, and perhaps the cabinet would find it pretty nearly as hard to agree about the matter, as you do at Herd's Hill. Nevertheless as Arnold used to say energetically *something* must be done. What the dominance of Protestantism has brought Ireland to, we see; and one sees small wisdom in keeping the spiritual instruction of the Irish people in the hands of those under whom the lower classes have grown up to their present frightful condition. When things are at the worst, some change seems likely to be for the better.

To T. W. BAGEHOT, AUGUST 1846

ms: Mr Norman St John-Stevas
date: probably earlier than next, from references to 'soon after I came up' and details of work; perhaps the previous week-end.

39 Camden St. August. 1846.

My dearest Father,

I wrote yesterday to my mother, and though I have not much time left will not let the post go out without a letter to you. The letters which I have received from my mother have been on the whole good, though not always quite clear. They are however quite as good as those which she is in the habit of writing hastily to me on matters that interest her at the moment. And as you say that she has been quite as well lately as she was when I left home there seems for the present to be necessary or proper for us but to be cheerful and thankful. I am now getting, or rather got pretty thoroughly into my work. I had a great deal of headache owing no doubt to the thunder soon after I came up, but this has now passed away, and I hope that I shall not be hindered in the

---

[2] Sir Henry George Grey, 3rd Earl Grey (1802–94). In the Lords, 23 March 1846, he had introduced his Motion on the State of Ireland with a speech in which he urged the necessity of giving the Roman Catholic clergy some independent means of subsistence, and had regretted that the Roman Catholic was not the Established Church of Ireland, according to the plan of 'the man whose character I admire and revere more than that of any man who has lived in our times, I mean the late Dr. Arnold' (*Debates*, LXXXIV, 1343–82). In the spring of 1846 Prince Albert expressed to Peel his apprehensions about future Whig policy towards the Irish Church question (N. Gash, *Sir Robert Peel*, pp. 670–1).

same way again. I am principally engaged on Pure Mathematics at present, and am going over carefully all the necessary ground. I am going rather slowly perhaps, but I do not wish to leave any enemies in my rear. It is best of course to take the Pure Mathematics before the applied, since unless you know a science well applications will certainly be obscure. After I have finished the Pure Mathematics, I shall read the classical books thoroughly, and then go to the Natural Philosophy, that is to say to the applied Mathematics. Of course I shall also read the Physiology, Logic &c but the main contention and difficulty is in the other and therefore I thought you would like to know the order in which I had taken the subjects. I took the classics in the middle for the sake of variety which will be refreshing. I have been reading some of the Theory of Numbers, which De Morgan says is the best exercise for the head possible and certainly is a hard stretch for my reasoning powers and memory. In most mathematics there are either figures or symbols, but here there are none of the first and few of the second. I read some of it with De Morgan this summer, and have been reading a little more now. The first proposition sounds very odd; it is to *prove* that a fraction, of which the numerator and denominator are not divisible by the same number (1 excepted) is in its lowest terms. Generally this is assumed as the lowest terms are defined to be those in which the numerator and denominator are not divisible by the same number. But 'lowest terms' are here taken in their natural sense for the fraction which being of a given value has its numerator and denominator as low as possible. So that the proposition really is to prove if a fraction is not divisible above and below by the same quantity, it has no fraction equal to it with a smaller numerator and denominator. This like most first principles looks obvious but is not easy of proof. Yet it is not to be compared in this respect to some others. I believe on farther as they say at school it gets harder, but I know now what *they* ask, if I can manage to remember it.

The last number of the Prospective Review[1] is interesting. It contains an article ascribed to Mr. Newman on the poetical origin of Roman

---

[1] The *Prospective Review* grew out of and replaced an earlier Unitarian quarterly, the *Christian Teacher*. Its founders and editors were a group of Unitarian ministers: James Martineau and John Hamilton Thom (1808–94) of Liverpool, John James Tayler (1797–1869) of Manchester, and Charles Wicksteed (1810–85) of Leeds. Thom had been editor of the *Christian Teacher* and the other three contributors. They founded the new periodical, which began publication in February 1845, as a vehicle for a more liberal Unitarian

history in the earlier ages.[2] It is impugning a fundamental idea of Niebuhr's system, in which it is supposed that the early Romans sang legendary and epic poems at private banquets and public festivities, from which later annalists set down the 'history'. Mr. Newman thinks that no poems ever existed such as Niebuhr supposed, and such as Macaulay has attempted to construct in his 'Lays', and that whether or no early Roman history was invented, or is trustworthy, it is wholly prosaic. Some of Niebuhr's arguments certainly are very weak, and their weakness is ably exposed in this review. But for my own part, as no one asserts that early Roman history is trustworthy matter of fact, I think we must assume that it was invented, and if it was invented the fine characters, beautiful episodes, and graphic descriptions seem to me to prove that its inventors must have been poets of a high order. Of course there must have been many such if the whole is an invention, but they might (and Niebuhr thinks they did) work one on the creations of another.

In this same number of the Review there is a review by Mr. Martineau of Whewell's systematic morality. He reviewed his 'Elements of Morality' in November last and Whewell replied to his criticisms in the lectures which he has now published.[3] I have not read Whewell's defence, but from what I read of the first work I thought that Mr. Martineau's criticisms though severe were quite just; and from the review I thought that Whewell had only made a bad matter a good deal worse by his recent publication. Originally the controversy turned mainly on two questions, 1st. whether or no it is possible or philosophical to accumulate a set of logically coherent precepts without stating the phenomenon in human nature that gives them their *authority?* This Whewell has attempted to do, and to justify and Mr.

---

theology and to appeal to a wider audience with articles on other subjects. The editors were the main contributors, but Francis Newman and John Kenrick also wrote regularly, and they soon attracted younger men, including R. H. Hutton, W. C. Roscoe and WB himself (see letter of ?6 February 1848, n. 7).

[2] 'The Poetical Element of Roman History', *Prospective Review*, II (Aug 1846), 322–337. by John Kenrick, not Francis Newman.

[3] William Whewell (1794–1866), Master of Trinity College, Cambridge, whose philosophical writings had not the authority of his earlier scientific works, had published in 1845 *The Elements of Morality, including Polity*, reviewed by James Martineau in the *Prospective*, I (November 1845), 577–610; Whewell answered Martineau in *Lectures on Systematic Morality*, 1846, and this volume was the subject of Martineau's article in the *Prospective* of August 1846 (II, 400–427). The *Prospective* articles enabled Martineau to express his view of the irreducibility of conscience, in opposition to Whewell's conception of morality as based on the revealed law.

Martineau said in his first article, that who ever did so must 'give up the title of philosopher to enlist himself among the compilers of receipt books'. The second point is 'whether duties take their origin from legal enactment alone'. A proposition undistinguishable from this was Whewell's original assertion, and he derived passive obedience to rules in all cases from this, which would be a good deduction. For if there is nothing higher than law, how [can] it be obligatory to disobey it? Mr. Martineau gave Whewell a great advantage in making the review turn on a 'Scholastic' question like the first. A person who wished merely to *cut up* Whewell's book would have easily made an amusing article by exposing the singularity of his language and the mistiness of his reasonings.[4] I must break off. Love to Watty and brother. Can't operatives write letters? Yours ever affly

W Bagehot

Please to remember kindly to Mr. Charles Bagehot[5]

To T. W. BAGEHOT, 15 AUGUST 1846

MS: Mr Norman St John-Stevas

39 Camden St. August 15th. 1846

My dearest Father,

Before your letter came yesterday I fully intended to have written to you, and after that I was certainly still more bound to do so. But I went out to wish Hutton goodbye, and he asked me to walk with him into the city and as I shall not see [him] for a year at least,[1] I thought you would not object to his infringing on your time. He was

---

[4] Martineau himself told a friend in July 1846 that 'the prospect of having to lift the lumbering Master of Trinity over all the gaps in his logic fills me with unutterable despair' (J. Estlin Carpenter, *James Martineau*, pp. 291–2).

[5] Charles Bagehot (1786–1856), cousin of Thomas Watson Bagehot; entered the Navy 1801 as Midshipman, Lieutenant 1808, from October 1823 until his death Inspecting Commander of the Coast Guard; married Amelia Bowden of Plymouth in 1825, and had two children, Watson (WB's foster brother) and a daughter (W. R. O'Byrne, *Naval Biography*, 1849; the *Navy List*, 1857).

* * *

[1] Hutton had gone to Heidelberg to study theology, returning to England in September 1847 to become one of Martineau's students at Manchester New College. While he was in

to leave London for Ostend last night, or rather perhaps this morning early. I shall miss him a great deal, and the more so as most of my other friends and acquaintances are out of town. However as I have only to work, this is no very great calamity perhaps, though it does not render working more agreeable. I have not yet done anything about the business as to the inns of Court, or the introduction to Mr. Newman[2] who is not yet, I understand, in London. It happens that if I understand rightly, the mathematical examination for honors falls exactly at the time at which if I went to the Middle Temple I should be eating my dinners. This will be rather an inconvenience but I suppose it could be got over. I am not aware if the other inns are exactly at that time but I will learn. I *believe*, that (if I am not plucked) my degree will save me at the Middle Temple from depositing a hundred pounds and that it will come just in time to do and no more. One can enter at any inn at any inn[3] at the beginning of any term. I have not yet got very complete information, but from what I have picked up, I think the question lies almost entirely between Lincoln's Inn, and the Middle Temple, and there is a pretty general opinion that the former is *rather* the most gentlemanly, and it is certainly the dearest. I will soon get more full and accurate information however. Apropos of the law I have just been reading in Foster's life two letters very strongly disapproving of the profession.[4] He seems to have had a dislike of

---

Germany he kept up a correspondence with WB, of which some of Hutton's letters have survived (MSS Norman St John-Stevas). The earliest, written from Heidelberg 30 August, welcomed his first letter from WB, and said that 'the want of our daily discussions and conversations on subjects so deeply interesting to both of us' would be a greater loss to his mind than to WB's, since 'I have always found myself arrived at the same stage of opinion and progress that you have passed some time'; he was anxious through letters to have the assistance of 'a more original thinker' in his study of German philosophy. He gave—as WB had asked—his impressions of places in Belgium and on the Rhine visited by his friend in July–August 1844, and said of Nonnenwerth: 'I visited the island . . . and stayed about it some time pleased to think you had been there before me, and do not in the least wonder at your love of it . . . I should not omit to thank you for your advice to stay in those regions.' The conclusion shows that WB's letter had asked for a definition of 'the appetites' as opposed to 'the affections', and their relation to the will and the conscience.

[2] F. W. Newman, Long's successor as professor of Latin at University College.

[3] Thus in MS.

[4] John Foster (1770–1842), essayist and Baptist minister, who had lectured at Broadmead Chapel, Bristol, in the 1820s. To a friend who intended to become a lawyer he wrote, in 1812, about 'that inglorious profession', whose practitioners had 'a much worse reputation for integrity than any other class of men not directly and formally addicted to iniquitous employments' and who 'fiercely and insolently opposed all manner of reforms' (*The Life and Correspondence of John Foster*, ed. J. E. Ryland, 1846, I, 426–30).

'lawyers' generally, and to have thought their standard of morality and their practice decidedly inferior to those of the rest of the community. He does not allege any proof of this however, nor does he say what branch of the profession he means by 'lawyers' which may mean attorneys or barristers or both. I believe there is an impression of the sort among many well intentioned persons, and from conversations which I have had with Dr. Hoppus at various times, I should think that a dislike of law and lawyers was rather general among the Independent dissenters. This seems too to be an old notion, as Cromwell who in general spoke the opinion of religious and scrupulous dissenters in his day, used to say that English Law was 'an ungodly jungle full of snares for the feet'. Do you think there is any ground for saying that the average morality of barristers is lower than that of the rest of the community? If it were so there would arise a presumption that there was something not right in their occupations and perhaps in the practice of advocacy which (though Foster does not mention it) is certainly the *most* disputable part of their calling. But surely public men who come from all ranks and all occupations are a fair test of the morality and honor of the different classes to which they belong, and it would be very difficult to prove that during the last fifty years distinguished lawyers had been found more wanting in probity and public spirit than other eminent public men. Indeed until very recent times Sir S. Romilly and Francis Horner who were both lawyers are the very strongest instances of a reputation depending very much on moral worth. Nor do Lord Eldon and Lord Stowell to take men very inferior morally to Romilly and Horner at all, I imagine, fall short of the average probity of the statesmen of their time.

If Brougham's youth be allowed to compensate for the aberrations of his old age, Lord Lyndhurst is the only instance that occurs to me, of a lawyer in recent times gaining very high eminence, and being notoriously dissolute of character.[5] It is probable that lawyers are opposed to alterations in law, which unprofessional philanthropists think so obviously advisable, that they impute unfairly moral obtuse-

---

[5] Sir Samuel Romilly (1757–1818) and Francis Horner were law reformers, admired by the Bagehots; John Scott, 1st Earl of Eldon (1751–1838), Lord Chancellor; William Scott, Lord Stowell (1745–1836), judge of the High Court of Admiralty; Henry Peter, Baron Brougham and Vaux (1778–1868), who after 1834 never again held office; John Singleton Copley, Baron Lyndhurst (1772–1863), succeeded Eldon as Lord Chancellor in 1827.

ness to all their opponents. But this seems like the mercantile men who came to Mr. Huskisson[6] and asked for Free Trade in every part of commerce but that in which they were concerned. No one who has fitted his mind to one system, likes to take it out again, and shape it to a new one; nor can a disinclination to see the possibility of this change being for the better be justly imputable to any one as a moral fault. The more I think of it, the more I incline to think the principle of advocacy quite defensible, though of the details I can of course know nothing. Indeed I am staggered more by the difficulties seen in it by Arnold[7] and persons partaking of his deeply conscientious character, than by anything which I can see myself in the practice. Perhaps the larger question is another instance in which very sensitive and scrupulous minds start back from a course of conduct that seems at first sight faulty, but is not so in fact.

Your remarks seem to me a sufficient answer to the Bishop of Oxford,[8] though the Bishop made out a very plausible case for his amendment. So long however as Free Traders have to do with Anti-slavery philanthropists, their victory will be easy; the only practical difficulty is with the West India Planters, the old opponents of the abolition of slavery, who have not a word to say in defence of their protection that does not throw deep censure on their own conduct in times not very remote. It is a misfortune that these men are to try the great experiment of overcoming the labor of slaves by the labor of freemen. But surely to give them protection while their productions are inferior to those of slaves states, is the surest way to make the compulsory work of slaves seem better and cheaper than that of freemen. And since if the emancipated slaves were intelligent, their labor would be the more profitable the protection would act as a direct encouragement to the planters to carry on the work which they begun in the days of slavery, and to keep the people as far as possible, that are beneath

---

[6] William Huskisson (1770–1830), whose tariff legislation of 1825 brought about modified free trade.

[7] Thomas Arnold expressed 'abhorrence' of the calling of an advocate, as 'inconsistent with a strong perception of truth' (A. Stanley, *Life of Thomas Arnold*, II, 71–2, 233).

[8] Samuel Wilberforce (1805–73), son of the great abolitionist. During the Lords' debate of 13 August 1846 he spoke against the removal of duty from sugar grown in Cuba and Brazil, on the grounds that it would lead to extension of the slave-trade; he argued that free trade would not do away with slavery, since the importation of full-grown slaves from Africa meant that free labour could not be cheaper. His amendment was lost (*Debates*, LXXXVIII, 649–667).

them in ignorance, and dullness. Mr Gladstone once said that all colonial monopolies were bounties on incapacity, surely this is also a bounty on the ignorance and degradation of a community. There is to be a great anti-slavery meeting[9] at which Mr. Garrison[10] and F. Douglas[11] are to speak and I should like to go, but I do not know whether I can or whether I ought. I have nothing to tell of my studies, which are going on in their ordinary routine, not so fast as I could wish, but I hope solidly. I am reading next to nothing else but degree work. I was surprized to see my Aunt and Uncle Edward at Hampstead. I did not know they were in town. Both my Aunt and Uncle Reynolds are better than they were.

Believe me ever
your affectionate Son
W BAGEHOT.

Love to Watty and Brother.

I cannot close this without telling you, that my letters from my mother have been very comfortable ones; although I see the want in them which you point out—One cannot wonder that her mind should be jaded by what she has gone through. It brings before one very strongly the loss of my Uncle Stuckey who would so easily have given her mind some of the freshness and elasticity which it wants now—Yet how much better is it than we expected 6 weeks ago.

Is there at home a small red mathematical notebook of mine? It is either in our room or in the cupboard in the passage upstairs. It can come by post if it is at home, and I cannot find it anywhere here.

I have made up my mind not to go to the A.S. meeting.

---

[9] On 17 August; its purpose was to form a society to abolish slavery in America (*The Patriot*, 20 August 1846).
[10] William Lloyd Garrison (1805–79), American reformer dedicated to the cause of immediate and complete emancipation of slaves; by this date the leadership of the movement had passed to more practical men than the inspiring but pugnacious Garrison, who had a talent for antagonizing even his own supporters.
[11] Frederick Douglass (?1817–1895), American negro who escaped from slavery 1838, and became an orator and journalist in the cause of abolition. In England and Ireland speaking against slavery 1845–7, partly to avoid being returned to slavery after the publication in 1845 of his *Narrative of the Life of Frederick Douglass*.

SEPTEMBER 1846

To T. W. BAGEHOT, 1 SEPTEMBER 1846

MS: Mr Norman St John-Stevas

39 Camden St. Sep. 1st. 1846.

My dearest Father,

Although your promised letter has not arrived yet I suppose that you will think it high time for me to answer your last. My work is progressing though more slowly than I could wish; but it does not afford any materials for correspondence. Have you observed the recent resolutions of the Inns of Court, as to Legal Education?[1] There really seems to be a propensity to move onward among the Lawyers on this matter. Some people (and the Times newspaper I believe among the number) are grumbling that some examination was not made indispensible previous to a student being called to the bar. But if they had done so we should have had grumbling enough, from those whom the Inns of Court have encouraged to look to the years of preparation for the bar as an easy lounge in London. Of course a certificate of attendance at lectures is *no* security for any knowledge; and therefore in time I suppose in common sense there ought to be an examination enforced on those who wish to be called to the bar, as a certificate of fitness for the numerous situations of which they have the monopoly. If you recollect in Horner's life, there are many allusions to his law Trials, which seem to have been an examination previous to his being called to the Scotch bar. I suppose we may look forward to seeing this done; but as it would seem opposed to the pecuniary interests of the inns of court, who would not perhaps have so many students as now when they have *both* idlers and workers, we cannot expect the inns of court to be overanxious and forward to impose the examination of themselves. I heard yesterday a piece of literary intelligence in which

---

[1] The report of the Select Committee on Legal Education (*P.P.*, 1846, X, 1) found that there was no formal system of legal education, and recommended that it should be undertaken by the universities and the Inns of Court, with the Inns combining to provide a system of class teaching and compulsory examinations. The resolutions of the Inns of Court were for the setting up of lectureships, but not for compulsory attendance and examinations, a scheme criticized as inadequate in *The Times* of 1 September 1846. The Inns of Court Commission of 1854 (*P.P.*, 1854–55, xviii, 1) found that the student was still left to educate himself, and in its turn recommended compulsory classes and examinations. See WB's 'Bad Lawyers or Good', *Collected Works*, VII, 245–65.

you may perhaps take an interest. It is that the articles on Puseyism &c in the Edinburgh during the last few years, were written by Baden Powell the professor of Natural Philosophy in the University of Oxford. The article on Mysticism and Scepticism is also by him in the last number.[2] The authority is the professor himself who told my informant. He writes a good deal in the Westminster, and seems altogether as odd a man for an Oxford Professor as one could well look for; he is an extreme Whig not to say a Radical. Like most of the university professors he has very few students in his class; perhaps in consequence of which he is a great vituperator of the Oxford system of education. He is a man of considerable reputation in the scientific world, as what they call a *valuable* writer, that is laborious and painstaking but not supremely original.

What do you think of the commotions in the Poor Law Commission?[3] It is impossible for anybody who had anything else to do to read the evidence, but the bits that are culled out by their enemies do not *look* very creditable to them as men of business. One is no judge however after hearing arguments on one side only and knowing nothing else of the facts of the case. Mr. Reynolds says that recent measures (including the Repeal of the Corn laws) are not of so much importance as the Bank of England's having lowered the rate of interest.[4] He thinks that the maximum fixed for their circulation of the Bank of England was eight millions too high, and will need to be reduced. They told me at Hampstead that Mr. Evans had met Mrs. George

---

[2] Baden Powell (1796–1860), professor of geometry at Oxford, was the author of 'Mysticism and Scepticism', *Edinburgh Review*, LXXXIV (July 1846), 195–223, though not of earlier articles on 'Puseyism'; WB must have been told that he was the author of such articles in the *British and Foreign Review* during 1843–4, as well as of a review of Blanco White's *Life* in the *Westminster* of December 1844, and of 'Tendency of Puseyism', *Westminster Review*, XLV (June 1846), 304–43.

[3] A Select Committee had been set up to inquire into charges of maladministration of the Poor Law in the Andover Union, of poor dietary and cruelty in Andover workhouse, and unjustified dismissal by the Commissioners of two assistant commissioners. The hearings were widely reported in the press; *The Times*, a consistent opponent of the New Poor Law, devoted several leaders to the subject and found the Report, presented to the House 20 August, a condemnation of the law as well as of the officials concerned. *The Economist*, on the other hand, supported the law and argued that the Report showed no blame to attach to the Board in London for the conduct of the Andover Union and workhouse (29 August 1846).

[4] The Bank of England at its weekly meeting on 27 August had lowered its minimum rate of interest to 3 per cent, as a response to the abundance of money (owing to the large deposits for railway calls payable at the beginning of October) with very little employment for it.

Stuckey[5] at Nice and was very *pleased* with her state of mind, but that she had a young lady with her whom he was very afraid would become a Roman Catholic! I quite admire Watty for walking from Bridgwater beside his sister's pony. It sounds quite like the patriarchal times. I expect to see paragraphs in the paper headed 'Primitive Simplicity among the working classes'. I cannot send you a completely satisfactory account of my eyes. They were a good deal better last week and I said nothing about it at Hampstead in consequence as they would send me to the Hospital if they could always. But yesterday my eyes gave me a good deal of pain, but they are again better today a good deal. It does'nt prevent working, but it is enough to make writing uncomfortable. I hope you will write to me soon.

Believe me ever
Your affectionate and obedient Son
WALTER BAGEHOT.

Many thanks to my Mother for her notes.

To EDITH BAGEHOT, [1 SEPTEMBER 1846]

Extract in Irvine, p. 23, dated 1 September 1846

He[1] is as you say the very opposite of a learned booby. He is a dry, withered looking man, who seems to be ready to go through any amount of labour. He is very clearheaded, though with rather a narrow disciplinarian mind, and is very suspicious and rather sceptical. He has a dry humour which used to make me cry with laughing.

---

[5] Maria Mary (?1780–1855), daughter of John Michell of Huish Episcopi, widow of George Stuckey (1775–1823). Possibly Mrs Bagehot's correspondent, 'Maria': see letter of 7 November 1841, n. 4.

* * *

[1] George Long, from whom Edith Bagehot had received a letter, according to Irvine.

SEPTEMBER 1846

To EDITH BAGEHOT, 9 SEPTEMBER 1846

MS: Mr Norman St John-Stevas

39, Camden St. Camden Tn. Sep. 9th. 1846

My dearest Mother,

As you say the time does go away *so* fast that one has no time to do anything. It sometimes seems to me as if by the time I was well and satisfactorily up in a morning, it was time to go to bed. One thing crowds after another so fast, that one has no leisure to think of the time which they each take. I hope my Uncle Edward did not raise a very melancholy report of me, as I told him ostentatiously that I was much better. My eyes are very nearly, if not quite well; and I have very little more headache than *we* always have. My nose has shown some symptoms of bleeding but has not done it effectually. Under these circumstances I do not think it would be doing right, to come down even for a week. I thought of it a good deal about a week ago when I was not very bright, as I thought my mind wanted freshening, and inspiring; but I changed my work and cured myself: so that I cannot persuade myself into thinking it necessary to come home for my health—What has Mr. Long been writing on education? He once had a controversy with Dr. Arnold on fagging, and the other parts of our public school system[1] but I did not know that he had written anything else on the subject.[2] He is always quoting Aristotle, whom he considers as the greatest thinker who ever lived. I do not think you or perhaps anybody would call him a *'converted'* man. He would indisputably say himself he didn't know in the least what it meant. What his religious opinions really are, I suspect no one but himself very well knows. He goes to Church I believe when he goes anywhere; but mainly I fancy because he thinks it the duty of a good citizen to conform to the national religion publicly, whatever be his private opinions. So that your arguments would not be much to him whatever they may be to others. You would do the state a great service if you could point any way in which the state could teach religion to *all* its subjects, when those subjects held different creeds, and believed many of them that the creeds

[1] 'On the Discipline of Large Boarding Schools', *Quarterly Journal of Education*, X (July 1835), 82–119.
[2] No book or article to which this might refer has been traced.

of others would doom them to misery for ever. The religion taught in a national system of education ought in my view to be a national religion. But in England we have no *national* religion. One part of the nation believes one thing, and another believes that the creed of the first is fatal to their salvation. Why the very rulers who are to select the religion have every sort of diversity of opinion, and are we to postpone all education till they agree?³ What you say about religion being 'the one thing needful' is true in one very important sense; but religion is not the *only* thing needful to make people intelligent and instructed. That reading and writing are quite necessary to give any degree of intellectual activity in this age, I cannot suppose that you doubt, though your expressions about religion being the only thing required would certainly seem to imply it. Really one does hope with Carlyle that after 'a thousand years of ineffectual consideration, England really will find courage and capacity to teach all Englishmen "the alphabet".⁴ It is' (he continues—I quote from memory) 'the belief of the present writer that such a task does *not* require superhuman powers'. It may be very true that in planning a Utopian community, one would give to the government supposed to be religious and agreed in opinion the task of providing a religious education; but here in England what are we to do? One thing at least experience and fact seem to show that *unless* the people are instructed, they will not be religious. Are they religious now? Can teaching the alphabet make them *worse*? Does my father think that Mr. Baines (whose letters⁵ he mentioned in one of his letters) makes out a case for our present system of education? He has not a very goodlooking case on the first blush.

---

³ Differences between the Church of England and nonconformists on religious education made the introduction of a national system of education impossible; the Committee of Council on Education provided the two great school societies with funds for particular purposes. In July 1846 Russell had announced that the Whig government would fulfil its pledge of introducing educational reforms by creating state supported apprenticeships and teacher training; the Committee of Council issued an outline plan in August, but delayed the formal Minute until 21 December, because of concern at its religious implications.
⁴ Perhaps a reminiscence of *Chartism*.
⁵ Edward Baines, later Sir Edward (1800–90), journalist and economist, son of Edward Baines, proprietor of the *Leeds Mercury*, and editor of his father's paper. Advocate of public education completely independent of the state, an attitude not shared by all nonconformists. Baines responded to Russell's announcement by expounding the voluntary principle in a series of letters in the *Leeds Mercury* (25 July–17 October); in the summer of 1847 he was active in making the Minute on teacher training an issue at the general election, with some success—among MPs who lost their seats was Macaulay.

SEPTEMBER 1846

The Prichards came home the day before yesterday. I saw them yesterday for a moment. James Prichard[6] was not looking so well, indeed he looked considerably older than his mother. My Aunt Reynolds is rather sore about the Catholics, and inclined to blow me up for agreeing with you. Mr. Reynolds seems to hope a good deal from the Evangelical Alliance[7] which his friends have just started, notwithstanding the opposition of Whately[8] and Chalmers.[9]

Has Watty *really* got a coat small enough for him? They must have amazing microscopes at Hyam's.

Believe me yours
affectionately and obediently
WALTER BAGEHOT.

Thursday morning. This letter was written yesterday, and ought to have been put into the post. But when I came in long after post time, I was astounded to see it on chimney piece still. As I was before after my proper time, I am afraid you will be expecting to hear, and wondering at my silence.

---

[6] The Revd James Cowles Prichard (1814–48), eldest son of Dr James Cowles Prichard; fellow and tutor of Balliol 1838–41; married Emma, daughter of the Revd T. H. Ley. In 1846 he had been ill for a year, following a bout of pleurisy; journeys to the West Indies 1845–7 proved useless, and he returned to England in May 1848, dying at Red Lodge on 11 September ('Memoir' prefixed to J. C. Prichard, *Sermons*, 1849).

[7] An interdenominational and international body to promote the unity of Evangelical Protestantism (and to counteract infidelity, Roman Catholicism and Puseyism), formed at the General Conference held in London 19 August–2 September 1846. It came close to splitting over a resolution that no slave-holder should be admitted, opposed by American representatives and eventually withdrawn. A full account of the Alliance is given in John W. Ewing, *Goodly Fellowship*, 1946.

[8] Archbishop of Dublin; he thought the Alliance would produce 'more dissension than union', and admonished the clergy of his diocese against its Associations (Ewing, *op. cit.*, p. 14).

[9] Thomas Chalmers (1780–1847), theologian, preacher and philanthropist; first Moderator of the Free Church after the schism of 1843. One of those instrumental in the founding of the Alliance, he was anxious that it should do some definite work; just before the conference (which he did not attend) he issued a pamphlet, *On the Evangelical Alliance*, advising it to become an anti-Popish association and a home mission working among the poor, and to avoid doctrinal discussions.

SEPTEMBER 1846

To T. W. BAGEHOT, [?16-20] SEPTEMBER 1846

MS: Mr Norman St John-Stevas
DATE: a few days after the Anti-slavery meeting of 14 September (see n. 3).

39 Camden St. Sep. 1846.

My dearest Father,

It is certainly now quite time that I thanked you for your remarks on the morality of the practice of advocacy which you made in your last letter. We have so often talked over the subject that nothing which I could find to say, would throw any new light on the subject. All that you say of the defensibility of the practice seems to me quite just. Perhaps one might wish to add to your description of the practice, that it would be *pleasant* when one was on the side of an interesting case that seemed, as far as one could judge, the right one. Though no doubt there is the set off, that in the opposite case the task of an advocate would often be irksome. I have not much difficulty about the matter myself; and am more staggered by the indignant disapproval with which some conscientious and scrupulous men like Arnold regard the practice, than by any other circumstance.

I have made some enquiries about the inns of court; and got a fact or two which I did not know before, but I will make some more enquiries, and write to you when I fully understand how matters stand.

I have lately been reading some parts of Mr Grote's history of Greece and have been very much interested with it. It is written in a very clear masculine and sensible style, with very extensive reading, and as far as I could judge very well digested. The part which he has published is not so favorable perhaps to his powers, as some others in his future labors will be. It is principally filled with persons and events whom Mr. Grote considers as wholly legendary, and to whom the most credulous authorities only give a very dim and disputable reality. As Mr. Grote is defective perhaps in the poetical requisites for a perfect historian, he was under very considerable difficulties, when Homer and other poets are the chief authorities for the times whose story he has to tell. He is not given to over-credulity certainly; indeed from his present two volumes it would be difficult to find half a dozen historical *events* in which he believes. He thinks that the Homeric poems were a good description of a *state of society* which the poet had before his eyes; but the personal existence of Agamemnon or Achilles he gives up entirely. Dr. Prichard told me not long ago that he thought the existence of Agamemnon was as certain as the existence of Charlemagne; and this is the old fashioned creed, but all modern writers seem to follow the great German scholars in discarding it. Dr. Thirlwall[1] (the Bishop of St. David's) goes very nearly as far as Mr. Grote; though Mr. Grote has criticized perhaps successfully some inconsistencies in his predecessor, who sometimes tries to elicit historical matter of fact out of writers whom he considers in his general estimate of them to be quite untrustworthy. Mr. Grote's history is essentially the composition of a *statesman*; just as Dr. Thirlwall's is of a *scholar*. In consequence of which the former's history is much the pleasanter book to read of the two. Did Mr. G. take up anything in Parliament beside the Ballot?[2] I never heard of him in any other connection and not believing much in the Ballot I had no idea that he was nearly so able a man.

On Monday Evening I was to have escorted my Aunt Emma to an anti-slavery meeting at Exeter Hall,[3] to hear F. Douglass the runaway slave and Garrison the American abolitionist. But my aunt was frightened at the probability of the meetings being long and noisy and did not go, and I went by myself. There was a great commotion in the meeting of which the object specially was to criticize the proceedings of the Evangelical Alliance (or EE' vangelical *Al*-liance as the Americans call it.) The meeting got into great commotion as there was a strong party that approved of the Alliance doing nothing in the matter of slavery, and as Mr. Garrison criticized them in many points in which *any* Exeter Hall audience would certainly approve of their conduct. He for instance criticized their setting up a creed to the exclusion of Quakers and Unitarians, which had not much to do with slavery, not to the naked eye at least. The mention of the Quakers was not

---

[1] Connop Thirlwall (1797–1875), historian and Bishop of St David's 1840–74; friend and schoolfellow of George Grote—they were buried in the same grave in Westminster Abbey, Grote pays tribute to Thirlwall's *History of Greece* (8 vols, 1835–47) in the preface to his *History*; both wrote before the excavations at Troy and Mycenae had provided independent evidence about the earliest period; Grote was the more sceptical about a possible basis in fact of Greek legend.
[2] Grote spoke on several other questions; in 1841, when he was strongly opposed to Palmerston's foreign policy, he made what was generally agreed to be an effective speech on the Eastern Question.
[3] The meeting on 14 September was advertised as being held to review the proceedings of the Evangelical Alliance in relation to American slavery and slave-holders (*The Patriot*, 10 September 1846). See also letter of 9 September, n. 7.

mal apropos as there were a good many there; but the mention of Unitarians was received with a perfect storm of hisses. He also wanted to convince the audience that the profanation of the Sabbath was not a crime like drunkenness with which the alliance had claimed to class it. He said that purely *ritual* observances made no part of Christianity and were Jewish, to which perhaps there is no great objection only that it was out of the way at an anti-slavery meeting.[4] Mr G. was staying with Mr. Estlin I believe when he was in Bristol, and he brought him to breakfast with Dr. Prichard when he was in London. He seems a bold benevolent man but not with much tact. F. Douglass seems a very clever man considering his disadvantages, but he has a sly look which I do not like myself. My work is progressing, and I am *particularly* well. I hope your deafness has ceased after the remedies. Many thanks to my mother for her *notes*. I am not exactly 'satisfied' with them as she construes thanks sometimes for I like *letters* better. But I do not *complain*, if she has other things to do.

Believe me ever
yours affly.
WALTER BAGEHOT.

To T. W. BAGEHOT, [SEPTEMBER–OCTOBER 1846]

MS: Mr Norman St John-Stevas
DATE: probably near in date to announcement on 1 October 1846 of discovery of Neptune.

My dearest Father,

I was not able to write to you on Saturday, and now I have only returned from the college Library in time for a note. To begin with business, you must please to send me £10 the fee for the degree. Next

---

[4] Garrison had already come into conflict with the Churches in America over their indifference to slavery. Although some of the 5000 present at the Exeter Hall meeting were indignant at his attack on the exclusion of Quakers and Unitarians from the Alliance and his contempt for Sabbatarianism, he succeeded in carrying a final resolution critical of the Alliance for its failure to come out against slavery.

SEPTEMBER–OCTOBER 1846

Saturday is the proper day for paying it, according to the authorities.[1] I believe it may be depended on that a person can enter at Lincoln's Inn at the beginning of any term, but I will make assurance doubly sure by further enquiries.

Mr. Taylor's lecture[2] (Dr. Hoppus tells me) was liked by the professors and was much cheered. A friend of mine says he can find it all in the Journal of Education which the Useful Knowledge Society published once. I did not hear it myself. My work is I hope progressing, but there is a good deal of looking over to be done yet; and this is the most serious work of all, as one is continually afraid of being stopped where one expected no difficulty, and of being thrown back and prevented by want of time from looking to things which one feels may require it. I will try and remember what you say, and to be calm, and not overanxious, nevertheless it is impossible not to feel that the occasion is one of importance to me; and as being overanxious is likely to make one take more pains it is erring on the right side. I did not see the account of the storm you mention but I will look to it when I get time.

There is a report in astronomical quarters of a new planet lately discovered more distant than Uranus, or the Herschel as it used to be called. Leverrier a French Astronomer (I believe his name is spelt this way) was examining the orbit of Uranus, and found that it was disturbed, and did not go in the orbit which it would have described if it had been acted on only by the sun and the known planets. He found by analysis which must be very difficult, where the body which would cause the observed disturbance, would be; and on looking there the planet is said to have been found.[3] Has there been anything in the papers about it?[4] It will be some time before it can be quite certain; as since

---

[1] The London University *Gazette* for 1846 gives the last Monday in October (the 26th) as the date of the BA examination, and rules that Certificates of Attendance and Good Conduct must be furnished a fortnight before the examination; the date for payment of the fee is not given (nor does it appear in the Examination Register, MS University of London Library), but it was probably between 26 September and 10 October.

[2] Not traced. The lecturer may have been the Revd John James Tayler of Manchester New College.

[3] The planet Neptune was first seen on 23 September 1846 by M. Galle of the Berlin Observatory, using the calculations of the French astronomer Urbain Jean Joseph Leverrier (1811–77); the Cambridge astronomer J. C. Adams had independently made the same calculations, which were referred to by Sir John Herschel in his address to the British Association 10 September.

[4] The discovery was reported in *The Times*, 1 October.

the planet is so far off, it would be difficult to make observations on it. It must be seen well not only by the alledged discoverer but by others also, before it will be *fully* believed. If it be true it is the more interesting from theory and previous knowledge having told us where to look for that which it is so hard to see. It will be a confirmation to the theory of gravitation if that can be said to be confirmed which is so indisputable already.

Love to all. Yours in haste

WALTER BAGEHOT.

I suppose Watty misses the Willtown[5] people; now that he has looked up his sister.

To T. W. BAGEHOT, 3 OCTOBER 1846

MS: Mr Norman St John-Stevas

39 Camden St. Oct 3. 1846

My dearest Father,

Many thanks for your note which I have just received. Is not my Aunt Reynolds in dismay at your having so much to do? I shall be very glad to hear from you; but I am certainly am[1] not a good correspondent enough to complain of your silence; and I shall not complain while you are so much occupied. From what I said in my last letter to you, I suppose you will be expecting to hear from me about the Inns of court; and though I have not got quite all the needful information it is quite time that I wrote to you on the subject. I have only thought it necessary to enquire minutely about the Inner and Middle Temple, and Lincoln's Inn. No one I believe goes to Gray's Inn scarcely. I do not make out very clearly why, but as it is got out of fashion, it is considered to be a decided disadvantage to a man to be called to the bar from that Inn.

---

[5] A hamlet two and a half miles from Langport where Watson's parents had lived.

* * *

[1] Thus in MS.

OCTOBER 1846

At the Inner Temple there is a slight examination 'in classical attainments and the general subjects of a liberal education'. This is I believe very little more than formal, but I enclose you a list of the examiners The certificates as to character &c have to be signed by two barristers belonging to that Inn Expense of admission is £29. 3. 2. and the entrance into commons is £7.17.6. and this last sum is to be paid annually, as it is the price of your dinners. I believe a deposit of 100£ is to be made here if you have not Oxford or Cambridge Degree. The Inner Temple is smaller than either Lincoln's Inn or the Middle Temple; but is reckoned a quiet gentlemanly place. The Middle Temple is as you know the only one where a degree of the London University takes off two years from the necessary 5 years of study. A London degree also saves the *deposit* of 100£ which is to be made here also by a person who has no degree, as a security that he will pay for his dinners. Two householders have to enter into a bond also that the person entered will do this. The certificates have to be signed by two barristers and one bencher, both of that inn; the benchers are few, and it is not very easy to get their signature. The expense of entrance fees is between 33 and 34 pounds and commons fee is 7£. The Middle Temple does not stand quite as well in point of gentility as the other Inns. I hear however that the prejudice does not extend to attorneys, and solicitors. Our cousin Kippie Watson[2] is I see a Middle Temple man, and he might help in getting the signatures if I went there. Roscoe whom you may perhaps remember to have heard me speak of, and who is the most gentlemanly young man I know is a Middle Temple Man. Lincoln's Inn has one great advantage. It is usual for all equity practitioners to have chambers there, and good chambers are more *easily* obtained by members of the inn than by those who are not members. However persons from other inns who wish to practise in the equity courts do constantly get chambers there. The entrance fees at Lincoln's inn are £31.13. and the commons fee 8 per annum. Here too I believe a deposit of 100£ is to be made; and the commons have to be paid for three years after a man is called to the bar, which is not the case at any other inn. Every where else no one pays any commons fee

---

[2] Andrew Kippis Watson (?1800–77), second son of the Revd Thomas Watson of Bath, was entered at the Middle Temple 20 October 1821, and called to the bar 25 May 1827. A special pleader, of 2 Plowden Buildings, Middle Temple, on the Western Circuit; remained unmarried, and died in the house of his brother, Dr Thomas Sanden Watson, of Bath.

but *students* of the Inn. Lincoln's Inn is reckoned the most gentlemanly, whether for any other reason than its being more expensive I do not know. The certificates of character &c have at Lincoln's Inn to be signed by 2 barristers of that inn. I *believe* a London degree of this year will be in time to save the deposit; if I were to enter in the ensuing term. It will be but just in time, but I believe that any time before the term divides, will do for entering; and supposing that I am not plucked, I shall know of my degree on or about the 3rd. of Novr. Your pocket book I know of old contains all necessary information about the Terms. Of course this about saving the deposit refers to the Middle Temple only. I have not yet learnt what are the rules of the different inns as to any person's being engaged in trade or banking. But I shall know this in a day or two and also whether there are any differences between them in this respect. It is now the question whether the advantages of Lincoln's Inn are sufficient to counterbalance the additional expense, which as you will see is considerable. I do not particularly wish to go to the Inner Temple as I know no one there; and I know several men at the Middle Temple and Lincoln's Inn. It seems to me that the advantages of L.N.[3] are hardly enough to counterbalance the additional expenses; but you can much better judge of this; and of course I shall be quite ready to do what you think best. I do not know that there is any other point necessary to be made out; but perhaps you will see some. This is so purely a letter of business that I suppose it will hardly be allowed to pass current for a letter *home*.

I hope I am getting on tolerably but I am not so forward as I could wish by a good deal. One makes very good resolutions about leaving nothing to the last; but when the last comes it generally finds its full share of employment. I have got to get up too such a mass of heterogeneous information, that I am teased with thinking constantly that I may be forgetting now, what I learnt some time since. A mathematical examination is peculiarly harassing, because if you forget one step in a demonstration, you are at fault completely. In classics or history where one thing does not depend on another it is otherwise; and one may make a shift to get on even if one has forgotten several things that ought to have been known, But if you have forgotten a step of a *proof*, especially in Analysis of Algebra, all the rest of what you remember

---

[3] Thus in MS.

cannot be used, and one breaks down completely. It is very difficult to be sure that one shall recollect propositions scattered over so large a field as is required for honors. I have never been without fears and am not entirely without hopes. Though as the time draws near my fears increase certainly faster than my hopes.[4] The post is going out, but I hope not gone.

Believe me
yours affectionately
W BAGEHOT

Love to *all*. Watty shouldn't have such undignified complaints. I hope his sister isn't really ill. Is Miss C. Law the tall slender one with the arched back.

To T. W. BAGEHOT, 5 NOVEMBER 1846

MS: Mr Norman St John-Stevas

Somerset House. Nov. 5th. 1846.

My dearest Father,

As I believe Dr. Hoppus wrote to you yesterday you will have had news of what I am afraid must be called my thorough breakdown. On Tuesday evening I was too ill and giddy to look over anything for the next day; and so went to bed early. I did nothing but toss about however. About four o'clock in the morning I tried to do some work, but could not make much of it and went to bed again, but I could not get any sleep. At breakfast time I had so much headache and pain in my side and giddiness that Dr. Hoppus said I ought'nt to go to Somerset House, and I had doubts as to whether I could do anything when I

---

[4] On 5 October Hutton answered a letter from WB (untraced) by telling him that his 'panic' was 'very natural and very useless', and assuring him that he was far better prepared than Hutton himself had been (he had been placed in the first class and obtained the scholarship in 1845); he was confident that WB would take the scholarship in mathematics: 'at all events I am sure you will *deserve* it far better than I did', gave some advice on preparation, and concluded that WB should 'most of all bully Jerrard about his questions and do well with Heaviside'.

got there. I have no doubt Dr. H. told you about Dr. Bright who said at first that I certainly ought not to go, but I told him all the facts, and at last persuaded him to let me. Dr. B. was very kind and sympathising, wrote a prescription and would not take a fee. I went but I am sorry to say did very badly. It was with a very painful effort that I collected my thoughts to *understand* the questions which I had been preparing for and some of which I had learnt up only a couple of days before. The effort of doing them was still more painful as my head was terribly hot and aching and the whole room spinning round with me. I went to bed as soon as I got home, and got some sleep though very dreamy, and very much taken up with mathematics and examinations. I was better this morning, and have done better at the one examination which I have just been at. However I ought to have done so well as to repair the disasters of yesterday, and as the table at which I write this has a very circular motion whenever I lift or move my head, I cannot now do this. The examiners have been very kind, seemed very sorry for my illness yesterday. Mr. Jerrard said that in my papers on Tuesday I [had] shown myself very well prepared, and as this is all the good I am likely to get from this examination, I had better make the most of the compliment. I am convinced that the papers I sent up yesterday were so bad, that *no* honors can be awarded to me. The examiners of course in their official capacity only look to what is written on the papers and I am quite certain that much of what I wrote yesterday afternoon particularly is sad stuff. I had prepared for most of the questions, and it is wretchedly painful to sit before questions, which one could have done tolerably at another time, and not remember more than a few disconnectd snatches of the proper answers. In many subjects these snatches would be some good, but in mathematics they are none, as when you are told to demonstrate a proposition, you must either demonstrate it or leave it alone. It is no use in mathematics to know something *about* a thing you must know the thing itself, and yesterday and in part today my knowledge of all things was confused and uncertain. Of course I am out of spirits and heart a good deal, but I hope to be able soon to bear this trial better. I hope you and my mother will be satisfied that this failure has not arisen from negligence or idleness. I have not much more time and holding down my head makes it very hot, and I wish it to be cool for the next three hours at least. It seems hard, that I should be ill only two days before it would have been no serious evil; but so it is and it must be borne. I thought you would wish me to go to Somerset House and try to do what I could, though the effort has been a painful one.

Yours ever affectionately,

WALTER BAGEHOT.

Many thanks for my mother's notes. They have given me some cheerful minutes and these are scarce with me now. My head is about the same today, and the giddiness rather worse but the pain in my side and tightness in my chest are better perhaps owing to Dr. B.'s medicine. I shall certainly come into the country as soon as ever I can.

To T. W. BAGEHOT, 7 NOVEMBER 1846

MS: Mr Norman St John-Stevas

Saturday 7 Nov 1846

My dearest Father,

Many thanks for you welcome letter which I received this morning. It has been a real comfort to me and I hope that I am now more able than when I wrote last to bestir myself to meet this trial as I ought. One certainly ought to be able to find reward enough in knowledge for its own sake; and I think that in general this has been with me the first consideration. At least I hope so. Notwithstanding this when one has been trying to obtain an honor, it is very disappointing to find oneself deprived of all one's chance of it. I hope that now however my natural good spirits are coming to aid my principles, and that the two together will enable me for the future not to be so much disheartened and confounded as I have been hitherto. I am better, I think, than when I wrote last, though my headaches are still troublesome, and my giddiness also. Indeed I do not think these are so much better, as that I am got better *generally*, and am better able to bear them and manage them. I have had some better sleep than I have had since I was taken ill though I still have a strong tendency to dream about mathematics.

I shall come down on Monday. I shall try to come by the train which leaves London at 12 o'clock but you must *expect* me by the 2 o'clock train. I have not as yet been able to learn anything of my fate whatever.[1] I shall go to Somerset House again on Monday, and If I can learn nothing then the report will be sent after me. I wish I had known that you wished me to see Dr. Bright again. I am afraid I shall not be able to get away in any tolerable time on Monday if I do so. He did not seem to think there was anything to be done for me but to take air rest and exercise. Under these circumstances I do not think I shall go to him, especially as if you wish me to have any advice when I get home, I can so easily get what is necessary from Mr. Estlin. I hope by the time I get home I shall be *looking* decent, as I am not so heavy eyed and disconsolate looking today. Every now and then my failure will come back upon me, and I shall be very glad when all suspense is over as to its amount. Purely personal calamities of this sort ought not to weigh long on one's mind; and I will try to do what I can to bear in mind what you say to me, as to submission, and calmness.

Dr. Hoppus showed me my mother's letter to him, which I was glad to see. Why didn't she write to *me*. I shall be *so* glad to get home after all this turmoil and failure.

Believe me ever
yours affectionately
W Bagehot.

---

[1] WB was placed in the first class and obtained the scholarship. Hutton, who had been waiting anxiously for news, expressed his delight in a letter of 16 November, and said: 'As to the farce of Somerset House, I feel it quite in regard to myself, but am very sure you deserved it far more than I did. However is it not curious that *explicitly* our University course has been so very symmetrical and as far as signs go, we shd. be so exactly side by side, I should indeed feel glad if I could think there was the same implicit equality, but that is absurd, the more I am away from you, the more I see how much I depended on you, and what a weak-headed person I am'.

FEBRUARY 1847

To EDITH BAGEHOT, 6 FEBRUARY 1847

MS: Mr Norman St John-Stevas

6 Great Coram St.[1] Feb. 6th. 1847

My dearest Mother,

I cannot say but that I was disappointed at none of my family at home taking any notice of my coming of age;[2] and I thought almost certainly that I should have heard from my father today. However if you thought of me that is main matter and as you say that you did, I must be contented, I suppose. Please not to write to me at Hampstead any more, as it causes a day's delay in my getting the letter, now that I am in my own abode. I like the abode very well indeed, and now that I have got my books into it and arranged them for work, and begun work everything goes on very comfortably. I have expended capital in a book case, and my Aunt Reynolds gave me [a] sofa on my birthday; so that I am become quite a proprietor of upholstery.

I went to Hampstead on Wednesday to dinner; Henry Sawtell and Alfred Norman were there. The former was still rather limp, *though* it is settled I believe that he is to be married in April.[3] Alfred Norman was especially gracious, and not at all like Mrs. Kent as he sometimes is. He says that Mr. Rowland Hill is very unpopular in the post office,[4] as his measures show a tendency to the reduction of salaries, which

---

[1] WB took these lodgings when he began to read for his MA; his subjects of special study were metaphysics, political economy and political philosophy. In his 'Memoir' Hutton notes that he was also devoting time to the reading of Shakespeare, Keats, Shelley and Wordsworth, and to Coleridge, Martineau and John Henry Newman (*Collected Works*, XIV).

[2] On 3 February.

[3] George Henry Sawtell (?1823–96), son of George Sawtell (1792–1836) and his first wife, Mary Jarvis; Sawtell's second wife, Edith Reynolds (1793–1836), was the sister of John Stuckey Reynolds. G. H. Sawtell was a solicitor, in partnership with Edward Futvoye, at 23 John Street, Bedford Row. On 25 March 1847 he married Sarah, eldest daughter of the Revd J. R. Sabin, Rector of Preston Bissett, Bucks (*Gentleman's Magazine*, n.s. XXVII [1847], p. 649).

[4] Rowland Hill, later Sir Rowland (1795–1879), inventor of penny postage, established by him in 1840, while an officer of the Treasury appointed to the Post Office (from which he was dismissed by Peel in 1842). He returned in November 1846 as Secretary to the Postmaster General, a post created for him by Russell's government, which brought him into conflict with Maberly, the Secretary to the Post Office. In spite of internal opposition Hill undertook reforms, including a thorough revision of the money order system and the extension of rural postal deliveries (in which he employed Anthony Trollope, then a surveyor's clerk in the Post Office).

is not the kind of Reform most agreeable to the *receivers* of salaries. Mr. Reynolds is rather strong on the introduction of railways as a means of employing the people of Ireland. I do not apprehend that like Lord George Bentinck he looks at them as providing *permanent* employment for the Irish people; but as a temporary measure in aid of the government scheme of waste lands; which many people think not extensive enough to supersede entirely the system of public works.[5] Supposing it to be the case that there will not be sufficient employment for the destitute population in cultivating the lands now lying waste, it certainly seems better to employ this labor of the people in railroads or something that will yield a return, than to throw away all the advantages that might be derived from that labor, by employing it as at present on works which are wholly useless and unproductive. But the whole system of public works is an evil, and one looks with some jealousy on these railroad schemes, as if they tended to perpetuate the growing disposition of the Irish lower class to look mainly to the Government for employment, and to leave their lands uncropped looking to English charity to give the food they ought to raise themselves. Nevertheless the system of public works once introduced cannot be withdrawn on a sudden; and one cannot help wishing something good could be realized from so much toil. It is the climax of grumbling even on the state of Ireland to say that the government are employing a great proportion of the lower classes in roadmaking; and after all the roads never were so bad, and are quite spoiled. Certainly the Railroad scheme would keep the old roads from the hand of the spoiler.

Now that the Miss Bagehots[6] tempestuous visit is come [to an end][7] I suppose that you are quite quiet again; and I hope it [means my

---

[5] These were the years of the 'great famine' in Ireland, and by January 1847 it was clear that, following the second failure of the potato crop, the measures of relief so far undertaken (distribution of food and a limited programme of public works) were ineffective, and that four million people faced disaster. Russell emphasized measures to improve agriculture by assisting drainage, waste-land reclamation, and the sale of incumbered estates, but on 4 February Bentinck brought forward as a substitute his railway scheme, involving large scale loans by the government to double the amount raised by private investment; although Irish members favoured the bill, when Russell made the vote on the second reading on 16 February one of confidence they joined with the government to defeat it (*Debates*, LXXXIX, 773–802, XC, 86–116). Subsequently the waste-lands proposal and the sale of incumbered estates were given up, and limited aid to railway companies introduced; this was of little value for relieving unemployment, which would not have been much helped even by Bentinck's measure.

[6] Possibly Edward Bagehot's daughters.

[7] Words removed by cutting out of stamp on reverse.

fa]ther[7] will now be able to find time to write to me. He says Bagehots are so beset with hostile forces at Langport that I wonder you did not take their part more, as you are generally so zealous on the weaker side. As you give me no facts, you leave me to suppose that you have pronounced judgment upon conjectures and suspicions (I do *not* mean in the matter of artificial vermilion); and this seems a little hard. I think some overt act ought to be proved, and I do not understand what that is in this case. However it is no business of mine to a certainty.

Dr. and Mrs. Prichard have been at York but are returned, and were gone to Greenwich when I called this morning; they are certainly possessed of the faculty of locomotion—I do not know exactly what Constantine has to do at Wells; nor do they I believe. He is under Mr Pindar[8] whom you know about and the college is a theological one. He went there about a week ago. Believe me ever

yours affectionately and obediently

WALTER BAGEHOT.

I left all my *white* pocket handkerchiefs at home. Can they come soon or must I buy some. Love to all.

To EDITH BAGEHOT, [28 JUNE 1847]

Test from RB, X, 178–9, written 'From Oxford'
DATE: Monday, 28 June 1847, since about the British Association meeting in Oxford, and referring to the Bishop's sermon as 'yesterday'

My dear Mother,

I am afraid the family will be wroth with me for not writing; but the philosophers[1] take up so much of one's time and tire one so during the rest of it that really not writing is excusable. Prince Albert has just been exhibiting himself here in the Ethnological Section of the

---

[8] John Hothersall Pinder (1794–1868), educated at Charterhouse and Caius College, Cambridge; President of Codrington College, Barbados, 1830–5, and Principal of Wells Theological College, 1840–65. Constantine Prichard, who had been ordained priest in 1847, was taking up an appointment as Vice Principal of the College, a post he held until 1850.

* * *

[1] The seventeenth annual meeting of the British Association for the Advancement of Science was held in Oxford, 23–30 June 1847; Prince Albert, accompanied by the Duke of

JUNE 1847

Association. Dr. Prichard and Chevalier Bunsen, and Dr. Latham went off about Ethnology, languages, ancient Egypt, &c.,[2] which the Prince tried hard to look as if he understood, but did not succeed completely. He was attended by Sir R. Inglis,[3] who contrives to look knowing very well, and attends the sections as diligently as any philosopher of them all, though he most likely does not know much more about the matter than persevering ladies who sit all day in the Mathematical section. Mr. Laverrier[4] and Mr. Adams[5] (the rival calculator of the position of the new planet Neptune) are the great philosophical attractions. Mr. Adams is the best to look at at good deal, as Laverrier is a yellow-haired pink little man with invisible eyes, and *no* expression of face at all. Dr Faraday[6] is here, and gave a statement that they can now by recent discoveries turn diamonds into coke, but it does not seem that they can turn them back again; so that the jewellers will not suffer. Sir J. Herschel[7] is the most interesting of the physical philosophers, and I think the most attractive mentally of them all. The most interesting Oxford man whom I have met here is is Mr. Stanley,[8] the writer of Arnold's life. He is a son of the Bishop of Norwich[9]

Saxe Weimar, was present at the proceedings of several sections of the Association on 28 June (*Athenaeum*, 26 June, 3 July 1847).

[2] Prichard spoke on 'The Relation of Ethnology to Other Branches of Knowledge'; other speakers included Christian Karl Josias von Bunsen, later Baron (1791–1866), Prussian diplomat, lay theologian and scholar, who was ambassador to England 1842–54, and Robert Gordon Latham, MD (1812–88), ethnologist and philologist, who became director of the ethnological section of the Crystal Palace in 1852.

[3] Sir Robert Harry Inglis (1786–1855), MP for Oxford University from 1829 (when he defeated Peel over the question of Catholic emancipation) until his retirement in 1851; in August 1847 he was returned at the head of the poll as a Protectionist. Took an active part in many religious and learned societies, and was chairman at the Oxford meeting of the British Association.

[4] Thus in printed text.

[5] John Couch Adams (1819–92), mathematician and astrologer; fellow and tutor of St John's College, Cambridge. He had begun his investigation of the disturbances in Uranus in 1843, but his prediction that they were caused by an undiscovered planet, sent to the Astronomer Royal in 1844, was not investigated until 1846, so that he was forestalled by Leverrier. Adams's claim to priority was first publicized by Sir John Herschel in a letter to the *Athenaeum*, 3 October 1846; Adams and Leverrier took no part in the controversy, and Leverrier's speech on the last day of the Association's meeting at Oxford paid tribute to Adams and expressed pleasure at making his acquaintance.

[6] Michael Faraday (1791–1867), experimental scientist, discoverer of electromagnetism; director of the laboratory of the Royal Institution from 1825, where his lecture courses popularized science and put the Institution on a sound financial footing.

[7] Sir John Frederick William Herschel, 1st bart (1792–1871), astronomer.

[8] Arthur Penrhyn Stanley (1815–81), later Dean of Westminster: see also letter to Edith Bagehot, ?December 1847, n. 1.

[9] Edward Stanley (1779–1849), Bishop of Norwich 1837–49.

whom I met at his rooms at breakfast the other morning. Ehrenberg[10] the great animalcule finder is there; he looks rather like a squashed animalcule himself. The Bishop of Oxford preached yesterday at St. Mary's, the University Church. It happened curiously that yesterday was the day for an old bequest sermon on pride and the vanity of human knowledge;[11] so that the physical philosophers kicked it in. The sermon was a good one on the whole, though too rhetorical for the Tractarians here who like plainness of speech. The Prichards are staying at Wallingford,[12] and come in daily. The doctor slid off the platform during the rush of Prince Albert to a neighbouring corner. Bunsen's speech was to a considerable extent an eulogism on the Doctor's book. Ethnology is only a subsection of the British Association. You seem to doubt a little whether you shall come on Tuesday, tomorrow, in your last letter. However, I mean to return tomorrow, and to go to Hampstead in the evening to receive you. *Possibly* something very attractive may turn up here, and I may stay, but it is not likely at all.

Believe me,
Yours obediently, though in great haste,

WALTER BAGEHOT

To EDITH BAGEHOT, [?1847]

Extract in RB, X, 179
DATE: placed after WB's letter of 28 June 1847 in RB, X, and described as written 'while paying another visit to the Prichards'; perhaps after WB returned from abroad (see letters of 10 February and 24 March 1848)

My dearest Mother,

I reached Oxford in perfect safety on Monday evening. The Prichards were all well and expecting me. They seem fitted in very

---

[10] Christian Gottfried Ehrenberg (1795–1876), founder of microgeology and micropalaeontology in Germany.
[11] Wilberforce's sermon, *Pride a Hindrance to True Knowledge*, was printed at the request of Inglis, that year's president of the British Association, Lord Northampton, the president-elect, and Sir Roderick Murchison, president of the preceding year; their letter to Wilberforce of 27 June 1847 is printed as a preface to the sermon, which Wilberforce inscribed to them. At the beginning of the sermon he remarked on the coincidence which led to its being preached 'when so many are gathered here together whose lives are devoted to the pursuits of science'.
[12] WB was staying with Constantine Prichard, presumably at Balliol.

nicely here, much better than they ever were in London. I am going to stay here till tomorrow Friday, as I am going to dine at Oriel with one of the fellows there who is a great logician and very ugly to the eyes.[1] The only great gun whom I have seen here that was new to me is Mr. Sewell, the moral philosopher and High Church divine.[2] I cannot say I much admire his books, but he is indisputably a capital talker, not much like a divine but with some shrewdness and a good deal of terrestrial knowledge and a large fund of clever stories. He was the life and soul of a dinner party given to the Coleridges[3] to which I was admitted.

To EDITH BAGEHOT, [DECEMBER 1847]

Extract in RB, X, 177, dated December 1847, which fits WB's reference to the publication of Stanley's book

Mr. Stanley, Arnold's biographer, has just brought out a volume of sermons and essays on the Apostolic age.[1] I admire the sermons exceedingly. Mr. Stanley is a little man with grissly black hair, and piercing

---

[1] Probably Charles Peter Chretien (1820–93), fellow of Oriel 1843–64 and tutor 1848–60; Dean 1850–59; Rector of Cholderton 1860–75. In 1848 he published *An Essay on Logical Method*, based on his teaching of logic at Oriel.

[2] William Sewell (1804–74), fellow and tutor of Exeter College; Whyte's professor of moral philosophy at Oxford, 1836–41; sympathetic to the Tractarians until the publication of Newman's Tract XC in 1841, but thereafter used his controversial skills against what he feared were Romanizing tendencies. In March 1847 he had established St Peter's College, Radley (Radley College), a public school run on high church lines, of which he was warden 1852–62; his financial mismanagement of the school left him heavily in debt, although the school was rescued and flourished under new management.

[3] Probably John Duke Coleridge, later 1st Baron Coleridge (1820–94) and his wife Jane Fortescue, *née* Seymour (*d.* 1878). Entered Balliol College 1838, where he was a contemporary of Clough and Matthew Arnold, and of Constantine Prichard; fellow of Exeter College from 1843 until his marriage in 1846. Coleridge was created Baron Coleridge of Ottery St Mary in 1874; be became Lord Chief Justice in 1880.

* * *

[1] Stanley had published in November 1847 *Sermons and Essays on the Apostolical Age*, the course he had preached as Select Preacher between February 1846 and January 1847. Stanley, tutor at University college since 1843, exerted great influence on the young men at Oxford, but his volume on the apostolical age made him an object of suspicion to their elders, evangelical and high church alike, because of its indebtedness to the broad church teachings of Arnold and to German theologians and its espnusal of free inquiry in Biblical studies.

black eyes that look like a Jew's; very singular and clever looking. I went to a queer party at Newman's[2] a night or two ago. He manages a party worse than anybody I ever saw. A good many ladies and a good many gentlemen, but none of the gentlemen knew any of the ladies except Mr. Newman, and one gentleman who, being married, vigorously fought shy of his own wife. All the ladies worked dismally in a meek way; and the men talked politics and metaphysics in another room, Newman peering through the folding doors at the ladies, being afraid, I suppose, they would make a rush and swamp his proof 'that all philosophy began in nonsense'. I have been there once or twice before; but none of the parties was so queer as this one. The last time he talked to Smith Osler (there were about twenty people there) and myself, leaving the rest to shift for themselves.

To R. H. HUTTON, JANUARY 1848

MS: Mr Norman St John-Stevas

Jan. 1848 Grt. Coram St.

My dear Hutton

I came to Town last Monday, and have been intending to write before, but have not fancied that I was able. When I received your last letter, I intended to write to you an invective against your remarks on Judaism in it:[1] but owing to delay my wrath has in great measure evaporated. The view of the character of God contained in it seems to me in the main coincident with the Christian: bearing somewhat the same relation to it that the grand does to the sublime. What you say of the Patriarchs seems to me to come to this much only: that notwithstanding particular acts of meanness or grossness, or cowardice, men who are on God's side in the great conflict between good and evil, and are in earnest on His side are in His favor, and therefore His friends. If you grant this, and it is difficult for a Christian to deny it, there is no difficulty in believing the view which the Old Testament takes of such men

[2] F. W. Newman.

* * *

[1] This letter from Hutton has not survived.

as Abraham or David. I have sometimes thought that anthropomorphism, (if the word is to retain its usual offensive sense) ought to be defined as the attributing to God any peculiarity of human nature not essential to our conception of perfect holiness: and perhaps it ought to include the taking this our conception as an accurate result, and not as an approximation more or less distant from the result. As however there are other names for this last form of irreverence, this much abused need not perhaps be stretched to include it. There are obviously two ways of holding the doctrine that man is God's image, one the Greek of fashioning the Gods on the exact model of interesting and attractive men; the other that of the Christians, and according to their light of the Jews viz the imputing to man the faculty of obtaining and in part also the possession of moral attributes resembling those of God so far as what is finite can resemble what is infinite. And the first is perhaps the most winning form of anthropomorphism. I have read Newman's book on the Jews[2] and think it very dull and poor. What does Martineau think of it? I do not like to speak evil of a book of Newman's but I cannot speak well of this one. There is no appreciation of the poetry in the religion of the Jews, nor of the great characters in the history: I do not so much mean no just appreciation as not attempt at appreciation at all. Speaking about the Jews in connection with your letter reminds me to tell you that there is an article in the last no. of the Chn. Remem[brance]r. by Mr. Mozley on Luther,[3] which is well worth reading. It is not so splendid as that on Blanco White, but still is striking. I think it one sided, and so will you; as it fails in appreciating Luther justly in connection with faith or the influence of affections in religion: nevertheless what he says is instructive as I had overlooked this view of Lutheranism in great measure.[4]

[2] F. W. Newman, *History of the Hebrew Monarchy*, 1847; an application of historical analysis to the Old Testament; the Unitarian *Christian Reformer* compared it to Strauss's work on the New Testament or Nieburh's 'destructive' treatment of Roman history (IV[1848], 137–46).
[3] James Bowling Mozley (1813–78), theologian; entered Oriel College 1830 and became a fellow of Magdalen 1840; friend of John Henry Newman, to whom he was connected by the marriages of his brothers Tom and John to Newman's sisters. In 1844 he became co-editor of the *Christian Remembrancer*, which succeeded the *British Critic* as the organ of the high church party, and many of his most forceful articles appeared there. WB was correct in assigning to him 'Autobiography of Blanco White' in the issue of July 1845 (X, 144–212), and 'Martin Luther' in that of January 1848 (XV, 93–188), both of which are reprinted in his *Essays Historical and Theological*, 1878.
[4] Mozley gives an account of the formation and nature of the Lutheran doctrine of justi-

JANUARY 1848

The defect of his writing to me is that it is not the writing of a man who has a personal feeling of great difficulties, that is not a deep feeling. It is the state incident to a mind that has acquiesced in the creed given to it by education: and not felt the need of personal search. Hence he is unintentionally unjust to eager men like Luther and Arnold:[5] who speak earnestly and hastily while their minds are yet running on, and are too impatient to speak to say always what is the truth. I think that his tone is more purely judicial, and his state of mind too quiescent: but his writing is excellent nevertheless, though perhaps with all the quickness of observation shown in it, there is also an indolence in not thinking out his explanations concerning the stars and the Earth.[6] I quite agree with you that its value is illustrative and not argumentative. I do not see the fundamental inference of the book, because we have no test of absolute magnitude, *therefore* all our idea of magnitude is subjective. And if this were admitted we might turn up not a few things which the writer does not contemplate. I think the value of the illustrations considerable. They have suggested to me this one of the foreknowledge and freewill difficulty. From the doctrine of the theory of probabilities as to the personal equation of individuals it is evident that we do not know exactly when any occurrence happens; one man notes say half a second too fast: another half a second too slow: and one immediately thinks that the whole human race may be 10 minutes too fast and not know it. But go further and suppose they were a whole eternity too slow; then everything wd. have been during that eternity known to God; but yet man may have been free in doing them nevertheless, when he did them ages upon ages ago. If anyone says that he knows when he does a thing exactly, though not when a star

---

fication by faith, and shows that its extreme, simple, and arbitrary character arose from Luther's own psychology. He also pays tribute to Luther as a creative mind, a subtle politician, and a man with 'marvellous richness of the social affections and sympathies'; Keble was surprised to find the German reformer 'so amusing and interesting' (J. B. Mozley, *Letters*, ed. Anne Mozley, 1885, p. 191).

[5] Mozley writes sympathetically of the German nature of Lutheran reform, remarking: 'Dogmatism in rejecting and dogmatism in enforcing were both condemned, and the spirit of Luther's reformation was in some aspects a remarkable anticipation of that modern Germanism which is associated among ourselves with the name of Dr. Arnold' (*Essays Historical and Theological*, I, 386).

[6] In this sentence WB begins to discuss some other unidentified piece of writing, since there is no passage about the stars and the earth in Mozley's article. It appears from what follows—'I quite agree with you' and 'fundamental inference of the book'—that his subject was a book WB and Hutton had both read; but this was not Newman's *Hebrew Monarchy*, to which WB's remarks do not apply.

comes to the meridian, I might deny the assertion if I wd.; but I might say also that for aught he knew he might have known it for a millenium but have lost the remembrance of having known it. It is a certain matter of fact that ideas must be before the mind *some* time before they can be remembered. How long this may be is not *certainly* known. For ought he can [7]

To EDITH BAGEHOT, [?9 FEBRUARY 1848]

MS: Mr Norman St John-Stevas
DATE: A note in his mother's hand, at the top of the first page, reads: 'Naughty Walter no date Received Feb. 10th 1848'; after WB's birthday (3 February) and not later than 9 February

My dearest Mother,

Many thanks for your congratulations and my father's on my birthday. I *do* seem to get very old as you say. I am not such a thorough boy as to spirits as I was a couple of years ago: but I am boy enough still: and more so than most of my contemporaries. Indeed as I am still in training I have no right to call myself anything else. It was Albert Prichard's[1] birthday also: and there was a party of diverse of the Molines[2] &c. and Alfred Estlin. I was not in great force having an amazing headache, though I hope nobody found it out: as I am not in favor of the publication of diseases. Alfred Estlin has taken to dancing the polka[3] with a terrific intensity. I slept at Hampstead last night as I had not been there the two last Sundays. Mrs. Vincent Reynolds[4] was there worn out with upholstery and her new house. My uncle deep in the Minutes of education, with some currency tendencies notwithstanding. He was also full of anecdotes out of Ld. Campbell's lives of the

---

[7] The remainder of the letter is missing.

* * *

[1] Albert Hermann Prichard (*b.* 1831), youngest of the ten children of Dr James Cowles Prichard; entered Merton College, Oxford, 1849, BA 1853; ordained 1869 and held various curacies 1869–78. He contributed an essay on Church Patronage to Orby Shipley's *Ecclesiastical Reform. Eight Essays by Various Writers*, 1873, and in 1888 published a translation of Bernadine a Picionio's *Exposition of the Epistles of St. Paul.*
[2] Cousins of the Prichards: see letter of 27 September 1840, n. 1.
[3] 'Polkamania' began in 1844 and the dance was still very popular.
[4] Marian (*d.* 1861), daughter of George Basevi (1794–1845); her father, a cousin of Disraeli, was a successful architect, who designed most of the houses in Belgrave Square 1825–40. In 1823 she married Vincent Stuckey Reynolds (*d.* 1843), younger brother of John Stuckey Reynolds.

JANUARY 1848

Chancellors, and especially Erskine.[5] I heard a good story myself of the last a day or two ago. In the last war there were some volunteer lawyers embodied who were rather an 'awkward squad'; and never could stand well in line, but zigzag. The Duke of Wellington happened to see them one day, and asked Erskine who they were. Lawyers your Grace: (and pointing to the crookedness of the line) as this *indenture* witnesseth. I do not think this is in Campbell[6] but it is like Erskine enough. Indenture is a common law-term, and indentures have often to be appealed to as evidence in more serious matters.

I have just been turning the leaves of the third edition of a poem called Festus recently written by a [man] named Bailey.[7] It is very good to be written by a living poet in these days: only the author seems to be not in his right mind exactly. In the first edition there was a great deal of stuff omitted in the second; but some of it has come back again I see in third. I wrote when I was abroad a review of the second edition which was published in the Prospective Review:[8] I think it is knocking about in my room somewhere, and I dare say my father could find it if you would like to read it. There are some passages new in this third edition, I see: though neither they nor any part of the book show a very well regulated mind in the author. I take it he is a man of more genius than sense. My eyes are got well again but they were weak for a long time till yesterday in fact; which was the first day that I have been able to read my full owance of hours. I am glad to hear that Mr. O. Michell[9] has come to terms so serviceably about the land; and hope the Bishop 'who is doing so much at Wells'[10] wont do so much evil at Huish. My Aunt Reynolds takes on amazingly about the trees.[11] She and Mrs. V.R. wanted to

---

[5] Vol. VI of Campbell's *Lives of the Lord Chancellors and Keepers of the Great Seal of England*, containing the 'Life of Lord Chancellor Erskine', had been published in 1847.
[6] WB is correct.
[7] *Festus*, first published 1839, second edition, 1845, by Phillip James Bailey (1816–1902).
[8] 'Festus', *Prospective Review*, III (November 1847), 511–41; reprinted *Collected Works*, I, 113–41. Bagehot's first known publication. For a full discussion, see the 'Introductory Note' in *Collected Works*, I, 108–112.
[9] Not identified.
[10] Richard Bagot (1782–1854), Bishop successively of Oxford and of Bath and Wells. Soon after leaving Oxford suffered a breakdown and the diocese was administered by the Bishop of Gloucester and Bristol. Bagot's *Charge* of May 1847 was concerned with church repairs, encouragement of weekday services and the existence of a few parishes where the Lord's Supper was administered only four times a year.
[11] His father's feelings about the trees are reflected in a letter quoted by Mrs Barrington: 'I do not know what you will say when you hear that some unsparing hand has commenced

know how you *bore* it. I said in substance that you felt middling: and that I rather doubted your having exactly learned up *which* trees were to go: I thought at any rate *you* would get over it. My father will be interested in hearing that Colonel Torren's pamphlet on the Currency[12] is *177* closely printed pages in length. What I have read is very clever and very well written but too long as my uncle would have said. I think it is meant to tell the members of the Banking committee[13] what questions to ask of the witnesses they examine: and it is good enough for this purpose because of its clearness. I have also seen Mr. Babbage's pamphlet on Taxation,[14] which is poor. I am afraid the family will think I am not writing very regularly, but owing to my eyes I have been dimmish lately, and *for me* out of spirits rather which is about in moderately good spirits for anyone else: and I cannot write letters when I am weak spirited and feebleminded. I must stop now.

Every yours affectionately and obediently

WALTER BAGEHOT.

Love to all. How is my hunter. Vincent Wood's[15] report was wretched.

---

the work of destruction at Wick and is cutting down the trees we have so long valued as one of our greatest ornaments. We shall be able to bear it I dare say; and I live in hope of finding many beauties beyond them. At all events we must have a beautiful home, while a virtuous and happy one' (RB, X, 9; dated 1843, but in view of this letter pehaps a misreading of 1848).

[12] *The Principles and Practical Operation of Sir Robert Peel's Act of 1844 Explained*, 1848, by the economist Robert Torrens (1780–1864). One of the works discussed in WB's "The Currency Monopoly", *Prospective Review*, IV (1848), 297–337; reprinted *Collected Works*, IX, 235–71.

[13] Parliamentary committee set up to investigate the monetary crisis of 1847, when Peel's Bank Act of 1844 was temporarily suspended; its first report (*P.P.* 1847–8, VIII, i.1) while approving government intervention in October 1847, concluded that the Bank Act should not be altered.

[14] *Thoughts on the Principles of Taxation with reference to Property Tax, and its Exceptions*, 1848.

[15] Vincent Stuckey Wood, later Stuckey (1829–1902), younger son of the Revd William Wood and his wife Julia, daughter of Vincent Stuckey. After his mother's death in 1832 Vincent, and his elder brother William, were brought up at Hill House; entered Stuckey's Bank, becoming a director 1851; nominated by his grandmother to succeed to her interest in the bank, he took the name and arms of Stuckey at her death in 1861.

MARCH 1848

To EDITH BAGEHOT, 24 MARCH 1848

MS: Mr Norman St John-Stevas

6 Gt. Coram St. March 24th. 1848.

My dearest Mother,

I was too dim to write yesterday. Today I am much better; quite well indeed, if my headache does not return to the charge. I do not know whether I can come down at Easter or not yet. I *want* to come home immensely. London all last week seemed mere diluted smoke. But I must see whether I can get on fast enough with my work to enable me to take a holiday. If I do come, it will be rather before Easter than after: I mean that I must be in London early in Easter week. I did not succeed in amassing many facts at Hampstead. My aunt was like myself, a little dimmish; and my uncle vituperative on the wet weather, and the state of the universe as a whole. My uncle had been saying the last week that the Provisional government[1] never would live over another Sunday. I thought they would live a week and I was right. 'I generally find I am right'. I think people are rather hard on the Provisional government. No doubt they are the most quizzable of existing men, and are not well up in Adam Smith. But we ought to consider that men who have to spout in answer to deputations five hours a day, must inevitably talk a mass of nonsense. And also that one cannot expect the rules of Political Economy to be very strictly observed in a time of such confusion when nations must be prepared to sacrifice national wealth to national preservation. Besides French statesmen (Turgot[2] excepted) never have understood much about Political Economy: nor have the present government in all their difficulties said anything so absurd as Guizot's[3] objections to Free Trade. Lamartine[4]

---

[1] Louis Philippe's July Monarchy, beset by a credit crisis, deteriorating relations with Great Britain, and ministerial corruption, had collapsed in the space of a few hours, as a result of hostile demonstrations during which soldiers fired on a crowd. Louis Philippe fled to England, and on 25 February a Provisional Government of eleven was set up; its seven leading republican members included Lamartine, Ledru-Rollin, and Louis Blanc.

[2] Anne Robert Jacques Turgot, Baron de l'Aulne (1727–81), Louis XVI's controller of finance 1774–76. WB's marked copy of Condorcet's *Vie de M. Turgot* is in the Goldsmith's Library, University of London Library.

[3] François Pierre Guillaume Guizot (1787–1874), Louis Philippe's prime minister, who had been forced to resign 23 February 1848. For WB's assessment of his career and of his responsibility for the revolution of 1848, see *Collected Works*, IV, 440–44.

[4] Alphonse Marie Louis de Prat de Lamartine (1791–1869), poet and republican politician;

271

MARCH 1848

has for some years been a free trader. People forget too that they only profess to be a temporary committee to keep things together until the National assembly can meet:[5] such a government cannot be expected to be very vigorous or united; if they can keep any decent order till their masters meet they will have done all that they profess to do. Of course *I* am very delighted to hear of Meternich's resignation.[6] If any one believes in old diplomatic, despotic governments now, they must be strangely insensible to facts: the oldest, the strongest, the ablest cannot stand a riot in Vienna not much greater *in itself*, than those in Trafalgar Sq[uar]e.[7] It shows the weakness of the system, and of every system which counts for nothing the opinions and convictions of the great mass of its most intelligent subjects. This is the second lesson of what king-craft and diplomacy are worth in the hour of trial. The weakness of Louis Philippe and Meternich—men of great diplomatic and administrative ability—has been really contemptible. I always thought they were scoundrels, but I did not think they were such atrocious *humbugs*: I knew they were cruel and selfish but I thought they were braver and stronger. I little thought when I was abroad this summer, and the whole continent almost seemed under the rule and influence of these two men that a few months and two mobs would be sufficient to annihilate all their power. The change of scenes is too quick for a comedy. Please to tell my father that I have seen and read Mr. Tooke's book about the currency.[8] He is vituperative beyond measure about Sir R. Peel's Bill: he cannot apparently find words to express his contempt for the theory on which it is founded,

---

defeated by Louis Napoleon in the presidential election of December 1848, and retired from politics after the *coup d'état* of 1851.

[5] Elections held in April 1848 on basis of universal manhood suffrage returned a moderate Assembly; it was unable to deal with the continuing economic depression, and in June used brutal measures to repress anti-government demonstrations in Paris. The Assembly drew up a new constitution with an executive consisting of a president elected for four years and a single chamber.

[6] WB's spelling. Prince Metternich (1773–1859), Austrian Minister of Foreign Affairs since 1809, resigned the day after mob riots of 12 March 1848 in Vienna.

[7] On 6 March a public meeting to demand repeal of the income tax was declared illegal; it then became a Chartist demonstration of support for the revolution in France, concluding with an attempted march on Buckingham Palace; there were collisions with the police on this and the two following days, but no serious disturbances (R. G. Gammage, *History of the Chartist Movement 1837–1854*, 2nd edn, 1894, pp. 293–95).

[8] Thomas Tooke (1774–1858), economist opposed to any attempt at monetary management; attacked the 1844 Bank Charter Act in the 1848 volume of his *History of Prices*, referred to here, which was one of the books dealt with in WB's 'Currency Monopoly' (*Collected Works*, IX, 235–71).

or his conviction of its practical failure. He thinks it has worked pure unmixed evil. A political economist in a rage is an amusing sight: his virulence is so meagre, and he has no rhetoric or eloquence to cover it with, and make it seem decent. Mr. Tooke recommends a return to the old system before 1844 with an understanding between Government and the Directors of the Bank, that they are to keep a basis of about 10,000,000 of bullion in ordinary times, and never to be easy when they have less. But above all things he recommends the abolition of the separation of departments, which he considers as 'mischievous and irrational pedantry'. The book is very tedious and prolix but contains some curious facts especially with regard to the Russian currency. I want to know what reference if any a country banker is to make to the exchanges in the management of his *banking* business. Mr. Tooke thinks that Sir R. Peel's bill has been a cause of improvident speculation, in giving bankers a notion that circulation only is important with reference to the exchanges. Mr. T. holds that banking accomodation[9] is important but that circulation is unimportant—It seems to me that he is all wrong. Excuse the Political Economy which you hate, and believe me ever

yours affectionately and obediently
WALTER BAGEHOT

I admit that the French Revolution is nothing to [?Taban Page's][10] copybook.

I also want to know from my father where to find an explanation of the *Comparative* Exchanges (vide Economist) I only know that they depend on the price of gold as compared with silver: the standard of Turin and Hamburgh being silver and ours being gold. But I want to have the *figures* explained, especially what 30 per mille means, it can't be poetry for 3 per cent I suppose.

---

[9] Thus in MS.
[10] Not identified; the reading is uncertain.

APRIL 1848

To EDITH BAGEHOT, 8 APRIL 1848

MS: Mr R. W. Lyman

6 Great Coram St.
April 8, 1848

My dearest Mother,

I am just returned from squeezing my way through a riotous mob of special constables at Lincoln's Inn. All the members of the inn have been struck with terror at the Chartist meeting &c on Kennington common on Monday, and notice has been given that 'it was expected' that all students would turn themselves into special constables on the occasion.[1] The benchers came down to be sworn: *not* looking very dangerous as they are old and ricketty and much addicted to port wine. However they hobbled down. The students are more vigorous certainly but decidedly as likely to make a row as to prevent it. If the Chartists have any pluck, I do not think they need be timid at our squadron. However in my opinion we shall only be set to guard some very quiet street in bodies of ten, while the police will be sent into the difficult posts and we shall have to take their places which will be pleasant if it is a drizzle. If they would send us en masse to Kennington Common we might see some good fun, but it will be a great bore to be muddling about Lincoln's Inn with an oak staff all Monday, which appears to be my fate. I wanted to shirk it but I found it was reckoned disreputable, and men talked patriotism and so I went and was sworn in. I suppose Government expect a real row or they would not have been so careful about the troops or dispatched the Queen to Osborne House: and a walk through St. Giles's is enough to convince anyone that there are *elements* for a riot in London which might be very serious. I suppose there is as much misery and recklessness there as in any equal space in

---

[1] The swearing in of 150,000 special constables was one of the measures taken to counter the expected Chartist revolution on 10 April, when the National Convention had announced its intention of meeting on Kennington Common and going in procession to the House of Commons to present the petition for the People's Charter. The government made use of a 17th-century law forbidding the presentation of a petition by more than ten persons; its proclamation, and the stationing of police and troops along the route and in public buildings, proved an effective deterrent: less than a tenth of the expected 150,000 assembled at Kennington, and after some disturbances and arrests, the petition was taken to the House in a cab.

APRIL 1848

the whole world: but I do not believe that these Chartists have any organized scheme that will prosper, or that they could hold their Irish troops in discipline; and a London mob though brutal and fierce is not inventive like the Parisians, and has not the spontaneous discipline of the French. The old act of Parliament about not congregating to present petitions about the houses of Parliament is very useful, as a procession through the streets of Chartists would almost certainly end in a riot; whereas now it is very uncertain. There is a great parliament or convention of them sitting in John St.[2] about half a mile from here; where very violent language is delivered to the world gratis by men in dirty shirts; one barrister whose business was not overwhelming presides—His name is Earnest Jones[3] with red whiskers and red hair. I do not think there is much *fight* in them; but there is a good deal of talk. However with the mass of wretchedness and recklessness that exists in London, the slightest spark is dangerous and must not be neglected. I am not quite sure I shall be able to come down on Saturday as I have several things which I particularly want to finish and I may be obliged to waste all Monday and Tuesday next week; but you shall hear and I shall come if I can possibly. I am much better generally though I have an unpleasant headache at the present moment. Indeed when I come down I think you will think me looking scandalously well for a person who makes an excuse of his health to get out of this smoke.

I dined with Mrs. V. Reynolds a day or two ago. It was very gracious of her to ask me as I have never called there. Vincent[4] goes twice to a week to Hullah's singing lessons[5] at Exeter Hall, which seems a horrid

---

[2] The National Convention had been in session at the John Street Institution since 4 April, with the gallery open to the public.
[3] The Chartist leader and powerful speaker Ernest Jones (1819–69), barrister of the Middle Temple, who had joined the working class movement in 1846; sentenced to two years' imprisonment for seditious speeches during the Convention of 1848.
[4] Vincent Reynolds (1825–83), elder child of Vincent and Marian Reynolds; educated Sherborne and Trinity College, Cambridge (BA 1847, MA 1851); admitted at Lincoln's Inn 1845, called to the bar 1850.
[5] John Pyke Hullah (1812–84), composer and teacher of choral singing, introduced singing-classes on the Wilhelm system at Battersea 1840, and by this date 50,000 were attending classes on his system; designed St Martin's Hall, Long Acre, opened 1849, for choral classes and concerts.

case of misdirected industry. Emma[6] seemed dismal and had a headache, but sang endlessly.

Ever yours affectionately and obediently

W. BAGEHOT

To W. C. ROSCOE, [20 APRIL 1848]

MS: Mr Norman St John-Stevas
DATE: 1848 from reference to *Saint's Tragedy*; Maundy Thursday fell on 20 April 1848

Herd's Hill
Maundy Thursday

Dear Roscoe

I left at your rooms a day or two ago a huge pile of books of yours which I hope turned up in due course: and also three dishevelled looking copy books of mine full of an essay on Shelley.[1] Concerning this latter if you, or Osler, or both of you, would send me your opinion I should be glad because I have an indefinite respect for it at times which makes me fear in moments of sanity that it is hopelessly and utterly bad. If you have read it and think the last you will please to write and say so in so many words. You need not write a detailed criticism if you do not like—or in any other case necessarily write but if you concur in the opinion of my reasonable moments. Have you seen a play called the Saint's Tragedy just come out written by a Mr. Kingsley a clergyman somewhere?[2] Buy it and read it if you have not seen it, as it will agree-

---

[6] Emma Louisa Reynolds (*d.* 1865), daughter of Vincent and Marian Reynolds; married 1850 Camille Felix Desiré Caillard (1822–98), later of Wingfield House, Trowbridge, Wiltshire, called to the bar at Inner Temple 1845 and became a judge of the county courts of Wiltshire.

* * *

[1] Perhaps inspired by the appearance of Thomas Medwin's *Life* of the poet in 1847; the essay was not published, but parts may have been incorporated in WB's 'Percy Bysshe Shelley', *National Review*, III (1856), 342–79; reprinted *Collected Works*, I, 433–76.
[2] Charles Kingsley (1819–75), ordained to the curacy of Eversley, Hampshire, 1842, and presented to the living 1844. His first published work, *The Saint's Tragedy*, a five-act verse drama, appeared in January 1848; it portrayed in the life of St Elizabeth of Hungary the conflict between married love and the mediaeval ideal of asceticism and celibacy, for which Kingsley felt a deep antipathy.

ably diversify your Easter holidays. I admire it *excessively*—it is more like the old English dramatists than anything since them: and takes up deeper problems than they for the most part meddle with. You are dreadfully fastidious about modern plays; but I will *answer* for your admiring this a good deal.³

I am in enormous haste as the post *ought* to be gone: but Somersetshire postmen are not incarnations of punctuality.

Ever yours

WALTER BAGEHOT

R. H. HUTTON to WB, [?APRIL 1848]

Extract in RB, X, 169
DATE: near in date to last, from reference to WB's essay on Shelley; before July 1848, when James Martineau left for a year in Germany

I was in Liverpool on Sunday and heard Martineau preach a very splendid sermon *indeed*. I was staying with the Roscoes, and they had a letter from William saying he had been looking over a critique of yours on Shelley; what is this? and may I see it? I enclose you the 'Jungfrau'.¹ Send me word how you like it, and whether you assent to my criticisms on your two pieces and adopt them or not. *Many* thanks for them. In themselves they are fine, but they look to me as if they had been written in pain or melancholy, and while they are certainly not the *less* fine for that, they are yet more interesting to me as coming more from your personality than your other things, which have generally been too *im*personal.²

---

³ In the preface to his *Violenzia*, 1851, Roscoe said that the *Saint's Tragedy* 'stands without a rival in the dramatic literature of the day, and in which the author has ventured to represent one of the most terrible and subtle conflicts in which a human soul can be engaged' (p. ix).

* * *

¹ A sonnet (RB, X, 169).
² During 1847–8 WB and Hutton sent verses to one another for criticism (RB, X, 170–1). Of Hutton's Mrs Barrington quotes only the sonnet 'To W.B.', written in 1847; but she

APRIL—MAY 1848

To R. H. HUTTON, [?APRIL–MAY 1848]

Extract in RB, X, 172, undated, but probably near in date to last

I send you Roscoe's criticism on my poems which will amuse you. I like both your sonnets, but the Pauline one the best; as the Star (which is he?) is in your personal equation and not in mine. Isn't it rather a petty form of fire worship? Also is not
>Cluster round thee *every* smile and sigh
>Spring from affections mocking times control,

rather a large consignment of feeling to send on so distant a voyage? Does not the attraction (or the attractiveness at least) vary *directly* as the square of distance? I met your family (i.e. your sisters and your

* * *

gives some lines from 'two shorter pieces' of WB's particularly admired by Hutton (perhaps those referred to in this letter):
>Since dull-eyed Love with idiot haste
>O'er human graves has restless paced,
>Musings have soothed at evening hour,
>As woman's words man's world-worn power.

and
>Since labours' weary curse began
>To dog the steps of anxious man.

She also quotes from verses WB wrote 'about this time', which 'betoken moods of profound melancholy':
>As an idiot mother prowling
>   For a lost and roaming brood;
>As a wild hyena howling
>   For her foul and cankered food;
>So ravenous pain strays scowling
>   Round lean life's banquet crude.

and 'Sonnet', 'on your speaking of "causeless melancholy"':
>The highest spirits deepest sorrows claim,
>   The noblest destinies are tinged with fear;
>To sadden careless instinct Jesus came,
>   From gladdest eyes to draw the scalding tear.
>*No* pain is causeless; o'er God's mightiest sons
>   Two angels Grief and Guilt divide their sway;
>He who affliction's icy tempest shuns
>   Must tread a path where *fouler* breezes stray.
>The heavy steps of sad repentance lie
>   Along the burning sands by passion spread,
>But they who shrink not from a wintry sky,
>   High o'er the Alps of *sinless* sorrow tread.
>The pilgrim bent Messiah's land to gain
>   Must pass a desert, or a mountain chain.

April, 1848.

In his 'Memoir' of WB, Hutton printed WB's poem 'To the Roman Catholic Church', written in 1849 or 1850, to show his concern with religion and the influence upon him of Newman's verses.

eldest brother)¹ at the Torrington Square Roscoes.² And I told them in a moment of temporary insanity that you seemed in good spirits; your last letter being *awfully* dismal. I hope I'm not a moral agent at times. I often say the exact contrary of what I should know very well, if I thought the least, in a calm tone of utter conviction.

To W. C. ROSCOE, 6 SEPTEMBER 1848

MS: Mr Norman St John-Stevas

6th. Sep. 6 Gt. Coram St.
1848.

My dear Roscoe,

I begun a letter to you in Somersetshire¹ the day after I received your account of Newman's address:² and as a reward for this piece of epistolary probity I never finished it. The only objection that any one could have to Newman as the head of a religious institution is that his own religion is such a thoroughly bad one. What he says about the

---

¹ The eldest of R. H. Hutton's three brothers was Joseph Henry, a schoolmaster; in 1860, when he was one of the executors of his father's will, he was living at Hove, Sussex.

² Robert Roscoe (1789–1850), solicitor; uncle of W. C. Roscoe, who looked up to him 'as to a second father; and probably no man ever influenced him more profoundly, mild and unassuming as his influence was' (R. H. Hutton's memoir of W. C. Roscoe, *Poems and Essays of W. C. Roscoe*, 1860, I, xciii). Robert and his wife, Martha, *née* Walker (1798–1884), had eleven children, including Henrietta (1821–69), who married Timothy Smith Osler in 1852, and Eliza (1823–97), second wife of R. H. Hutton, whom she married in 1858.

* * *

¹ WB took his MA in June 1848, and was awarded the gold medal in Moral and Intellectual Philosophy; he then went to Herd's Hill to recover from the strain of the examination.

² F. W. Newman had been appointed the first Principal of University Hall, erected in commemmoration of the passing of the Dissenters' Chapels Act of 1844 as a hall of residence which would enable students to receive non-denominational theological instruction. WB and his father were among the subscribers, each contributing £50. A Council of prominent Unitarians, including James Martineau, Henry Crabb Robinson, and Edward Tagart was set up in 1847, and on 20 July 1848 the foundation of the building in Gordon Square (now Dr Williams's Library) was laid. Crabb Robinson recorded that the excellence of Newman's inaugural address 'lay in the skill with which he asserted, without offence, the power of forming an institution open to all opinions whatever, even Jew and Mahometan' (H. Hale Bellot, *University College London*, pp. 298–9; Minutes of the Council, MS Dr Williams's Library; *Diary, Reminiscences, and Correspondence of Henry Crabb Robinson*, ed. T. Sadler, 1869, III, 291, 297, 320–21).

magnanimity of founding an institution independent of opinions is marred to me by my being convinced that if the Council *had* known his creed they would never have appointed him.

I am come to London in September to read law and write a review of John Mill's Pol. Ec. for the Prospective.[3] I have got a great reverence for my own virtue in consequence, and am in immense danger of doing nothing now I am here; one likes so much to reward merit. The fates seem to think or feel differently however as I am in much trouble about John Mill, who is very tough and rather dreary. I am trying to discuss his views about the labouring classes: most of his peculiar views come in there, and the subject is of more interest than any other that I could select. The theory of population is in an unpleasant state; and it is very difficult to find sure ground upon it. It wont do to say with Ricardo and Malthus that *every* increase of comfort or decrease of misery tends to produce an increase of population: but it is difficult to find formulae to suit the case. Do you believe that the English law of Partnership is good? I mean does it seem to you that every one who shares in the profits of a concern ought to be liable for its losses to the whole extent of his property. John Mill thinks decidedly otherwise and would give any persons the power of forming partnerships with limited liability if they like with due notice to the public. I incline rather to agree with him. I am rather impressed by the fact, that it is a growing opinion among bankers that it is impossible to have stable joint stock banks under the present law. And I think this opinion is most likely true for very few would be willing to risk their whole property for a small profit on a few shares. There *are* such people: I know a large landowner who for the sake of £20 lets his whole property be liable for the mismanagement of bankers of whom he knows nearly as little as the majority of Australians: but the supply of fools of that magnitude, is, I fear, exceedingly limited. It is exceedingly advantageous to have joint stock

---

[3] 'Principles of Political Economy', *Prospective Review*, IV (Nov 1848), 460–502; reprinted *Collected Works*, XI, 157–194. On 3 July J. J. Tayler told F. W. Newman that the editors hoped they had 'secured a very able young writer to give us a notice' of Mill's *Principles* (*Letters Embracing his Life*, I, 264). Hutton and James Martineau thought the article inferior to that on the currency; Hutton wished that WB had been more critical of Mill's theories on the future of the working classes. Later, Hutton referred to WB's own 'hatred' to the article, and went on: 'I only said *you* could write a better, but if I had read it first in the *Prospective* without knowing by whom it was, I should have been astonished and delighted with it' (extracts from letters of Hutton to WB, written from Berlin, ?December 1848, in RB, X, 176–77).

banks; because the old system of banking by individuals is not applicable to extensive districts, throughout which it is hardly possible for the characters and circumstances of individuals to be certainly known: and the economy of banking on a large scale is obviously considerable. I own I am much inclined to think that the present law amounts to giving the bank of England a monopoly of secure joint stock banking.[4] This is a serious evil. Moreover the prima facie view of such questions is that they are like games of chance where a man risks a certain sum for a certain chance of profit: and he either gains the profit or loses the sum paid down. J.M. says that the French law admits of partnerships in which the managing partners only are liable without limit, and the rest only to the extent of the sum subscribed: these are called partnerships *en commandite*[5] and seem to me the most likely to answer of any. What do you think of this? I have just seen Osler and Sandford[6] at the British Museum. I'll tell you a way of reading German law that seems to work. Put a Savigny[7] on the table before you: and an unwholesome looking white hat beyond it: then look over the Savigny plaintively at the white hat. If any one seems watching, turn over a leaf and read with your lips voraciously. It seems to work. Sandford was reading a dreary looking book with long S's. called England's Recovery.[8] I made a speech of some length to a man with flaxen hair and a peaked nose under a belief that he was Osler. I didn't ask him anything but he said 'No Sir' with a snort: and I departed.

I suppose you have seen Keats' Letters[9] which are curious. I do not like any of them much till the two or three last written on his way to

---

[4] For WB's expansion of these arguments, see his articles 'Sound Banking' and 'Unfettered Banking' (*Collected Works*, IX, 305–316), written after the passing in 1856 of the Limited Liability Act, from which joint stock banks were excluded.
[5] The Limited Liability Act began as an attempt to introduce this continental system, which was considered by the Select Committee on the law of partnership (P.P. 1851, XVIII, I).
[6] John Langton Sanford (1824–77), historian; became a close friend of WB, Roscoe and Hutton, while a student at University College, from which he entered Lincoln's Inn and read in the chambers of John Richard Quain; called to the bar 1855. Joint editor of the *Inquirer* 1852–55, and from 1861 a contributor to the *Spectator*.
[7] Friedrich Carl von Savigny was one of the founders of historical jurisprudence; his *Treatise on Possession* was translated by Sir Erskine Perry, 1848.
[8] Not identified.
[9] Before the appearance in August 1848 of Richard Monckton Milnes's *Life, Letters, and Literary Remains of John Keats* few young men had even heard of Keats. Milnes had been assembling material for years, and his volumes provided the first biography of the poet, 67 of his peoms, and many letters.

Italy. I never heard of a mind with so little stamina: I mean with so little of settled realized principle, intellectual, moral, or religious. I was not prepared for his possessing so much energy: and his pugnacity was another unexpected good quality, and one which I could appreciate. I should not have thought that the imagination could have attained such excellence with so much poorness in the other parts of the mind. He never seems to have had any thought and Endymion seems to have been written before he had experienced much feeling. It was a shame to publish Otho the Great, though the blank verse is good. I laughed more over it however than over the 'Cap and Bells' which seemed to me a trifle dismal. The last sonnet[10] is excellent: the rest seem to me thoroughly weakminded: but I failed to read them quite all.

I hope your asthma is departed according to Osler's report. He also states that you are finishing your tragedy[11] which I am rejoiced to hear. It wd. be a charity to write to me for London is dull even to me who am always a solitary animal.

Ever yours affly
WALTER BAGEHOT

Will you remember me to your family and tell Richard Hutton that I will write to him soon.

To R. H. HUTTON, 20 SEPTEMBER [1848]

MS: Mr Norman St John-Stevas
DATE: 1848, from reference to *Saint's Tragedy* and Manning's *Charge*

6 Great Coram St. Sep 20th.

My dear Hutton,

I have left your letter so long unanswered, that I fear you will have forgotten the points which you told me to write about. I concur with

---

[10] 'Bright Star!'
[11] *Violenzia:* see letter to Roscoe, ?early March 1851.

SEPTEMBER 1848

you in thinking, that minds not self-conscious[1] must be comparatively deficient in aspiration in the sense of being but little occupied with the future state of their own minds. I do not know exactly how far to agree with you about J.H.N's[2] personal character. I rather doubt his having less than the average of self-consciousness. Do not you unconsciously take Martineau as the standard whose self-consciousness is many million sizes above that of ordinary mortals? I do not think F.W.N much if at all below the average: he (and his brother perhaps also) has quite enough to make him a much better metaphysician than he is: but it seems to me, that perhaps owing to overactivity and restlessness of mind both the Newmans combine with a great facility of analyzing to a certain extent, a great disinclination (and almost an inability) to analyse further. Also I think he is quite imaginative enough to realize futurity or anything else as definitely as he pleased: I am not sure that he does want aspiration (much at any rate) in the sense of not desiring to do his duty better. Martineau's aspirations very often amount to wishes for harder or higher duties than those which he has at the time: and this M. wd. not think it *right* to indulge: he would think it his duty to put forth his strong will and drive them off. I quite think with you however that his imagination is singularly dependent on his will: and that it is neither self-acting as I suppose it was in Shakespere, or an instrument of mere desire as in St. Paul or St. Augustine. As to St. Paul I think Martineau[3] expresses the truth very well, by saying that his whole soul was absorbed in a wish for the triumph of the truth: this was inextricably connected no doubt with a love of God and Christian persons: beyond these he had only one intense wish, as far as I can see, viz to do his duty whatever that might be: I do not imagine that he was defective at all in the sense of personal sin: but I do not think he cared the least what his own position hereafter might be so long as the truth triumphed: he had an intense wish to perform whatever *work* was given him but no anxiety about what the nature of that work might be. Of course it is in the nature of a buoyant

---

[1] Their discussion may have been inspired by James Martineau's discourse, 'Christian Self-Consciousness' (included in Vol. II of his *Endeavours after the Christian Life*, 1847, pp. 85–103), on this consequence of a high state of civilization, which, although it may be abused, is a condition of thought and conscience.
[2] John Henry Newman.
[3] This suggests that WB had heard or read in MS one or more of the course of sermons on St Paul first given by Martineau in 1841, and published after his death.

mind not to be sad in seasons of activity, such St. Paul's were for the most part. To finish about Newman, I do not think his want of self-consciousness can be the reason for his wanting precise moral convictions: Arnold who was not self-conscious at all scarcely, had a very precise notion of duty: I think in N.'s case the reason is that his intellect is more subtle than his moral sense is discriminating: he can conceive finer shades of feeling and motive, than his conscience will confidently estimate—As to the peaceful nature of Prot[estantis]m. I only meant that it repudiated the characteristic work of the Catholic military ages; viz the organized *living* authority to be obeyed in all points of faith and practice; the notion of 'an oracle' is essential to a positive Revelation: and I do not imagine that the Protestant belief in this is to be accounted for from the circumstances of a period but simply from the truth of the doctrine. If by the construction of the human intellect truth has an advantage on the whole, we need only seek in social circumstances for the sources of *error*. I have just read (in a charge of Archdeacon Manning's)[4] rather a good sentence on ecclesiastical history. 'The world persecuted the church in the beginning: espoused her in the middle ages: is divorcing her now'.[5]

It must have been an immense gain in the middle ages that all their systematized thought was Christian and spiritual. Ever since Hobbes in England, there has been a systematic Unchristian philosophy constructed by men of this world (i.e. men who have not much cultivated the moral sense): and one picks up scraps of this in ones infancy, and it takes much trouble to be rid of them. There was much worldliness in the middle ages no doubt, but there seems to have been no organized philosophy to keep it in countenance. However anyone who can understand Hume, will not be in a hurry to believe any *ir*religious philosophy: the choice for a man is whether he will believe in God and duty or whether he will believe in nothing. I agree with you quite in saying that the Saint's Tragedy is deficient in severity of moral feeling. Does not this amount to saying that there is a Germanism about it: I mean is not this the point in which the German character is defective; a severe discrimination as to voluntary acts? There is

---

[4] Henry Edward Manning (1808–92), Archdeacon of Chichester, 1840; became a Catholic in 1851; Archbishop of Westminster, 1865, and Cardinal, 1875; not a Tractarian, but helped to rally the high church party after Newman's departure.
[5] *Charge Delivered at the Ordinary Visitation of the Archdeaconry of Chichester in July 1848*, 1848, p. 41. A comment on the role of the church in the 'year of revolutions'.

SEPTEMBER 1848

(as it seems to me but I am a poor judge) a rich overflow of feeling, but a want of strictness in the details of action. Please to answer this. I am inclined altogether to disbelieve the thesis which the St.'s tragedy is to prove about celibacy. I think it may be held, that the highest life is an imitation of Christ's not only in its spirit, but in its characteristic circumstances. For perhaps these circumstances comprize the maximum of opportunities for self-denial and for a form of action that will morally improve mankind. About celibacy I think St. Paul argues satisfactorily that it is essential to an *absorption* in the highest end of human action: this is undoubtedly the teaching religion in such a manner as effect a diminution of sin among mankind. This cannot be the unremitting pursuit of anyone who is a member of a family; daily and secular cares will lay hold on a large fraction of human life: to follow in the highest manner our Lord's earthly profession we must be as He was *home*less. There is an important principle which seems to me to qualify this however: it is that no man should begin to put down the disinterested part of his original nature, unless he has thoroughly put down the selfish and the unnatural: it wd. be an awful thing and yet it must have happened often after conquering the affections to succumb to the appetites. The affections are the bastards in what may be called the *inevitable* sphere of human action: while necessary duties are neglected, it is sin to dispense with any aid in getting through them; and to undertake harder ones beside. To those who have to lead a secular life, marriage is, I suppose, in the majority of cases an assistance in the performance of duty: it is necessary to keep a strong habitual feeling of disinterested affection (in the case of most men) toward existing persons whom they habitually see, and it is very difficult to do this in the case of friends, because they are dispersed so widely, and have such different spheres of duty. You know Arnold's saying that a family or religious intercourse with the poor was necessary for an Englishman.[6] I think it might with pains be generalized into a complete view of the subject.

About divine self-denial I think we quite agree. I only meant that it ought to be kept consistent with the truth that the manner of virtue

---

[6] 'The most certain softeners of a man's moral skin, and sweeteners of his blood, are, I am sure, domestic intercourse in a happy marriage, and intercourse with the poor. It is very hard, I imagine, in our present state of society, to keep up intercourse with God without one or both of these aids to foster it' (letter of 7 July 1832; A. Stanley, *Life of Dr. Arnold*, I, 287).

depends on the unitedness of the mind in point of active motive, and the greatest strain of executive volition.

When do you come to town? I wish you had been up when I first came here. I was in immense force and we might have had some good talk. I am rather dimmer (as this letter will evidence) from ten days of *exciting* headaches. I can think then, but writing or any execution is generally done weakmindedly and irksomely. I am better today though. I like the second verse of your hymn, the 1st. and 3rd. not so well: they strike me as written under the orders of your will. Nobody but Newman can contract with his imagination for a supply of verses.[7] I send you some of mine which are gloomy and I fear dull.

Ever yours affly

WALTER BAGEHOT

I wont be in town more than a fortnight more My family wont stand it. Bring the sermon you mention. Remember me very kindly to your brother.

R. H. HUTTON to WB,
[?OCTOBER–DECEMBER 1848]

Extract in RB, X, 18–19, dated Berlin, 1848; Hutton joined James Martineau in Berlin in October (J. Drummond and C. B. Upton, *Life and Letters of James Martineau*, I, 186)

I do not take a one-sided view of your character.... But this does not in the least diminish my faith and expectation that you have a most important influence to exercise over us all, I hope as a *Nation*, one which I cannot *bear* to think should be diminished or destroyed either by the modifying or incapacitating influence of bad health on genius such as yours. I think myself I understand your character pretty thoroughly, both its wants and its powers, at least I feel as if I could

---

[7] On WB's reading of Newman, Hutton said that he 'was intimate with all Dr. Newman's writings. And of these the Oxford sermons, and the poems in the *Lyra Apostolica*... were always his special favourites. The little poetry he wrote... seems to me to have been obviously written under the spell which Dr. Newman's own few but finely-chiselled poems had cast upon him' ('Memoir'). *Lyra Apostolica* (1836, and frequently reprinted) is a collection of 179 poems, 109 of them by Newman, first published in the *British Magazine*, 1833–6. See also letter of April 1868.

analyse it as well as any character I know; and certainly I know none so capable of exerting the highest permanent influence over England. I think your influence is essentially more fitted to be exerted over bodies of men, than over *persons*; through institutions, by reason and by moral power, rather than through individuals by authority and persuasion and affectionate powers. Even in reasoning you can adapt yourself far better to convince mankind than to alter individual views, because you generally choose the natural universal road to Truths, even Truths the most difficult and obscure and often seem unable to wind along the particular paths of fallacy or truth by which specially contented minds so often reach their own views. . . .

This is partly what makes me think your genius is fitted for a statesman's position; and I cannot help trusting that your influence may be so wide and essential in our national distress and need, as to give you a *permanent* place in our history. It is strange I should feel such confidence as to this: that you are fitted for it, I feel *certain*. My only fear and anxiety is about your health and prudence.

To T. W. BAGEHOT, [?MID-DECEMBER 1848]

MS: Mr Norman St John-Stevas
DATE: probably near in date to the first meeting of the University Hall trustees about Clough's appointment, held 11 December 1848

6 Gt. Coram St. Dec. 1848

My dearest Father,

I am now thoroughly involved in the routine of a law student's life. I go to chambers every day at ten and return at five with exemplary regularity. While I am there, I read law and copy precedents, or read the cases that are sent into the pupil room or draw any paper that is easy and that Mr. Hall[1] deems suitable to my uninitiated mind. I like what I have seen of Mr. Hall exceedingly. He explains points very clearly, and, what is not so usual a merit in a lawyer, very concisely. He seems to me to be an excellent man of business. The work he gets

---

[1] Charles Hall (1814–83), barrister, of the Middle Temple; became recognized leader of the Chancery bar and foremost authority on real property law; appointed Vice-Chancellor and knighted, 1873.

through in a day is very great, and all that he does is correct. I was going through a huge pile of papers with him two days ago, about some fens in Lincolnshire which there were three acts of Parliament for draining, each of them giving the commissioners different powers, and taxing different districts at different rates with many other complicated details. Mr H. had previously been conversant with some portions of the subject, and this made it easier to him; but nevertheless I was quite amazed at the rapidity and practised facility with which he mastered and combined so much involved and complicated matter. The commissioners wanted to mortage some of the taxes, and no[t] others; some they had mortgaged already and others they had no power to mortgage at all: and so on with details ad infinitum. This strikes me more and more in law, that its difficulties are mainly difficulties of quantity. No one thing is to a mind that has been properly disciplined, very difficult to grasp and master in and by itself: but unless great care is taken, while new matter is being laid hold of, the old matter slips away. So that the great requisite for success in law is roominess of mind, to take in and hold at once a large number of considerations.

I find the work rather fatiguing at present. My eye is not practised enough to see easily the contents of a law paper. I do not know what are the material and what the immaterial parts; and groping all through masses of papers is a tiring operation, and a capital way of picking up a headache. I am I hope however already acquiring more facility than I had at first. But the progress is slow, and the process of learning this part of the subject not the most agreeable. Reading law treatises however is much easier and pleasanter. I was at Hampstead on Sunday. I thought my aunt very tolerable on the whole, though she said she [had] been very much tried by the journey up and did not feel that she had recovered her strength. My uncle was not very animated, I thought, but Dr. Crawford[2] was there pouring out stupid medical stories, which were rather a dead weight on society in general.

You will have seen that Mr. Newman has resigned the headship of University Hall. He invented [a] mass of architectural reasons about a staircase and a roof,[3] but the real reason of his resignation seems to be

---

[2] Probably Adair Crawford, MRCP, MD; assistant physician London Fever Hospital.
[3] The Council of University Hall received his resignation at the meeting of 7 November and it was accepted at that of 14 November; Crabb Robinson recorded that most of the Council were relieved, especially the 'religious party' (MS Diary; Dr Williams's Library).

that Mrs. Newman[4] jibbed. She did not like housekeeping on a large scale I suppose and the commissariat is not exactly her line. The council talk now of electing a Mr. Clough[5] who was once a fellow of Oriel college, and who has a great reputation, and is a friend of Constantine Prichard's[6]—By the way you have no doubt heard that Dr. Prichard has been rather seriously ill at Salisbury. Mr. Proctor came home without him and Constantine went down directly and Mrs. P soon followed. They do not expect to [be] able to move him for some days, I believe, and he seems to have suffered a good deal though he is now better.

Ever yours affectionately

WALTER BAGEHOT

I am sorry to say that I have just heard an unfavorable account of Dr. P. He has not got at all better, they say, and I shd. fear he was rather worse if anything. Constantine came to town today to fetch Dr. Tweedie.[7] I did not see him as I was at chambers when he was here.

---

[4] Maria (*d.* 1876), daughter of Sir John Kennaway, married F. W. Newman 1834.
[5] Arthur Hugh Clough (1819–61) had resigned his Oriel fellowship 18 October 1848, on the grounds that he could not subscribe to the Thirty-nine Articles; the Provost of Oriel, Edward Hawkins, strongly advised against this course, as did Jowett and Stanley, and Hawkins did not formally announce his resignation until February 1849. On 27 November Clough wrote to Tom Arnold (whom he had considered joining in New Zealand): 'I have an invitation to stand for the headship of the new University Hall (on the Oxfd and Cambridge college system) to be attached to University College, London. One would have to read prayers in the morning—stomachable by all parties specially Unitarians, of which creed come the chief contributors to the Institution. Only two hours' work a day, which is tempting. This offer, though *offer* it hardly is, I have not made up my mind about.' (See *The Correspondence of Arthur Hugh Clough*, ed. F. L. Mulhauser, Oxford, 1957, I, 219–25, 247.) WB was among those instrumental in securing the post for Clough (see letter to Hutton, 1 March 1849, and ns), and this began his friendship with one who had, said Hutton, 'a greater intellectual fascination for Bagehot than any of his contemporaries' (see 'A Short Biography', *Collected Works*, I, 47).
[6] Of the University Hall appointment Prichard wrote to Clough: 'I disagree too much with what I conceive to be your present state of mind not to hope that it may not last, but being such as it is, I can well imagine you could not stay happily at Oxford. And I dare say you will have opportunities of doing good at U.H.' Although unable to enter into Clough's doubts he tried, in this and two further letters, to suggest arguments against them (*Correspondence of Arthur Hugh Clough*, I, 235–6, 238–40, 249–50).
[7] Alexander Tweedie (1794–1884), MD, FRCP; FRS, 1838; physician to the London Fever Hospital, 1824. James Cowles Prichard contributed to Tweedie's *Cyclopaedia of Practical Medicine*, 1831–5.

DECEMBER 1848

R. H. HUTTON to WB, 10 DECEMBER [1848]

Extract in RB, X, 67–8, where the date is printed '1845' in error; 10 December was a Sunday in 1848, the year when Hutton was in Berlin with Martineau

Sunday, 10th December [1848]
Bei der Madame Schmidt 13 Behrenstrasse—
Berlin

Mr dear Bagehot,

It is a great pleasure to sit down to answer your letter which was indeed with its enclosure exceedingly welcome. I am glad to hear you have been nearly free from giddiness which I fear most, and not had much headache. I don't care for your apathy much, for it is not a state likely to last. Only I wish you had more interests around you, not merely of intellect but of feeling, which are with you too much limited to the exclusive interests of home. In London you always appear to me to be a *perfect* expression of the class idea of a young man studying in lodgings, without *differentia specifica*. Of course as regards *social* relations you go to places and to fellow-students, but *biding* nowhere; and while others seem to be always definable with respect to some distinct circle of individuals, there is no particular distance from your lodgings that enters more than any other into your functional equation. I don't think this is either good for you, or your intellect; the apathy you describe I think arises from this absence of positive interest and forces in your London life, which none can help missing though in very different degrees. I know I could never work well and with energy without *real* friends near me, to whom my thoughts and attention may sometimes turn entirely. I do not mean simply men one *likes*, but men one loves; and I should be here in a state of quiet apathy, just like yours, if I had not Martineau near me to supply the attractive force that intellectual pursuits must often fail in, when the mind is ill or weary. All your friends you seem to *like*, but they do not seem to be resources that instantly and spontaneously fill the vacuum that rational, moral, and even religious interests will often leave. And I know when this is the case, a kind of reverie, which is not over-beneficial to the mind, supplies the place which human interests were, I think, meant to fill. I wish you had not simply more friends but more attachments.

To C. C. ATKINSON,[1] 24 FEBRUARY 1849

MS: University College, London

6 Great Coram St. Feby. 24 1849.

Sir,

A short time since a committee was appointed by the 'New Debating Society' of University College to report upon the best mode of employing the surplus funds which the Society now has at its disposal, and which as its probable income seems to exceed its regular expenses, the Society will most likely have at its disposal for some time to come—this Committee reported to the Society that in their judgment the best mode of expending the surplus funds (supposing that the Council of the College would allow of it) was the Establishment of a prize of books for the best English Prose Essay on a given subject to be open to all Students attending lectures at the college—Accordingly the society at a recent general meeting passed the enclosed resolutions in conformity with the report of the committee to which I beg to direct your attention. The surplus fund in the present year available for this purpose will be £5 and it is hoped and expected that the same sum will be forthcoming for the same purpose in future years. It is of course understood by the Society though it is not expressed in the enclosed resolutions that the permission of the Council must [be] obtained before anything else can be done and that the authorities of the College will have a veto on the subject chosen for the essay, and the person selected by the Society to be Examiner in each year. If the [Council] should allow the plan to be carried into execution, Professor Malden has kindly consented to be the first examiner—with the proviso however that some different or supplementary arrangement should be made, if the Essays sent in for Examination should chance to be exceedingly numerous—In pursuance of the enclosed Resolutions a Committee has been chosen (from among those members of the Society who are excluded from competing for the prize) to choose the first subject and to communicate with you; and I have been desired to write to you on their behalf. As we wish if possible to give the first prize in June next

[1] Charles Cales Atkinson (1793–1869), barrister of the Middle Temple 1834; Secretary of University College, London 1835–67.

there seems to be no great deal of time to spare, and it would therefore be very agreeable to us if the subject could be brought under the notice of the Council within as short a period as may be consistent with their convenience.[2]

I am, Sir
Your obedient servant
WALTER BAGEHOT

To C. Atkinson Esqre.

To R. H. HUTTON, 1 MARCH 1849

MS: Mr Norman St John-Stevas

written ages ago March 1st. 1849

My dear Hutton,

I have begun two letters to you both of which are now mouldy and superannuated Would you like to take the Chaplaincy of Univ. Hall? Clough has been appointed, but declines to read prayers[1] Therefore a chaplain has to be appointed, and Roscoe and I want to know whether you would dislike to take it for a year or two. Roscoe and I have a scheme of going to live there ourselves. I should certainly settle to do so but I do not know very well whether my mother would like it or not. But at any rate I should be living close. So that you would be living with your own friends instead of being stuck down in the country with a congregation that you hated, a prey to all manner of dyspeptic ideas. I do not know so well about the article salary, but you would certainly have rooms rent free and £100 a year, or *perhaps* more—what would you take it for? You would have to read prayers,

---

[2] Council accepted the Prose Essay Prize (see letter of 25 April 1849), but University College has no record of its award.

* * *

[1] On 3 February Clough wrote to Bagehot from Liverpool, asking whether the 'Chaplain matter' was settled, and saying: 'If there is any difficulty, I shall have no objection to read chapters of the Bible—something corresponding to Church of England Psalms and Lessons,—for any length of time that may be convenient. I should like it' (R. H. Tener, 'Clough to Bagehot: A New Letter', *Notes & Queries*, CCII[1977], 14–15).

say grace, and have a fixed time for explaining things to men in De Morgan's classes, which Clough cannot undertake. You might coach men in Mathematics to obtain coin. I think myself independently of wanting to have you in London, that you would be better able to study theology, and get through difficulties in London than in any other place, and there does not seem to me much object in your taking a congregation for a couple of years or so. You could preach in Carter Lane[2] quite as often as *I* should think good for your mind at your age. Clough is guaranteed £150 for the first two years, for which [he] is to attend to the discipline and business of the house, and answer men's difficulties in classics and everything but mathematics. I can't tell what the council would think to be the proportion that the amount guaranteed you ought to bear, and the funds are not flourishing especially but half would be the minimum, that I should think right. Say £75, and Roscoe and myself could we think, oust Davison[3] the secretary, and get you this place which is £50 per annum for doing next to nothing. Clough you would like very much, I think. He is a man of strong, and clear though not very quick intellect: so that I feel like a gnat buzzing about him. He has a great deal of imagination, and has written a good deal of poetry; a proportion of which is good, though he unfortunately has been in the Highlands and talks of barmaids and potato-girls and other operative females there in a very humiliating manner as it seems to me though Roscoe defends it.[4]

You would I think, agree with me in thinking that his mind was defective in severity of moral feeling and in the conception of law generally as applied to morals. But he is evidently a man of great honesty and moral courage with an immense deal of feeling. C. Prichard says his mind was injured he thinks by an overstrained asceticism when he first knew him at Oxford, and has never recovered from the evil.

[2] The Unitarian chapel in Carter Lane, Islington, of which his father, Joseph Hutton, was minister 1835–52.
[3] David Davison (1795–1858), Unitarian minister, was secretary of the Council of University Hall. MA Glasgow 1815; minister of the Jewin Street, Old Jewry, congregation 1825–40; after five years in Germany, he devoted himself to the cause of education and to literary work; trustee of Dr Williams's Library and member of the Presbyterian Board. Left London 1851, following an attack of paralysis (obituary in *Christian Reformer*, n.s. XV [1859], 62).
[4] A reference to Clough's *The Bothie of Toper-na-Fuosich*, published in November 1848; in his 'Mr. Clough's Poems', WB focusses on Clough's later narrative poem in hexameters, *Amours de Voyage*, but mentions the 'artistic skill' and excellence of the *Bothie* (*Collected Works*, II, 257–8).

MARCH 1849

Roscoe and myself put him into the Principalship. There was a committee to see him composed of Busk[5] a Chancery barrister, Le Bretton[6] an amateur furniture broker, and Tagart. They came back with no end of blunders and said nothing could be got out of Clough, and he would bind himself to nothing: and Tagart disgusted Clough by delivering fractions of bad sermons on general subjects. Everybody at the meeting was ready to concur in breaking off the negotiation with Clough, except Roscoe and myself. Roscoe became extra-crafty and I made a great noise, and so we got it adjourned. And I saw Clough and talked him over, and Roscoe and I divided the Council between us and had endless fun talking them over. We went together to Tagart over to Bayswater, and Roscoe threw his conscience overboard and agreed with Tagart that Ch[ristianit]y. was essential, and Deism out of the question; meaning (which he swears (! !) he didn't know) by Ch[ristianit]y. exactly what Tagart meant by Deism. In the end we carried the election of Clough nem. con. Tagart rather disapproving, but not having pluck enough to vote against it.[7] We consider that we did this 'rather well', and it was great fun in the doing. After this we think that the council must succumb in future to what the junior members may think fit to exact.

[5] Henry William Busk (1806–86), grandson of Sir William Busk, bencher of the Middle Temple, who held his chambers 'for two lives', the second of which was Henry's; called to the bar 1830, and became a skilled conveyancer. Busk did much legal work for nonconformist chapels and charities and drew up the documents for University Hall. His father was a Unitarian and his mother a churchwoman, and he was given a Unitarian education (studying under Lant Carpenter at Bristol and at Manchester College) before entering St John's College, Cambridge, which he left without taking a degree, having decided that he could not conscientiously sign the Thirty-nine Articles. (*Inquirer*, 13 November 1886).

[6] The Revd Philip Le Breton (1779–1860), son of Very Revd Francis Le Breton, Dean of Jersey; educated Exeter College, Oxford, and succeeded his father as rector of St Saviour's, Jersey, but resigned 1814 because of doubts about the Trinity. Established a school in London, which he gave up because of poor health; a trustee of Dr Williams's Library, on committee of British and Foreign Unitarian Association, and interested himself in the foundation of the Ladies' College, Bedford Square (later Bedford College). As a member of the Council of University Hall, he took an active part in its proceedings, including the erection of the building. His eldest daughter Mary Anne married H. W. Busk. (Obituary in *Christian Reformer*, n.s. XVI[1860], 756–60.)

[7] Before the Council meeting of 21 December, Crabb Robinson thought Clough certain to be appointed, though he recorded the exertions of Tagart to secure a Unitarian principal as a symptom of the 'schism' in the London Unitarians between orthodox and liberal. At the meeting it was discovered that a letter of recommendation from Dr Arnold's widow did not guarantee Clough's religious views, and it was decided that he should be interviewed by a committee. This committee laid before the meeting of 11 January a letter from Clough saying that he was not 'competent to undertake the conduct or superintendance of any prayers', although he would 'facilitate devotional arrangements', and

Write me word about the Chaplaincy,[8] and consider the financial part carefully. What is the income of such a congregation as you would be likely to get? We could make this £125 per ann. rooms rent free and a dinner in Hall gratis. I decidedly think it would be best for you, independently of my own wishes. By the way I should feel obliged if you wd. assault Martineau or singe off his children's eyelashes, or hurt his feelings somehow. He wrote me a very affected and disagreeable letter about Clough, saying that the less could not comprehend the greater and that he could not therefore give an opinion &c &c, and it was all in rhythmical sentences like the most labored parts of the 'Endeavours'. Taste in letter writing certainly is not his forte. Is he writing his book on Morals or what is he doing? I think his letter had some weight with the council and you may thank him for it from me, but I had rather you struck him at the same time if you don't mind.

I suppose you have forgotten the letter which this is an answer to, and I have lost it for a time at least. What you said about Mill and the population question, I thought was true, except that you did not say what I do not doubt you meant that in so far as an improvident marriage was a sin it was good to have an unfavorable public opinion operating as a penal sanction against it. I suspect that Mill thinks profligacy a less crime than a marriage on insufficient means, and taking only

---

explaining the unsettled state of his own convictions. Tagart and Richard Martineau (a cousin of James) thereupon brought a motion against the appointment. After Roscoe and WB had succeeded in deferring a vote they induced Clough to write a further letter (dated from WB's rooms in Great Coram Street), expressing willingness to dine in Hall, and giving two further assurances 'at Mr. Bagehot's suggestion': that he would lecture on Aristotle's *Ethics*, and that he repudiated the notion that religious convictions or sentiments were 'simply a matter of *taste*.' Roscoe also called on Crabb Robinson, 15 January, to enlist his support. At the meeting of 18 January Clough's letter, and letters of support from James Martineau and Samuel Smith (Clough's future father-in-law) were read out; a motion in Clough's favour (proposed by Busk and seconded by Crabb Robinson) was then carried, Tagart and Martineau having withdrawn their previous motion. Robinson, who did not want the Hall to be exclusively Unitarian, told his brother that he was 'glad to have such a man as Clough who professes to have strong convictions of the truth of Christianity, but to be unfixed on points of doctrine.' (See G. P. Johari, 'Clough at Oriel and at University Hall', *PMLA*, LXVI (1951), 420–22; Diary of Henry Crabb Robinson, November 1848–January 1849, MS Dr Williams's Library; *Correspondence of Arthur Hugh Clough*, ed. F. Mulhauser, I, 230–1).

[8] The meeting of 18 January had agreed there should be a chaplain, but could not agree about the title of the office; they advertised in the *Inquirer*, 26 May, for a minister as 'Domestic Chaplain', willing to give instruction in theology and mathematics. In November it was agreed that Hutton should be invited to become 'Secretary', who would read prayers, a means (as Crabb Robinson noted) of reconciling 'the pro-religionist and anti-religionist parties'; the eventual solution was to give Hutton the title of Vice-Principal (Crabb Robinson, MS Diary; Dr Williams's Library).

rather extreme cases of the latter, it would not be easy to find a proof that the consequences (which is the only test of morality that he would allow of) were not worse in the former case than in the latter. Of course on higher grounds it is clear that profligacy is far the worst. I did'nt go into it in my review because I thought that if touched at all, the whole moral question ought to be argued out which would have taken up a good deal of room, besides the subject not being a very pleasant one to write about: Mill's axiom, that it is an indubitable moral principle that children ought not to be begotten unless they can be maintained in 'comfort', is very vague to say the least for an ultimate truth, and not practically true in many cases where he would cite it. The real principle as it seems to me, is that persons ought not to marry unless they are morally sure that the moral dangers to themselves from remaining single are greater than those to wh. their children would be exposed from the poverty and suffering into which they would be born. A person who knew his strength of character to be more than the average might do more than this but no more can be expected as a compulsory duty from the mass of mankind. And against gross breaches of this a moderate degree of moral censure would not be undesirable, though I do not believe there is any hope of getting it from the English labourers. Of course it should be accompanied with at least an equal amount of public censure on profligacy which no English men can for any long time be expected to impose. I think myself that the censure on profligacy ought even to be greater than the comparative amounts of guilt would seem to require, because the penalty can only be imposed on the few cases which are discovered among the enormous no. which exist; and since this renders all punishment for it [subject] to a species of decimation, it seems reasonable to counteract the influence of this uncertainty in favor of the species of crime by making the penalty heavier when it comes upon those that commit them. Something like this appears to me to be the moral government of the world itself irrespective of man's intervention. I mean that it has often been observed that punishments which are long delayed are sensibly heavier than those which are immediate, and the principle of this is that the notion of intervening has given men a notion also of possible escape, and weakens the impression made by anticipated pain, and a greater intensity is therefore required to produce any given alteration in human conduct. Of course there is nothing unjust in this because the pain which it is proposed to inflict by public opinion, and that which actually is inflicted in the moral government of the world are neither of them greater than that which the particular sins in each case may happen to deserve.

Your *note* has just (that is severally[9] days ago but I really and truly had had no time to write since) turned up. I have not the shadow of an excuse for not writing. I am pretty well I believe, but I'm sluggish[10]

To HENRY CRABB ROBINSON,[1] 1 APRIL 1849

MS: Dr Williams's Library

Herd's Hill
Langport
Taunton
1 April 1849

My dear Sir,

I hope you will not be offended at my writing to ask you to be a Steward of the University College dinner this year. On the last occasion we were deserted by every member of the Council, and I think that the governing body of the College are bound not to withdraw their support from an institution so nearly connected with it—I ought perhaps to mention that there has usually been a deficit in the finances of the dinner and that in theory perhaps any Steward might be called on to contribute. But it has always been the practise hitherto for the former Students of the college to settle this among themselves without calling either on the

---

[9] Thus in MS.
[10] The remainder of the letter is missing.

* * *

[1] Henry Crabb Robinson (1775–1867), famous diarist, of whom in 1869 WB gave a sympathetic and diverting portrait (*Collected Works*, IV, 476–88), based on a friendship which began in 1849. Robinson, on the Councils of University College and University Hall, often asked the young men to his celebrated breakfasts; he first records WB's presence on 11 February 1849, when Roscoe and Osler brought with them this 'young man of talent' (MS Diary, Dr Williams's Library).

professors or on members of the Council and I have no doubt such will be [the] course adopted on the present occasion. I should add that the dinner is fixed for the 14th of May and that I write to you upon the matter in my capacity of Secretary for the present year.[2]

I am
yours sincerely
WALTER BAGEHOT.

H. C. Robinson, Esqre.

To C. C. ATKINSON, 25 APRIL 1849

MS: University College, London

6 Great Coram St. April 25th 1849.

Sir,

I am directed by the New Debating Society to acknowledge the receipt of your letter containing the notification of the assent of the Council to the foundation of the Prose Essay Prize according to the terms proposed. I am also directed to inform you that the Society at its last meeting resolved that in addition to the regulations formerly adopted, the subject chosen in each year should be submitted to the Dean of the Faculty, and also that the Examiner chosen by the Society should be submitted to the Council for their approval or rejection.

I am Sir
your obedient servant
WALTER BAGEHOT

C. Atkinson Esqre.

---

[2] Robinson wrote 5 April declining to be a steward, since he thought members of the Council should not take an active part; at the dinner he responded to the Founders' toast, recording that he 'spoke tolerably well tho' too long—But I was well received on my rising and much applauded. I went over the old topics of the first principles of the College and I spoke of myself as the representative of the last age' (MS Diary).

MAY 1849

To T. W. BAGEHOT, [15] MAY 1849

MS: Mr Norman St John-Stevas
DATE: the day after WB's University College dinner, 14 May

6 Great Coram St. May 1849.

My dearest Father,

I did not write to you on Saturday not so much on account of my University gaiety as because I had a rather important point in my professional education to consult you upon, and matters were not then in so convenient a state for writing as I knew they would be today. The point is whether it would not be better for me to postpone the rest of the conveyancing time which I have with Mr. Hall, and to commence my studies in pleading immediately. It appeared to me that I had mastered the elementary portions of real property law with tolerable completeness, and that though I cannot pretend to be a very skilful and accomplished draftsman yet that I had acquired a tolerable share of the skill in drawing and conveyancing essential to a common law barrister. Under these circumstances it became advisable for me to look out for those parts of the study and business of a conveyancer's chambers which would hereafter be most useful to me at the Common law. But upon trial I found that I was too much in the dark as to what would really be of importance to me to make anything which I could do in the way of selection quite as likely to do harm as good. In consequence of this I asked several of my friends in whose judgment I have most confidence (especially Roscoe and Richmond)[1] first whether such a scheme as my postponing the rest of my time with Mr. Hall for a year would be very unusual, and secondly whether in [their] judgment it would be an advisable course for me to adopt. The answer which I received from them was that so far as they could judge such a course of proceeding would be the best for me under the circumstances and also that there would be nothing in it opposed to established precedent and usage. I was rather quickened in the matter by learning that Mr. Quain[2] a pleader whose reputation as a teacher is very high among

[1] Christopher William Richmond (1821–95), barrister of the Inner Temple, who read with Lewis Duval and Charles Hall; went to New Zealand 1853, where he was a puisne judge from 1862.
[2] John Richard Quain (1816–76) had read law at University College and was appointed one of its first fellows 1842; after reading with Thomas Chitty he practised as a special

299

MAY 1849

young men here and who has a very considerable business had a couple of vacancies which were not likely to remain long open. I therefore asked Mr. Hall whether he would object to this course on his own account and whether he thought it would be inadvisable in me to take such a course. He told me that he would give me an answer today and he has accordingly told me two or three hours ago that he had no objection to my going to a pleader for a year on his own account and that he should be quite ready to take me back this time next year of course with a proviso that he should have due notice of my movements, and receiving a power to make any future arrangements that might be mutually convenient. As to the question whether it would be best for me to do this, he said with the caution that is habitual to old conveyancers that he must decline taking the responsibility of advising me either for or against it, but on the whole he appears to think that it would not be a bad thing for me to make the change, and he pointed out the advantage that if I should find the common law not so much to my taste as I expected I could come back without any further break to conveyancing and the kindred pursuit of equity drawing. He further advised me to consult some of my friends a little older than myself whose opinion he seemed to think was the best attainable advice under the circumstances. I had previously done this but I left the matter quite open with Mr. Hall in order that your opinion might be taken before I came to any arrangement with him. My own judgment is that this change would under my particular circumstances be highly advisable, and unless you would disapprove of it I should like to make it forthwith. I have assumed that you will not particularly care whether you pay a hundred guineas to a pleader now [or] in December next. I had nearly decided independently of this change in my plans that Mr. Quain would be the best pleader for me to go to. I hesitated for a time between him and a Mr Edye[3] who has a stupendous business, but who also I found had the reputation of taking more people than he can attend to or than even his business will employ. I have one or two more inquiries which I wish to make on this point but I do not expect that they will particularly affect the result. The upshot of the whole is that the question

---

pleader until 1851; called to the bar at the Middle Temple 1851. Became a judge of the Queen's Bench 1871, and was knighted 1872.
[3] Walter Oke Edye of 5 Paper Buildings, Temple, who appears in the *Law List*, 1849, as a certificated special pleader not at the bar.

whether or not I shall migrate to a pleader immediately stands waiting for your consideration and decision.

My dinner came off yesterday and went off very well in everybody's judgment that I know of—The music was voted *excellent*! We had three singers of eminent reputation from Exeter Hall and Westminster Abbey and a choir boy who came for his feed, and was considered to be an 'infant phenomenon'[4] of stupendous merit. I made a considerable speech principally pathetic about Lord Auckland[5] who had been kind enough to die and exultatory about the recent reforms at Oxford and Cambridge[6] which may be said without foolish boasting to be following in the track previously taken by University College and the London University. Everybody behaved with great spirit, and I think, enjoyed themselves. The principal blot was the Chairman[7] whom the committee elected last year, and who was a feeble minded Jew with an atrocious squint. He was chosen because he was the oldest student extant, but it was a mistake having him.

The levee at Somerset House[8] the other day also is considered to have gone off well. The Chancellor[9] was not quite up 'to the swing of the humbug' and did not comport himself with much dignity or éclat. His method of proceeding was to lurk behind the door and when any one was announced to rush out and shake hands with him greedily. A good many people took him for a waiter and wondered at the intensity of his affection. Of all people Sir Robert Inglis was there looking very jovial and complaisant. Lord Brougham looked very old and horribly

---

[4] Phrase often used in playbills: cf. Miss Ninetta Crummles in *Nicholas Nickleby*, ch. XXIII.
[5] George Eden, Earl of Auckland (1784–1849), one of the founders of London University and president of the Senate of University College, had died on 1 January.
[6] In November 1848 Cambridge voted for the introduction of triposes in the Natural Sciences and Moral Sciences and of a Board of Mathematical Studies; during 1849–50 Oxford revised the examination statutes and introduced new Schools for Natural Sciences and for Law and Modern History. Both were anticipating the work of the Commission on the Universities, appointed 31 August 1850.
[7] Frederic David Goldsmid (1812–66), son of Sir Isaac Lyon Goldsmid (one of the founders of University College) and the brother of Sir Francis, who fought for the removal of Jewish disabilities.
[8] On 9 May; the university's first soirée, at which those who had obtained degrees since its foundation were formally presented to the Chancellor; the *Inquirer*, 12 May, reported that some 250 graduates attended, many having come from a distance. Held in response to the graduates' petition to the Senate that degrees might in future be publicly conferred, as they were from 1850.
[9] William Cavenidsh, 2nd Earl of Burlington, afterwards 7th Duke of Devonshire (1808–91), first Chancellor of the University, 1836–56.

ugly. If he were on his trial I think a jury would not require much evidence beside his face to convict him of a sufficient number of crimes, and the older he gets the worse he looks. It was pleasant on the whole to see a great many men whom I had known, and should not otherwise have seen. Th examiners were in great force and all of them in academical clothing except Mr. Alford the poet[10] who was morbidly affectionate to me by the way and who had been mystified into believing that there were to be no gowns. I wish there had not been as mine is not paid for, and as the pleasure of wearing it is not quite worth nine guineas.[11] The only real *use* of the meeting is that it shows that the graduates take an interest in the University and this brings us nearer to certain alterations in the present charter which we wish Sir George Grey[12] to concede to us.[13] The post is going out. With love to all believe me your affectionate Son

WALTER BAGEHOT

My kind remembrances to the Bridgwater squadron if they are with you.

---

[10] The Revd Henry Alford (1810–71), later Dean of Canterbury; his *Poems and Poetical Fragments* had been published anonymously in 1833, and *The School of the Heart and Other Poems* in 1835; appointed examiner in logic and moral and intellectual philosophy in the University of London 1842.

[11] The *Inquirer* reported that to the graduates 'the scene was evidently one of high exhilaration; and their hoods and robes with their rich velvet facings—the distinctive mark of this University—added in no slight degree to its effect upon the spectator'.

[12] Sir George Grey (1779–1882), Home Secretary.

[13] The graduates had been campaigning since 1848 for a new charter which would give them—like graduates of Oxford, Cambridge, and Durham—a recognized place in the university. In April 1849 their committee (which included Timothy Smith Osler, J. R. Quain and W. C. Roscoe) sent Grey a draft charter, by which the University was to incorporate and give a share in its government to the graduates in convocation; the Senate, to whom the Secretary of State referred the draft, refused, at its meeting of 20 June, to recommend the committee's propositions, and postponed indefinitely consideration of a motion granting part of what they asked. It was not until 1858 that the evasiveness and inactivity of Senate and Secretary of State was overcome and a new charter incorporated Convocation (seeP. Dunsheath and M. Miller, *Convocation in the University of London: the First Hundred Years*, 1958, pp. 6–31). The *Inquirer*, which supported the graduates' campaign, devoted a leader to the subject, 19 May, saying that the soiree was both a recognition by the Senate of their existence and an expression of the graduates' eagerness to support the movement for incorporation.

MAY 1849

To T. W. BAGEHOT, [?MAY 1849]

MS: Mr Norman St John-Stevas
DATE: sonn after last, from subject matter

6 Great Coram St.

My dearest Father,

I think I have weighed all the objections you state to the course which I wish to take, and I confess they seem to me to be outweighed by the advantages which I expect to derive from adopting it. I think I had considered them thoroughly before and since I received your letter I have gone over the whole ground in my mind afresh. First as to what you say as to the shortness of the time between this and the long vacation. It is to be remembered that I have about four working months longer to remain with Mr. Hall. This is a considerable time and it is very important to me that it should be spent in the most profitable manner, and it seems to me quite long enough to give the plan which I propose a fair trial, if it should seem in other respects desirable.—I do not attach much weight to the advantage of confining my studies to the subject of real property law. I think indeed that it would be a mistake to spend the vacation in the study of that part of law alone. It is not *possible* to run up the knowledge of one part of law to a great height without laying the foundation of others. I find my ignorance of the common law a perpetual hindrance in my conveyancing studies now, and I expect to find it more and more so every day if I pursue them exclusively. I am met by this difficulty especially in the perusal of common law cases which ought now to fill a very important place in my legal reading. I have experienced this difficulty sooner than most men because I have from my previous studies more facility than many others in learning the book work of law. I am quite certain that I now spend a great deal of time less profitably than I might from not knowing those portions of the common law which are akin to that of real property. For instance I am now come to the time when I ought to read Coke upon Littleton[1] but I could not do so with much profit without immense labor as I should have to search in all directions for the principles of common law and pleading which he assumes his readers to be acquainted with.

---

[1] The first book of Sir Edward Coke's *Institutes*, 1628, known as *Coke on Littleton*, is virtually a legal encyclopaedia, constantly re-edited and brought up to date.

This is not theory but experience as I have been, and am trying to read him. On the whole I am not prepared to accuse myself of any impatience with my present course of study. In some respects a change would certainly not be unpleasant to me, but then I know that I am going to a new set of preliminary difficulties which are not attractive objects in general. I am a little jaded at present certainly, and the change might give me some additional freshness and vigor, but if it were in my judgment inadvisable on other grounds, I should not allow myself to be decided by this, and therefore I do not wish you to advert to it in the least. The main advantages which I expect from the plan are 1st. greater facility and profit in my reading as I have explained, 2ndly. what I dwelt on in my last letter, deferring the rest of my conveyancing studies till I should know what portions of it would be most profitable to me. At present I feel that I am working in the dark and this is not pleasant. 3rdly. an earlier opportunity of deciding whether my present preference of the common law is well founded or not.

There are other advantages but none comparable to these which seem to me sufficient to outweigh your objections when taken in connection with the observations which I have just made upon them. On the whole as I told you my judgment is strongly in favor of the plan, but of course I should not wish to adopt it if you had a strong opinion that it was undesirable. There is not anything very unusual in it after all. Many men take six months with a conveyancer at first and six months afterwards. It *is* unusual to pay the whole fee for both at once but I do not attach much weight to this. Please to write by return of post as I leave the matter quite in your hands.

Ever yours affly
W Bagehot

Love to all. My mother's letters to me have been very good value, and therefore I was surprised as well as grieved to hear that you did not think her so well as usual.

To C. C. ATKINSON, 6 AUGUST 1849

ms: University College, London

6 Great Coram St.
6 August 1849.

Sir,

I beg to acknowledge the receipt of your letter dated this morning. I have only to say in answer to it that I have very great pleasure in accepting the office of 'Fellow' which the Council of University College have thought fit to confer on me.

I am Sir
your obedient Servant

WALTER BAGEHOT

C. Atkinson Esqre.

To C. C. ATKINSON, 4 OCTOBER 1849

ms: University College, London

Langport 4th. Oct. 1849

Sir,

I beg to acknowledge the receipt of the Certificate of Proprietorship in University College[1] which you forwarded to me some days back, but which owing to my absence from town did not reach me until this morning—

I am, Sir
your obedient Servant

W BAGEHOT

C. C. Atkinson Esqre.

---

[1] Money had been raised for the foundation of the College by the selling of £100 shares, the shareholders being known as 'Proprietors'. Proprietors might cede their shares to the College by reversion, and these, with others which had become forfeit, might be conferred by the Council upon Fellows; no fee was payable for the registration of any such Fellow as a shareholder.

DECEMBER 1849

To EDITH BAGEHOT, 8 DECEMBER 1849

MS: Mr Norman St John-Stevas

6 Great Coram St.[1]
8 December 1849

My dearest Mother,

You complain of my silence and certainly not without strong reason. I have nothing to say, why judgment should not be passed against me, for I am conscious of having lazily put off writing from day to day. But in mitigation of the punishment to be imposed I have to plead that I have been very busy indeed as in addition to my usual work I am attending certain lectures on law delivered at Gray's Inn, and as I did not begin quite at the beginning of the course I had some arrears to work up in the shape of copying other peoples notes &c &c which have occupied me a good deal. Nevertheless you are entitled to maltreat me for not having written to you long ago.

I was at Hampstead on Sunday. My Uncle was in excellent force and my Aunt very tolerable. My Uncle was talking off in great style on Political Economy. I lent him John Mill's big new book nearly two years ago but he never read it at all till this summer, when as there was not much going on at Cromer he betook himself to this rather terrific publication. He seemed much pleased with a good deal of Mill's doctrine and teaching although he did not adopt the ne plus ultra views upon the currency,[2] whereof you have 'heard tell' *occasionally*. He had also been reading Southey's life which he blew me up for praising, and so did my Aunt which I told her was inconsistent with her general literary views seeing that the said life of Southey is an autobiography[3]

---

[1] In the autumn of 1849 Edward Fry, now at University College, came to lodge here with WB, remaining until he went to reside in Lincoln's Inn in 1854. He recalled WB as 'very epigrammatic and witty, and had in conversation much of the brilliance which his writings often display'; he 'used to like to talk of the career of Henry Crabb Robinson ... and how he succeeded at the Bar by the force of his chin, and Bagehot used to say that he hoped he should do the same by staring at the jury with his own big eyes' (Agnes Fry, *Memoir*, p. 45).
[2] i.e. Reynolds espoused the 'banking' school, while Mill effected a compromise between that and the 'currency' school.
[3] The incomplete autobiography in the recently published Vol. I of the 6-volume *Life and Correspondence of Robert Southey*, ed. C. C. Southey, 1849–50. The evangelical and liberal Reynoldses doubtless regarded Southey as a reactionary in religion and politics.

of extreme minuteness and simplicity beginning from the very beginning of all, and tells every possible and conceivable fact during the period of his life over which it extends. This plan of writing an autobiography has this trifling defect that no man would have patience to keep it up and to narrate on so large a scale any great portion of his history, and so it has proved in Southey's case as he stops about the time when he is thirteen. But nevertheless it is an amusing book to read and I was quite surprized at being so taken to task for liking so inoffensive a book especially as it is just in my Aunt's usual line. Mr. Newman the Catholic has been publishing a volume of sermons[4] lately which are rather remarkable both in themselves and as he has not published anything with his name[5] since he joined the Catholic Church. They are very keen and acute like all his writings and much more decisive and conclusive than his writing used to be, and he seems altogether much more in his natural place than in former times.

I will write again soon. Many thanks for your letters. With love to all

Believe me ever
Yours affectionately and obediently

WALTER BAGEHOT

To C. C. ATKINSON, 1 FEBRUARY 1850

MS: University College, London

6 Great Coram St.
1 Feby. 1850

Sir,

I am directed by a meeting of certain of the Fellows of University College to forward to you the inclosed letter addressed to the

---

For WB on Southey as a writer who had 'no events, no experiences', see *Collected Works*, I, 184.
[4] J. H. Newman, *Discourses Addressed to Mixed Congregations*, published at the beginning of December 1849. Newman had been received into the Catholic Church in 1845.
[5] WB may have heard that Newman was the author of *Loss and Gain*, published without his name in 1848; the name was given in the edition of 1853. It is the 'recent novel' from which WB quotes in his essay on Bishop Butler, published in the *Prospective Review*, October 1854 (*Collected Works*, I, 220–2).

FEBRUARY 1850

Council—[1] It is right that I should add that this letter has been signed by all the Fellows with whom we have had an opportunity of communicating; and I hope in a few days to be able to communicate to you the concurrence of the remaining Fellows.

I am, Sir
Your obedient Servant
WALTER BAGEHOT

C. C. Atkinson Esqre.

To T. W. BAGEHOT, 7 AUGUST 1850

MS: Mr Norman St John-Stevas

6 Great Coram St. 7 August 1850

My dearest Father,

You will I fear have been expecting to hear from me for a considerable time but I have not been very well—almost though not quite laid up with an unpleasant batch of headaches and my work as well as my correspondence is in considerable arrear. My mother ought to be much condoled with on the slow pace at which her recovery advances,

---

[1] At the meeting of the Council of University College on 9 February there was read 'a Memorial dated 1st. February on behalf of the Fellows of the College with 20 signatures, requesting consideration for a proposal by them that a certain number elected from and by their body should have seats in the Senate or that there should be adopted some other plan by which all the Fellows might attain what they conceive to be their legitimate place in the Constitution of the College.' The Memorial was referred to the Senate, which set up a Committee (Professor Scott, Dean of the Faculty of Arts, and Professors Carpenter, De Morgan, Foster and Newman) to consider it; their report (which has not survived) was circulated to members of Council, 6 July 1850, and on 8 February 1851 Council resolved that they concurred with the Senate that it was 'inexpedient to admit persons not being Professors . . . to a seat in the Senate' and that it was not in the Council's competence 'to constitute the Fellows any such corporate body, as is suggested in their Memorial, entrusted with a share in the discipline and management of the College'. This resolution was communicated to the Senate 11 February. (Minutes of the Senate and Council of University College, MSS University College London.)

AUGUST 1850

especially as I fear she does not appreciate the luxury of not being required to be down to breakfast. I hope I shall be able to come home in a fortnight or thereabouts more or less but more probably I hope less than more. Mr. Hall talks of leaving town sooner I believe than that as he meditates a continental tour of some extent,—and work has been ebbing at Lincoln's Inn for a fortnight past. In the Temple there was promise of a very fair assize just at the last—Quain had more to do than he could very well get through, two of his men being ill and I went down and did a couple of days' work for him in consequence. You see more business and more points of law in two days in the Temple than you do in a week at a conveyancers—or in a fortnight when work is slack. The County Courts you will have observed have turned out not so bad as might have been anticipated. I should not[1] imagine that under the amendment of the House of Lords they will produce any great change and their competition will be a very serviceable stimulus to the simplification of the procedure in the superior courts:[2] so that on the whole perhaps they will rather do us good than harm—

The judges have power to make a set of new rules for reforming both pleading[3] and other parts of the procedure of the superior courts and Lord Campbell[4] is said to have shown great disposition to make their reforms really efficient and extensive. It will be difficult to get Baron Parke[5] (who from his great ability knowledge and experience has very great weight) to concur in anything very sweeping. His judicial reputation which is greater than that of any other living

---

[1] Added in another hand.
[2] Set up by the County Courts Act of 1846, as a remedy for delays and expense in the superior courts; by the Extension Act of 1850 their jurisdiction in actions for debt and for recovery was extended to £50, or to a higher sum if both parties agreed.
[3] By an act of 1850 (13, 14 Victoria, c. 16).
[4] John, 1st Baron Campbell (1779–1861), who had succeeded Denman as Lord Chief Justice in March 1850.
[5] James Parke (1782–1868), Baron of the Exchequer Court 1834; known for his attachment to the technicalities of special pleading—it was supposed that their abolition by the acts of 1852 and 1854 led to his resignation in 1855. In 1856 he was created a life peer, a dignity which the Queen had been advised to revive in order to improve the appellate jurisdiction of the House of Lords; but the letters patent creating him Lord Wensleydale were referred to the Committee of Privileges, which ruled that he was not entitled to sit or vote in Parliament. In July 1856 he was granted an hereditary peerage. The revival of life peerages was one of the reforms recommended by WB in the *English Constitution* (*Collected Works*, V, 284): it was brought about in 1958 (see V, 122).

common law judge, a good deal rests on a series of decisions which would be much lessened in value by any extensive changes in pleading; and it is hard to ask a man to depreciate his own work and impair his own reputation. Nevertheless I think we may expect that some measures of considerable value will be soon forthcoming either from the judges or from the commission which is now sitting on the subject[6]—

I was at Hampstead on Sunday last. My Aunt was very tolerable and my Uncle recovering his good looks rapidly, though like my Mother he has been a good deal pulled down by his illness. He was much interested about Baron Rothschild as my Mother also seems to be—

I suppose Lord John will carry his resolutions without difficulty though Page Wood has a very fair case and has argued it very ably.[7] Probably I suppose Lord John's view is the correct one, though it involves what is at first sight an odd anomaly, that Baron Rothschild might, if he had so chosen been sworn upon the *Old* Testament to an oath purporting to be 'on the faith of a *Christian*'. As the Jewish formalities are adopted in part, there is some ground for keeping them throughout. I suppose the answer is that a Christian *might* prefer being sworn on the Old Testament, and in matter of fact a crotchetty individual who said he was a Christian did once desire to be sworn in that manner—So that perhaps this oddity is not much of an objection to Lord John's view in reality though at first it struck me forcibly.

If you wish me to come home, you must please to send me £35 at an early period, to pay off incumbrances. Is Watty returned from his pilgrimage? I hope he did'nt find it slow being *on duty*—

Love to all.

Yours affly.

W BAGEHOT

---

[6] The Common Law Procedure Commission was set up in May 1850 and issued its report in June 1851 (*P.P.*, 1851, XXII, 20). The commissioners criticized the system of written pleadings (by which the form and course of pleadings and therefore the issue to be tried was settled by counsel before the parties came to court), because cases were often decided on points of pleading without reference to substantial merits. The defects they found were removed by the Common Law Procedure Act of 1852, and that of 1854 which followed the second report.

[7] Since 1830 the Lords had thrown out five bills passed by the Commons, to enable Jews to take the oath. Baron Lionel Nathan de Rothschild (1808–79), banker and philanthropist, elected for the City of London in 1847 (with Lord John Russell as his colleague)

JANUARY 1851

To EDITH BAGEHOT, [?JANUARY 1851]

MS: Mr Norman St John-Stevas
DATE: paper watermarked 1850, and reference to cardplaying suggests WB's return from Christmas holiday

> 6 Great Coram St.
> Tuesday morning

My dearest Mother,

I arrived here last evening with exemplary punctuality—the express train being only two minutes behind its time—I contrived to get through the evening without any loo.[1] I suppose the family find existence easier without the perpetual wear and tear of my row. I think I shall go to Hampstead tonight—Love to all—

> Yours affly and obediently
> WALTER BAGEHOT

accordingly sat for four sessions below the bar of the House, unable to take his place or vote; in 1850 he tried his rights under the existing law, and after discussion was allowed to take the oath on the Old Testament 30 July. He took the oaths of allegiance and supremacy in the accustomed form, but from that of abjuration omitted the words 'on the true faith of a Christian'. William Page Wood (1801–81), later Lord Chancellor and Baron Hatherley, one of the campaigners for the removal of Jewish disabilities, argued that the legislature had severed the oath in two parts—that which was sworn to and that which was sworn by—and that the Baron was excused from swearing 'by the true faith of a Christian' without any dispensing power being needed. Russell, himself a zealous supporter of bills enabling Jews to take the oath, could not agree that it was in the power of the House to dispense with those words. It was eventually resolved that Rothschild was not entitled to vote or sit, and that the form of the oath should be taken into serious consideration next session (*Debates*, CXIII, 769–815). It was not until 1858 that Rothschild was permitted to take his seat, following a compromise by which the oath was administered in either House in the form determined by its members. The words 'on the true faith of a Christian' were removed by the Parliamentary Oaths Act of 1866.

* * *

[1] WB had played this card game, with counters known as 'fish', since childhood: in *Physics and Politics* he recalled 'a set of boy loo-players, of whom I was one', and their superstition about 'a certain "pretty fish" ' which brought luck (*Collected Works*, VII, 91).

To EDITH BAGEHOT, MARCH 1851

MS: Mr Norman St John-Stevas
DATE: probably late March, see n. 3

6 Great Coram St.
March 1851

My dearest Mother,

My 'well' headaches are quite gone and I am completely well again now, except that the laziness and languor of the influenza hang about me still. It is odd that it wont go away: it has professed to be going away so long. As to what you ask, I am not aware that a dissenting minister has any legal right to the title of 'Reverend'. Indeed the secular law of this country does not I fancy recognize any such title even in the case of clergymen of the English Church. The title is never given them in pleadings, they are called 'clerks'. Indeed it is usual to add 'Revd.' but this is a courtesy.

In the Ecclesiastical courts where they administer the peculiar Church law, I suppose that English clergymen have a right to the title as Catholic priests have by the Canon law of the Catholic Church— dissenting sects I fancy have no law about the matter.

As you have heard from my Aunt I was at Hampstead on Sunday. The family were by no means brilliant and Dr. Crawfurd was there preying upon society which [does] not tend to elevate the spirits of mankind. It is a bad habit to set up for *instructive* conversation: it generally ends in making a man a *bore*. I have just been turning the pages of a new edition of *Hartley* Coleridge's Poems which has just come out with a memoir of him by his Brother Derwent—[1] the Principal of St. Marks. It is a very curious life. He had exactly the same sort of weakness, vice, want of self-controul or whatever you choose to call it which his father had, only the latter took opium and Hartley only drank beer. In the intervals of the beer he used to talk they say like the wisest philosopher and his poems especially the sentimental ones are very religious indeed, but he could not stand thirst. It is very curious that the same kind of weakness should be found both in father and son— in so extreme and remarkable a degree: it looks so like an hereditary

---

[1] The Revd Derwent Coleridge (1800–83), first principal of St Mark's College, Chelsea, established by the National Society 1841.

disease, and goes to support what the Medical men want now to call
'*Moral* Insanity'.² And for aught we can tell there may be such a
thing, though it would never do to allow it to be an excuse for crime
in courts of justice as the Medical Men wanted at one time to make it.
The Coleridges knew what they were doing was wrong, but, it rather
seems as if they could not help doing it which would be exactly what
is called 'Moral Insanity'. I confess, I think it was so in their case.

I am glad how quick Easter is approaching and Lent advancing.³
I shall be home *soon*—

Yours affly and obediently

W BAGEHOT

To W. C. ROSCOE, [?MARCH 1851]

Text from RB, X, 187–8, dated Great Coram St
DATE: probably March 1851, the date of the Preface of *Violenzia*, which WB has just received

My dear Roscoe,

I send you the final proofs of *Violenzia*.¹ I received yesterday from
R.H.H. the Preface which I have sent to Parker. I read it with much in-
terest and like the Sonnet² and what you say of the play, exceedingly.³
I suppose it is true and it is certainly excellently said; but I altogether

---

² WB would have met this theory in the writings of Dr J. C. Prichard: *Treatise on Insanity*, 1835, and *On the Different Forms of Insanity in Relation to Jurisprudence*, 1842.
³ In 1851 Ash Wednesday fell on 5 March and Easter Sunday on 20 April.

* * *

¹ W. C. Roscoe's verse tragedy, published by John W. Parker in May 1851; publication was anonymous because, according to Hutton, 'the reputation of a poet, even if attained, might have injured his prospects' at the bar, which he did not give up until 1852 (W. C. Roscoe, *Poems and Essays*, ed. R. H. Hutton, 1860, I, xcvi). The book was seen through the press by WB and Hutton because Roscoe was abroad (RB, X, 187).
² Following the title-page; its subject is Roscoe's receding from poetry in a life that is 'outward bound'.
³ Roscoe contended that the struggle of a religious spirit to conform to duty in difficult circumstances was a 'fit and lofty subject for a dramatic poet'; he compared the conflict

object to the introduction of Kossuth and the Hungarian refugees.[4] I can't see that they have anything to do with the matter in hand. If it appeared on affidavit that Ethel was a Magyar, and the king an Austrian, no doubt there would be a connection, and I would strongly advise the introduction of this link. And seriously I think a dedication—still more a dedication requiring an argumentative defence—should have *some* reference to the matter in hand, and this plainly has not, and will strike readers, at least it did me, with alarm and consternation. Moreover you can't afford space enough to give the real reasons for your opinion, and I doubt whether it is very accordant with that superexcellent taste for which you,—,—,[5] to give a [mere][6] *obiter dictum* on a point whereon the public mind is so divided. This should only be done when the writer has shown, by his familiarity with kindred topics or otherwise that he knows more of the matter than his readers. Now it does not appear from this play that you know anything about Hungary, it *does* appear that you know a good deal about *women*, but perhaps there is no necessary connection in these cognitions. I don't think opinions of this sort much affect the public, there is a national feeling against convictions which a man is very eager to express, they are to be suspected.

Yours ever speaking plainly,
W. BAGEHOT

---

in his play to that in Kingsley's *Saint's Tragedy*, but said that his had been begun before Kingsley's appeared, and its theme had been suggested to him by the preface to Shelley's *Cenci*. He had tried to make it a 'real play', although aware that its character would 'exclude it from the stage': at its climax the hero, Ethel, has to resist the temptation to take violent revenge on the king, who is responsible for the violation and death of the girl Ethel loves. Kingsley himself, while finding the plot 'revoltingly coarse and horrible', praised the 'terse racy style of its language' and the conception of Ethel, and hailed the author as 'a true creative poet' (*Fraser's*, XLIV [December 1851], 626–8).

[4] The play is dedicated to Louis Kossuth (1802–94), the Hungarian patriot, in exile in Turkey since July 1849; came to England October 1851. In his preface Roscoe defends the dedication on the grounds that Hungary is the noblest battle-field of the cause of constitutional freedom, while England is engrossed with an 'appreciation of material improvement' typified by the Great Exhibition (pp. xi–xiii).

[5] Thus in printed text.

[6] Printed text reads 'more', clearly in error.

APRIL 1851

To W. C. ROSCOE, [?APRIL 1851]

Text from RB, X, 185–7, dated Herd's Hill, March 1851, but probably after Easter, since WB says he will be in London 'this day week'

My dear Roscoe,

Would you be so kind as to look for me at 'Rex V. The Churchwardens of Crossley',[1] 5 Adolphus and Ellis,[2] page 10, and send me an account thereof. The point for which I want it, is of this sort. Under the 59 George the 3rd, chapter 134, churchwardens have a power to mortgage church-rates to obtain any sum they deem necessary for the repairs of the church, Vestry, Bishop and incumbent thereto assenting. Now, some of my family being bankers, have been weakminded enough to lend £1,000 or so, on such a security without requiring anybody to be personally liable. Everybody in the parish has quarrelled with everybody, and the security is not forthcoming. By the deed of mortgage the money was to be paid by six instalments beginning in '46. In fact they only paid the first instalment and the first year's interest and then quarrelled and the vestry or majority thereof refused to make any rate and the churchwardens and minority made one which they can't get paid and the validity of which is being contested up at Wells in the Spiritual court. This was in '48 and since then they have made no rates whatever, and the mortgagees have had nothing. They now imagine that it would have a good moral effect, if they went for a mandamus[3] to the churchwardens to make the rate. Montague Smith[4] whose opinion they took rather throws cold water on them and seems to say that the aforesaid case decides that each instalment should be paid annually when due and that the mortgagee loses his money, if he does come *that very year* for a mandamus to get a rate made, and if possible collected. I confess this strikes me as monstrous. I can understand that Lord Denman may have held, say as

---

[1] In fact 'Dursley'; perhaps an error in transcription.
[2] J. L. Adolphus and T. F. Ellis, *Reports of Cases Argued and Determined in the Court of the King's Bench*, Vol. V (Trinity and Michaelmas Terms 1836), 1838.
[3] Prerogative writ granted at the discretion of the court of the Queen's Bench, where there is a legal right to have a function of a person or corporation exercised but no specific legal remedy for enforcing that right or the alternative legal remedy is less convenient.
[4] Montagu Edward Smith (1809–91), barrister of Gray's Inn, joined the Western circuit

against a parishioner, that the proper mode of managing the parochial business was to make and levy annual rates to discharge annual liabilities, but I can't fancy that a mortgagee is to lose his money unless he applies to Q.B. the very moment it becomes due.[5] John Lotd Campbell will look at that, I think. In this very case the mortgagee simply waited because the validity of the rate actually made being contested, they thought it useless to compel others to be made in the same form. They may be wrong in this very likely but I can't think they deserve on that account to be mulcted of their money. No rates could *now* be made except by mandamus as the parish churchwarden sticks out and refuses, but I think the farmers would pay a rate that the Q.B. directed to be made. I should therefore be immensely obliged if you would tell me about this 'anomalous' case which seems to me very hard, as I rather back up my family to go for a mandamus on the general principle of going ahead when you have the moral merits with you and also on Notteram's rule 'Bagehot always recommend[6] proceedings'. It is a happy case altogether, they got one suit on for judgment in the Bishop's court when the Defendant maliciously *died* and of *course* the suit abates and it will take several years apparently to work another up to the same critical point. Brilliant system altogether church-rate law. I recommend [Quain's][7] being sent in for a mandamus and hope to carry it. I believe (this case excepted) they would win and there does not seem to be anything even in the objections taken to the rate which has been made, but it isn't easy to get the money for all that—so out of the suavity of your disposition tell us about Lord Denman's decision. He muddled a good deal in his time. I shall be up this day week, and have settled to go into equity. I couldn't live cheerfully down here, and though I regret immensely that I ever opened a law

---

and was admitted to the Middle Temple 1839; appointed justice of the Common Pleas and knighted 1865; MP for Truro 1859.

[5] The cases were not parallel: at Dursley money had been borrowed to pay for repairs six years after the repairs had been done; Denman's judgment was that parish rates were 'not to be made retrospectively' (Adolphus and Ellis, V, 15–16).

[6] Printed text reads 'recommends' in error. In 'Bad Lawyers and Good' WB recalls: 'When, years since, I was reading law, I had laid for me a peculiar rule for pleasing the less honest sort of attorneys: "Always," said a very experienced man, "always recommend *proceedings*, and then you will be sure to succeed."' (*Collected Works*, VII, 256).

[7] Printed text reads 'Main's'; no 'Main' appears in the *Law List*, and 'Quain's' (easily misread in WB's hand) must be correct.

MAY 1851

book, I must stick to London now come what may, and I am sure of enough to live on, in any case.

Ever yours,

W. BAGEHOT

I am responsible for some delay in sending you the account of *Violenzia* for which I apologise. My old landlady had a really profound idea that it was too big for foreign postage.

To EDITH BAGEHOT, 8 MAY 1851
MS: Mr Richard W. Lyman

6 Great Coram St.
8 May 1851

My dearest Mother,

I took a start yesterday and went to see the Queen open the Exhibition.[1] It went off very well though her Majesty looked matronly and aged and the ladies in attendance on her were an affecting spectacle. The only accurate idea that I can give you of the Exhibition is that it is a great fair under a cucumber frame: the booths very numerous and the glass case very well painted: only it must be one of the Swiss fairs where they sell everything from the best jewellery down to needles and thread. The day was most brilliant and the crowd[2] enormous both of which were essential to the goodness of the spectacle as the palace

---

[1] The Great Exhibition of the Art and Industry of Nations, originated in 1849 by the Prince Consort and Henry Cole, President of the Royal Society of Arts. The greatest difficulty facing the Commissioners (whose president was Prince Albert and chairman Lord Granville) was the design of a building suitable to house the Exhibition on its 16-acre site between Albert Gate and Princes Gate, Hyde Park. This was solved by the inspiration of the Duke of Devonshire's gardener, the remarkable Joseph Paxton, who in June 1850 presented his revolutionary plan for a vast replica of the new *Victoria Regia* lily-house at Chatsworth, a structure of glass, iron and wood, which could be taken down, extended or reduced in size; it was soon popularly known as the Crystal Palace—the name invented for it by *Punch*. Full details of the Exhibition, from its inception to the removal of the building to Sydenham—where it burnt down in 1936—are given in Yvonne ffrench, *The Great Exhibition: 1851*, 1950.

[2] On 20 April an earlier decision—prompted by fears for the Queen's safety—that the opening should be private, had been reversed, following widespread public protest.

would be cold and icy without inhabitants and sun is required for the proper apportionment of light and shade and the due appreciation of the painted roof. The form of the building is that of a cross—the long stroke from an analogy to Church architecture being called the nave, and the short stroke the transept. The Queen sat in the centre with the crowd around and behind her,[3] and I was lucky enough to get a place in the front row of one of the galleries immediately overlooking the chair of state, and almost exactly over the head of your aged and infirm friend the Duke of Wellington. The proceedings were in the nature of pantomime as I could not hear a single syllable either of the address or the answer to it, and ninety-nine hundreds of the audience were similarly circumstanced: a great majority not being able to see anything either. I fancied that I caught two or three words of the archbishop's grace or benediction but I am not sure: at any rate I heard a sermonic tone of voice which was a great satisfaction. I suppose the Archbishop was inserted in the program to please the foreigners who are in the habit of consecrating railways and all sorts of secular places: otherwise I think he might as well have been left out as there was nothing there in keeping with him,—[4] nobody minded him and the Queen looked as if she wished that he would leave off. The court looked brilliant enough as far as the men went: the foreign magnates very well got up, our Cabinet ministers like town criers and the Lord Chancellor like a Butler on the stage—There was a strong light upon them, and a tree behind—a real tree[5] growing in the ground and just coming into leaf—which threw them out well and was original and picturesque looking. I walked about for an hour or two when the Queen went. There is an immense amount of wealth industry and ingenuity and all that sort of thing: and I suppose the best of all things that can be manufactured is there: but no one thing can make much im-

---

[3] Victoria recorded: 'The sight, as we came to the middle, where the steps and chair (which I did *not* sit on) were placed, with the beautiful Crystal Fountain just in front of it—was magical—so vast, so glorious, so touching. . . . The tremendous cheers, the joy expressed in every face, the immensity of the building, the mixture of palms, flowers, trees, statues, fountains,—the organ . . . and my beloved husband, the author of this "Peace Festival" ' (diary entry, quoted ffrench, *op. cit.*, p. 188).
[4] There had been some uneasiness about the inclusion of a religious aspect in the ceremony; Sumner, Archbishop of Canterbury, delivered a specially composed prayer of thanksgiving and national pride.
[5] The vast transept with its curvilinear roof had been added to the original design in order to protect a clump of elms at the north entrance: the trees became a special feature of the Exhibition.

pression in such a mass: the point of the scene is their number and the good effect of the whole. In the exact centre is a stunning fountain of glass made by the Oslers of Oxford St.[6] The foreign departments are much behindhand: the United States especially: indeed at present nothing satisfactory can be collected except that in that country they are extremely well off for soap. They have an immense compartment all to themselves at the end of the nave and nothing hardly in it except busts in soap of the Queen and other people.[7] It must be amusing to wash yourself with yourself and a great relief from the wretchedness of the employment. There were a great many Americans in the crowd. Quain—with whom I went—got hold of one who swore he was member in Congress for California and looked like a Smithfield drover. Otherwise there were much fewer foreigners than I expected. They were certainly not a twentieth part of the crowd. There are a good many of questionable aspect in the streets, but few I take it that abound in coin. I hear that the house-letting people are at a low ebb in consequence. Hope you can read this scrawl. I write in a hurry as I want to go to bed—

Yours affly

W BAGEHOT

I shall go to Hampstead on Sunday. Love to all.

---

[6] Follett and Clarkson Osler, glass chandelier, lustre and table glass manufacturers, of 44 Oxford St. They were sons of Timothy Smith Osler's father, Thomas, by his first marriage to Fanny, daughter of Abraham Follett.
[7] The United States had applied for more space than they could fill, although their exhibits included inventions and the very popular statue of the Greek slave by Hiram Powers. *Punch* commented: 'their contribution to the world's industry consists as yet of a few wine-glasses, a square or two of soap, and a pair of salt cellars' (quoted ffrench, *op. cit.*, p. 238).

To EDITH BAGEHOT, 20 OCTOBER 1851
Text from RB, X, 190-1

41, Rue de Vaugirard,[1]
20th October 1851.

My dearest Mother,

I have not heard from you for a long time but I suppose that you will write to me soon. Your friend Madame Meynieux[2] desired to be remembered to you with such exceeding vigour that it seems a plain duty to put her affection in the very front of my letter. I had the honour of dining with her some days ago, and she made a really splendid panegyric on her 'bien ancienne amie' as she calls you (antiquity of course being your line) for the benefit of a stout and impressive French lady to whom she was introducing me. She stated that a few centuries back when she had the pleasure of knowing you she had been of all your many 'idolateurs' and 'idolatrices' by far the greatest. I was fumbling for a Christian answer to this heathenish sentiment and feebly striving to be agreeable to the French lady aforesaid, when I was surprised to hear, in a voice that seemed familiar to me, 'Hello, I say, Bagehot'. It turned out to be a legal friend of mine, Adams[3] by name, who in his surprise at seeing me very nearly overturned Monsieur Meynieux (a round man fit to bowl with) who was advancing with numerous bows to receive him. I admire your old friend exceedingly.

There is rather an interesting crisis in politics here just now. Prince Louis[4] has changed his tack and his ministers won't change with him. The whole object and idea of his present policy is to secure the Revision

---

[1] WB went to Paris in August, 'ostensibly to perfect himself in the French language, but more exactly to change the mental atmosphere' (RB, X, 189); see also letter to Roscoe, ?10-11 January 1852.
[2] Whom Mrs Bagehot had met during a visit to Paris with her brother, Vincent Stuckey, many years before.
[3] Probably Francis Ottiwell Adams (1826-89), entered at the Inner Temple 1847 and at Lincoln's Inn 1850; barrister, Lincoln's Inn, 1852; entered the diplomatic service 1854; knighted 1886.
[4] Charles Louis Napoleon (1808-73) had been elected President of the Republic in December 1848. Article 45 of the Constitution prohibited re-election of a president to a further term of office, and France was faced with the prospect of losing President and Assembly in the spring of 1852. In July 1851 the President had failed to get the three-fourths majority in the Assembly, necessary for a change in the Constitution, to allow him a further term. After failing in November to change the character of the Assembly by

of the article of the Constitution which renders him ineligible at the next Presidential Election. This is rather a self-seeking end for the head of a great nation, but he has this excuse that the country really wish him to remain where he is, and all the better sort of people are ready to revise the constitution in order to keep him. Some of this attachment he owes to the good sense and the strength of character which in the main he has shown during his time of office, but much to the general spirit of timidity and depression which is the general sentiment here in the middle and especially in the commercial classes. Anybody who is in will be supported by people who dread any change and live by the mercantile credit that Revolutions are certain to destroy. On this account I think the President has a very good chance of beating, though the legal difficulties imposed by the constitution are very great. It required three-fourths of the assembly to consent to the revision and there is an organised opposition, partly Socialistic and partly factious which is about, or rather more than a fourth, and which won't hear of it at any price. The present plan is to break up this opposition by proposing the repeal of a certain electoral law which requires three years' continuous residence in a district before you can vote there. There is a good law enough in itself, but perhaps scarcely wise here now. The only sort of institution for which the Red Republicans have any respect is Universal Suffrage and unless it could be really and substantially allowed it seems unwise to tamper with it and weaken the attachment to the one constitution which can really pretend to any. It is hardly consistent also with the Constitution of which Universal Suffrage is a main feature. However, this may be the offer to the Red Republican opposition that he will consent to the abolition of this law if they will on their side consent to the revision.[5]

Lamartine who is now from personal grounds in opposition, Emile de Girardin,[6] a sort of French Cobbett, the head of the news-

---

enlarging the electorate (see n. 5), he staged a *coup d'état* on 2 December: 20,000 opponents were arrested (including Deputies, Republican journalists, and army officers), the Assembly was dissolved, and proclamations were printed, appealing to the people and the army for support. WB was present at the unsuccessful attempt by Republicans to oppose the *coup* on 4 December: see next.

[5] The law which disenfranchized almost a third of the electorate had been passed in May 1850, in order to keep republicans out of the Assembly; Louis Napoleon proposed its repeal at the opening of the new session on 4 November 1851; the proposal was narrowly defeated.

[6] Emile de Girardin (1802–81), pioneer of cheap journalism in France; editor of *La*

paper world, and a member of the Assembly, are all ready to consent to this compromise. But it is yet doubtful whether the law of election can be repealed, or whether if repealed, enough of the opposition would be willing to vote for the Revision. 'The board has not determined on the result of what has taken place'. But there is a general impression that somehow or other the President will win, whether by removing or quashing the technical difficulties is to be seen. The present constitution is not liked, and the Republic is felt to be rather a lame and impotent conclusion after being introduced with so great a flourish of trumpets four years ago. The ouvriers use the phrase *Vous avez diné sur la République*—'You've been and dined on the Republique' as equivalent to the Anglican compliment, 'What a muff *you* are'.

Yours affectionately,

W. BAGEHOT

To T. W. BAGEHOT, 5 DECEMBER 1851

MS: Mr Norman St John-Stevas

Paris, 5 Decr. 1851

My dearest Father,

I forgot the electric telegraph[1] and thought that my note would be the first—or about the first intelligence that you would receive of the new Revolution. Wednesday was extremely quiet—unnaturally so almost —and everybody seemed to have stood in the streets to know as soon as might be what would turn up, however no one seemed to like to stay still in any place for fear that something of great importance might have happened or be happening somewhere else—

I assisted in the evening at a great gathering in the Boulevards and a man whose name I could not learn read a paper announcing the déchéance of the President, but the appearance of a very few soldiers sent the

---

Presse 1836–56, 1862–66; member of Chamber of Deputies 1834–51, 1877–81. Supporter of Louis Napoleon's election to the presidency, but now in opposition. WB speaks of him with contempt in his *Inquirer* letters: see *Collected Works*, IV, 43, 72–3.

My dearest Father,

I forgot the electric telegraph and thought that my note would be the first — or about the first intelligence that you would receive of the new Revolution. Wednesday was extremely quiet — unnaturally so almost — & every-body seemed to have stand in the streets to know as soon as might be what would turn up; however no one seemed to like to stay still in any place for fear that something of great importance might have happened or be happening somewhere else — I assisted in the evening at a great gathering on the Boulevards & a man whose name I could not learn read a paper announcing the decheance of the President. but the appearance of a very few soldiers sent the swarm in all directions, for they were mere peaceful citizens or curious foreigners & had no fighting attitude. Altogether the characteristic of that day was exactly what Lord Byron in some letter calls "Quiet inquietude". Yesterday Thursday — the coup d'état you will remember was on Tuesday — was much

Letter to his father, 5 December 1851.

swarm in all directions for they were mere peaceful citizens or curious foreigners and had no fighting aptitude. Altogether the characteristic of that day was exactly what Lord Byron in some letter calls' quiet inquietude'. Yesterday Thursday—the coup d'état you will remember was on Tuesday—was much more disturbed—the Palais Royal was closed and a formidable notice was affixed to all the walls informing all persons that the 'enemies of order' had begun their operations. Being curious to see their tactics, I immediately hied to the Boulevard St. Martin which I fancied would be the centre of operations for it is in the narrow streets leading out of that great thoroughfare that all the most 'exalted' of the *ouvriers* are said to reside. I had not been misinformed for as soon as I got on the ground, the preparations for barricades were immediately visible. It is a simple process, though there being no paving stones on the Boulevards was a difficulty—but the stones of a half-built house supplied the place excellently well for the one where I was. These with palings, iron rails, planks, &c and three overturned omnibuses and two upset cabs completed the bulwark. It took about half an hour to make *mine*—as the Boulevards are about there very wide, but others especially in the side streets were run up much more rapidly. The people making them were of two very unlike sorts—immensely the greater number were mere 'boys' or lads—*gamins* is the technical word I am told—the lower sort of shop boys and some of the better artisans, not bad looking young fellows at all, liking the *fair*, and in general quite unarmed. Beside these and directing them were a few old stagers who have been at it these twenty years—men whose faces I do not like to *think* of—yellow sour angry fanatical, who would rather shoot you than not.

Each barricade that I saw was constructed under the eye of one or two, not more, of such fellows—the most of them do not I was told show until the building is over and the fighting begins. They were implicitly obeyed—indeed a man must have a great deal of pluck not to do as they said, for they were armed and a trifle bigotted in their temper. These—Montagnards[2] is their name technically—I very studiously

---

[1] Between London and Paris; the Dover-Calais section had been completed in October 1851.
[2] The term 'Montagnards' for extreme Republicans and revolutionaries came from the time of the first French Revolution, when the extreme party led by Robespierre and Danton was known as 'la Montagne' because it occupied the highest position in the chamber. For WB's description of the 'Montagnard' in his first letter to the *Inquirer*, see *Collected Works*, IV, 32–3.

DECEMBER 1851

avoided but I asked a question or two of some of the young fellows and found that *they* thought that all the troops were out of Paris, that the provinces—Lyons especially—were rising, and that all the military would be wanted to prevent *their* march on the capital. It was likely enough that there was a row at Lyons, but not likely from the distance that they could yet be at the gates of Paris. Why the troops did not come I do not know, but for I suppose a couple of hours the barricade-people had it all their own way, and erected I think *five* in that part of the Boulevards, one after another, with about a hundred yards between them. I scrambled over two and got as far as I dared towards the centre. The silence was curious. On the frontier a raging though industrious multitude, within the kingdom no one—a woman hurrying home, an old man shrugging his shoulders, all as quiet as the grave.

I did not stay long in the inside, as I feared the troops would come and I might be shot that Napoleon might rule the French or some Montagnard might be so kind as to do it just to keep his hand in. The moment the barricades were done, they begun to break into the shops and houses, not to rob, but for arms. As soon as they were satisfied there were no more weapons to be had, they chalked 'death to robbers' or something of that sort on the shutters and went away. I should not think they stole sixpennyworth of any matter except powder and guns. The Montagnards would have shot any young fellow that tried it on. I tried hard to hire a window to see the capture of the fortress as well as its erection but this was not to be for everybody said they meant to *shut* their windows, and indeed it would not have been very safe to look out of them in the firing. I therefore retired, though not too quickly. It is a bad habit to run in a Revolution—somebody may think you are the 'other side' and shoot at you—but if you go calmly and look *English*, there is no particular danger. As I retired I met the troops at some distance, slowly and cautiously hemming in the insurgents. Anybody might go out who would but no one come in. The whole operation reminded me very much of the porteous mob in the Heart of Midlothian.[3] If you will read over that again you will have the best idea of the thoroughbred Parisian émeute that I know. There is the same discipline, order, absence of plunder and

---

[3] The storming of the Tolbooth in Ch. VII.

in the leaders the same deep hatred and fanaticism. I am pleased to have had an opportunity of seeing it *once* but once is enough, as there is I take it a touch of sameness in this kind of sight, and I shall not go again into the citadel of operations. In no other part is there any danger for a decently careful person. Today is much quieter. The troops soon cleared my barricade, though I heard canon and musketry, the latter in plenty, and there was blood,[4] a good deal of it, in the approachable parts of the Boulevards. The field of the hardest battle was not to be approached for soldiers. I have not got time for a word more. You will have better accounts in the English papers than we have here. Only those of the Government are allowed to appear and these I know from the description of what I saw are written to tranquillize the provinces etc. and diminish the disorder much. However *my* notion is that the President will hold his own.

Many thanks to my mother for her note and also for your letter. I will write in a day or two.

Yours ever

W BAGEHOT.

I hope and believe that this letter is true. People spreading false news are liable to be brought before a military commission which is apt to shoot and imprison.

To EDITH BAGEHOT, 7 DECEMBER 1851

Text from RB, X, 197–8

7th December 1851,
Sunday.

My dearest Mother,

At this moment Paris is as tranquil as a tea-party, at any rate to the eye. The barricaders have been quashed, and *according to me* there will be no more fighting of consequence for some days and it may be for some months. I do not think it possible for a populace to rise with

---

[4] The 30,000 troops waited until 3 in the afternoon, when the 1200 defenders were within their barricades, to go in. By 9 in the evening all was over: barricades were smashed, defenders overwhelmed by musketry and bayonet charges, with no quarter given and many prisoners shot out of hand.

bayonets so close upon them; the Government have as yet been very determined, cruel and bloody according to their enemies, and I cannot imagine that if they continue to pursue the same policy there can be any insurrection of importance; but no one can know this. The Montagnards *may* turn dexperate, but they are much broken, their best leaders being in prison and in London. I wish for the President decidedly myself as against M. Thiers[1] and his set in the Parliamentary World; even *I* can't believe in a Government of barristers and newspaper editors,[2] and also as against the Red party who, though not insincere, are too abstruse and theoretical for a plain man. It is easy to say what they would abolish, but horribly hard to say what they would *leave*, and what they would *find*. I am in short what they would call a *réactionnaire*, and I think I am with the majority—a healthy habit for a young man to contract. M. Bein whom I live with said to me, 'I do not approve of this violence and *coup d'état*, but I am for the President because he's for "the tranquillity".' People want to be let alone; it is clear that the Republic has been *burgled*, and if the President were turned out no one knows who would come in. For the moment, the alternative is between him and the Socialists. How long he may last is another question. Your friend Madame Meynieux pitched into his private character yesterday at a great pace. She was arguing with a French lady whom I did not know. I have never heard two people talk so fast and so well at the same time. M. Meynieux and myself looked on openmouthed and in perfect silence. I could not talk that pace in English, much less in French, where I require five minutes to express four ideas. I listened patiently for a long time. The French lady was for the President and your friend violently against. She is allied with some of the Parliamentary people whom he has knocked about. She professes to be a Socialist but *not* a Republican; on the contrary she disdains forms of government and is exclusively strong on the principle of 'association'. I can't tell you, for I do not know, *who* is to associate with *whom*? She don't at all approve of the common Red Socialist, indeed the weak point of the system is that no Socialist will ever associate with any other; all I know is that, as they say in the kitchen,

---

[1] Louis Adolphe Thiers (1797–1877), statesman and historian; in 1848 a moderate republican under whose influence the *Constitutionnel* had taken Louis Napoleon's side. Among the 16 deputies arrested after the *coup d'état*. For WB's assessment of him, see *Collected Works*, IV, 43–4.
[2] As WB says in the *Inquirer* letters: see *Collected Works*, IV, 34, 75.

somebody is to 'keep company' with somebody. M. Meynieux didn't seem so strong on that, he is a man with good notions of food but not much general ability, though jolly, and awake to the existing world. *His* idea was that if he said anything on the Boulevards, he might be 'had up' for it, which he didn't like However, in fact, people say what they please, and your friend did not please to spare the President. Don't suppose society here is at an end. People eat their meals—the shops are open. Rachel[3] is to play tomorrow. But of course there is uneasiness, great uneasiness, though as my Father will have observed the funds keep up miraculously. The English papers have all stopped today. I do not know if there is row in the provinces which we are not to hear about. That would floor the Government, at least if they had to withdraw troops from Paris.

To R. H. HUTTON, [DECEMBER 1851]

Extracts in R. H. Hutton, 'Memoir', pp. xliii-xliv.
DATE: close in date to last

Of late, I have been devoting my entire attention to the science of barricades, which I found amusing. They have systematised it in a way which is pleasing to the cultivated intellect. We had only one good day's fighting, and I naturally kept out of cannon-shot. But I took a quiet walk over the barricades in the morning, and superintended the construction of three with as much keenness as if I had been clerk of the works. You've seen lots, of course, at Berlin, but I should not think those Germans were up to a real Montagnard, who is the most horrible being to the eye I ever saw,—sallow, sincere, sour fanaticism, with grizzled moustaches, and a strong wish to shoot you rather than not. The Montagnards are a scarce commodity, the real race—only three or four, if so many, to a barricade. If you want a Satan any odd time, they'll do; only I hope that *he* don't believe in human brotherhood. It is not possible to respect any one who does, and I should be loth to confound the notion of *our* friend's solitary grandeur by supposing him to fraternise ... I think M. Buonaparte is entitled to great praise. He has very good heels to his boots, and the French just want treading

[3] Elisa Rachel Filix (1821–58), great tragic actress of the Comédie Française.

down, and nothing else—calm, cruel, business-like oppression, to take the dogmatic conceit out of their heads. The spirit of generalisation which, John Mill tells us, honourably distinguishes the French mind, has come to this, that every Parisian wants his head *tapped* in order to get the formulae and nonsense out of it. And it would pay to perform the operation, for they are very clever on what is within the limit of their experience, and all that can be 'expanded' in terms of it, but beyond, it is all generalisation and folly. . . . So I am for any carnivorous government.

Till the Revolution came I had no end of trouble to find conversation, but now they'll talk against everybody, and against the President like mad—and they talk immensely well, and the language is like a razor, capital if you are skilful, but sure to cut you if you aren't. A fellow can talk German in crude forms, and I don't see it sounds any worse, but this stuff is horrid unless you get it *quite* right. A French lady made a striking remark to me:— '*C'est une révolution qui a sauvé la France. Tous mes amis sont mis en prison.*' She was immensely delighted that such a pleasing way of saving her country had been found.

To HENRY CRABB ROBINSON, 25 DECEMBER 1851

MS: Dr Williams's Library

41 Rue de Vaugirard
Paris.
25 Decr. 1851.

Mr dear Sir,

I have often heard you say that you do not disapprove of young men's being overbearing dogmatic obtrusive and irreverent. Now I am going to be *impertinent*. Of course I concede that this by no means falls within the list of vices which you so kindly tolerate in us youth but I submit to you that it is closely allied to them: that a Catholic theologian would class it among their 'natural developments' or 'preservative additions'—[1] and that finally according to *yourself* no one young man

---

[1] In writing of the new constitution in his *Inquirer* letter of 20 January 1852, WB speaks

be expected to go far enough (even in a vicious direction) without going *too* far. My impertinence is this, and it is *considerable*. I have broken loose from law for a month or two and am living here tranquilly observing the barricades and Revolutions of this agreeable capital. And it has seemed to me *possible* that besides knowing and having known (as all the rising race reverently believe) the very *élite* of all mankind might perhaps have condescended to be acquainted with one or two persons so low down in Parisian society as not to be offended with the introduction of a crude and unformed lawyer whose meekness is his sole and only title to respect; and my insolence craves that you 'mero motu' and out of your abounding benevolence would address and direct unto such person or persons such letters missive as to you might seem reasonable and fit and would furthermore transmit the same to me here to be by me served upon and delivered to the same person or persons so aforesaid as before.[2] I entreat you to observe that I do not defend this insolence or in the least excuse or by any means palliate it— I only *commit* it—which though I cant *hope*, I pray may be forgiven. I was here during the only day of hard fighting which we have had and shall be able to give lectures on the construction of a barricade if that noble branch of Political Economy ever become a source of income in England. The elections will be in favor of N. Bonaparte by at least five million.[3] The stupid people are with him though the clever ones are against and you are aware which even here are slightly the majority. A free press, a Parliament, and other the little comforts

---

of what 'Newman would call a "preservative addition" or a "necessary development" ' (*Collected Works*, IV, 46); a reference to the sixth test of a 'true development' in J. H. Newman's *An Essay on the Development of Christian Doctrine*, 1845.

[2] On receipt of this letter, 26 December, Crabb Robinson considered giving WB an introduction to a Miss Niven, but 'doubted the expediency' of this, since she was 'all in favour of Louis Napoleon'. Instead, he sent on 8 January a letter of introduction to Mme Mohl. Mary Mohl, *née* Clarke (1793–1883), was a member of an old Scots family who had been educated in France, became an intimate of Mme Récamier, and in 1846 married the naturalized French orientalist Julius Mohl; during his stay in Paris WB was a visitor to her salon at 120 rue du Bac, which attracted celebrities for nearly forty years (RB, X, 192). Robinson also asked him to call on Mlle LeConte, a friend of Mrs Elizabeth Jesser Reid (1789–1866), Unitarian philanthropist and founder of the Ladies' College, Bedford Square (Crabb Robinson MS Diary, Dr Williams's Library). The letter of introduction to Mme Mohl, sent by Robinson, came from Mrs Reid and her sister, Miss Sturch, according to Eliza Bagehot: see M. C. M. Simpson, *Letters and Recollections of Julius and Mary Mohl*, 1887, p. 136.

[3] In the plebiscite of 21 December seven and a half out of eight million voted for the maintenance of his authority and delegated to him power to establish a constitution; the new constitution was promulgated 14 January 1852.

of a free people are not appreciated here and now—people want to be quick and to mind the shop—and perhaps they are right—for though journalists deny it, leading articles may be bought too dear. I observe that the arrest of conspicuous persons is pleasing to the people. A naive French lady—a keen Bonapartist observed to me 'C'est une Revolution qui a sauvé la France. *Tous mes amis sont mis en prison'.* She was delighted at so agreeable a mode of saving her country.

Yours with much respect
(though it mayn't seem so)
W. BAGEHOT—[4]
of University Hall and sometime of 6 Great Coram St.

I ought to add that I can speak French pretty freely—though with a *horrid* accent.

Once more excuse my insolence, and *bad* writing—

H. C. Robinson Esqre.

To EDITH BAGEHOT, [?26 DECEMBER] 1851

Test from RB, X, 192
DATE: printed text reads 'October', but WB's 'Decr.' is easily misread 'Octr.' and content shows this to be a December letter, almost certainly Friday the 26th, from reference to Palmerston's resignation (see n. 1)

Paris, [Decr.], 1851.
Friday Evening.

My dearest Mother,

I have added what *I* call waltzing to my other accomplishments. It differs from what other people call by that name, not only in the step which is of my own invention, but also in its having no relation whatever to the music, and by preserving its rotatary motion in a great measure by collisions with the other couples. It's very amusing running small French girls against some fellow's elbow, it's like killing flies years ago. There is, however, the inconvenience that one does not like to ask the same girl twice; she might say she had not insured her life, but if you are careful to select a fresh subject for each experiment, the

---

[4] Crabb Robinson annotated this letter: '*Bagehot*. A bel Esprit and very able man. In 1864 Editor of the Economist, author of Estimates of English and Scotch authors'.

JANUARY 1852

pastime will succeed. I do not fancy it pleases the girls; he dances *tout seul* ('all by himself') I heard one of them say with great indignation to her female friends, as if a fellow of my age could be expected to keep time with her or with the music either, and it pleases me, it being a new, if not humane excitement, and is better than talking feeble philosophy in out of the way corners.

People here take great interest in Lord Palmerston's retirement.[1] The minister for foreign affairs is here, in general, the first minister; he was so always in Louis Philippe's time, though in consequence of the domestic confusion the minister of the Interior[2] (the Home Secretary in our nomenclature) has naturally cut him out, and they know nothing of Lord John Russell scarcely, and wonder at his having the power to turn out Lord Palmerston who has been their *bête noir* for years and whom they fancied was omnipotent. The reason seems to be that he and Lord John got in a rage and the Queen cut up rough (hard phrase that to do into French) for they don't really seem to differ much about Louis Napoleon, so I expound this, but the expression of my auditors is still puzzled. 'You don't explain it to me' as Brother would say. Of course they are too polite to impute the difficulty to my mode of expression (they only cut you up afterwards like a rotten potato) but ascribe it all to the complicated wheel-within-wheel nature of the English constitution.

To W. C. ROSCOE, [? 10–11 JANUARY 1852]

Extract in RB, X, 189, written from Paris
DATE: Since WB has heard that his 1st letter of 8 January 1852 is to appear in the *Inquirer*, 10 January, and will send another (that of 15 January) 'next week', this is probably 10 or 11 January

I was very unwell mentally and bodily when I came here. I had a good deal to put me out. Everything of all kinds had gone wrong with me

---

[1] On 3 December Palmerston had told the French ambassador that he thought the *coup d'état* in the best interests of France; this private expression of approval was reported in Paris as the British Government's view, to the fury of the British ambassador in Paris, Lord Normanby, who wrote direct to Russell about it. The Prime Minister and the Queen were relieved, as WB surmises, to have this pretext for removing Palmerston, who was forced to resign 19 December and replaced by Granville on the 26th; Normanby was removed and replaced by Lord Cowley.
[2] The Duc de Morny, who had helped to organize the *coup d'état*; an Orleanist, he resigned after the confiscation of Orleanist property in January 1852.

for a long time, and there were some family matters which much annoyed me besides, so I was in a very weak-minded state and what you did for me was a real satisfaction just then, and I am very *much* obliged to you. I am much obliged also to Sanford[1] for putting in my letter[2] which is a queer thing I fancy. Please to tell him to send me a copy. There is no difficulty. I have half written another which I will send you next week,[3] as soon as I have read over the other. I am rather full on the subject—perhaps in error—as my maxim just now is that a man's *favourite* ideas are always wrong. But there are moments of truth about my view that I should not have known if I had been in England, and may be good for other people in consequence.[4] I confine my immorality to speculation, and to the perusal of De Béranger[5] who is really a great poet.

---

[1] Langton Sanford had taken over the editorship of the leading Unitarian weekly newspaper, the *Inquirer*, in 1851; he was assisted by 'a knot of young Unitarians'—R. H. Hutton, Timothy Smith Osler and W. C. Roscoe—who were critical of their readers 'optimist and philanthropic politics', literary works and liturgy (R. H. Hutton, 'Memoir', p. xxxix).
[2] 'The Dictatorship of Louis Napoleon', dated 8 January 1852, the first of seven letters WB wrote over the pseudonym 'Amicus' on the *coup d'état* of 1851, published in the *Inquirer* between 8 January and 6 March (*Collected Works*, IV, 29–84).
[3] Dated 15 January and appeared in the *Inquirer*, 17 January.
[4] On the views expressed by WB in the letters, see *Collected Works*, IV, 15–17; on the reactions of readers to his defence of the *coup d'état*, I, 51–2. Hutton supposed that Clough might sympathize with WB's 'fast' politics, but himself thought 'his doctrines detestable, almost as much as the measure he defends' (letter of ?January 1852, *Correspondence of Arthur Hugh Clough*, ed. F. Mulhauser, I, 304). After the appearance of the second letter Roscoe confirmed Crabb Robinson's suspicion that WB was the author of these 'clever letters but proving only this, that a coup d'etat was necessary, but not the actual one with all its needless atrocities and flagrant injustice.' When on 19 August 1852 Robinson read WB's article on Oxford in the *Prospective* (see letter to ?W. C. Roscoe, ?August 1852) he recognized the authorship from 'a tone of sarcasm which is not inappropriate here and which resembles the letters from Paris in the Inquirer signed Amicus—But these are [*sic*] better' (MS Diary, Dr Williams's Library).
[5] Pierre Jean de Béranger (1780–1857), the subject of an article by WB in the *National Review*, October 1857 (*Collected Works*, II, 11–43); in the fourth *Inquirer* letter WB characterized his poetry as a 'manual of the philosophy of this world' (*Collected Works*, IV, 56).

JANUARY 1852

To EDITH BAGEHOT, [?10–15 JANUARY 1852]

Text from RB, X, 196–7
DATE: after the Decrees of 10 January 1852 and near in date to the *Inquirer* letter of 15 January

41, Rue de Vaugirard,
Paris.

My dearest Mother,

... When I have not got this Parisian complaint—for everybody now has at least a bad cold here—I am extremely well, quite stout, gross and ruddy. I lost three parties by being ill last week, to one of which, I believe, a big one, your friend Madame Meynieux was to have chaperoned me. However, I observe that dances like wheelbarrows are much the same in all countries, and nowhere propitious to people too muffish to waltz. One has to fall back on elderly creatures and express edifying sentiments in bad grammar. Not having 'been any place' as Watty used to say, I have not got anything to tell you.

Politics are as dull as ditch-water here now after the excitement, the only new thing is decree of banishment apparently for life against some socialists of note, and of temporary exile against M. Thiers and the African generals, and M. de Girardin,[1] the great journalist, and others. The African generals are much to be pitied, I think, for they are a fine race of men; the list of exiles is thought numerous,[2] I think, even by the President's friends—at least the people on his side whom I have happened to hear of—of course his enemies say there never was such 'tyranny' or oppression since the commencement of mankind. The Constitution hangs fire, that he may have more time to fill up the Consultative Commission—his privy Council, as he wants to get all the creditable names he can. I will write again[3] in a day or two when I am less stupid and have more to say.

Yours most affectionately,
W. BAGEHOT

[1] Text reads 'Madame', but WB's 'great journalist' shows that this is a transcriber's error for 'M. de Girardin', named along with Thiers in the *Inquirer* letter of 15 January. Girardin's wife, Delphine, née Gay (1804–55), was a novelist, dramatist and occasional journalist.
[2] In the *Inquirer* WB said that he was 'not prepared to defend the *number* of the transportations', and regretted the fate of the African generals (*Collected Works*, IV, 42–3).
[3] No further letters written before WB's return from Paris have been traced. He was in

P.S.—I was very sorry to hear of poor Mr. Spark's death[4] whose mild manners and valuable qualities everybody I think respected. What a horrid loss of the Amazon,[5] the French papers live and thrive on it since the *coup d'état*, except the government organs; they are at low life, and obliged to criticise old prima donnas and 'fill their columns' with accounts of the state of the *Navy*,[6] pleasant reading that, careful deportations on old copy.

My love universally.

To T. W. BAGEHOT, [?3 AUGUST] 1852

MS: Mr Norman St John-Stevas
DATE: WB's '31 August' is an error either for '3 August' or for '31 July', in view of his reference to a 'little article on the "money-market" ' (see n. 7): no such article appeared in the issue of 28 August

9 Spring Gardens[1]
31 August 1852

My dearest Father,

I have been considering carefully the question which we almost decided upon when I was at home—I mean my abandoning the law at the present crisis—and in accordance with what we very nearly resolved

---

London on 25 April when he breakfasted with Crabb Robinson, who noted that his mind had 'taken a start', and that he had written 'Lord Jeffrey' in the *Inquirer*, 10 April 1852 (*Works*, I, 343–8); although the 'Amicus' letters were not mentioned, Robinson discovered that WB was 'not a partisan of Louis Napoleon' (MS Diary, Dr Williams's Library).

[4] Samuel Sparks, of Huish Episcopi, Somerset, died 28 December 1851 (*Gentleman's Magazine*, n.s. XXVIII ([1852], 213). In his will (copy, PRO) he is described as 'of Langport. Merchant'; the will appointed the Revd James Stratton Coles and Thomas Watson Bagehot as executors and trustees for Spark's four children (three of whom had the middle name 'Stuckey'). He may have been a descendant of one of two daughters of Vincent Stuckey's brother, George Stuckey (1731–1807): Sarah Stuckey married 23 August 1765, at Langport, Samuel Sparkes, of Cheapside, London; Martha Stuckey married 11 September 1754, at Langport, Isaac Sparks of Forthington, Dorset.

[5] The West India mail steamer *Amazon* had been destroyed by fire 4 January in the Bay of Biscay with the loss of most of the 110 crew and 50 passengers (*Annual Register*, 1852, pp. 462–9).

[6] In the *Inquirer* WB says 'the government papers deal in asterisks and "details unfit for publication," and the rest are devoted to the state of the navy, and say nothing' (*Collected Works*, IV, 41).

* * *

[1] Jn Charing Cross; the occupant in 1852 was Henry Bennett, commission, shipping,

AUGUST 1852

upon when I was with you. I have decided to do so at this juncture—utterly and for ever. You are aware that the determining circumstance which principally decides me, is the present confused of[2] the legal business and profession. Law was always a fair risk—it is just now an immense one. The County Courts and other changes have all but abolished the old Common Law practice which was the attraction that originally beguiled me to the bar and the more recent alterations in Chancery[3] have made a new Chaos of which no one pretends to see very confidently the effect or the end. I suppose that these changes will very likely be beneficial to the public at large—but I am not sure the public at large, and their benefit won't of itself earn *me* an income. Most likely too when the whole legal world is newly arranged, law will be a more satisfactory profession than it is at this moment—but that must take a long time, and twenty years—though a short time for arranging and consolidating a new system of legal practice is notwithstanding a great fraction of my life. Besides what will issue from the confusion is a difficult speculation, and it would be foolish to venture my success on the chances of *any* difficult speculation;—it is too dangerous. Moreover I see the men around me leaving it in great numbers and as fast as they can—and I wish to follow a multitude to do *well*.[4] Nothing, in my judgment, would at all be gained now by additional delay—on the contrary I am inclined to believe I should have made the *wrench* before. I shall therefore practically be called as soon as I can,[5] and when I have achieved that complicated exploit, I shall exile myself immediately from the legal circle.

I am reluctant, I own to do this as I like law, and have spent a good deal of time upon it, and if I thought that my chances of success were reasonably sure I should still—go on—but I do not think so—on the contrary imagine that 'under all circumstances' the common sense is to leave it and therefore I do leave it—What I mean to do in other pursuits,

---

transit, continental and French wine agent, also at 10 Mark Lane; from 1853 it was the address of the Church of England Scripture Readers' Association, with Henry Bennett as one of the lay secretaries (*Post Office London Directories*).
[2] Thus in MS.
[3] The Court of Chancery Acts, 1852 (15, 16 Victoria, cc. 80, 86) reformed the system of procedure and pleading in these courts, which dealt with disputes about legacies, trusts and mortgages by the principles of equity; the delays of Chancery were attacked in Dickens's *Bleak House*, the first monthly part of which appeared in March 1852.
[4] cf. Exodus, xxiii. 2.
[5] WB was called to the bar 17 November 1852.

must be entirely decided by what it is found I can do, when I am tried in them, but I assume that we quite resolved on the first step—that I should go into the counting house and remain there under your direction until I am decently fit to go elsewhere. And this is all which need be stated in this letter. I am not acquainted with any news—except this concerning my personal fortunes.

I hope that the bride and bridegroom[6] thrive. My best love to them. Many thanks to my mother for her notes, and my love also. I know she has long been inclining to my giving up law, but I am not quite sure she will exactly like it now that it comes to be done. I don't profess to *like* it much myself[7] though I am clear that it is prudent and proper.

Ever yours

W BAGEHOT

There is a little article on the 'money-market' of all subjects in the world of mine in the Inquirer[8] of this week. It is not very lengthy or elaborate as I had to write it at the last possible moment for a friend who had to do something else.

To [?W. C. ROSCOE], [?AUGUST 1852]

Extract in RB, X, 205–6, addressed to the Editor of the *Prospective Review*
DATE: probably near in date to the publication of 'Oxford' in the *Prospective*, August 1852. *Addressee:* one of the editors of the *Review*—perhaps W. C. Roscoe, who had become an editor in July 1852

I think that my article on Oxford[1] has got off extremely well. I should very much like to write for you an article on Hartley Coleridge, a

---

[6] His cousin William Stuckey Wood (1826–70) had married 26 June 1852, at Monkstown, Co. Dublin, Mary (1827–1916), daughter of Richard Armit of Monkstown.
[7] Life as a banker proved more congenial than he feared at the outset, partly because he was able to use his leisure for writing in, and later editing, periodicals. In a letter almost certainly of December 1855 (when he was joint editor of the *National Review* and writing 'Edward Gibbon' for the January issue), he said: 'You see I have hunting, banking, ships, publishers, an article, and a Christmas to do, all at once, and it is my opinion they will all get muddled. A muddle will print, however, though it won't add up—*which is the real advantage of literature*' (extract in Hutton's *Spectator* obituary of WB: *Collected Works*, XIV).
[8] 'Investments' in the issue of 31 July: *Collected Works*, IX, 272–5. This was followed by three articles, beginning in the *Inquirer*, 14 August, on John Lalor's *Money and Morals: Collected Works*, IX, 276–94.

* * *

[1] 'Oxford', on the report of the Commissioners on the University, in the *Prospective*

review of the edition of his *Biographia Borealis* recently brought out. I am rather strong on him myself, as I was an admirer before his death and renovation. I am rather afraid his 'poems' were reviewed in the *Prospective*[2] not very long ago, and I don't know whether you would think it desirable to have any second article on him or them so soon, but if you could strain a point for us, I should like to write it very much indeed. It would not be a long article—about thirty pages. I should make it an estimate of him as a whole—though including of course a criticism on his poetry—and elucidating him by his father.

To T. W. BAGEHOT, [?14 AUGUST 1852]

MS: Mr Norman St John-Stevas
DATE: Summer 1852, from address and content; perhaps Friday 14 August, to allow time for receipt of letter and note from his father in answer to letter of ?3 August

9 Spring Gdns
Friday.

My dearest Father,

Many thanks for your note which I received this morning. I should like to come down the last two or three days of this month. I mean *on* one of them or on the first of September. I do not know what my uncle and Aunt Reynolds's present plans precisely are—but I talk of running down to see them for a day or two, and will let you know. My love to my mother. I hope she will support my change of plans with Equanimity, if you have announced it to her. I did not understand your last letter quite correctly, and I had previously announced my resolution here before I received [it]. I confess also that I doubt if it would have been possible to try business adequately, without such an absence from law as would be equivalent to abandoning it, but we need scarcely now discuss this.

As to what you say of business itself, I hope I shall always be ready to do my best—though I certainly do not imagine that I shall set the Parret on fire, at any rate not immediately. I saw William Wood

---

Review, VIII (1852), 347–92: *Collected Works*, VII, 327–370.
[2] Not the subject of an earlier article; WB's appeared in the *Prospective*, November 1852: *Collected Works*, I, 142–71.

AUGUST 1852

and his bride on Sunday last at his father's[1] lodgings in Sloane St. The bride was very gracious, and pleasing. She is a little like Mrs. Caillard[2] in manner—at least I thought so, but more animated. She is not imperiously beautiful but pretty and calm. The young generation were, I thought, an admirable contrast to the old.

Ever yours affly,

WALTER BAGEHOT

To W. C. ROSCOE, [?AUGUST–SEPTEMBER 1852]

Extract in RB, X, 213
DATE: after 12 August, when Hutton did not know for certain that WB had written 'Oxford' in the *Prospective* (letter to Clough of that date, *Correspondence of Arthur Hugh Clough*, ed. F. Mulhauser, I, 321)

I saw him[1] on Sunday and he was as well as one could hope, but I can't but *fear* very much about him.

---

[1] The Revd William Wood (1798–1871), educated Exeter College, Oxford; vicar of Staplegrove, near Taunton, 1826–39, after which he was without a living until 1858. His first wife, Julia Stuckey, died 1832, and he remarried in 1835. Between 1839 and 1858 the Woods divided their time between London and Martock.
[2] Emma Louisa (*d.* 1865), elder daughter of Vincent and Marian Reynolds; married 1850 Camille Felix Désiré Caillard (1822–98), barrister of the Inner Temple, later judge of the county courts of Wiltshire.

* * *

[1] R. H. Hutton. While Vice-principal of University Hall Hutton had married, 26 June 1851, Roscoe's sister Ann Mary (1821–52). At the end of 1851 the Council of University Hall had made use of the pretext of Clough's application for another post to remove him from the principalship, because they found him insufficiently concerned with building up the number of students and wanting in energy (see G. P. Johari, 'Clough at Oriel and at University Hall', *PMLA*, LXVI [1951], 424–5). Hutton was appointed Principal; WB's comment, Hutton told Clough, was that 'I shall do better for the post, as a lower style of man was wanted to be in sympathy with the Council of the Hall to *some* extent. He says you "never understood a shopkeeper who had been 'carefully brought up'," and thinks as I agree with them more, I shall do better' (letter of January 1852; *Correspondence*, I, 304). In order to guarantee Hutton £250 a year as Principal a subscription list was opened, to which WB, T. S. Osler, Roscoe and Crabb Robinson each contributed £10 (*Inquirer*, 3, 10, 24 January 1852). But in May Hutton became seriously ill with lung disease, and gave up his post at University Hall (Dr W. B. Carpenter was appointed in his place); at the end of September the Huttons went to the West Indies.

To A. H. CLOUGH, [OCTOBER 1852]

MS: Bodleian Library
DATE: not long before Clough's departure at the end of October 1852

Herds Hill
Langport
Monday

My dear Clough,

I have just heard incidentally that you are talking of going to America[1] perhaps for a visit, perhaps indefinitely. Indeed it seems possible that you are gone, but if you are not I should like you to have a line from me congratulating you on this new source of 'experience' and exhorting you to *try* to bear me in mind. Of course you will fail, but I should be very grateful for the attempt. Do you expect to find America 'instructive'? I should think for a visit it wd. be very much so. I rather like that rough active pecuniary life, but I doubt whether it wd. be *perfect* for a very long time. Besides they are so dyspeptic. I have changed my own plans in life since I saw you last. I have given up law, and taken to banking and gone into trade. I do not think that I shall like it so well as I shd. have liked law, if I had seen a reasonable certainty of speedy or even eventual employment, but I did not see any in the existing confusion of the profession—and I possess connections and advantages here which make the mercantile alternative a reasonable certainty.

I find the poor fellow[2] is sailed for the W. Indies. I have very little idea that I shall ever see him *in health* again. *Do* remember me.

Ever Yours

WALTER BAGEHOT

---

[1] Clough had come to this decision in June, and sailed for Boston at the end of October; he returned to England July 1853, and married Blanche Smith in 1854.
[2] R. H. Hutton.

JANUARY 1853

To WILLIAM KILLIGREW WAIT, 5 JANUARY 1853

MS: Mr Norman St John-Stevas

Herds Hill
Wednesday 5 Jany. 1853

My dear Wait,

Your very kind letter gave me great pleasure. I have very often of late had a strong but ineffectual intention of writing to you (for my conscience reproaches me, that I was the first defaulter in our ancient correspondence) which was only prevented taking effect in action by the horrid inertness of my nature. It was a great gain to me therefore to find that you still remembered me and had forgiven my laziness. I can't say that I am going any great pace in life myself. I find that life is not the easy thing which in early youth one demonstrated it to be. As you suggest I have had the honor of being called to the bar by the Hon'ble Society of Lincoln's Inn,[1] which, as it only requires eating dinners, I was found in the day of trial to be equal to accomplishing. But there I made a pause. I had intended for obvious reasons to come [to] the Western in preference to any other Circuit, but when it came to the point, and I made a mathematical computation, of the extremely small amount of business thereon, the number of years it would require to try the law, and the small chance I seemed to have in it altogether, I decided to give it up. Owing to these miserable County Courts, and other crotchets of Reform the number of men of old standing that are going out of the profession is enormous, and it was, I think, their utter discomfiture, and total inability to succeed in anything else which most of all determined [me] to run away in time, as it seemed immensely likely that it would of necessity come to that in the end. I was sorry though to have to do this since in some respects legal studies suited me very much better than any other pecuniary pursuit is ever likely to do, and I give myself credit for a certain mastery of chaff (partly exemplified perhaps in our ancient theological correspondence) which I should have been peculiarly proud to bring to bear on the intelligent residents in this County, but the fates would not have it so,

---

[1] In his 'Bad Lawyers or Good' (*Collected Works*, VII, 246–7) WB describes 'the Lincoln's Inn way of giving its degree of "Barrister" twenty years ago.'

JANUARY 1853

and therefore here I am in my father's counting house trying (and failing) to do sums, and being rowed ninetynine times a day for some horrid sin against the conventions of mercantile existence. My family perhaps you know, are merchants, shipowners, and bankers &c &c here and elsewhere—but of their multifarious occupations I hope to be able to find though I cannot precisely say that I have yet found, some one to which I am not contemptibly unequal. As to your notion of doing anything *well*, it so many years since I abandoned the idea that I cant now quite enter into the feeling. My difficulty is in doing anything *at all*. The only thing I ever really knew was Special Pleading, and the moment I had learned that, the law Reformers botched and abolished it. It was a very pretty art and the only trade in which the logical faculties appear to be of any particular service. It was therefore the champagne of life. But this people which knoweth not the law[2] went and abolished it. I suppose you like business by this time. I think I might if I knew anything about it and if my relations would admit that sums are matters of opinion. I can't claim to be very familiar with German matters. I like to read English Books best, because I am partially acquainted with the language in which they are composed. Besides I fancy they are the truest books after all. The German ideas *may* be true hereafter, but in the existing world, it seems to me that they a good deal mislead.[3] If a man knoweth not what he hath seen (and no German ever does) how shall he know that which he hath not seen.[4] Besides they say there is *no* such thing as nonsense in which I think them quite wrong. I do not know that I can tell you 'what I am thinking about' for I am a good deal inclined to believe that I have ceased to think about anything. In one's Infancy one woke up daily with a new *Weltansicht* every morning. My friends say I am too sceptical, but *I* say that I am only lazy in believing, as I am in everything else. Indeed it seems to me that I do that better than I do most other things.

I am very sorry indeed to hear that you have lost your father.[5] Your deepedged envelope prepared me for some such calamity. I am not destitute of domestic anxiety myself, as my mother who many years ago

---

[2] John, vii. 49.
[3] cf. the opening of WB's 1855 essay on Cowper, and its jokes at the expense of German scholars: *Collected Works*, I, 263, 265–6.
[4] cf. I John, iv. 20.
[5] William Killigrew Wait, Bristol merchant, had died in 1852 (his death was registered in the January–March quarter).

was subject to attacks of delirium, has of late fallen into a good deal of habitual delusion and aberration, which, I fear, will end in ultimately disqualifying her for society. Indeed except with her oldest friends who are quite used to her, it has done so already. I suffered a good deal when I first put this steadily before me, but this is some time since and one can 'grieve down' a good deal. But it is an odd world after all. I should like exceedingly to look in on you some time soon in conformity with your kind invitation—but just now I am rather under a vow to go to the counting house daily—but I hope to see you at no distant period. We should revive our old friendship more in an hours talk than centuries of correspondence. If you feel any curiosity, I recommend you to read two articles of mine (if indeed you can get hold of them) in the two *last* nos of an out of the way review called the Prospective—one on Oxford, the other on Hartley Coleridge. You comprehend, I don't say they are worth reading, but the only chance of readers is to bore ones friends.

Ever yours
most sincerely

WALTER BAGEHOT

I almost think I should know your mother[6] if I met her, so deeply does 'terror' imprint features upon the mind.

To R. H. HUTTON, 7 JANUARY 1853

MS: Mr Norman St John-Stevas

Herds Hill
Langport
Jany. 7th. 1853

My dear Hutton,

I was in hopes I should have heard from you by the mail which is just come in, but no letters have appeared, and therefore I will not any longer delay writing to you. I was very glad indeed to hear from

---

[6] Frances Newman Wait (*d.* 1856), daughter of the Revd Newman Newman of Thornbury Park, Gloucester.

JANUARY 1853

Roscoe of your safe arrival in Barbadoes, and I thought the account which he sent me of you on the whole a good one. It always seemed to me that any good effect from a change of climate must be very gradual and that no sudden or violent recovery etc. from any such cause be looked for in such a case as yours. But I hope a good deal from a continued residence, which will give the natural *wiriness* of your nature time to operate. You have more of it than you get credit for. You must employ yourself moderately on *something that you like* and keep up your spirits. I hope you will do the latter, and indeed I think you will, for I have observed that people who are naturally inclined to melancholy and like you would never be made awfully happy by any good fortune, are not (after the care) so much depressed when they have *invested* their low spiritis in real care. A buoyant person like myself who is rarely dismal, and not inclined to bemoan himself for other peoples calamities, is liable to be much disturbed when he has to be dismal because something has happened to *himself*. But this is not your way. By the bye we hear a great deal about the yellow fever being in Barbadoes.[1] I hope you will leave it if there is anything serious. You cannot afford to run any risk—besides there is excitement in it. I am going on in a very torpid state of mind myself. I have devoted my time for the last 4 months nearly exclusively to the art of book-keeping by double entry, the theory of which is agreeable and pretty but the practice perhaps as horrible as anything ever was. I maintain too in vain that sums are matters of opinion—but the people in command here do not comprehend the nature of contingent matter and try to prove that figures tend to one result more than another which I find myself to be false and they always come different. But there is no influencing the instinctive dogmatism of the uneducated mind. In other respects I approve of mercantile life. There is some excitement in it, if this does not wear off—always a little to do and no [we]aring[2] labor, which is something towards perfection. It is stupefying to live in the country: one gets into a rut of ideas and society, the same since our great grandfathers fell asleep, from which living tomb nothing after a short time will ever save one. But it is lazy which is still something: but I regret to observe that idleness is

---

[1] WB had not yet heard that Hutton's wife had died of the fever 21 December 1852.
[2] Paper torn; two letters missing.

JANUARY 1853

less agreeable as we advance in life. At least I begin to feel rather strongly a restless craving for more action irrespectively of the end, which once was quite foreign to me, and is now gaining great strength. I used to laugh at people who liked doing things and did not care for them when done, but fear I shall end in that state.

I was in town about six weeks ago, and was called to the bar, and saw all our friends. Osler has a cryptogramic establishment at Twickenham, very nice indeed, and his wife[3] and he seemed on really *friendly* terms. It was a very amusing visit. I think they will pull together. Roscoe and Sanford were exactly in appearance *in statu quo*, though it struck me they were getting tired of the Inquirer which I cannot wonder at. I never would write regularly for baldheaded people if I were them. They don't comprehend anything wh. is not erroneous. Osler said *he* shd. abandon it.

In the book world there is not much going on. A new novel from Lady G. Fullerton[4] is the most remarkable thing. It is a good deal like Ellen Middleton in the leading characters, though there is a Christian hero with 'almost *marble* temples covered &c &c' who is quite new. The plot is that a girl is so much in love with him that she runs off with someone else and marries him which wd. irritate you. There is a great deal of power of course in many parts of the work and a great deal of monstrosity too. The Xtian. hero is very splendid. Several of the women are good, especially the heroine notwithstanding her being called 'Ladybird' at which some years [ago] you would have dashed your foot against the wall.

Chevalier Bunsen has published a huge book on 'Hippolytus',[5] a Xtian. writer in the 3rd. century. At least on a book which he says was written by Hippolytus, but wh. other people say is Origen's. Bunsen's book is 4 volumes and contains a mass of learning shovelled together as ill as possible, and not working out anything clearly or well. But there is a German earnestness and solidity about the book which makes it agreeable to read and the facts are very good.

---

[3] Osler had married 14 September 1852 Henrietta (1821–69), daughter of Robert Roscoe.
[4] *Lady-bird, a Tale*, 1852; Lady Georgiana Fullerton (1812–85) had a great success with her first novel, *Ellen Middleton*, 1844; influenced by the Tractarian movement and became a Catholic in 1846. During WB's courtship of Eliza Wilson she recorded that he 'told me all the plots of Lady Georgina [sic] Fullerton's novels' (*Servant of All*, II, 9).
[5] Bunsen's *Hippolytus and his Age* was favourably reviewed by J. J. Tayler in the *Prospective*, February 1853 (IX, 118–64).

He proves in a beautifully Germanic manner that this book was written by Hippolytus because it is a collection of heresies and Photius mentions a book by H[ippolytu]s. on Heresies 33 in no. beginning with A, and ending with B. Now the book in question does not end with B or begin with A or contain 33 heresies, but Bunsen says it is all quite consistent and has a special subsidiary hypothesis for each inconsistency which is very amusing. I believe he is right about the book on the whole and that it was certainly *not* written by Origen and perhaps by Hippolytus but you would be delighted with the manner in which he goes round and round the subject, and the unspeakable importance which he attaches to it. His own evidence wd. not require a keener argument or obtain it. It is splendid to see such a bookish turn; as if it mattered who wrote such a book, for it is certainly stupid, that is agreed upon. I read with interest your huge article on Mr. Lalor's book,[6] and regret to say that you have no way altered my very low estimate of it. I think the economical part especially erroneous in all its main ideas. I think you answer him perfectly in the beginning, and then go and admit a modified diluted extract from his theory in the conclusion. It seems to me that the whole matter comes in the end about to this: 1st. that in a state of barter when only one new person saves, his new commodity wd. be a new demand without a new supply and would tend to raise the price or value of other commodities; but if on the other hand two new persons saved, it is possible they may supply one another; and if a large no. of persons saved habitually with a view of supplying one another (the actual case in every civilized society) the probability is that the savers will do what they wish to do, and that they will supply one another. In no case is there any oversupply if the right article is selected. Now I deny that the introduction of money alters this in the least, except to this extent, that as money is by the hypothesis required to circulate commodities, every increase in the quantity of commodities to be circulated requires necessarily a proportionate increase of money. Suppose I save a to obtain b from B, B, b, to obtain c from C and so on down to Y who saves y to obtain a from A, Mr. Lalor wd. say the trade was at a permanent standstill, but this is only true till the arrival of Z the coiner and miner who has coined and mined to obtain y from Y. When he has bought Y's article, Y can

---

[6] *Money and Morals*, on which WB had written in the *Inquirer* in 1852. Hutton's article appeared in the *Prospective*, November 1852 (VIII, 423–55).

buy A's, A's B's and so on ad inf. and according to me there is nothing else of principle in the matter. You modify Lalor's opinion to the extent of the profit of the producer, which you justly say is a new demand for money. I say that as the production of money is regulated by just the same laws and conditions as any other trade, money will be suplied in general and as a rule to meet that demand. The fact is that money, even metallic money is a peculiarly delicate article, and the slightest tinge of demand is followed by an increase in the supply, and this is much more still the case with the subsidiary forms of representative currency.

I therefore think Mr. Lalor's book about the most erroneous I have ever read, just as it is nearly the most uncomfortable. I deny as a fact that the profits of trade have recently fallen. The interest of money certainly has and also possibly the peculiar remuneration to a certain species of skilled services, but I am not aware of any evidence of a great fall, as Mr. L. thinks or of any fall, and I deny too what his book throughout assumes, that money produces no effect while it is lodged as a private deposit (the actual case of the Australian Gold) in the walls of the Bk. of England. I believe it is more efficient there than any where else, and that the whole problem of 'its getting into circulation' is founded on a misconception as to the nature of our circulation and of the purchasing power which really acts on actual prices.

But I shall not send you any more Political Economy at the distance you are. Have you seen anything of the blacks? It can't be a pretty study, but it may be an instructive one. People are quite wild here again about slavery, as strong as they ever were when there was a *bonâ fide* agitation in this country on the point. I should like to know accurately what comes from emancipation, taking it as a question of sacrifices. I can imagine many cases in wh. slavery is good for a population, but none or not many in which *traders* can be trusted to be slaveowners. It may answer in rural villages where they only supply their own demand, and where the notion of the slaves being 'capital' is extremely secondary, but never in a mercantile community where that notion is the main one and the notion of moral and personal dependence extremely faint. I hear you took my Goethe with you. Do you seriously think of giving us a sketch of him? The more I have thought of it, the more I fancy it wd. suit you well as an occupation for this time, but mind *not* to use abstract words or assume that people know the

Integral Calculus. They don't and it puzzles them. Don't criticise the books too much, except as elucidating the character of the man, which is what will interest his public. Write out your real mind, but do not make it an *exposure* of him, because he was a great man after all.

You will know that we have a change of ministry in England. Lord Derby is gone out and Ld. Aberdeen with everybody else is come in.[7] I think it is an excellent ministry myself, though Sir. J. Graham[8] is in it, whom I detest. They are the best men we've got, though they are frightfully old, and have many of the notions of very old people. I am afraid what they will do about the franchise. I doubt if they have really studied the subject. They are the old Reform Bill people and have not any new ideas since that time. Otherwise I think they'll do. You see my friend Louis Napoleon is Emperor.[9] I think there is no doubt his foreign policy will be mainly aggressive, and this country must look sharp or he'll be upon us. I don't mean now or tomorrow but soon.

My best remembrances to your wife. Believe me

Ever yours most affly.

WALTER BAGEHOT

Write to us when you *like* but not before. In a warm climate one can't ask for much.

To W. C. ROSCOE, [16 MARCH 1853]

Text from RB, X, 215, dated Taunton, 16 March 1853

My dear Roscoe,

Good-bye. Give my kindest and best remembrances to Hutton.[1] I hope indeed you will be of service to him and I hope you may bring

---

[7] Gladstone's attack on Disraeli's budget brought down Derby's Conservative government 18 December 1852; Aberdeen formed a government in coalition with the Peelites.
[8] Sir James Robert George Graham (1792–1861), the most prominent Peelite in the coalition; appointed First Lord of the Admiralty, the position he had held in Grey's ministry until his resignation in 1834; an efficient administrator, but never popular: as Home Secretary in Peel's government he had been implicated in the 'letter-opening' scandal of 1844, when Mazzini's letters were opened on Graham's authority and sent to the Foreign Office.
[9] Became Napoleon III, Emperor of the French, by a plebiscite in December 1852.

* * *

[1] Roscoe, undeterred by prevailing panic about the yellow fever epidemic, went to the

him home to us better than I can now get myself to expect. I will arrange about the *Prospective* though what to write about[2] I know no more than the people in the street. I write with ever so many people talking figures about me and I hardly know what I write, but good-bye and God speed you.

To R. H. HUTTON, 20 [?JULY 1853]

MS: Mr Norman St John-Stevas
DATE: reference to the *Prospective* suggests 1853, when Wednesday fell on the 20th in April and July, and probably near in date to next

Herds Hill
Wednesday 20th.

My dear Hutton,

Many thanks for your note. I am much better—indeed pretty well in everything except energy—but I have an amount of difficulty in setling[1] to anything which you cannot well conceive, and a stupidity when I do, that is not agreeable or encouraging. I have nearly got over the lameness, but not the *jar* quite as yet.

I agree, I think, with you that it wd. scarcely be wise in you to accept the *partial* Editorship of the Prospective.[2] In a pecuniary point of view, I always thought that the plan of your becoming *sole* Editor, a bad one for you, as it wd. take up your strength, and prevent your getting on more lucrative periodicals; but on general grounds I thought you wd. like the conduct of such a review so well, and wd. do it so well, and I have so good an opinion of the prospects of the Prospective (a very good opinion considering my distrustful turn of mind) that I had no scruple in advising you to take it, though against your immediate money-interest. But now the case is altered. The half-conduct

West Indies and brought his brother-in-law home.
[2] During Roscoe's absence WB wrote only 'Shakespeare', for the issue of August 1853: *Collected Works*, I, 173–214.

* * *

[1] Thus in MS.
[2] Hutton began an informal assistant editorship of the review in the summer of 1853; he would have been able to work closely with J. J. Tayler, who moved to London in September to become principal of Manchester New College there.

of the Prospective can only bore anybody who has to do with it—
must be unsatisfactory to every body—the *Contributors* included
who will never know, if their articles will be inserted or not—and
would not give you the arbitrary sort of satisfaction which [I] thought
you wd. enjoy so much. The objections remain, and besides this I
think if the Inquirer scheme[3] is carried out, it wd. have in *equity* a
first claim on your time, and at any rate, before you have tried it, and
know how much of your strength and *energy* it will involve, you shd.
not contract any other permanent Engagement. As to the reason
of one person's not editing the Inquirer and the Review, it seems to
me wholly *parsonic* and worth nothing—

I had a note from James[4] a day or two ago, wh. seemed encouraging
about the Inquirer—

Read Trench on the Miracles[5]—not a bad book—good quotations in
the notes—a little muddled but no harm.

Yours ever

WALTER BAGEHOT

To R. H. HUTTON, 15 AUGUST 1853

MS: Mr Norman St John-Stevas

Langport
15 August 1853

My dear Hutton,

I saw De Morgan before I left town but I am sorry to say got very
little out of him. He seemed to think mathematics themselves of very
little good in a pecuniary point of view, and was quite helpless (as

---

[3] This suggests that after Hutton's return from the West Indies he had been asked to undertake the editorship of the *Inquirer*, which Sanford and Roscoe had been talking of giving up (see WB's letter to Hutton, 7 January 1853); Sanford remained editor until[1] 1855.
[4] Not identified.
[5] *Notes on the Miracles of Our Lord*, 1846, by Richard Chenevix Trench (1807–86), professor of divinity at King's College, London, and later Dean of Westminster (1856–63) and Archbishop of Dublin (1863–84). Trench accepts the Gospel records of the Miracles, and provides a series of exegetical homilies on them, with comments and illustrative material from the Fathers and other Christian writers.

you can fancy) when it came to suggesting anything. He said that an actuary's business nowadays consisted merely or mainly in pushing the office, that the mathematical work was done, that the tables were made &c &c. The only thing he could think of being Scientific that paid was Popular Physics and mentioned that Rushton (of all people in the world) had been enquiring of him some time back about something of the sort which he was to edit for Longman.[1] He did not know Rushton's address but said Longman's care wd. no doubt find him, though I should hardly advise you to have anything to say to it. It occurs to me that you might write to *Long* and ask him if he has anything in his gift. He is the 'editor' general. I remember Rushton telling me that he had been of service to him. I believe his address is College, Brighton. On the whole if I were you I should rather rest on my oars and occupy myself with the Prospective &c for a little time—rather than exert myself in too many quarters at once. Something will turn up gradually, in all likelihood, for so good a *worker* (doing work *quite* right is very rare) as you are and *Connection* is everything in every Profession and can only be obtained gradually. I have not been able to see James but send a copy of what I have written to him. I did not find Crabb Robinson or Parker[2] in town, but will write to the *former*. By way of the next step I strongly advise you to write the article on Atheism which you mentioned and to get the review[3] made over to you as soon as may be. I should like to write for you a short article on the new series of M. Arnold's poems.[4] They are not very much in themselves, but they show character and afford I think matter for a short paper and no reading up of any subject will be necessary, which is a great blessing and consideration. Or I will write on the 'Principles of Taxation', a dreary article if you like it better on the Chancellor of the

---

[1] Neither Rushton nor the Longman series has been identified.
[2] Publisher, and proprietor of *Fraser's Magazine*.
[3] The *Prospective*.
[4] *Empedocles on Etna, and Other Poems*, 1852. WB's 'short article' suggests that he intended the review for the *Prospective* rather than the *Inquirer*, which did not publish long articles. In the event the review, unsigned, but clearly by WB, appeared in the *Inquirer*, 27 August 1853 (reprinted Vol. XIV). Other articles identifiable as WB's by internal evidence appeared in the *Inquirer* of 7 May 1853, 28 April 1855 and 4 August 1855; there was also a series of articles on University Extension, over the signature 'Amicus' (employed by WB for his *Inquirer* letters on the *coup d'état*), March–April 1854, and which must be WB's (see *Collected Works*, XIV. The articles were first identified in R. H. Tener, 'Walter Bagehot: Some New Attributions', *Studies in Bibliography*, 29 [1976], 346–57).

Exchequer's speech and the Report of the Income Tax Committee.[5] Only make your election in due time, so that I may have a long time to waste and then do it in any[6] very great hurry exactly at the last.

You can hardly imagine the relief it has been to me to have seen you and to have a new and not unmixedly painful picture of you in my imagination, and to see your mind so clear and healthy and firm. I did not fancy for a moment that the suffering which you feel and have felt would weaken your intellect or obscure your judgment. But I was not sure that it would not increase the tendency to mere melancholy, which I (characteristically enough) used to hold to be morbid. I think it has diminished it. The real and daily pain which you do not express but cannot conceal and the constant habit of *putting down* serious and solemn thoughts—give a distinctness and coolness to your views which I think they sometimes used to want. There is more of the pure steel in them as if they came from a solider and clearer ηθος.

Ever yours most affly
WALTER BAGEHOT

R H Hutton Esqre.

To HENRY CRABB ROBINSON, 17 AUGUST 1853
MS: Dr Williams's Library

Langport.
17 Augt. 1853.

My dear Sir,

I did myself the honor of calling on you a few days since, when I was in town, but heard only that you had left it. I was *disinterestedly* vexed at this—for I wanted to ask you a favor. You do not know of any *lucrative* literary employment just now in the market. It is not for my-

---

[5] Gladstone had renewed income tax for seven years, but with the hope of gradually reducing and eventually dispensing with it; he also extended legacy duty to real property. The Income Tax committee set up in 1851 to consider its readjustment and amendment had not been able to frame a report, and was not reconvened. No article on the subject appeared in the *Prospective* or the *Inquirer*.
[6] Thus in MS.

self (which would be too absurd) but for a much sounder man my friend Mr. R. H. Hutton, who used to be Principal of U. Hall. He is a first rate German scholar, a capital mathematician, a very fair classic, and writes a very clear and strong style. These late articles in the Inquirer are his about the Professorship of M. Phily. at Univ. Hall.[1] He has been very ill and in much distress of mind, as he lost his wife in Barbadoes, but though from loss of voice, he is unable to teach or preach (his old profession) he is quite equal to anything with the pen and a certain amount of literary exertion would be good for him, independently of financial considerations. He is the sort of man to get on, I should say, in literature for he has great energy and accuracy and is to be depended on for doing any sort of work right which you will agree with me, is not very common. If you could think of any way in which he could be employed *I* should be very *grateful*, and he much obliged and you would have done a piece of great kindness *and* goodness.

I am
Ever yours faithfully

WALTER BAGEHOT

If you wish to read *bad* writing let me recommend to your attention an article on Shakespeare in the last No. of the Prospective.

---

[1] The articles appeared 9, 16, and 30 July, and 13 August. It had been decided that Manchester New College should be established in London 'as a Theological Institution in connection, for literary and scientific purposes, with University College', sharing the premises of University Hall, though remaining a separate body; the move was made in October 1853 (H. Hale Bellot, *University College London*, pp. 301–2). Hutton was one of those campaigning unsuccessfully for a chair of Moral Philosophy at the college, to be filled by James Martineau. Instead a lectureship was created, and Martineau travelled from Liverpool to deliver his lectures until 1857 when he was appointed Professor of Mental, Moral and Religious Philosophy at the college, and moved to London to share the theological teaching with the Principal, J. J. Tayler.

End of Volume XII